ARNOLD AND GOD

ARNOLD AND GOD

———— *Ruth apRoberts* ————

UNIVERSITY OF CALIFORNIA PRESS
BERKELEY • LOS ANGELES • LONDON

University of California Press
Berkeley and Los Angeles, California

University of California Press, Ltd.
London, England

Library of Congress Cataloging in Publication Data

apRoberts, Ruth.
  Arnold and God.

  Includes index.
    1. Arnold, Matthew, 1822–1888–Religion and ethics.
2. God in literature.   3. Religion in literature.
4. Bible–Criticism, interpretations, etc.   I. Title.
PR4024.A54   1983   821′.8   82–10847
ISBN 0–520–04747–8

Printed in the United States of America

1   2   3   4   5   6   7   8   9

Contents

Preface

Thomas Carlyle has said a man's religion is the chief fact about him, religion being understood broadly as man's relationship to the Eternities and Immensities. I have tried in this book to review Matthew Arnold's career from the perspective of that chief fact, thinking that this perspective best reveals the principles of his literary criticism and the urgency of his program for politics, for education, and for "culture." Arnold's works on religion and the Bible have been neglected: secularists have sometimes felt nervous about them, suspecting a frowsty "Victorian" interest, and even—since the works profess to be Christian—an indecent supernaturalism; while supernaturalists have been nervous about the secular approach and the rationalism. The result of the neglect has been, I think, a notably incomplete view of Arnold: that chief fact, which makes sense of the whole, is missing. It seems to me that the religious perspective reveals a hundred hitherto unperceived concords in his work. The religious question was for him the greatest challenge of his career, and it is in the religious context that he best formulates his own broad criticism of life. The Bible was for him the greatest textual challenge, and it is in his Bible criticism that he does his most systematic literary criticism. The oneness of literature and religion was his principle, and with a touching consistency he labored to produce his edition of the book of Isaiah as literature for the schools. His Isaiah is in a way a suitable crown of his career.

Arnold's sense of the wholeness of culture had its roots in German Historicism and the complex of developmental thought associated with it, of which Darwinian evolution may be perceived as part. The Higher Criticism was a recognition of development in religion; the great doctrine of *Bildung* was a recognition of man's ever-incomplete development and the cognate infinite capacities. To cultivate all our distinctively human powers harmoniously, always *becoming* because the process is infinite—this is the law of our being, of *Humanität*, and this is Arnold's Culture. This Culture, or movement in the direction of an idea of perfection, is the essential religious office. Such a view of Arnold's thought is substantially confirmed by new evidence from unpublished manuscript material that shows how Arnold drew on Johann Gottfried Herder and Wilhelm von Humboldt.

Bildung and Culture are ideas of process, and I am myself sufficiently impressed by these ideas to make process my method in this study. Synchronic treatments of Arnold's thought risk obscurity and distortion. It has seemed to me easier as well as more just to discover diachronically his development through the poetry and early essays. I trace a variety of themes—poetic vocation, the function of myth and of metaphor, education or the transmission of tradition, the nature of religion and of language itself—which all, I hope it is clear, come together in *Literature and Dogma* and its corollary *God and the Bible*. As Arnold's literary, social, and educational ideas draw together to form the religious doctrine of these books, so in turn the religious doctrine shapes and directs the ensuing writings.

In Germany the Historicist line developed the doctrine of *Bildung*, the dialectical method of Hegel, the provisionalism of Nietzsche, and in our century the philosophy of fictions of Hans Vaihinger. Just as Historicism and *Bildung* ultimately imply the philosophy of fictions, so, I think, do Arnold's works; it seems to me that in his analyses of the phenomenology of myth and of metaphor he proceeds toward this philosophy. I, in turn, find it a clue to the unifying element in his work, the idea of the provisional as alternative to the dogmatic. This I explore in a central chapter called "Metaphor." And I end with Arnold's treatment of a "fiction" in the usual literary sense—*Anna Karenina*—which implies "fiction" in the philosophical sense.

Czeslaw Milosz, in his Nobel lecture of 1981, reaffirms the old Arnoldian principle, in a generation now too often characterized by a terrible "refusal to remember." "For we all who are here, both the speaker and you who listen, are no more than links between the past and the future."[1] The Arnold who in youth knew the anguish of being born "between two worlds" comes to find that this narrow strait itself conditions his vocation, makes it possible and makes it necessary. *Links*, says Milosz; *Kette*, said Herder, *die Kette der Bildung*, the chain of culture, in a passage that Arnold made his own. Culture may be the saving grace, which makes sense of our lives and constitutes the chief fact about ourselves as human beings.

1. *New York Review of Books* 28 (March 5, 1981): 11–15.

Most of this book was written in the period of a Guggenheim Fellowship, for which I am deeply grateful. The University of California at Riverside has given generous auxiliary support, and its library and librarians have been an unfailing resource. The Beinecke Library at Yale and the kindness of Miss Marjorie Wynne were invaluable to me, and I have appreciated also the resources of the Library of the University of Virginia, the Huntington Library, and the Library of the University of California at Los Angeles.

I owe a great debt to R. H. Super, both for his beautiful edition of Arnold's prose and for an immensely helpful reading of my manuscript. An anonymous reader for the University of California Press was very generous and helpful. To Park Honan, I give heartfelt thanks for sustaining encouragement in the course of my work, and also for his fine, humane *Matthew Arnold: A Life*. It has been a great pleasure to have the friendship of Arnold Whitridge, the writer's grandson, who has himself maintained the Arnoldian virtues in this country. I have received kind interest and help from Dwight Culler, David DeLaura, Stanley B. Greenfield, J. Max Patrick, Gordon N. Ray, William Robbins, Georg B. Tennyson, S. O. A. Ullman, and Alexander Welsh. My friend John Irving has been my guide and inspiration in some German matters, and many of my colleagues have aided me: Edwin M. Eigner, Robert Essick, Milton Miller, Marshall Van Deusen, Jules Levin, Josef Purkart, Günther Rimbach, David Kemp, and Elizabeth Lang. I am much blessed in my wise typist, Antonia Turman. My husband has steadily administered books, criticism, and encouragement.

As for shortcomings and errors, I am comforted only by Arnold's own doctrine of provisionality: this book is no more than an essay, perfectly expendable, on the way to a better understanding of Arnold, of God, and of man's metaphorical ways.

The frequently used editions of Arnold's works are cited parenthetically in the text by the following code:

The Poems of Matthew Arnold. Edited by Kenneth Allott. Second edition. Edited by Miriam Allott. London: Longmans, 1965/1979.

Cited by page number alone.

Collected Prose Works. Edited by R. H. Super. 11 volumes. Ann Arbor: University of Michigan Press, 1960–77.

Cited by volume and page number, e.g., III: 88.

The Letters of Matthew Arnold. Edited by George W. E. Russell. Two volumes in one. New York: Macmillan, 1900.

Cited as *Letters*, with volume and page number, e.g., *Letters* I: 57.

The Letters of Matthew Arnold to Arthur Hugh Clough. Edited by H. F. Lowry. Oxford: Clarendon Press, 1932.

Cited as *Clough*, with page number.

The Note-Books of Matthew Arnold. Edited by H. F. Lowry, Karl Young, and W. H. Dunn. London: Oxford University Press, 1952.

Cited as *Note-Books*, with page number.

All translations of foreign languages are my own, unless specified otherwise.

—————————————— I ——————————————

—————————————Vocation ———————————

ARNOLD'S pensive Scholar-Gipsy, "in hat of antique shape, and cloak of grey," once known, stays in the mind as a sort of token that things may be worth their while, that one's quest is not in vain. The Scholar-Gipsy's source, however, Joseph Glanvill's *The Vanity of Dogmatizing*, is remembered only as a source; no one seems to have noticed that Glanvill's title makes a motto for Arnold's whole career. Glanvill tells how *The Vanity of Dogmatizing* was undertaken as a "Corrective of Enthusiasm, in a Vindication of the use of Reason in matters of Religion."[1] Arnold aims to rout the "enthusiasm" of the literalist Evangelicals with a true understanding of the function of texts and to vindicate "sweet reasonableness" and a Christianity acceptable to scientists. Arnold, like Glanvill, is dedicated to skepticism and empiricism. The Scholar-Gipsy is, in Glanvill's book, an emblem of Glanvill's mission, and the figure takes on a similar function for Arnold.

Arnold is one of those authors who is remarkably consistent: his professional career fulfills many anticipations in the poems, so that his later work in prose actually illuminates the poetry, and one can discern how the poetry shaped and sustained the career. To see him steadily and whole, we need to correlate his early work with his later. Arnold scholars are fortunate in having the masterly and now complete editions of his works, and Kenneth Allott in the *Poems* and

1. Joseph Glanvill, from "The Epistle Dedicatory," *The Vanity of Dogmatizing*, facsimile of the edition of 1661 (New York: Columbia University Press, 1931), n.p.

1

R. H. Super in the *Prose* both make generous cross-references within their editions and between them.

For this study of Arnold's religious thought, I propose now to separate one strand or theme out of the poetic works that seems to me particularly premonitory: the theme of vocation. Obviously a great many of the poems are in the class of poetry-about-poetry, most especially about the role of the poet,[2] and I believe that they adumbrate the writings about culture and the role of the critic. It does some violence to the poetry to consider it as a *Prelude*, or "Growth of a Critic's Mind," but not to know the outcome is to risk distortion of the poetry. And if we stay too long with the criticism of the poetry, we may be left with an academic fiction, an "Arnold" who is a "foiled circuitous wanderer," doomed to "fluctuate idly without term or scope," a Matthew-Sohrab forever being destroyed by a father-Thomas-Rustum, stranded on "the vast edges drear and naked shingles of the world." But the fact is that he found his vocation as critic, knew his powers, exercised them with great discipline and energy, and was profoundly effective, so profoundly that on the one hand we take many of his achievements for granted and on the other hand we have yet to exhaust the virtue of his influence.

Arnold himself thought the poems valuable as cultural history: "My poems represent, on the whole, the main movement of mind of the last quarter of a century" (*Letters* II: 10), he wrote his mother in 1869. They have become for us, of course, much more. Arnold's nineteenth-century crisis has become our norm; his "wandering between two worlds" seems less a diagnosis of the Victorian malaise than a statement of the human condition. His great symbols—the two worlds, the Sea of Faith, the ignorant armies' clash by night—are so successful that they have become almost too overriding as keys to "the Victorian Age" and to our own as well. They tyrannize over our minds, as it were, so that we see ourselves in their terms. We forget what Arnold later taught us about the provisional nature of figures, a language not "rigid, fixed, and scientific" but "fluid, passing, and literary." Perhaps Nietzsche's brilliant Death-of-God metaphor has be-

2. As G. Robert Stange well says, poetry as the subject of poetry was very much a contemporary concern. "Like Browning, Arnold's interest is fundamentally intellectual; and unlike Tennyson, he is concerned less with the existential agony of the poet than with . . . the artist's task." (*Matthew Arnold: The Poet as Humanist* [Princeton: Princeton University Press, 1967], p. 14).

come too rigid and literal now among academics, and the receding tide of the Sea of Faith has become too much like an article of literal faith. It might be better now to say that the "melancholy, long, with-drawing roar" has given place to a most ominously advancing tide of irrationalism, surging around and threatening our bulwarks of Hel-lenism. New philistines announce God reborn on bumper stickers. And where Arnold anticipated an ever-increasing scientific rational-ism, the masses now cultivate pseudo-science, space monsters, and demon possession. For his own time, Arnold's great figures are largely heuristic: they invite hypotheses rather than absolutes, and they help him to certain diagnoses. He was, as he himself describes Goethe,

> Physician of the iron age,
>
> . . . .
>
> He read each wound, each weakness clear;
>
> . . . .
>
> And said: *Thou ailest here, and here!*
> ("Memorial Verses," 240)[3]

The poet Arnold is mainly the diagnostician, while the essayist pre-scribes the treatment.[4] "Rugby Chapel," coming comparatively late, celebrates the father, Thomas Arnold, who would not alone be saved, and it may be seen as a kind of rite of passage: Matthew receives the father's mantle on his own shoulders, undertaking to lead the way to joy, and love, and light; a kind of certitude, and peace, and help for pain. Just because the diagnosis was so brilliantly objectified in his poetic symbols, he is the better qualified to devise a treatment that may go to the root of the malaise. But the positive action of the phy-sician is implicit in the poems.

Even the adolescent rhetoric of "Alaric at Rome" calls for "a min-strel of diviner might," "a holier incense" (12), to celebrate rightly his great subject, the eternal city. It is true that the figure of the poet's "divine" power, along with poetry as worship or "incense," is the merest commonplace, quite to be expected in adolescent academic poetry. But in the light of Arnold's later insistence on the common ground of poetry and religion, his use of this figure even here is signifi-

3. George Ford identifies Arnold as "physician of the iron age" (*Keats and the Victorians* [New Haven: Yale University Press, 1944], p. 66).

4. Or as Lionel Trilling put it: "The poet's vision gave the prose writer his goal" (*Matthew Arnold* [New York: Norton, 1939], p. xi).

cant, for it is one of his own particularly characteristic data. It is developed in "The Strayed Reveller": the poet is the "divine bard," *vates*; he is, moreover, something of a *poète maudit*,[5] a kind of martyr to art who, endowed with godlike vision, is nevertheless doomed to suffering beyond the normal lot of humanity (76). "The Future" aligns the poet with the prophet Moses (280); "The Youth of Nature" mourns the "sacred poet" Wordsworth, who "was a priest to us all" (261).

"Resignation" is marked by a developing sense of the poet's mission, a kind of distancing that makes sorrow bearable:

> Before him he sees life unroll,
> A placid and continuous whole—
> That general life, which does not cease,
> Whose secret is not joy, but peace;
>
> .   .   .   .
>
> [He] Breathes, when he will, immortal air,
> Where Orpheus and where Homer are.
>   (96–97)

This is the work of the critic who was to hypothesize a "general" life of our united best selves, who was to recognize God in the Eternal, or that which does not cease, and in the "immortal" air of culture, the tradition, which includes both religion and poetry. Kenneth Allott rightly, I think, sees the appeal of John Henry Newman in "The Voice"—"Those lute-like tones"

> Blew such a thrilling summons to my will,
>   Yet could not shake it.
>   (37)

5. Did Arnold borrow the concept from Alfred de Vigny's *Stello* (1832)? Did he know the *Winterreise* (with or without Schubert's music) of that Wilhelm Müller whose son was the Max Müller later to become Arnold's friend at Oxford? "Was vermeid' ich denn die Wege, wo die andern Wand'rer gehn?" Park Honan connects Arnold with the continental "Sentimental" school ("Fox How and the Continent . . . ," *Victorian Poetry* 16 [Spring-Summer 1978]: 58–69). This connection seems to me to best explain the nature of the "Marguerite" series and the "Faded Leaves" series. G. Robert Stange argues persuasively that the main generic prototype is the *Liederzyklus*, and he mentions the cycles of Heine, Müller, and Chamisso (*Matthew Arnold*, pp. 222–24).

Here we see Arnold steadfastly rejecting the supernatural. "The World and the Quietist" relates the Indian religious idea of detachment (from his reading of the *Bhagavad Gita*) to the poet's role in society (106). Slighter poems often anticipate later critical positions: one recognizes in "the barren optimistic sophistries" of "To a Republican Friend, 1848" (108) the vanities of "Our Liberal Practitioners" in *Culture and Anarchy*. The lines "Written in Butler's Sermons" reveal an early impatience with the habit of taking as absolutes the fictive abstractions of language:

> Affections, Instincts, Principles, and Powers,
> Impulse and Reason, Freedom and Control—
> So men, unravelling God's harmonious whole,
> Rend in a thousand shreds this life of ours.
>
> Vain labour!
>
> (42)

in the face of the "majestic" and mysterious unity of being. Arnold later elaborates his criticism of Bishop Butler (VIII: 12), but this poem indicates the early impatience with dogma and promises the development of a Spinozist experiential gauge of ethics. What might be called the approach to religion by way of language is developed in the late "The Divinity," which is based in his meditation on the words of St. Bernard, "that the Divine Essence, nature, form, deity, goodness, wisdom, virtue, power, magnitude, truly is God."

> "For God of these his attributes is made". . . .
> *God's wisdom and God's goodness!*—Ay, but fools
> Mis-define these till God knows them no more.
> *Wisdom and goodness, they are God!* what schools
> Have yet so much as heard this simple lore?
> This no Saint preaches, and this no Church rules;
> 'Tis in the desert, now and heretofore—
>
> (530)

the young Arnold cries out in the wilderness against literalism. "Progress" anticipates Arnold the comparative religionist: all religions, he insists, fill a deep human need.

Which has not taught weak wills how much they can?
Which has not fallen on the dry heart like rain?
Which has not cried to sunk, self-weary man:
  Thou must be born again!
(278)

There are many clues here to *Literature and Dogma*: the energizing power of religion; the ecumenical appreciation of other religions— Moslem, Hindu, Buddhist; the intensity of man's need; the ubiquitous biblical water metaphor (doctrine shall drop as the rain, my soul thirsteth, etc.); the focal Christian new-birth metaphor. As Carlyle before Arnold has been at pains to say, religions develop and change. "Leave then the Cross as ye have left carved gods, / But guard the fire within!" (277). Leave miracles, that is. I, Arnold, will dedicate myself to guarding "the fire within," or "The True Greatness of Christianity."[6] This evolution of religions is similarly touched on in "Monica's Last Prayer"; Arnold draws the Monica material from Augustine and comments:

Creeds pass, rites change, no altar standeth whole.
Yet we her memory, as she prayed, will keep,
Keep by this: *Life in God, and union there!*
(534)

Rhetoric itself at times reveals Arnold's sense of mission, as when he indulges in preacherly imperatives or homiletic concluding exhortations: "Fool . . . rest her slave!" (44), "Know thou the worst!" (61), "Live by thy light!" (111), "Resolve to be thyself!" (150), "Sink, O youth, in thy soul!" (269), "Think clear, feel deep, bear fruit well" (278). Arnold, I think, adopts the Victorian-Sage voice more often than the other poets. Sometimes it sounds Carlylean, but we can at times catch the note of Thomas Arnold's peroration in Rugby Chapel:[7]

How fair a lot to fill
Is left to each man still!
(286)

6. Chapter 12 of *Literature and Dogma* (VI: 395–406).

7. Wendell Stacy Johnson is surely right to argue that Arnold's "oracular" voice is his least effective (*The Voices of Matthew Arnold* [New Haven: Yale University Press, 1961], especially p. 139).

Or:

> On, to the City of God!
> (490)

Or:

> *"More strictly, then, the inward judge obey!*
> Was Christ a man like us? *Ah! let us try*
> *If we then, too, can be such men as he!"*
> (527)

All these various scattered references in the minor poems combine
to indicate the nature of the Arnoldian mission: there is, first, the
clear obligation to serve society; second, the service is apparently to
be through combining the office of poet with seer, prophet, or priest;
and third, in the poet-priest's sphere of activity, poetry and religion
seem to be undifferentiated. These concepts unquestionably have an
ancient lineage, but their more immediate forbears are—to stay for the
time only with the local and English—Coleridge and Thomas Arnold.
Coleridge's vision of the "Clerisy" is a vision of agents in charge of
what Arnold is to develop as the idea of Culture; the "Clerisy" over-
see both education and religion. Influenced by Coleridge, Thomas
Arnold as spokesman of the Broad Church Movement declares "the
essential unity of the secular and religious, of Church and State, and
the universal priesthood of the laity."[8] The importance of the inherited Broad Church principles is more closely explored in subsequent chapters. For now let me propose that it was Arnold's own
distinction to found, on a Coleridgean basis, a realm where poetry
and religion are undifferentiated. "Poetry" and "Religion," he might
have written in the margins of Butler's *Sermons*, are fictive entities
unraveling what is really a harmonious whole. He apprehends something which I propose we might call the poetry-religion continuum.
Its agency is the Broad Church, its agents are the Clerisy (example:
Thomas Arnold—poet, scholar, teacher, clergyman), and its model
might be Rugby itself, and later, Oxford. This focal sense of continuum guides the developing idea of vocation in the poems. It is
variously intimated in the lesser poems, not necessarily in proportion

8. This summary is from the "Thomas Arnold" entry in *The Oxford Dictionary
of the Christian Church*, ed. F. L. Cross (London: Oxford University Press, 1974),
p. 91.

to their merit as poems. But it is most significantly elaborated in the best poems, and although they have been much explicated, they will yield yet new light on Arnold's career, I think, if we survey them from the perspective of the poetry-religion continuum.

Arnold's eventual turn from poetry to prose is associated with a major question of the technique of the poems, and this is the important question of symbolism. Arnold would not have been sympathetic with the Symbolist movement, but I think we may venture to speak of his own theory and practice as being in the symbolist mode even if he did not use the term. We have his important statement in a letter: "More and more I feel bent against the modern English habit (too much encouraged by Wordsworth) of using poetry as a channel for thinking aloud, instead of making anything."[9] I take this to be occasioned by his sense of his own work: where it is less good, it is discursive, it thinks aloud; when it is best he has "made something"—a metaphor, a myth, a symbol. Such "making" is by no means new in English poetry. Louis Cazamian declared of symbolism that while the French may have "taken the initiative of the term," English poets have given themselves "to the thing, before our French symbolists, with fullness and intensity." And he illustrates by turning to Arnold, for Arnold "organizes his poetic expression around images so rich and potent in meaning that they become symbols."[10] It is no accident that the use of symbols in both ancient and recent times is recognized as common to religion and poetry. Maximus of Tyre in the second century defended "images" as serving both religion and art; Aquinas asserted, "Modus symbolicus utrique communis est" (The symbolic mode is common to both). This concept has been made central in our time by Susanne Langer: man is a symbolizing animal; his capacity to symbolize is his most interesting and satisfying function. In all the arts, and in religion too, Langer claims, symbols stabilize things inaccessible through the necessarily limited spectrum of our referential language.[11]

9. *Unpublished Letters of Matthew Arnold*, ed. Arnold Whitridge (New Haven: Yale University Press, 1923), pp. 15–16.

10. Louis Cazamian, *Symbolisme et poésie: L'Exemple anglais* (Neuchâtel: Editions de la Baconnière, 1947), pp. 24, 169.

11. Susanne Langer, *Philosophy in a New Key* (Cambridge, Mass.: Harvard University Press, 1942).

Arnold's best poems all exploit the symbolic method in a well-observed peculiarity identified as the "parable" or "analogy" ending by Arnold's contemporary R. H. Hutton, the "tableau-ending" or "endnote of relief" by C. B. Tinker and H. F. Lowry, the "coda" by Lionel Stevenson, the "end-symbol" by Dwight Culler.[12] It is a break near the end of the poem, a shifting of ground, a turning away from discursiveness to something else. "Mycerinus" has the mysterious picture of "the moving Nile"; "The World and the Quietist" ends with the unarticulated "message" of the slave; "Stanzas from the Grande Chartreuse" ends with the children by the abbey wall; "Sohrab and Rustum" ends with the river and the Aral Sea; and then there are the Tyrian trader of "The Scholar-Gipsy" and the signal-elm of "Thyrsis." In each case Arnold turns to symbol as a solution to a technical problem, to "say" for him something that even in the poem itself he may have tried saying in a prosy or literal or abstract way. It gives him a new perspective and a kind of extension of meaning, with no loss of precision. But if we are asked to define the quest in "The Scholar-Gipsy" or to say what is the omen of the signal-elm in "Thyrsis," we find ourselves hard pressed. "A piece of music," said Mendelssohn, "expresses not too indefinite a thought to be put into words, but too definite a thought."[13] It is a kind of honesty in Arnold, I think, that drives him to the definite precision of symbolism. He is not one of the "abhorred . . . self-proclaimed poets" Auden castigates, "who, to wow an audience, utter some resonant lie" ("Ode to Terminus"). In an early essay he acclaims in Joseph Joubert a principle we may take to be one of his own: Joubert, he says, makes "no compromise with words in spite of their difficulty" (III: 197). Park Honan has referred us to the parents' view of two kinds of poetry. The one was, for Dr. and Mrs. Arnold, descriptive, superficial, and occasional; but the second kind was "inward, sincere, deeply felt, serious, often religious; it means what it *says*, as Mrs.

---

12. R. H. Hutton as quoted by David DeLaura in *Victorian Prose: A Guide to Research* (New York: Modern Language Association, 1973), p. 260; C. B. Tinker and H. F. Lowry, *The Poetry of Matthew Arnold: A Commentary* (London: Oxford University Press, 1940), p. 213; Lionel Stevenson, "Matthew Arnold's Poetry: A Modern Appraisal," *Tennessee Studies in Literature* 4 (1959): 37; A. Dwight Culler, *Imaginative Reason* (New Haven: Yale University Press, 1966), p. 146.

13. *Letters of Felix Mendelssohn-Bartholdy*, trans. Lady Wallace (London: Longmans Green, 1864), p. 276.

Arnold put it, and does not strive for effects."[14] This concern to mean what he says, this honesty, is what makes Arnold's poems difficult and at the same time worth our trouble. Some critics do give up: this or that poem, in spite of lovely passages, is a "failure." But many have persevered and have amassed a large body of significant interpretative comment, often drawing on Arnold's prose. Tinker and Lowry, Lionel Trilling, Dwight Culler, J. P. Curgenven, W. Stacy Johnson, G. R. Stange, Alan Roper, R. H. Super, Kenneth Allott, and David DeLaura have all enabled us to return to the poems with reassured understanding. Like poetry, criticism succeeds when it eschews the resonant lie and finds new ways to be guarded in explication—as Alan Roper does in his comment on "The Scholar-Gipsy": "As often as it is read, the poem confirms the possibility of good dreams in bad times, and if the poem also questions the validity of such dreams, it never quite commits itself against them: that, after all, is what the Gipsy Scholar does for you."[15] This is admirably and properly minimal.

In the light of Arnold's later career as essayist, I propose to reconsider some of the symbols in his best poetic work and to move on carefully toward some minimal explication of the vocation theme. For the Scholar-Gipsy, as I have said, we need to turn back to Glanvill's *Vanity of Dogmatizing.*[16] We can imagine the octavo volume in Arnold's pocket, or—as the poem says—lying beside him on the grass during his pastoral meditations in the Oxford countryside. Glanvill was an Oxford man but a little defective in loyalty: he was friends with the Cambridge Platonists and traditionally counts as one of them. He and Henry More seem to have had between them a regular research project in extrasensory perception and were much interested in witches. The Cambridge Platonists were anti-Calvinistic and were called "latitude men"; they were the precursors of the Broad Church of the nineteenth century, that party of which Thomas Arnold was a prime leader, and its principles of free inquiry. Glanvill has a strong

14. Honan, "Fox How and the Continent . . . ," p. 60.

15. Alan Roper, *Arnold's Poetic Landscapes* (Baltimore: Johns Hopkins University Press, 1969), p. 224.

16. J. P. Curgenven, who is otherwise perceptive, does not think Arnold read it through (" 'The Scholar-Gipsy': A Study of the Growth, Meaning, and Integration of a Poem," *Litera* 2 [1955]: 43).

sense of the limitations of reason. "The knowledge I teach," he says
in his preface, "is ignorance,"[17] and he anatomizes the limits and un-
trustworthiness of our senses and intellects to demonstrate the absurdity of the dogmatists, anticipating Arnold's attacks on Arnold's
own dogmatists and their "insane license of affirmation" (VI: 152) :

Did we but compare the miserable scantness of our capacities, with the vast
profundity of things; both truth and modesty would teach us a dialect, more
becoming short-sighted mortality. . . . The best Principles, excepting Divine,
and Mathematical, are but Hypotheses; within the Circle of which we may
indeed conclude may things, with security from Error: But yet the greatest
certainty, advanc'd from supposal, is still but Hypothetical.[18]

This is Arnoldian, except that Arnold is so bold as to make no exception for the Divine, and in spite of his love for Pascal he did not
much appreciate mathematics. Twentieth-century science has redis-
covered the "vanity of dogmatizing"; we know that the best we can
manage are hypotheses, or "convenient supposals," as Glanvill calls
them.[19]

Finally, the marks of Glanvill are widespread in Arnold's work. The
very odd word "sciolist," for instance, which turns up in "Stanzas
from the Grande Chartreuse" (11. 99 and 102), is a favorite word of
Glanvill's, [20] a nice pejorative for the kind of "smatterers" he has it
in for. Basil Willey acclaims Glanvill for inventing the phrase "climate
of opinions."[21] Though Arnold does not to my knowledge use the
phrase, the climate of opinion is really what he is concerned with in
all his writings about the *Zeitgeist*. Both "climate of opinions" and
Zeitgeist are figurative ways of insisting on change, on the relative,

17. Jackson I. Cope reveals Glanvill as not so much a philosopher as above all
the apologist for the Anglican establishment, and in this also of course he is deeply
attractive to Arnold (*Joseph Glanvill, Anglican Apologist*, Washington University
Studies [St. Louis: Washington University Press, 1956]).

18. Glanvill, *Vanity*, pp. 193, 195.

19. Ibid., p. 212.

20. Ibid., pp. 143, 218, 223, 225 et passim. But R. H. Super notes Carlyle's use
of the word in the heading to book 1, chapter 10, of *Sartor Resartus* (*The Time-
Spirit of Matthew Arnold* [Ann Arbor: University of Michigan Press, 1970], p. 25).

21. Basil Willey, *The Seventeenth-Century Background* (London: Chatto and
Windus, 1949), p. 193; Glanvill, *Vanity*, p. 227.

on the non-absolute. Glanvill's careful observations of our efforts to observe and assess our own mental processes[22] might well be the basis for Arnold's lines in *Empedocles on Etna*,

> We shut our eyes, and muse
> How our own minds are made.
> What springs of thought they use,
> How rightened, how betrayed.
>
> (179)

Glanvill's remark "that every being uncessantly aspires to its own perfection"[23] may well have mediated the old theological concept to result in some Arnoldian propositions.[24] Glanvill attacks on the one hand the enthusiasts—so closely parallel to Arnold's Puritans—and on the other hand the Peripatetic School, the Aristotelians—parallel to Arnold's systematizers: Comtists, Utilitarians, and dogmatic theologians. As Glanvill outlines his own skeptical position, he asserts that in philosophy he is a *seeker;* and this is the best indication of the centrality of Glanvill to Arnold's two Oxford elegies. Faithfulness to a quest is probably the best statement of the unifying idea of the two poems: "A fugitive and gracious light he seeks, / Shy to illumine; and I seek it too" (548). The object of the quest is an elusive, perhaps shifting truth, and the condition is skepticism. The questing scholar is integral to Glanvill's message: he leaves the dogmatism of the schools and resorts to the unconventional gipsies; this withdrawn position gives him a new vantage point and the opportunity to acquire a non-dogmatic lore which he will in time bring back as a benefit to society. This new lore is literally thought-transference (Arnold very deliberately omits this when he quotes Glanvill in the summary headnote to his poem), but since Glanvill in his skepticism finds no disproof, he thinks it possible, and there is no odor of cheap magic about it. It suggests, rather, the power of the gipsy's imagination, potent to influence the minds of his fellows.

Just as the Scholar-Gipsy eschews dogma, so does Arnold the poet eschew dogma and even discursive statement, at his best "making something," symbols, by which he affects us, his fellows, when we en-

22. Ibid., pp. 95–105.
23. Ibid., p. 107.
24. By both Hebraism and Hellenism, man seeks his own "perfection" (V: 164); "*All things seek to fulfil the law of their being*" (VI: 10).

counter him in that lasting Oxford country of the mind, by the power
of the "Imagination" his "Phancy" binding ours.[25] The withdrawal
theme is frequent in Arnold's poetry: revelers stray, Callicles leaves
the party, Obermann seeks an Alpine retreat. In the eloquent "Palladium," the withdrawal is into a sort of citadel of the self, that part
of us that is engaged not with the multitudinousness of the world but
with what is permanent and one. It is a place to gather strength and
power, from which to return to battle on the plains of Troy, to be an
influence in human affairs. In each case of withdrawal the concept is
quite parallel to that of "retreat" in the religious sense. In the larger
context of Arnold's career, the Scholar-Gipsy's withdrawal may be
taken as a withdrawal into poetry itself, whereby one acquires a lore
of inestimable value, and builds strength and power to become a force
in society. The gipsies' lore in this light symbolizes that great humanistic cause for which shallow contemporary science allows no
rationale; Arnold dedicates himself to founding this rationale—the
rationale for the value of the classics, the tradition, the Celtic element
in literature, the "Oriental" poetry of the Hebrews. And the projec-
tive power of the Scholar-Gipsy's imagination becomes Arnold's
power in society to criticize and to promulgate the tradition of poetry
and religion. The quest, or process, does not end, because "truth" is
not single and absolute; but one remains faithful,

> Still nursing the unconquerable hope,
> Still clutching the inviolable shade,
> With a free, onward impulse brushing through—
> (367)

the syntax itself suggests process and continuance. Though the quest
can never be ended, it is not in vain. It is dogmatizing that is the
vanity. Later, in "Thyrsis,"

> long the way appears, which seemed so short
> To the less practised eye of sanguine youth;
> And high the mountain-tops, in cloudy air,
> The mountain-tops where is the throne of Truth.
> (545–46)

But there is nothing else worth seeking. This Scholar-Gipsy may be
after all the most suggestive symbol in all of Arnold's works, illus-

25. Glanvill, *Vanity*, p. 198.

trating Arnold's own skepticism while confirming possibilities. The skeptical Glanvill was a cleric, that is, one whose business was religion. And I think we need to look at Arnold more as one who makes his business religion. We have that interesting 1869 letter of his to Frederick Temple, later Archbishop of Canterbury: "In the seventeenth century I should certainly have been in orders, and I think, if I were a young man now, I would take them."[26] Glanvill, we must remember, is part of Oxford (although he himself might rather have been at Cambridge), and in both elegies Oxford itself becomes a symbol. We may find the explication in the preface to *Essays in Criticism*: Oxford, "this queen of romance," in her "warfare against the Philistines" (III: 290) takes on the meaning of the religion-poetry continuum.

In "Lycidas" Milton had brought together the poet's vocation and the religious vocation; Arnold's version of pastoral makes the same link in the thoroughly Anglican locus of Oxford. Pastoral—flowers, river, hunters, wattled cotes, Thyrsis himself—is truly domesticated here. In a famous passage Arnold is to deplore English names as unpoetic—Wragg, Stiggins, Bugg—but he himself has metamorphosed the very English Oxford "Hinksey" into something Theocritan, an autonymous version of the Lityerses song.

The gnomic symbol-endings of the two elegies can in the perspective of the vocation theme be further explicated. On the much debated Tyrian trader of "The Scholar-Gipsy", lights come from various sources, out of Herodotus, Thucydides, Alexander Kinglake, Isaiah, Thomas Arnold's *History of Rome*, Ward's translation of Curtius's *History of Greece*, and Grote's *History of Greece*.[27] In Grote's *His-*

26. Quoted by Kenneth Allott, *Poems*, p. 564n.

27. R. H. Super supplies "Arnold's 'Tyrian Trader' in Thucydides," *Notes & Queries* 201 (1956) : 397; Kenneth Allott gives the relevant Herodotus passage and a reminiscence of Isaiah's Tyrian "Traffickers" (*Poems*, p. 369); Earl E. Stevens brings in Ezekiel ("Arnold's Tyrian Trader," *Victorian Newsletter*, no. 24 [Fall 1963]: 24–26), as Louis Bonnerot had done (*Matthew Arnold, poète* [Paris: Didier, 1947], p. 474n); Dwight Culler brings together Kinglake's *Eothen*, Herodotus, Thucydides, Diodorus Siculus, Thomas Arnold's *History of Rome*, Curtius's *History of Greece*, and George Borrow's gipsy lore (*Imaginative Reason* [New Haven: Yale University Press, 1966], pp. 190–93); David R. Carroll brings in Grote's *History of Greece* and mentions also the comments of G. Wilson Knight and A. E. Dyson ("Arnold's Tyrian Trader and Grecian Coaster," *Modern Language Review* 64

tory, the Greek with all his large experience was easy in his social and commercial exchanges, and in this ease he risked his own integrity. The Phoenician (or Tyrian) retreated from the dangerous involvement and found a way of dealing in the essentials without being distracted by cultural flotsam and jetsam. Beyond the Pillars of Hercules were a people who did not like hand-to-hand trade; for them, the Phoenician spread out his wares on the beach and withdrew. If the goods pleased, these people would take them and leave payment. And so for once it looks as if Arnold's admired Greeks are on the side of "sick hurry" and "divided aims," and it is the Tyrian trader of all people who is the "best self" by which we are "united, impersonal, at harmony . . . , the very self which culture, or the study of perfection, seeks to develop in us" (V: 134–35). For Arnold the poet, the problem is to reach the audience: it has become so hard; it used to be so easy: "O easy access to the hearer's grace / When Dorian shepherds sang to Proserpine!" ("Thyrsis," 543). I suggest that Matthew Arnold intimates with his Tyrian trader his turn to ironic prose with its "distancing" as his medium for the hard-to-reach if not shy Iberian-Philistines. We may glimpse none other than himself undoing his corded bales of the-best-that-has-been-thought-and-said-in-the-world on a distant northern shore. In prose, he was to find, one may veil oneself in persiflage and nevertheless deliver the goods. Furthermore, the indirect Tyrian method suggests the superiority of the indirect mode —metaphor—over the direct mode—the literal.[28]

In the more elegiac "Thyrsis" the main images—the Gipsy, the light from heaven, the quest—are more closely related to the idea of vocation, and in the ending symbol of "the tree" all these images converge:

[January 1969]: 27–33). Carroll sees the figure as a successful solution to some problems in the poem: "Here, thanks again to his trading analogy, Arnold has found a character who can withdraw from the dangers of involvement, and yet, unlike the Scholar-Gipsy, can be seen to act decisively in his withdrawal. He is able to act in accordance with the values of an older culture in which the self is not jeopardized" (p. 33).

28. The Tyrian trader might be considered not quite an artistic success; he functions as symbol at the cost of some strain. Certainly he defies New Criticism, and probably one should not have to bring to an explication so much material from outside a poem.

The light we sought is shining still.
Dost thou ask proof? Our tree yet crowns the hill,
Our Scholar travels yet the loved hill-side.

(550)

Some time ago, Louis Bonnerot, drawing on Louis Cazamian, tentatively proposed that the signal-elm of "Thyrsis" is a symbol of symbolism.[29] Perhaps we can say this again now with new confidence and
new reverberations. If the method of symbolism is recognized as
common to both religion and poetry, the tree adumbrates Arnold's
religion-poetry continuum. Happy omen, hail! It promises *Literature
and Dogma*, and a theory of metaphor, in the hope of revalidating the
Bible.

The five songs of Callicles in *Empedocles on Etna* are lyrics that,
as Arnold knew, may each stand by itself, open-ended in their symbolism. But Arnold did not know well enough their powerful function
in his own poem when he explains his dissatisfaction with *Empedocles*
and his reasons for omitting it from the *Poems* of 1853 (I: 1–15).
Without the songs the poem would still be immensely interesting and
memorable, but it might conceivably be objected to on Arnold's
ground as less than classical in vigor, "modern" in Arnold's negative
sense of enervating. But the songs *are* part of it and make on the figurative level a radical modification of the meaning of the whole. The
first concerns the traditional subject of the education of Achilles by
Chiron the Centaur. The lore imparted to Achilles is clearly different
from the tortuous and tortured intellectual discursiveness of Empedocles. May one not say that here "all the wisdom of his race" invokes
the tradition, which Arnold understands as "steadying" and benign,
potent against the "multitudinousness" of modern intellectual life?

29. Bonnerot, *Matthew Arnold*, p. 486. Bonnerot was drawing on Louis Cazamian's "Literature and Poetry," *University of Toronto Quarterly* 5 (1936) : 520–
43. The matter is more fully treated in Cazamian's *Symbolisme et poésie*, which
was published too late for Bonnerot to take account of except in a footnote (p. 489).
Bonnerot endorses Cazamian generally, and in many places notes the importance
of the religion-poetry link: "Défendre la Bible, c'est défendre la Poésie" (p. 265 et
passim).

If the tree of "Thyrsis" is a symbol of symbolism, it should be added that "The
Scholar-Gipsy" has been seen as "an elegy for elegies" (Roger B. Wilkenfeld, "The
Argument of the Scholar-Gipsy," *Victorian Poetry* 7 [Summer 1969]: 117–28, espe-
cially p. 117).

The Cadmus and Harmonia song comes after the philosophic chant or homily of Empedocles to Pausanias, and it has a curious power: Robert Frost said it was "his favorite poem long before he knew what it was going to mean."[30] Does it promise a kind of armor against grief? Can we say it effects somehow an ennoblement of ordinary suffering? We have heard Empedocles' advice to society, represented by Pausanias, on how to accommodate to life; now we hear him in soliloquy, confessing he has himself lost the power of accommodation, "broken" by the world. It is at this point that Callicles' third song is heard from below, the song of the Typho myth—Typho, "the rebel o'erthrown" writhing under his defeat by the gods. "He fables, yet speaks truth!" exclaims Empedocles in an ecstasy of literary criticism. His explication follows. As Arnold is later to do in the case of biblical texts, Empedocles rejects the literal statement of the myth, and explains its import:

> What suffering is there not seen
> Of plainness oppressed by cunning,
> As the well-counselled Zeus oppressed
> That self-helping son of earth!
> (192)

Is this reading legitimate? Empedocles is confessedly "prisoner of his consciousness," and being "dead to life and joy, therefore I read / In all things my own deadness" (200). Accordingly he reads (or hears) the Typho song as a fable of himself victimized, and misses the life and joy of it. In the song, there is pity that Typho's groans

>   almost drown
> The sweet notes whose lulling spell
> Gods and the race of mortals love so well,
> When through thy caves thou hearest music swell.
> (190)

Empedoclean groans, that is, make inaccessible the sound of music, or art, which is the meeting ground of man and gods. Callicles' Typho song moves into the numinous picture of the Olympian council "appeased," charmed by music, as the Thunderer

30. Quoted by Douglas Bush, *Matthew Arnold* (New York: Macmillan, 1971), p. 58n; *The Letters of Robert Frost to Louis Untermeyer* (New York: Holt, Rinehart and Winston, 1963), p. 240.

lets his lax right hand,
Which the lightnings doth embrace,
Sink upon his mighty knees.
And the eagle, at the beck
Of the appeasing, gracious harmony,
Droops all his sheeny, brown, deep-feathered neck,
Nestling nearer to Jove's feet;
While o'er his sovran eye
The curtains of the blue films slowly meet.
                                        (190)

Empedocles rejects his vocation—"Lie there, / My golden circlet, / My purple robe!"—while Callicles maintains: "The music of the lyre blows away / The clouds which wrap the soul" (192–93), and sings of the martyrdom of Marsyas, the suffering that art entails for the classical *poète maudit*. After Empedocles' gloriously ambiguous suicide, Callicles below on the mountainside sings all unknowing his serene praise of the Father and the Muses. The song acclaims the beauty and divinity of Apollo, god of poetry, and the nine Muses—"The leader is fairest, / But all are divine" (205)—and accepts the timeless hierarchy of all things.

In criticism, the discourses of Empedocles have received much attention, and indeed rightly so. Uneven in form, occasionally prosy, frequently sublime, they comprise in fact a most astounding compendium of Victorian intellectual concerns and of Arnold's own reading, expressed with a pungency that reveals most of them as our own concerns still. Arnold, in his mood of rejection, castigates the poem as part of the enervating modern "dialogue of the mind with itself," and yet the Empedocles sections taken by themselves are by no means ignobly that. In his last apology, Empedocles proclaims the kind of heroism which the intellectual life, however tortured, can take pride in.

Yea, I take myself to witness,
That I have loved no darkness,
Sophisticated no truth,
Nursed no delusion,
Allowed no fear!
                                        (203)

This is his grace, by which he can die a hero. And in the right circumstances this "life of mind," as the Victorians called it, can be lived joyously: "When with elated hearts we joined your train, / Ye Sunborn Virgins! on the road of truth" (196). The maidens of the sun, Heliades, seem to suggest the intellectual quest not yet cut off from the Apollonian world of art: "We had not lost our balance then, nor grown / Thought's slaves" (197). Something has gone awry. The dialogue of the mind with itself has become self-consuming. One must recognize, I think, in Empedocles' complaints against the "Sophists" what was to become Arnold's attack on "Our Liberal Practitioners" in *Culture and Anarchy,* and in Empedocles' complaints against the popular appetite for spells and magic tricks one can see what was to become Arnold's deprecation of miracles and literal interpretation of the Bible—that literalism which vitiates the true function of the great religious texts. The Empedocles discourses are the richer for their two phases: one, to Pausanias, the thinker to the ordinary good man; two, in soliloquy, the true honest dialogue of the mind with itself, the mind trying to mean what it *says.*

But the integrity of the work is missed if one misses the symbolic dialogue, the central drama of the poem. Callicles' songs are by no means mere lyric relief, but agents of action, making the case for art at the same time as they function as art in opposition to discursive logic. However wide-ranging and illuminated that discursive logic can be, it has limits; it tends to be self-canceling and self-destructive at last. Callicles to Empedocles is as art to science, as religion to theology, as Literature to Dogma. I offer this not as an arcane reading which may with difficulty be discerned in the poem, but rather as a representation of what really happens when we read it, speaking phenomenologically. Each of Callicles' songs takes us each time to a different level of discourse, and because they are such good art, they make the case for art tellingly. The last word is Callicles', and it is a hymn, connecting religion and poetry. This connection is to become Arnold's great theme in the essays. But the poems present it *best,* in a way—by means of symbolism, which can mediate thought with greater precision than statement. These poems retain their efficacy, and in their open-endedness present a continuing invitation to the reader.

All this by no means exhausts the theme of vocation in Arnold's poetry, but only fastens on some loci that seem especially central to

me. And my sense of Arnold's vocation is somewhat different in
emphasis from what has been current: I see his religious mission as
paramount. I do not mean to discount the delightfully worldly, *enfant-
terrible*, dandiacal young Arnold. Arnold tends to talk about multiple
selves and levels of being because he himself is a man of many levels.
The letters to Clough show the variety: ironic, mercurial, insouciant,
posturing—along with a steady ground bass of concern for First
Things, which the references to Spinoza, to the *Bhagavad Gita*, and
to the Bible repeatedly demonstrate. There is, moreover, a drive I believe very like that of a religious vocation, toward an integration of
religion with one's other dearest concerns:

Modern poetry can only subsist . . . by becoming a complete magister vitae
as the poetry of the ancients did: by including, as theirs did, religion with
poetry . . . . an immense task.

(*Clough* 124)

One Rugbeian writes here to another, in the joint understanding of
the Rugbeian sense of "call." This "called" self of Arnold was to assume increasing importance. He himself said of *Literature and Dogma*,
"I think it, of all my books in prose, the one most important (if I may
say so) and most capable of being useful" (VI: 141).

The late poem "Obermann Once More," which I will consider below, is most explicit on the religious mission. In it, briefly, Obermann
redivivus explains how the old grounds of faith are gone, and calls
upon the poet to reestablish Christianity on grounds which are "true."
It must be granted that Arnold felt himself to be answering to this
challenge. And for all his cool Tyrian irony, he felt himself, with a
rather Miltonic arrogance perhaps, to be rejustifying the ways of God
to man—God the force not ourselves that makes for righteousness,
God the stream of tendency by which all things seek to fulfill the law
of their being, God the metaphor. And by means of that tact which
the study of letters alone can provide, he undertakes to rejustify the
Bible and to provide a religion which is acceptable to a new scientific
or rational age. Tinker and Lowry some time ago read the poem in
this way: "His vocation—one must make bold to say it—was no less
than the task of civilizing his fellow countrymen and setting up for
them a new religion!"[31]

In 1876 Arnold published an essay, "A Psychological Parallel,"

31. Tinker and Lowry, *Poetry of Matthew Arnold*, p. 273.

which he felt to be a kind of envoi to his writings on religion. In this he returns, significantly, to Glanvill and his associates; he had been reading John Tulloch's *Rational Theology and Christian Philosophy in England in the Seventeenth Century* (1874) and was freshly inspired by the Cambridge Platonists. The "parallel" of the title is between St. Paul and one of the Platonists, John Smith, and the word "psychological" very well indicates the phenomenological nature of the approach to religion. The essay is a sort of reprise of Arnold's religious thought, and is particularly explicit. For him, the Cambridge Platonists offer "a conception of religion true, long obscured, . . . for which the hour of light has at last come. . . . [They] base it upon a ground which will not crumble under our feet" (VIII: 123). And he recounts his concept of how the metaphorical language of the Bible and of the liturgy work as "poetry" and exclaims: "It is a great error to think that whatever is thus perceived to be poetry ceases to be available to religion. The noblest races are those which know how to make the most serious use of poetry." I think this shows Arnold in the full sense of his mission; his literary theory would appear to be handmaiden to his main vocation: to revalidate religious texts, and to regain the joy whose grounds are true.

II

The Fathers of
the Higher Criticism

A S an old man of seventy-five, Robert Browning wrote an ingratiating autobiographical poem about his experience of the Iliad.

> My father was a scholar and knew Greek.
> When I was five years old, I asked him once
> "What do you read about?" "The siege of Troy."
> "What is a siege and what is Troy?" Whereat
> He picked up chairs and tables for a town,
> Set me a-top for Priam, called our cat
> —Helen, enticed away from home (he said)
> By wicked Paris . . . .[1]

That humane old banker, the senior Browning, with a rare peda-gogical sense, helps the little boy to act out the essential Homeric narrative.

> This taught me who was who and what was what . . .

and it was "a huge delight," and it caught on. A few years later the father comes across Robert and his playmates "playing at Troy's siege" and invites him to know more about it. Pope's translation will give you a good account, he says, and perhaps some day you'll get it "from Homer's very mouth"—and he makes Buttmann's *Greek Grammar* available.

1. Robert Browning, "Development" (1889), in *The Complete Poetical Works* (New York: Macmillan, 1915), pp. 1312–14.

> So I ran through Pope,
> Enjoyed the tale—what history so true?

Thus *motivated*, as we say now, the child worked away at the *Grammar*.

> Time passed, I ripened somewhat: one fine day,
> "Quite ready for the Iliad, nothing less?"

And so he proceeds to work at the standard Heyne text (1802) with his lexicon.

> I thumbed well and skipped nowise till I learned
> Who was who, what was what, from Homer's tongue,
> And there an end of learning.

We see then the complacent twelve-year-old prodigy showing off to the family friends that he knows all there is to know about Homer. There is no reason to doubt the autobiographical authenticity of the account.

> Thus did youth spend a comfortable time;
> Until—"What's this the Germans say is fact
> That Wolf found out first? It's unpleasant work
> Their chop and change, unsettling one's belief . . . .

It was Friedrich August Wolf who in 1795 published his *Prolegomena* to Homer, proposing the origin of the Iliad to be in oral tradition, multiple ballad-type sources, from which the written version was "edited" to give unity to the whole.

> So I bent brow o'er *Prolegomena*.
> And after Wolf, a dozen of his like
> Proved there was never any Troy at all,
> Neither Besiegers nor Besieged,—nay, worse,—
> No actual Homer, no authentic text,
> No warrant for the fiction I, as fact,
> Had treasured in my heart and soul so long—
> Ay, mark you! and as fact held still. . . .

The reader may now begin to sense overtones here. Certainly the child's first "doubts" about the passionately felt, passionately believed story of Troy would be traumatic, but the analogy of the

Bible leaps to mind. This poem is in fact a deft allegory of the Higher Criticism of the Bible.[2] In just such a way one would "bend brow" over Eichhorn's *Introduction to the Old Testament* (1780–83), which proposes that the Bible accounts existed in oral tradition a long time before being written down, that they were composed by many different people at different times, and that it was the priestly editors who gave the material a kind of unity.[3] So these new Bible critics, Eichhorn and a dozen of his like, proved there was never any—Eden, neither Abraham nor Isaac, no escape from Egypt nor entry into the Promised Land; nay, worse—no Moses, perhaps no actual Deity! no real Scripture, no *warrant* for the myth that I, as fact, had treasured in my heart and soul so long—

> and as fact held still, still hold,
> Spite of new knowledge, in my heart of hearts
> And soul of souls, fact's essence freed and fixed
> From accidental fancy's guardian sheath.

There is a kind of truth here, in this Homer/Bible, an *essence* to be understood in the myth, something *fixed* or lasting, within this *accidental* imaginative exterior. But—

> ah, Wolf!
> Why must he needs come doubting, spoil a dream?

The pity of it! Browning seems to say. Pain often accompanies the move from one phase of understanding to another. Should I blame my father for not explaining the nature of myth to me from the start? (Jeremy Bentham, one remembers, felt it was reprehensible to expect children to be taught to *believe* in things they could not understand.)

> Suppose my childhood was scarce qualified
> To rightly understand mythology,
> Silence at least was in his power to keep.

2. I presume this is the accepted view of the poem; it is well explained in De-Vane's commentary (William Clyde DeVane, *A Browning Handbook*, 2nd ed. [1955; New York: Appleton-Century-Crofts, 1963], pp. 547–49).

3. Gladstone believed firmly in a personal Homer, somewhat as he believed in a personal God (John L. Myres, *Homer and His Critics*, ed. Dorothea Gray [London: Routledge and Kegan Paul, 1958], p. 106).

But of course it was right to give the child that "huge delight"; the rhetoric of the poem communicates filial pride in the parent's wisdom. In our allegory, that is, the Church (or Chapel) is to be perfectly condoned for letting youth dream his Bible dreams. It is conceivable, the poet grants, that he might have learned ethics if he had not had his Homer/Bible, might have learned "by forthrights not meanderings,"

> to loathe, like Peleus' son
> A lie as Hell's Gate, love my wedded wife,
> Like Hector, and so on with all the rest.
> Could not I have excogitated this
> Without believing such men really were?

The father *might* have given him a translation of the *Nichomachean Ethics*. But ah,

> 'tis a treatise I find hard
> To read aright now that my hair is grey,
> And I can manage the original.

I don't have any trouble reading Greek, that is, even philosophic prose. But even when we are old, how infinitely preferable, how infinitely superior, are those myths, those stories, those *meanderings*, those delights of metaphor, to the *forthrights*, the literal abstract prose of dogma. The aged Browning did, in fact, find Homer his most companionable reading, still. It is not irrelevant, I think, to note that the friendship between Arnold and Browning at this stage appears to be deep and sympathetic. There are no notable long letters, but there are many short notes of invitation to small dinners, and there must have been much intimate talk. This poem, "Development," is a miniature allegorized *Literature and Dogma*, making an Arnoldian point in its own way.

Not only does it allegorize the Higher Criticism of the Bible, but it also allegorizes a whole theory of history, and this theory is a larger phenomenon, embracing the new criticism of Homer and the Bible. The Higher Criticism is best understood as just one aspect of this new theory, Historicism. Vico first articulated it, in reaction against Cartesianism and the primacy of the study of the physical sciences. Vico advocates the study of history as the supremely *human* science, rejecting the standard notions of the human condition as fixed and

static. He propounds a cyclical theory of history. All societies are
perpetually changing: they start in a "bestial" stage, move into an
"age of gods" when brutal impulses begin to be curbed by fear of
supernatural powers, then move into an "age of heroes" in which
societies become organized, hierarchically; then the inequities of the
heroic age give way, by social pressure, to democracy and equal justice, but the weakening of tradition in this stage leads at last to disso-
lution and barbarism. Vico's cyclical theory, especially in later hands,
such as the influential Herder's, takes on a certain spiral movement,
implying a slow, eddying "progress." Vico and Herder had important
direct influence on Matthew Arnold, and this will be taken up later.
For Browning's poem, it should be said now that with Vico and
Herder the early stage of a society is marked by the use of unex-
amined symbols and metaphors, or myths. This use constitutes the
"poetry" of that early stage and is coextensive with religion and ritual.
Herder, following Vico, considers that Homer's poetry is early-phase
Greek culture; the Bible early-phase Hebrew-Christian; the legends of
Aeneas, Romulus and Remus, and Numa Pompilius the early-phase
Roman; while the ballads Bishop Percy collected in his *Reliques*, and
Herder's own collections of Germanic folk poetry, constitute the early
phase of Northern European culture. The idea that Browning uses in
his poem is that these poetic myths are all taken literally at first, and
then in later stages of the culture they are understood as symbolic yet
invaluable in teaching us what we need to know to relate ourselves
morally to one another and to eternity. By a Higher Criticism we can
find the essence of the folk poetry, "free" it from accidental literalism
and reveal it as "fixed" or of eternal value. Browning uses his own
childhood, then, as the analogue of the early phase of culture when
the myth is accepted uncritically and joyfully. Man's development re-
capitulates society's development. In old age, or in later stages of the
culture, we may appreciate the Stagirite, but even then we still turn to
our great fictions, rightly understood as such and all the more valuable
for that, for delight, sustenance, and humanity. For Herder, the central principle of the philosophy of history is *Entwicklung*, most often
translated into English as *development*. Brownings title "Development" has indubitable echoes of this influential German historical
concept, and the poem demonstrates the connection of Historicism
with the Higher Criticism. This connection, I think, is vital to an understanding of Arnold's religious thought.

With this in mind, I propose an outline review of the Higher Criticism, and for that we need to go back rather far into history—to Aristotle, who first claimed for poetry a "higher" truth than history has. And it is for literary criticism to search it out and establish it, and this is the genesis of the Higher Criticism. For the use of the term "Higher Criticism" in its nineteenth-century sense, most commentators turn first to Johann Gottfried Eichhorn. He writes in his foreword to the second edition (1787) of his *Introduction to the Old Testament* that people have been reading the Old Testament with no sense of its place in history or of the peculiarity of its language:

> My greatest labor I have had to devote to a hitherto unworked field, to the investigation of the inner nature of the various scriptures of the Old Testament, with the help of the Higher Criticism (not a new term to any humanist).[4]

With great hopes and a devout spirit this prodigious philologist set the pattern for the new biblical criticism, implying by his very terms that he would use the methods that had been used in the study of the classics of Greece and Rome. The history of Higher Criticism, so important to nineteenth-century studies, is often traced in brief in those books called "backgrounds" to Victorian literature, but we are in fact lacking a fully developed history of the subject, for certain specific reasons. On the one hand there are the theological Bible scholars working in their own tradition, which was broad at first but too often now perpetuates only one side of the early German academic achievement in an ossified vocabulary, like "Form Criticism" and "Sitz im Leben," as though no other terms had developed in the mainstream of English historical and literary studies. "Form Criticism" is simply genre criticism, and "Sitz im Leben" is simply historical background. On the other hand there are the literary scholars who talk about the great importance of the Bible in our tradition but seldom do anything about it. They tend to suspect the biblical specialists as naive religion-

4. Johann Gottfried Eichhorn, *Einleitung in das Alte Testament*, 3 vols. (Leipzig, first published 1780–83; 2nd. ed., Jena, 1787; 3rd. ed., Leipzig, 1803): "Die meiste Mühe musste ich auf ein bisher noch gar nicht bearbeitetes Feld, auf die Untersuchung von der inneren Beschaffenheit der einzelnen Schriften des Alten Testaments durch Hülfe der höheren Kritik (eines keinem Humanisten neuen Nahmens) wenden" (p. vi). Whether Eichhorn refers to some specific humanist use of the term I do not know, and I should like to know, if anyone can tell me. He may merely be referring to Aristotle.

ists and yet are somewhat afraid to touch the area as too much the province of specialists. Secular culture seems disinclined to take up its biblical heritage. Even when a bona fide literary figure like Matthew Arnold embraces the Bible as literature, some scholars are somewhat embarrassed and feel this material speaks only to the "Victorian crisis of faith" which is now mere history and has been sufficiently dealt with in the "backgrounds" books; any Victorian Bible criticism *must*, they think, be dated. Even Douglas Bush, arguing that Arnold's "vision of man and society and literature, far from being out of date, is in some essential respects well ahead of our own," declares nevertheless that "his biblical scholarship has long been superseded"![5] But his biblical scholarship, I think it will appear, is an important part of that "vision of man and society and literature," and it is so because it is *literary* analysis. It connects the specialist study of the Bible with a broader humanism, and it does not suffer from the separateness described above. It has been neglected by both Bible critics and literary critics because it has appeared to fall into neither camp. And it has not been "superseded"; on the contrary, it has been hardly noticed. As John Holloway says, it "contains some of his most interesting ideas . . . ; it had been first attacked, then misrepresented, and then neglected."[6]

But the first desideratum would be a history of the Higher Criticism in breadth and depth. In a pioneering study of its influences on literature, E. S. Shaffer deplores the lack of such a history as a kind of scandal. *Faute de mieux*, she proceeds to supply an outline, useful because it is from the point of view of a comparativist, and this, if there ever was one, is a comparativist matter.[7] But to be a comparativist is

5. Douglas Bush, "Arnold's Prose: 'The Humanisation of Man in Society,'" *The Arnoldian* 5 (Fall 1977): 2.

6. John Holloway, "Matthew Arnold and the Modern Dilemma," in *The Charted Mirror* (London: Routledge and Kegan Paul, 1960), p. 158.

7. Her book, E. S. Shaffer, *"Kubla Khan" and The Fall of Jerusalem: The Mythological School in Biblical Criticism and Secular Literature, 1770–1880* (Cambridge: Cambridge University Press, 1975), is a provocative consideration of how the Higher Criticism impinges on four literary works: Coleridge's "Kubla Khan," Friedrich Hölderlin's "Patmos," Browning's "A Death in the Desert," and George Eliot's *Daniel Deronda*. But her literary sense falters when she acclaims, for instance, *Daniel Deronda* as George Eliot's *summa*, on account, in part, of the Daniel-Mordecai-Zionism elements, which are generally agreed to be a painfully inferior

to take risks, and it is not really so outrageous or surprising that we lack the full study of the Higher Criticism. One would have to be at least as learned as some of the early Higher Critics, having Hebrew, Arabic, Greek, and Latin of course; English, French, and German for the main modern lines of it; and Italian and Spanish for other important contributions. We may have to make do with partial views.

Meantime, I propose to touch on some points of an outline history that will be scattered, tentative, and selective according to my sense of what is relevant to Arnold's development. The term "Higher" itself, to start with, offers some difficulty. It is sometimes understood as opposed to the "lower" or textual criticism: the ascertaining of the authoritative text, involving linguistic study, editions, and translations. "Higher" in this context would imply a more generalized criticism, philosophical and theological, involving matters of genre, historical background, anthropology, archaeology, origins and analogues in other literatures, etc. The term has a sort of sense in that from a "higher" or removed standpoint one may discern contours that are invisible close up, just as air photography of fields may reveal ancient earthworks. Eichhorn and his school were "Orientalists," and being able to stand off high enough to view the Bible in the same field as other near-Eastern myths, could discern parallels. When Northrop Frye discovers archetypes in biblical and other literature he is following a line which is very "high" indeed. But then at times the "lower" or textual criticism discovers such things as linguistic evidence that Moses did not write all the Pentateuch; the record shows that different parts of the document come from different periods in history and that as historical record it cannot all be true. But, it is said, Scripture embodies nevertheless a "higher" or spiritual kind of truth than literal truth, and the critics who deal in this do Higher Criticism. By this declension, "lower" criticism now means literal criticism and implies the doctrine of plenary inspiration—and so we have an illogical set of terms.

There is yet another sense of "Higher" as "more evolved" that grows out of the developmental ways of thinking that Browning's metaphor of childhood suggests. Sometimes this presupposes the cycli-

---

and sentimental part of Eliot's work. She says the historical novel "dominates the century's prose" and is very confused on Arnold's St. Paul and Protestantism.

cal Viconian view, the Bible being written in the early phase of
Hebrew culture; sometimes it presupposes a kind of Darwinism, that
man is continuing in a biological progression from simple brain to a
more complicated brain, from consciousness to a consciousness-of-
being-conscious, that this progression is toward "higher" forms of intelligence, and that we are now ready for a new understanding of
myth as symbol. Tennyson speaks for this vision of moral, religious
evolution; his friend Arthur Hallam was a "type" of the man of the
future, and Christianity will take new forms:

> Ring in the valiant man and free,
> The larger heart, the kindlier hand;
> Ring out the darkness of the land,
> Ring in the Christ that is to be.[8]

What these senses of Higher Criticism have in common is that they
were all an offense and anathema to the Evangelicals, or literalists,
and Higher Criticism earned diabolical overtones. Comparing the
Bible to other literatures and traditions impugned its uniqueness;
textual, literary, anthropological, historical study impugned its absolute sufficiency. The passion with which this literalist view can be
held has been well instanced in an often-quoted passage from John
William Burgon, Dean of Chichester:

*The Bible is none other than The Voice of Him that sitteth upon the Throne!
Every book of it—every chapter of it—every verse of it—every word of it—
every syllable of it—(where are we to stop?) every letter of it—is the direct
utterance of the Most High! The Bible is none other than the word of God—
not some part of it more, some part of it less, but all alike the utterance of Him
who sitteth upon the Throne—absolute—faultless—unerring—supreme.[9]*

And yet, at the age of two months, the tiny John Burgon, born at
Smyrna, had been dedicated to Athena at the Acropolis![10] *Tantum
religio potuit suadere malorum!*

---

8. *In Memoriam*, CVI, in *Poems*, ed. Christopher Ricks (London: Longmans,
1969), p. 959.

9. John William Burgon, *Inspiration and Interpretation* (Oxford: Parker, 1961),
p. 89. Burgon was not an Evangelical but a High Churchman. An ingratiating side
of him appears in his study of some Victorian Anglican worthies: *Lives of Twelve
Good Men* (London: John Murray, 1888).

10. *Dictionary of National Biography*, vol. 22, pp. 335–38.

At times there is yet another shade to "Higher," suggesting transcendence: the Higher Criticism is that which takes us away from the temporary and impermanent into a sense of the One. And at yet other times "Higher" is used, just as we have used Latin *superior*, merely for "better," sensible criticism, or *my* way rather than *your* way. In this meaning it tends to be used only by its proponents. With all these ambiguities it might seem better to call it Literary Criticism, or, more guardedly, New Bible Criticism; and yet because Higher Criticism is the conventional term and we pretty well understand each other when we use it, I think we need not strain to avoid it.

Everyone remembers the medieval tradition of the fourfold exegesis: literal (historical), allegorical, moral, and anagogical (mystical). Milton seems to have been the latest great Protestant continuator of the method, and he exercised a kind of comparativism, insofar as for him classical myth could stand as figure for Christian truth, at its service. The degree to which he saw the Christian mythos itself as *figure* is, I suppose, problematical. The degree to which it *can* be figurative —or not—is the problem Arnold addresses. The development that Puritanism took in the late eighteenth century into the pietistic movement reduced the fourfold exegesis by a kind of purifying passion into the single operation of literalism. Oddly enough, the rationalist impulse of the Enlightenment had often had the same effect, tending to reduce exegeses to the one "correct" literal sense. And from this limitation came the need for a counter criticism, a "Higher" extension to make a rationale for the allegorical, moral, and even anagogical exegeses.

But at the time of the Renaissance, one could apparently have it both ways; Bacon, for instance, seems to me impressively compartmentalized—or hypocritical— in *The New Atlantis* (1626), where he covers himself with conventional piety while the tenor of his matter is highly unorthodox. As W. Neil puts it, "Bacon and Descartes, while both professing orthodoxy, had raised doubts as to the authority of the Bible, in so far as they insisted on the supremacy of reason as the ultimate criterion."[11] Hobbes at least had the candor to get himself into some trouble with *Leviathan* (1642), where he disputes (among other things) the Mosaic authorship of the Pentateuch. But Spinoza, as Arnold himself tells us, got into much more trouble: he was anathe-

11. W. Neil, "The Criticism and Theological Use of the Bible, 1700–1950," in *Cambridge History of the Bible*, vol. 3, ed. S. L. Greenslade (Cambridge: Cambridge University Press, 1963), p. 239.

matized by his coreligionists, the Portuguese Jews (III: 159), and this "God-drunk man," of all people, earned the reputation of atheist.

The Higher Criticism is a many-fathered thing, but for Arnold studies it is Spinoza who best deserves the parental title. For in his *Tractatus Theologico-Politicus* (1670) he insists on the Bible as open to the exercise of reason; in fact, it demands scholarship. Spinoza is essential background to the Germans—Herder, Goethe, Schleiermacher, and Hegel—but his influence on Arnold is direct and early; in a letter to Clough of 1850, Arnold acclaims his "positive and vivifying" force (*Clough* 117). H. F. Lowry declares that to have mastered the thought of Spinoza is to have mastered half of Arnold's religious teaching.[12] Arnold's own essays on Spinoza, with their synthesis of Spinoza's teaching, best illustrate the point,[13] and their place in his career—before the writing of *Culture and Anarchy* and *Literature and Dogma*—indicates Spinoza's shaping force.[14]

The French pioneers of Higher Criticism do not, so far as I know, directly influence Arnold. Richard Simon, although he considered himself orthodox and anti-Spinozist, did in fact apply Spinozist hermeneutics in his *Histoire critique du Vieux Testament* (1678), which denies Mosaic authorship of the Pentateuch. Simon is considered the father of French Bible criticism and along with Pierre Bayle and Jean Astruc established its important French tradition, formative for Ernest Renan, who is so closely relevant to Arnold's thought, and formative of the French intellectual milieu of the *Revue des deux mondes* and the *Revue germanique et française* from whose coverage of German scholarship Arnold regularly profited.

In England the seventeenth-century Cambridge Platonists and their Oxford confrere Joseph Glanvill, Arnold's tutelary spirit, fostered the exercise of reason on the Scriptures, anticipating the Broad Church of the nineteenth century. John Locke continues the Cambridge-Platonic tradition of tolerance; and although he accepts the divine inspiration of the Bible, he holds nevertheless, in *The Reasonableness of Christianity* (1695), that the Bible may be tested by reason, being con-

12. Lowry, introduction to *Letters to Clough*, p. 51.

13. "The Bishop and the Philosopher," "Tractatus Theologico-Politicus," and "Spinoza and the Bible" (III: 40–55; 56–64; 158–82).

14. The authoritative assessment of Spinoza's influence is in chapter 3 of R. H. Super's *The Time-Spirit of Matthew Arnold* (Ann Arbor: University of Michigan Press, 1970).

fident that Christianity is rational and simple. Berkeley is probably a more intimate influence on Arnold than Locke; his engaging *Siris* (1744) was on Arnold's early reading lists (1845–47).[15] Points of sympathetic understanding would be Berkeley's interest in the pre-Socratics, especially Heraclitus and Empedocles, and the idea of the retreat of the soul into itself; and then Arnold's studies in anthropomorphism must owe something to Berkeley's understanding of God as wisdom, order, law, virtue—although, says Berkeley, "it may seem more pious to some to take God as a substantial being."[16] Arnold's commentary on the Tetragrammaton would seem to owe something to Berkeley's noting that Plato describes God as Moses does, by his *being.* And Berkeley anticipates Arnold's sense of the power of criticism in creating the climate of the state, the conditions in which we meditate on the nature of God.

Prevailing studies are of no small consequence . . . , the religion, manners, and civil government of a country ever taking some bias from its philosophy . . . . Whatever the world thinks, he who hath not much meditated on God, the human mind, and the summum bonum, may possibly make a thriving earthworm, but will most undubitably make a sorry patriot or a sorry statesman.[17]

The Deists' controversies further opened up the interpretation of Scripture, and there ensued a peculiar dialectic: on the one side are the scoffers—Voltaire, Rousseau, Gibbon, Tom Paine, and on the other the defenders of orthodoxy—William Whiston, Bishop Butler, and so on, and each one of the defenses provides ammunition to the scoffers. In 1753 in France, Jean Astruc proposed the first substantial argument for composite authorship of the Pentateuch by discriminating the "Elohist" and "Jahvist" texts and theorizing on the duplication of narratives. In England, Richard Bentley became yet another father of the Higher Criticism, bringing philology and history to classical and biblical texts alike. In his *Hexepla* (1720) he created a tool for the learned study of the Old Testament, comparing the Hebrew vocabu-

15. Kenneth Allott, "Matthew Arnold's Reading-lists in Three Early Diaries," *Victorian Studies* 2 (March 1959) : 254–66.

16. *Siris: A Chain of Philosophical Reflexions and Inquiries Concerning the Virtues of Tarwater, and Divers Other Subjects Connected Together and Arising from One Another,* first published 1744 (*Complete Works,* ed. A. C. Fraser, 4 vols. [Oxford: Clarendon Press, 1901], 3: 115–299, especially p. 285).

17. Ibid., pp. 282, 291.

lary with the Chaldee, Syriac, Vulgate, and Septuagint; he espoused
the idea of multiple authorship of Homer, if not the Bible, and proposed a new edition of the New Testament on sound principles.

In 1753 in England Bishop Robert Lowth published his Oxford
lectures *De Sacra Poesi Hebraeorum*. The lectures are best known
for the recognition of Hebrew poetry as a genre, for the demonstration of parallelism as its formal element, and for the demonstration
that the Prophets are for the most part poetic in form, as well as
Psalms, the Song of Solomon, Job, and incidental songs. But the lectures are also a landmark in the history of literary criticism; Lowth
argues responsibly and precisely, and his practical criticism is hardly
to be surpassed, especially in the analysis of metaphor. He might be
describing Arnold's very method of biblical criticism when he declares, "The mind should . . . exert itself to discover . . . the connexion
between the literal and figurative meanings."[18] Samuel Holt Monk
finds that Lowth anticipates Burke and Kant "in his explanation of
what occurs when the imagination strives to grasp a reality beyond
the possibility of literal description."[19] Some of Lowth's importance
for the Romantic poets has been appreciated,[20] but his own study of
the Bible is of overriding significance in itself. Friedrich Meinecke
claims he is of signal importance for the history of history:

Lowth's book was perhaps the most intellectually important product of the
whole Pre-Romantic movement in England. It was free of all dilettantism and
superficiality of taste, and had the indirect result of contributing to the liberation of historical research from the bonds of theology by displaying the purely
human and historical content and value of the Bible. It set forth a genuine
science of the humanities and gave it new organs.[21]

Lowth was taken up by the Germans, and his influence made its way
back to England through them, often unrecognized. But Arnold knew

18. Robert Lowth, *Lectures on the Sacred Poetry of the Hebrews*, ed. Vincent
Freimarck, trans. G. Gregory (1787), 2 vols. (Hildesheim: Georg Olms Verlag,
1969), 1:155.

19. Freimarck, referring to Samuel Holt Monk, *The Sublime: Critical Concepts in XVIII Century England* (New York, Modern Language Association, 1935),
in his introduction to Lowth's *Lectures*, p. xiv.

20. Ibid., pp. xvii–xviii.

21. Friedrich Meinecke, *Historism: The Rise of a New Historical Outlook* (*Die
Entstehung des Historismus* [Munich, 1936]), trans. J. E. Anderson (London: Routledge and Kegan Paul, 1972), p. 206.

Lowth's work (VII: 61, 64; X: 124) and himself understood the principles of parallelism and their essential value for exegesis (X: 102), and he used Lowth's edition of Isaiah in making his own and—as I think—profited by Lowth's analysis of metaphor. Otherwise, some of the effect of Lowth's work came to Arnold as to his countrymen indirectly through the Germans.

The *Lectures* were soon translated into English, and the German scholar Johann Michaelis, who had heard one of the lectures at Oxford, brought out in Germany a new and annotated Latin edition, in 1758 (volume 1) and 1761 (volume 2); they were widely known and acclaimed on the continent. A recent English scholar reports that Heinrich Gesenius (the great lexicographer of Hebrew, whose Hebrew grammar is still standard) occasionally differs from Lowth, but when he does he is generally wrong.[22] It is curious to see Thomas Arnold, as Arthur Stanley tells us, making much of "the general coincidence of two men so different as Lowth and Gesenius in their interpretation of Isaiah"; Thomas Arnold "used to instance [this coincidence] as a satisfactory proof that the meaning of the Hebrew Scriptures could be readily ascertained,"[23] where in fact Gesenius was borrowing from Lowth. T. K. Cheyne in his standard *Founders of Old Testament Criticism* (1893)[24] hardly grasps Lowth's significance, though he does give him a page, and in Cheyne's own edition of Isaiah (1880–81) he does astutely grant that Lowth "began that important *aestheticising* movement in Biblical criticism" (my italics). *Aestheticizing* looks very important indeed from where we stand now.

The case of Alexander Geddes is a melancholy example of the British biblical effort: a learned Scot and a Roman Catholic, he knew Astruc's work and that of the Germans, and was himself respected by Eichhorn; he projected a new translation of the Bible with critical apparatus and was supported by Lowth. His first volume, however, was prefaced by a declaration of multiple and late authorship of the Pentateuch, and this drew the disapprobation of the Anglican Church and the universities, and of the Roman Catholics as well, and he was sus-

22. R. S. Cripps, "Two British Interpreters of the Old Testament: Robert Lowth (1710–87) and Samuel Lee (1783–1852)," *Bulletin of the John Rylands Library* (Manchester) 35 (March 1953): 385–404.

23. A. P. Stanley, *Life of Arnold* (1844; London: John Murray, 1904), p. 351n.

24. T. K. Cheyne, *Founders of Old Testament Criticism* (London: Methuen, 1893; reprint ed., Jerusalem: Raritas, 1971).

pended from his priestly office. Cheyne observes in his English way that Geddes was "socially and intellectually on a level with the best English Protestants . . . *though* [my italics] a Roman Catholic."[25] He died in 1802, a martyr, we might say, of the Higher Criticism.

The "best English Protestants" had perhaps learned their lessons from the Deist controversies and resorted to a certain hypocrisy; they might consider literalist interpretation a legitimate support to the faith of the simple while they themselves might savor the new scholarship in their studies. But with John Wesley and the growing Evangelical movement the idea of the Bible as the word of God becomes a principle, and literalism becomes a prime tenet of Evangelicalism. The battle lines against the Higher Criticism are drawn up. There was probably also some general hostility to it as part of the revulsion from all things associated with the French Revolution. "Rationalism" leads not only to the well-known political excesses but also to the other excess of undermining the Christian faith.

But it was different in Germany, "learned, indefatigable, deep-thinking Germany. . . . But for that same unshackled and even sequestered condition of the German Learned, which permits and induces them to fish in all manner of waters, with all manners of nets, it seems probable enough, this abstruse inquiry might . . . have continued dormant."[26] So Thomas Carlyle has it, learned, indefatigable, deep-thinking Carlyle, who embraces, mediates, and transforms the new learning. The German universities were secular foundations, and so the radically new approach to the Bible developed in comparative academic freedom.[27] Yet the motive force in Germany was often Protestant Pietism, related to the Evangelical movement in England: if the Bible is to be our sole guide, it is our most urgent task to determine its meaning. When this pious impulse touches these secular universities at a time of great scholarly ferment, biblical criticism flourishes. It is part, often it may seem the motivating part, of the new Historicism, which combined the study of historical records with comparative philology, comparative religion, astronomy, geology, biology, mythol-

25. Cheyne, *Founders*, p. 11.

26. Thomas Carlyle, *Sartor Resartus*, vol. 1, pp. 2, 4; in *Works*, Edinburgh edition, 30 vols. (London: Chapman and Hall, 1910).

27. Arnold acclaims the *Lehrfreiheit* and *Lernfreiheit* of the German universities in "Superior or University Instruction in Prussia" (IV: 263).

ogy, and folk poetry, to achieve a singularly broad and unified vision. Here is Carlyle again:

Criticism has assumed a new form in Germany; it proceeds on other principles, and proposes to itself a higher aim. The grand question is not now a question concerning the qualities of diction, the coherence of metaphors, the fitness of sentiments, the general logical truth, in a work of art, but properly and ultimately a question of the essence and peculiar life of the poetry itself. . . . [Take Shakespeare:] Are these dramas of his not verisimilar only, but true; nay, truer than reality itself, since the essence of unmixed reality is bodied forth in them under more expressive symbols? . . . Criticism stands like an interpreter between the inspired and the uninspired; between the prophet and those who hear the melody of his words, and catch some glimpse of their material meaning, but understand not their deeper import.

And how do they do this? By an overflow of the poet's own "Pythian raptures"? No, says Carlyle,

Nowise in this manner do the Germans proceed; but by rigorous scientific inquiry.

Not that the science is complete or certain, but it is methodical. And, moreover, Carlyle insists,

It is a European tendency, and springs from the general condition of intellect in Europe.[28]

When one knows Carlyle's priorities, and his own sense of the oneness of things, one realizes that all this concerns the Bible primarily, in a kind of allegory.

This new German learning that concerns Carlyle—and Arnold— has Goethe for its greatest exemplar, but the greatest original force in it, and the most influential, is Johann Gottfried von Herder. He more than any other activated the Historicist line of thought, including the Higher Criticism, and he is so particularly important for Arnold studies that he demands attention here. It is always a question with Arnold whether he took in his German thought directly or by way of Carlyle. His well-documented reading of Herder's *Ideen* (1867–69) demonstrates a direct influence, but in all probability he knew much

28. Carlyle, "State of German Literature" (1827), *Critical and Miscellaneous Essays*, vol. 1, pp. 43–45; in *Works*.

of Herder early, through Carlyle. We have learned that the Carlylean elements in Arnold's thought are hardly to be overstressed, from Kathleen Tillotson's and David DeLaura's classical essays on the subject.[29] R. H. Super has further demonstrated the Carlylean elements in the area of religion particularly.[30] Even Arnold's Goethe is often a Goethe in Carlylean terms, and Arnold's most distinctive achievements seem often to have a Carlylean germ—even the concept of the Philistine, for instance. Arnold's attitude to Carlyle is curiously ambivalent, at times oddly hostile, considering the great debt.

A somewhat similar situation obtains in the case of Carlyle's debt to Herder, and the definitive study here is that of Hill Shine.[31] Shine recounts the record of Carlyle's reading of Herder and demonstrates the enormous influence of Herder on Carlyle's actual writing, with an abundance of parallel passages. As Shine says, some Herder passages could be translated and "inserted in *Sartor* and 'Characteristics' without injury to unity of meaning or, in some instances, without injury even to the figurative style."[32] Herder used, before Carlyle, the figure of institutions as ruined buildings, the *Sartor* clothes-metaphor, the phoenix-figure, *Palingenesia* or rebirth, and the notion of the relativity of time and space. It seems to me further that Carlyle's sense of Organic Filaments binding all together is a version of Herder's holism, that *Sartor* itself is the very text and flower of Herder's *Entwicklungsphilosophie*, and that this *Entwicklung* is Carlyle's "Eternal Growth" and Arnold's "Becoming" (as well as Browning's "Development"). Hill Shine concludes that Herder's influence on Carlyle "was at the high level where religion, philosophy, and history merge into one."[33] Precisely. It is Herder's distinguishing thought that *they do merge*, and this characterizes the Higher Criticism.

Carlyle was troubled about Herder. He writes in an early notebook of 1826:

29. Kathleen Tillotson, "Matthew Arnold and Carlyle," *Proceedings of the British Academy* 42 (1956) : 133–56; David DeLaura, "Arnold and Carlyle," *Publications of the Modern Language Association* 79 (March 1964) : 104–29.

30. Super, *Time-Spirit of Arnold*, pp. 61–91.

31. Hill Shine, "Carlyle's Early Writings and Herder's *Ideen*," *Booker Memorial Studies*, ed. Hill Shine (Chapel Hill: University of North Carolina Press, 1950), pp. 3–33.

32. Ibid., pp. 25–26.

33. Ibid., p. 33.

Everything is the effect of circumstances and organisation: *Er war was er seyn könnte* [he was what he was able to be]. . . . This is surely very dubious. . . . Strange ideas about the Bible and Religion; passing strange we think them for a clergyman. Must see more of Herder: he is a new species in some degree.[34]

Shine directs us to another passage, in Carlyle's "Life and Writings of Werner" (1828), on "the general state of religious opinion in Germany":

It is a common theory among the Germans, that every Creed, every Form of worship, is a *form* merely; the mortal and ever-changing *body*, in which the immortal and unchanging *spirit* of Religion is, with more or less completeness, expressed to the material eye, and made manifest and influential among the doings of men. It is thus, for instance, that Johannes Müller, in his *Universal History*, professes to consider the Mosaic Law, the creed of Mahomet, nay Luther's Reformation; and, in short, all other symptoms of Faith; which he scruples not to designate, without special praise or censure, simply as *Vorstellungsarten*, "Modes of Representation." We could report equally singular things of Schelling and others, belonging to the philosophic class; nay of Herder, a Protestant clergyman, and even bearing high authority in the Church.[35]

We can see here the opening up of the Calvinist consciousness to the large German comparativistic, anthropological vision of Herder, above all, as the fount and main force of the movement. In spite of Carlyle's dubiety, whole tracts of Herder's thought are incorporated into the base of his fabric, and in spite of Arnold's frequent ostensible rejection of Carlyle, these same tracts undergo a further incorporation by Arnold. Herder is barely acknowledged, while Goethe receives the praise. Carlyle professedly planned a study of Herder but never wrote it. Arnold should have planned a study of Carlyle, but he never comes to terms with his Carlylean debt directly.[36] I think we can suspect in

34. Quoted by Hill Shine, ibid., p. 7.
35. Carlyle, *Critical and Miscellaneous Essays*, 1: 123.
36. Kathleen Tillotson proposes that Carlyle is the real subject of the essay on Emerson (X: 165–86) in "Matthew Arnold and Carlyle," pp. 151–53. Her demonstration throughout of Carlylean elements is wonderfully rich and just, but at one point I should like to offer an amendment that may be significant. She speaks of the

both cases what Harold Bloom has designated "anxiety of influence": the relationships are so close, the debts so large, and the influences so great as to be of the very essence. Arnold's reading of Herder's *Ideen* in the late sixties (which reading we shall consider in due course) must have been an experience of returning *ad fontem*, an experience of recognition of what had become part of him through Carlyle.

But now let us consider Herder himself. The culmination of the *Aufklärung* in Germany, in the court of Frederick the Great and his guests, Voltaire and Madame de Staël, seems to have made the climate that produced great men: Lessing, Kant, Herder, Goethe, Schiller, the Humboldts, Eichhorn, each prodigious on his own and yet all the greater for their interaction. Lessing, one of the first of the neo-Spinozists, had questioned conventional biblical scholarship and had spoken against dogma. As an *Aufklärer* Michaelis felt the earthy language of the Old Testament could hardly be regarded as the Word of God; God would be sure to talk in an intellectual sort of way. But Johann Georg Hamann (1730–88) attacks the materializing tendency of the Enlightenment, holding there is no thought apart from language, and deplores Michaelis's language of *Verstand*, abstract reason; it is language castrated and dehumanized. The proper human mode is the language of *anschauende Vernunft*, intuitive reason (worth mentioning here if only as a prototype of Arnold's "imaginative reason").[37] This is a language full of concrete images (*Bilder*),

---

"notorious" discrepancy between Empedocles' suicide and the preceding statement of his creed in the great philosophical stanzas. I see no discrepancy, for the stanzas, which embody the Carlylean doctrine, are clearly *dramatic*, i.e., addressed to Pausanias, while the later soliloquy represents, as is traditional in soliloquies, the speaker's real state of mind. The central *Sartor*-ideas in the stanzas, then, offer justly and sympathetically the Carlylean creed as one to live by. But the soliloquy and suicide constitute Arnold's criticism of Carlyle: there are some who come to a point where this creed is not sufficient to live by. So the poem might be taken as an early representation of Arnold's ambivalence about Carlyle: in Empedocles as teacher to Pausanias we see "the beloved man" (*Clough* 75); in the soliloquy we see the "moral desperado" who "led us out into the wilderness and left us there" (*Clough* 111).

37. I am indebted here to James C. O'Flaherty, "Language and Reason in the Thought of Hamann," *Creative Encounter: Festschrift for Herman Salinger*, ed. L. R. Phelps (Chapel Hill: University of North Carolina Press, 1978), pp. 86–104. The mystical Hamann, called the *Magus* and often dismissed as wild, draws new

analogy, parataxis, and it addresses itself to the whole man, both feeling and intellect. Such is the language of the Bible; God is "the Poet at the beginning of days," who, being the word made flesh, uses the human idiom of images. "Perception and passion speak and understand by images alone. In images subsists the whole wealth of human knowledge and happiness."[38] Hamann had begun a *Metakritik* against Kant's *Critique of Pure Reason;* Herder's *Metakritik* (1799) completes it. He belabors Kant's *Critique* "as a linquistic monstrosity, an unparalleled word jugglery" and a perpetuator of the untenable faculty psychology.[39] The *Metakritik* maintains, as Robert T. Clark says, "the purely positivistic, downright behavioristic position . . . . [Its] chief result . . . is the identification of thought with language, and this identification is that of a poet. Poetic discourse *is* identical with its language."[40]

One of the remarkable things about Herder is how reminiscent of Vico he appears to be. Isaiah Berlin, in his recent *Vico and Herder*,[41] explains how the actual influence is problematical; the similarity is incontestable. Berlin considers both as keys to our counter-Enlightenment ways of thinking and being. Vico's great discovery, in Berlin's words, is of "the study of the human past as a form of collective self-understanding."[42] Like Vico, Herder aims to bring "all the sciences of man and his environment, his origins, his history, into a single integrated whole."[43] Among Herder's works are *Vom Geist der Ebräischen Poesie*,[44] which starts off by acknowledging the debt to Lowth

---

interest now for connections with Nietzsche and Kierkegaard. See Isaiah Berlin, *Against the Current* (New York: Viking, 1959), passim.

38."Sinne und Leidenschaften reden und verstehen nur als Bilder. In Bildern besteht der ganze Schatz menschlicher Erkenntniss und Glückseeligkeit." Hamann, *Aesthetica in Nuce;* quoted in O'Flaherty, "Language and Reason in Hamann," p. 88.

39. Robert T. Clark, *Herder, His Life and Thought* (Berkeley: University of California Press, 1955), p. 399.

40. Clark, *Herder*, p. 405.

41. Isaiah Berlin, *Vico and Herder: Two Studies in the History of Ideas* (London: Hogarth Press, 1976).

42. Ibid., p. 98.

43. Ibid., p. xxi.

44. Johann Gottfried von Herder, *The Spirit of Hebrew Poetry*, trans. J. Marsh (Burlington, Vt.: E. Smith, 1832).

and proceeds with rather general appreciation of the Old Testament poetic books—this Arnold owned—and *Gott, Einige Gespräche*,[45] which is profoundly Spinozist.

But his great and influential work is the *Ideen zur Philosophie der Geschichte der Menschheit*[46] (Ideas Toward the Philosophy of History of Mankind).[47] It is this two-volume work which Arnold read intensively and marked liberally—the volumes are preserved in the Beinecke Library at Yale. Arnold's reading lists of 1867–69 record his reading of volume 1 up to page 282 (*Note-Books* 579, 581, 584, 586). This point marks a division: up to here it has been a philosophy of history; from here Herder embarks on his massive history of mankind beginning with China and the rest of the Orient; then Babylon, Assyria, Chaldea; Greece, the Etruscans and Latins, Basques, Gaels, and Cimbri; the Finns, Letts and Prussians, Germans, Slavs; and on to the history of Christianity and Europe with its connections up to the sixteenth century. It is the cosmic, comparativist, and anthropological philosophy of history in the first ten books that would have been crucial for Arnold, and these are what he read and marked. Like Goethe, Herder combines a broad knowledge of science with his humanism, and the science is much less dated than might be supposed. He shows man in his largest context, cosmic and biological, as a creature *developed* from lower forms (there are certain anticipations of Darwinian evolution here).[48] Just as every man is unique, so is every society unique; it has grown and developed in its own way, in

45. Johann Gottfried von Herder, *God, Some Conversations*, trans. Frederick H. Burkhardt (New York: Hafner, 1949).

46. Johann Gottfried von Herder, *Ideen zur Philosophie der Geschichte der Menschheit*, first published 1784–91. The edition of Arnold's own copy is Leipzig: Johann Friedrich Hartknoch, 1828. References will be to this edition.

47. There are three versions in English: one early complete translation by T. Churchill, *Outlines of a Philosophy of the History of Man* (London, 1800; rpt. ed., New York: Bergman, n.d., but fairly recently); an abridged edition of Churchill's translation with some modernizations by Frank E. Manuel, which unfortunately omits the first six books of the twenty (Arnold's intensive reading covers the first seven), *Reflections on the Philosophy of the History of Mankind* (Chicago: University of Chicago Press, 1968); and F. M. Barnard's *J. G. Herder on Social and Political Culture*, which has an excellent introduction and selections from books 3 through 9, following Churchill but occasionally amending (Cambridge: Cambridge University Press, 1969).

48. In scope, these chapters are remarkably parallel to Carl Sagan's *Dragons of Eden* (New York: Ballantine Books, 1977).

response to conditions of its time and place. The historian must try to rid himself of the perspective of his own time and place, and of his own self for that matter, to achieve a sympathetic understanding of cultures other than his own. Each is unrepeatable and exists in its own terms and must be judged by its own standards. Each society undergoes its own *Fortgang* (progress), more or less fulfilling its own potential, and societies yield place to one another in constant *Entwicklung* (development).[49] Process and metamorphosis, conditioned by historical time and geographical space, is the way of the human species.

The corresponding phenomenon for the individual is *Bildung*. This ruling concept, originating with Herder, characterizes the whole German movement and is, as I believe, the essential element in Arnold's theory of culture and religion, and it therefore deserves our close consideration. Our common literary-critical term *Bildungsroman* has somewhat debased the idea of *Bildung*, suggesting often merely a novel of the hero's education and establishment of himself in his life's course. *Bildung* is, rather, the willed harmonious development in the individual of all aspects of the human—as distinct from animal—potential, which Herder calls *Humanität*. Herder writes, in a passage which Arnold marked with double emphasis:

Few men make humanity, in the pure and extensive signification of the word, the proper study of their lives; most begin very late to think of it, and even in the best of men inferior propensities draw down the exalted human to animality. Who among mortals can say that he will reach or has [reached] the pure image of man that lies in him? . . . Every beast attains what his organization can attain; man only reaches it not, because his end is so high, so extensive, so infinite, and he begins on this earth so low, so late, and with so many external and internal obstacles.[50]

49. The concept illuminates many points in Arnold's poetry. "Progress," for instance, can be seen as representing the developmental view of religions. R. H. Super recognizes the concept by making "Development" an index item in *Prose*, vol. III (in the vol. XI addenda). There are several references in vol. III; they peak in vol. VI (which includes *Literature and Dogma*), and there are some also in vols. VII and VIII.

50. Herder, *Ideen*; Churchill, trans., *Outlines*, pp. 182–83. Churchill omits *gottähnliche* ("divine," modifying *Humanität*):

Bei wenigen Menschen ist die gottähnliche Humanität im reinen
und weiten Umfange des Wortes eigentliches Studium des Lebens; die
meisten fangen nur spät an, daran zu denken, und auch bei den besten ziehen

This idea constitutes, I believe, a model of the quest in "The Scholar-Gipsy" and "Thyrsis." Another passage to which Arnold gave double emphasis:

Horrible is the view that finds in the revolutions of the earth only rack and ruin, ever beginnings without ends, eddyings of fate without lasting design. *The chain of development* [*Die Kette der Bildung*, Arnold's emphasis] alone makes out of this rubble a whole, in which indeed individual human forms pass away, but the human spirit lives, immortal and prevailing.[51]

On the inside front cover of the volume, Arnold had jotted "The object:—über den gang des menschlichen Lebens zu ein festen ansicht gelangen zu können [*sic*]" (To be able to arrive at a firm view concerning the course of human life).[52] The chain of *Bildung* or culture here represents his vision of the firm view, the saving, sense-making principle.

One of the very few unidentified items in Arnold's published *Note-Books* is a German item for 1867: "In den umwälzingen des Lebens ein Dauerndes, in sich Gutes und Vernünftiges, zu erkennen!"[53] This can be recognized now as a passage from Heinrich Luden's introduction to the *Ideen*, a passage, again, that Arnold had marked: "dass er [Herder] in den Umwälzungen des Schicksals eben das Schicksal, ein Dauerndes, in sich Gutes und Vernünftiges, zu erkennen wünschte" (that Herder wished to recognize in the eddyings of destiny

---

niedrige Triebe den erhabenen Menschen zum Thier hinunter. Wer unter den Sterblichen kann sagen dass er das reine Bild der Menscheit, das in ihm liegt, erreiche oder erreicht habe? . . . Jedes Thier erreicht, was es in seiner Organisation erreichen soll; der einzige Mensch erreicht's nicht, eben weil sein Ziel so hoch, so weit, so unendlich ist, und er auf unsrer Erde so tief, so spät, mit so viel Hindernissen von aussen und innen anfängt. (Pp. 182–83)

51. Grausenvoll ist der Anblick, in den Revolutionen der Erde nur Trümmer auf Trümmern zu sehen, ewige Anfänge ohne Ende, Umwälzungen des Schicksals ohne dauernde Absicht! *Die Kette der Bildung* allein macht aus diesen Trümmern ein Ganzes, in welchem zwar Menschengestalten verschwinden, aber der Menschengeist unsterblich und fortwirkend lebt.

These are Herder's words, quoted by Heinrich Luden in his introduction to *Ideen*, p. xix.

52. Shortened by Arnold, from ibid., p. xxxvi, of Luden's introduction.

53. *Note-Books* 48.

[the true force of] Destiny itself, something enduring, in itself good and rational).[54] Arnold's inaccuracy in his jotting—he puts *Leben* for *Schicksal*, "life" for "destiny"—shows that he was writing from memory, and indicates how he had appropriated, even adapted, the passage, recognizing in it something that he was to envisage as the *Dauerndes*, the "Eternal." To give just one more passage that he doubly emphasized:

It is culture [*Bildung*] alone which binds together the generations which live one after the other as men who see [but] one day, and *it is in culture [Bildung] that the solidarity of mankind is to be sought*, since in it the strivings of all men coincide [Arnold's italics].[55]

In Herder's vision, the links or chain of culture bind all men together as fellows in *Humanität* in all its vast variety, over all the world, and all through history. The marks of *Humanität* are the capacities for language, for society, and for religion—all these being aspects of a whole. Religion, then, as well as all other aspects of man, shares in the perpetual becoming, the ever shifting relativism of history. Herder sought out *Volkslieder*, folk poetry (and he invented the term), not in the antiquarian way of Bishop Percy but because he believed literary culture the most precious product of a society and believed also that it *created* that society in a way that Isaiah Berlin has called *expressionism*.[56] Herder says: "We live in a world we ourselves create."[57] And one of the most important of created worlds is that of the Bible. Herder's attitude constitutes one of the great energizing forces in the Higher Criticism. By insisting on the Bible's humanness he believed he best served God.

One must read the Bible in a human way: for it is a book written through human agency for human beings; human is the language, human were the external means whereby it was written and preserved; human, finally, is the sense with which it must be grasped, and every aid that elucidates it, as well as

---

54. Herder, *Ideen*, p. xxxv.
55. Herder, Ideen, p. liv.
Die Bildung allein die Geschlechter verbinde, die nach einander leben, wie die Menschen, die Einen Tag sehen, und dass *in der Bildung die Einheit der Menschheit mit sich selbst zu suchen sey*, weil in ihr die Bestrebungen aller Menschen zusammenfallen.
56. Berlin, *Vico and Herder*, p. 153 and index.
57. Quoted from Herder by Berlin, *Vico and Herder*, p. 143.

the entire purpose and use to which it should be applied. You can, therefore, safely believe that the more humanly (in the best sense of the word) you read the word of God, the closer you will come to the purpose of its Artificer, who created man in His image and acts humanly for us in all works and benefices in which He shows Himself to us as God.[58]

Herder has a sense, moreover, of the metaphors of the Bible as of the essence.

When I hear . . . much talk about imagery which must be translated into good, pure, intelligible German, that is, into metaphysical, abstract German, then I often do not know what to do. The former [imagic] language is understood by everyone; the latter is understood by no one.[59]

Here are principles that Arnold makes his own in his Bible criticism.[60]

"Herder's greatest single educational act," writes Robert Clark, was "the awakening of the young Goethe from a complacent Rococo irrationalism to a fuller development as Germany's greatest poet."[61]

58. Johann Gottfried von Herder, *Maran Atha*, vol. 10, p. 7; translated and quoted by Clark, *Herder*, p. 273.

59. Quoted in Clark, *Herder*, p. 281.

60. There are few exceptions to the general neglect of Herder in Arnold studies. Louis Bonnerot recognizes the influence of Vico and Herder's Historicism, points out a possible influence of Herder through Carlyle (quoting from a French version of the *Ideen*), and further suggests a Herderian influence on Arnold's idea of poetry (*Matthew Arnold, poète* [Paris: Didier, 1947], pp. 122, 213n, 415). David DeLaura observes that "Herder's *Humanität* would have appealed [to Arnold] because of its insistence on the need for beauty balanced by its deeply ethical strain. At times Arnold's Hellenism—and certainly his Hebraism—sound closer to Herder's ideal than to Goethe's" (*Hebrew and Hellene in Victorian England* [Austin: University of Texas Press, 1969], p. 186). The insights of DeLaura's "Matthew Arnold and the Nightmare of History," in *Victorian Poetry*, Stratford-on-Avon Studies, no. 15 (London: Edward Arnold, 1972), would come into still better focus if seen as related to the Herder-Barthold Niebuhr-Thomas Arnold matrix. Peter Allan Dale's recent *The Victorian Critic and the Idea of History* (Cambridge, Mass.: Harvard University Press, 1977), a study of Carlyle, Arnold, and Walter Pater, has a good consideration of *Empedocles* and its relationship to Historicism. However, the book is vitiated by ignoring the centrality of Herder and Bible studies to the Historicist issues and by an appalling condescension to Carlyle.

61. Clark, *Herder*, p. 123. Essential texts for this whole field are W. H. Bruford's *Culture and Society in Classical Weimar* (Cambridge: Cambridge University Press, 1962) and *The German Tradition of Self-Cultivation: "Bildung" from Humboldt to Thomas Mann* (Cambridge: Cambridge University Press, 1975).

The friendship and the education is too large a subject to survey here, but it can be noted that Goethe appropriated Herder's enthusiasm for Shakespeare; the sense of language as the distinctively human capacity; the Historicism and its implications for folk poetry, Homer and the Bible; the Herderian holism[62] and the doctrine of Development and its concomitant ideal of *Bildung*—to which he dedicated himself. On religious issues Herder and Goethe were sympathetic up to a point, as Clark writes: both were "convinced of the transcendent importance of Christianity in the culture of the Occident, but both had fought themselves free of the orthodox superstitions about the letter of the Scriptures."[63] Herder continued to consider himself Christian and continued to be a clergyman, parting company with Goethe, who felt Christianity restrictive. Goethe writes in a letter to Johann Jacobi:

With the many divergent tendencies of my being, one mode of thinking is not enough; as a poet and artist I am a Polytheist, as a scientist on the other hand I am a Pantheist,—one as firmly as the other. If for my personality, as a moral being, I need one God then I can manage that too.[64]

Or, more wittily: "In our father's pharmacy there are many prescriptions."[65] Arnold's great debt to Goethe has been traced by others,[66] and so I only suggest here some points of contact on the subject of religion. *Wilhelm Meister*, which Arnold read early in Carlyle's distinguished translation,[67] is, as is well known, the *Bildungsroman par excellence* and embraces the concept, developed from Herder, of *Bildung* as a sort of secular salvation. The "Confessions of a Fair Saint"

62. Herder can be considered a forerunner of *Gestalt* psychology. See Berlin, *Vico and Herder*, p. 216n.

63. Clark, *Herder*, p. 301.

64. Quoted in James Simpson, *Matthew Arnold and Goethe* (London: Modern Humanities Research Association, 1979), p. 129.

65. Quoted in Bruford, *Culture and Society in Weimar*, p. 139.

66. Simpson's *Matthew Arnold and Goethe* is detailed and helpful but must be used with care. His sections on religion, for instance, do not show a sound knowledge of Arnold. Goethe's sentence, "He who has art and science has religion too," is quoted as an Arnoldian principle, when in fact Arnold quotes it only to disagree.

67. An interesting memento of his reading stayed with him in "The Scholar-Gipsy"; compare Carlyle's "we stop with rapture if among the dingles we are crossing the voice of the nightingale starts out" (*Wilhelm Meister*, bk. 2, chap. 2) with Arnold's "listen with enchanted ears, / From the dark dingles, to the nightingales!" ("The Scholar-Gipsy," 368).

(volume 2, book 6) constitutes a thoroughly sympathetic account of the pietistic experience, in a female persona who represents certain elements of Goethe's own encounter with the Herrnhuter Brethren, or Moravians (who also affected John Wesley and Schleiermacher). "Fair Saint," Carlyle's translation of "schöne Seele," loses a special German meaning. Kant had posited two motive forces in human behavior, inclination and duty, which are at odds. Schiller proposes that there are certain individuals, *schöne Seelen*, "beautiful souls," in whom inclination and duty are in harmony.[68] The term stays with Arnold, and he is later to apply it to Wilhelm von Humboldt, the apostle of *Bildung*.[69] Goethe's "schöne Seele" evinces his own passionate interest in science and a rather feminist determination of self separate from relations with the opposite sex and exemplifies both *Bildung* and the *schöne Seele* idea.

I am still advancing, never retrograding; . . . my conduct is approximating more and more to the image I have formed of perfection. . . . I scarcely remember a commandment; to me there is nothing that assumes the aspect of law; it is an impulse that leads me, and guides me always aright. I freely follow my emotions, and know as little of constraint as of repentance.

The later part of *Wilhelm Meister*, the *Wanderjahre* or *Travels*, communicates much of Weimar humanism in general and outlines Goethe's own supra-Christian position and his concept of perpetual self-cultivation. Goethe himself supplies the *loci classici* of the term *Bildung* in the lexicons:

Whatever great, beautiful, or significant experiences have come our way must not be recalled again from without and recaptured, as it were; they must rather become part of the tissue of our inner life from the outset, creating a new and better self within us, continuing forever as active agents of our *Bildung*.[70]

And again:

If we consider structures [*Gestalten*] in general, particularly organic ones, we never come across anything stable or completed, but always things trem-

---

68. Friedrich Schiller, *Über Anmut und Würde* [Concerning Grace and Dignity].

69. V: 161. He acclaims his self-development and his public service.

70. Keith Spalding, ed., *An Historical Dictionary of German Figurative Usage* (Oxford: Basil Blackwell, 1952–   ), fasc. 7 (1956), s.v. "Bildung."

bling in constant movement. Accordingly our language, appropriately enough, is wont to use the term *Bildung* both of the product of formation and of the process.[71]

The relevance of this German concept to Matthew Arnold's "Culture" in its religious aspect will become clearer, I think, as we trace it through his prose.

For Goethe's influence on the narrower matter of Bible criticism, we can turn to the countless and often repeated extracts from Goethe that Arnold copied into his note-books over the course of many years. In about 1870, before the composition of *Literature and Dogma*, we find him musing on this:

Man streitet viel und wird viel streiten über Nutzen und Schaden der Bibel-verbreitung. Mir ist klar: schaden wird sie wie bisher, dogmatisch und phantastisch gebraucht; nutzen wie bisher, didaktisch und gefühlvoll auf-genommen.[72]

(*Note-Books* 142)

People contest much and will contest much about the use and harm done by the dissemination of the Bible. To me it is clear: it does harm as heretofore when it is dogmatic and fantastic; it does good as heretofore when it is done in an instructive way, and sympathetically.

In the next year he copied out again the *Bibelverbreitung* passage, and added:

Ich bin überzeugt, dass die Bibel immer schöner wird, je mehr man sie versteht, d.h. je mehr man einsieht und anschaut, dass jedes Wort, das wir allgemein auffassen und im Besondern auf uns anwenden, nach gewissen Um-ständen, nach Zeit und Ortsverhältnissen einen eignen, besondern, unmittel-bar individuellen Bezug gehabt hat.[73]

(*Note-Books* 168–69)

I am convinced the Bible becomes even more beautiful the more one under-stands it; that is, the more one gets insight to see that every word, which we

71. Johann Wolfgang von Goethe, "Vorwort des ersten Heftes 'Zur Morpho-logie,'" in *Goethes Werke*, 60 vols. (Stuttgart: J. C. Cotta, 1827–42), 58: 7; cited in Jakob and Wilhelm Grimm's *Deutsches Wörterbuch*, 16 vols. (Leipzig: S. Hirzel, 1854–1954), s.v. "Bildung," 2: 33. Passage translated by Bruford, *Culture and Society in Weimar*, p. 4.

72. Goethe, "Maximen und Reflexionen," *Werke*, 59: 86–87.

73. Ibid., 59: 117.

take generally, and make special application to our own wants, has had, in connexion with certain circumstances, with certain relations of time and place, a particular, directly individual reference of its own.

(Arnold's own translation, VII: 68)

And again,

Die Religion selbst, wie Zeit, wie Leben und Wissen, in stetem Fortschritt und Fortbildung begriffen ist.[74]

(Note-Books 173)

Religion itself, like time, like life and knowledge, is engaged in continual advance and further development.

These recurrent Goethean meditations in the Note-books indicate perhaps better than anything else the scope of Arnold's religious sense.

J. G. Eichhorn is the first great professional Bible critic, and the breadth of his approach is suggested by the fact of his friendship with both Herder and Goethe. He was the student at Göttingen of Michaelis, who had published Lowth in Germany. He fell in love with the languages and culture of the Near East and became professor of Oriental languages at Jena, and so, as Cheyne tells us, he approaches the Bible as one "Oriental" book among others. Cheyne also tells us that it is Eichhorn and Herder who established the custom (continued by Matthew Arnold) of referring to the Bible as "Oriental."[75] Eichhorn and Herder indubitably each endorsed and enriched the other's work, Herder as a theologian among the littérateurs, and Eichhorn a littérateur among the theologians.[76] This sort of interplay distinguishes the German movement as a sort of ideal university in action. Herder envisaged a holistic approach, and he and the others made it, and Bible criticism moves forward in one wave with historiography, philology, anthropology. Eichhorn was the first to take myth as a kind of "sinnliche Denkungsart der Urwelt" (a sensuous [or reifying] thinking-mode of the ancient world), specifying, I think, what Herder understands by the Bible as "Poesie."[77] His Einleitung

---

74. F. W. Riemer, Mittheilungen über Goethe (Berlin: Duncker und Humblot, 1841), 2 vols., 1: 130.

75. Cheyne, Founders of Old Testament Criticism, pp. 14–15.

76. Ibid., pp. 16–17.

77. This is adapted from the article on Eichhorn in Neue Deutsche Biographie, vol. 4 (Berlin: Duncker und Humblot, 1959), pp. 377–78.

ins Alte Testament (3 volumes, 1780–83) distinguishes multiple authors of the Pentateuch (as has been noted above) and instigates much of the work that is to follow. Eichhorn sees nothing irreligious in his research, and it is all informed with delight. "Well does the aged Goethe," exclaims Cheyne, "congratulate himself on having known the time when Herder and Eichhorn together opened up to himself and his contemporaries a new source of pure delight in the Biblical literature!"[78]

Schleiermacher's experience of the Herrnhuter movement left him convinced of the supreme validity of *feeling* as the essence of religion; he rejects pietistic literalism but rationalizes this element of feeling, and thus he takes his place in that Spinozist-Arnoldian-William Jamesian line that takes experience as paramount. He is introduced into English thought with Connop Thirlwall's translation of his essay on Luke in 1825, and he was revered by both Thomas and Matthew Arnold as a man who accepted science but kept the faith on grounds of experience. He contributed, moreover, to Matthew Arnold's idea of culture. W. H. Bruford traces *Bildung* from Herder, through Humboldt, Goethe, and Schleiermacher (and on through Nietzsche and Thomas Mann), and in his discussion of Schleiermacher distinguishes between *Kultur* and *Bildung*, *Kultur* being the continuing influence of the mind of earlier generations and *Bildung* being the inward self-cultivation which alone makes *Kultur* possible.[79] Bruford notes that Schleiermacher puts forward with religious fervor a kind of gospel of *Bildung*.[80]

Schleiermacher, though considered "liberal," was still among the faithful, but D. F. Strauss ultimately left the fold. In his *Leben Jesu* he presents a new way of viewing the historicity of the gospels:

We have to realize that the narrators testify sometimes, not to outward facts, but to ideas. . . . [The result is] a narrative, legendary, mythical in nature, illustrative often of spiritual truth in a manner more perfect than any hard, prosaic statement could achieve.[81]

78. Cheyne, *Founders of Old Testament Criticism*, p. 19.
79. W. H. Bruford, *The German Tradition of Self-Cultivation*, (Cambridge: Cambridge University Press, 1975), p. 70.
80. Bruford, *German Tradition of Self-Cultivation*, pp. 70, 75.
81. As quoted by Neil, "Criticism and Theological Use of the Bible," pp. 275–76; in *Cambridge History of the Bible*, vol. 3, ed. S. L. Greenslade (Cambridge: Cambridge University Press, 1963), pp. 238–93.

The *Leben Jesu*, over fourteen hundred pages long, was translated with great endurance and some pain by George Eliot in 1846, and it sealed her enfranchisement from Evangelicalism. English readers encountered Strauss in George Eliot's translation and also could see the man himself in Browning's vivid satire of the Christmas Eve lecturer at Göttingen in "Christmas Eve and Easter Day" (1850).[82] Strauss's *Leben Jesu* was translated into French, and it is from this French version that Arnold transcribes a passage in the note-books for 1874; and there is another in English in 1878, presumably George Eliot's (*Note-Books* 222, 304). Much more impressive is a lengthy transcription in the "General Note-Book" at Yale, which is yet unpublished, of about four thousand words, from a review of Strauss by Charles Dollfus (one of his French translators) in the *Revue germanique et française* for 1864.[83] Dollfus gives an overview of the whole German school as well as Strauss's place in it, and all with a minimum of what the French call *brume nordique*. Arnold owes much, I believe, to this clear synthesis of German scholarship, and I will refer to it where I believe it contributes to his essays.

For biblical scholarship proper, the two great names are Heinrich Gesenius and Heinrich Ewald. Gesenius is above all a Hebraist and a great teacher. His *Handwörterbuch* first came out in 1810–12 and is the basis of our best modern *Lexicon*. His *Grammar*, still standard, came out in 1813, and his commentary on Isaiah in 1820. The *Grammar* and the Isaiah were among Arnold's books. Heinrich Ewald, who worked under the presiding portraits of Herder and Eichhorn in his study, felt himself divinely appointed to continue in the recovery of the true meaning of the Bible[84] and had a Carlylean sense of wonder in "God's greatest gift," language.[85] He extended Gesenius's Hebrew studies and sustained his biblical exegeses with Arabic, Sanskrit, Persian, Turkish, Armenian, and Coptic, as well as the more usual languages. Arnold excerpts in his *Note-Books* passages from Ewald's *Commentaries*, and he owned his *Geschichte des Volkes Israel* (1843–

---

82. W. C. DeVane affirms that the original is Strauss. *A Browning Handbook* (New York: Appleton-Century-Crofts, 1955), p. 257.

83. Charles Dollfus, "À propos de la nouvelle Vie de Jésus par David Strauss," *Revue germanique et française* 21 (November 1, 1864): 358–64. This unpublished "General Note-Book" is catalogued in the Beinecke as Tinker 24.

84. Cheyne, *Founders of Old Testament Criticism*, p. 71.

85. Ibid., p. 79.

45), which was the basis of A. P. Stanley's *Lectures on the History of the Jewish Church*, which Arnold reviewed (III: 65–82). And then there is Ferdinand Christian Baur, founder of the Tübingen school, a thoroughgoing rationalist but carried away by his "rigour and vigour," as Arnold is to show in *God and The Bible* (VII, passim), to an absurdly reductive view of the Gospel of John.

Michael Timko, in an important essay, has given us a fresh perspective on "Victorianism" as distinct from the precedent "Romanticism" and whatever it is we are now embarked on in the twentieth century.[86] He sees it, first, as characterized by an engagement with the epistemological problem—where the Romantic asserted his subjective sense of self, the Victorian questions his identity, and even questions the possibility of ever knowing his identity. Second, the Victorian is characterized by an anxious effort to differentiate man from that Nature the Romantics were for the most part glad to be one with. Nature is "red in tooth and claw": let me not be one with that! Timko's perspective makes for an enriched reading of the poets with their explorations of consciousness and self-consciousness, explorations of the distinctively "human," whether it is love, or art, or mystical transcendence. Carlyle, for instance (and Carlyle should more often be included among the poets), roundly asserts "It is in Society that man first feels what he is; first becomes what he can be" ("Characteristics"). "Close thy Byron, open thy Goethe!"—forsake "the dandy of sorrows," that is, and turn to the whole world of history and art. "Know what thou canst work at!" Arnold explores the epistemological question more subtly, perhaps, than any of the other poets: consider the limits of self-consciousness, say, in *Empedocles*, or the sense of inner self in "Palladium"; and he recognizes the challenge of Darwinism, very precisely in a poem Timko refers us to, "To an Independent Preacher, Who Preached That We Should Be 'In Harmony with Nature' ":

> Restless fool,
> Know, man hath all which Nature hath, but more,
> And in that *more* lies all his hopes of good.
> Nature is cruel, man is sick of blood;
> Nature is stubborn, man would fain adore.
>
> (44)

86. Michael Timko, "The Victorianism of Victorian Literature," *New Literary History* 6 (Spring 1975): 607–27.

Arnold closed his Byron, and opened his Goethe, and his Herder and
Humboldt, where he found the prime concern was with that *more*.
This is what Herder addresses in developing his concept of *Humani-*
tät: man, and only man, is organized, biologically, with a capacity for
reason, for art, for language—and for religion.[87] Out of Herder's work,
and Humboldt's and Goethe's, emerges the great concept of *Bildung*,
that process of moving toward fulfillment of the capacities of *Humani-*
tät, both in individual civilizations and in individual human beings,
the process which Arnold denominates "Culture" and makes his subject. What Timko sees as Darwinism—recognizing that Darwinism
existed before Darwin—can I think be best viewed as one aspect of
the larger concept, Historicism, Herder's philosophy of history with
its *Entwicklung*, or "development," its relativism and its humanism.
Darwin's *Descent of Man* is really understood as an *ascent*, into ever
higher forms. (And these higher forms will need a Higher Criticism.)
It is a twentieth-century habit to try to reassociate man with animality,
sometimes with the all-too-successful effect of resuscitating the Yahoo,
sometimes with a wistful feeling that we can never be quite so amiable
or "humane" as dolphins. But the Victorian way was to develop away
from the beast, and in Arnold's case this flowered in his exploration
of the State as the collective "best self" and his abiding concerns with
education (in the distinctively "long childhood" of man, in Herder's
terms), with art, and with religion. Goethe's Germany saw one of the
greatest flowerings of scholarship ever, in which the Higher Criticism
was integrated with a new view of mankind, and it changed the face
of European culture. The story of the century is in large measure the
story of the adjustment to this new learning. Carlyle appreciated the
situation as early as 1827:

> To the charge of Irreligion . . . the Germans will not plead guilty. On the
> contrary, they will not scruple to assert that their literature is, in a positive
> sense, religious; nay, perhaps to maintain, that if ever neighbouring nations
> are to recover that pure and high spirit of devotion, the loss of which, how-
> ever we may disguise it or pretend to overlook it, can be hidden from no
> observant mind, it must be by travelling, if not on the same path, at least in
> the same direction in which the Germans have already begun to travel. . . .

---

87. "Der Mensch ist zur Vernunftfähigkeit organisirt . . . zur Kunst und zur
Sprache, . . . zur Religion." From Herder's chapter titles in book 4 of the *Ideen*.

Religion, Poetry, is not dead; it will never die. Its dwelling and birthplace is in the soul of man, and it is eternal as the being of man.[88]

So wrote Carlyle, prophesying. So read Arnold in his formative years. And the first chapter of *Sartor Resartus* concludes with the prayer that this new thing out of Germany, this "clothes-philosophy," might flourish also on British soil—"Möchte es auch im Britische Boden gedeihen."

88. Carlyle, conclusion of "State of German Literature," 1 : 72–73.

III

The Higher Criticism
in the Home

M AT T H E W Arnold stood in a particularly privileged position with respect to the new German learning: his father's circle was the one group in England that was closest to it. Carlyle, the single English writer most deeply read in the Germans, stands outside this group, and there was no particular privileged friendship; Matthew Arnold read him just as his contemporaries did. Thomas Arnold admired Carlyle particularly, however, and wrote him an interesting letter in 1840, in which he said he recognized in the *French Revolution* "an understanding of the true nature of history"; this would be that Viconian-Herderian historicism that he and Carlyle had both arrived at by their somewhat different routes.[1] The radical religious implications of *Sartor Resartus*, which are the ground of Arnold's religious thought, would have escaped Thomas Arnold.

For the particularly domestic influences on Arnold's religious thought, Coleridge comes first, the prime shaper of the Broad Church Movement. Coleridge's nephew, John Taylor Coleridge, later Justice Coleridge, was from 1811 Thomas Arnold's fellow student at Corpus Christi and remained one of his closest friends. Through him, Thomas Arnold came to read the Lake poets with enthusiasm and became something of a Laker himself: in 1834, Matthew being twelve years old, Thomas bought the Fox How property at Ambleside, the beloved permanent home of the Arnold family. It is close to Rydal Mount, and

1. An exchange of letters with Carlyle is available as appendix 2 to Arnold Whitridge's *Dr. Arnold of Rugby* (New York: Henry Holt, 1928), pp. 236–41. Their encounters are described in A. P. Stanley's *Life of Thomas Arnold* (London: John Murray, 1904), pp. 532–34, 641, 649.

56

the Wordsworths were intimate friends. The great poet was a kind of presiding rural genius over the boy Matthew's holiday haunts.

The new Higher Criticism in England has its first great spokesman in Coleridge. Coleridge's *Constitution of Church and State* (1830) sets a direction of thought of which Thomas Arnold's is a development, and Matthew Arnold's a further development. If a mark of pre-Romantic thought can be called compartmentalization—Bacon professed orthodoxy but practiced rationalism; Lowth hardly troubles to reconcile his Bible criticism with his bishopric; and as Gibbon remarks of the sophisticated clergy and the Articles, they "subscribed with a sigh or a smile"—so it is a mark of Romantic thought to decompartmentalize, to reconcile, to move toward oneness. With Coleridge, the integer becomes a passion. His vision of church and state as related in a kind of association of duties becomes in Thomas Arnold a vision of church and state as virtually identical. Matthew Arnold in his work for the schools must deal with the practical implementation of a state school system and the part religion will play in it; *his* vision of the state as the collective "best self" implies a relationship of church to state, which may depend ultimately on a kind of integration of literature and religion. Coleridge conceives of the "Clerisy" as guardians and disseminators of both religion and education; Matthew Arnold's developing idea of "Culture," or poetry-religion, would constitute the united field of action of such Clerisy. Coleridge in his marvelous prescience was one of the first to anticipate the need to define—in Timko's terms[2]—the uniqueness, the beyond-Nature-ness, of humankind. In something like Herder's mode, he sees the distinguishing mark of humanity as a need for and capacity for religion. Basil Willey explains:

Coleridge helped to teach his century wherein the genuine superhumanness of Christianity really lay. Moreover, he taught this before the main attacks of the higher criticism and of science were launched, so that when the crisis came . . . the defensive positions were already laid down.[3]

Arnold recognizes that Coleridge affirms the value of the Bible by the one sure test—the experimental: "In the Bible there is more that

2. Michael Timko, "The Victorianism of Victorian Literature," *New Literary History* 6 (Spring 1975) : 607–27.

3. Basil Willey, *Nineteenth Century Studies: Coleridge to Matthew Arnold* (London: Chatto and Windus, 1949), pp. 31–32.

finds me than I have experienced in all other books put together"—
finds me, his "excellent expression," his "happy phrase," Arnold calls
it.[4] He recognizes that "the great Coleridgean position, that apart from
all question of the evidence for miracles and of the historical quality
of the gospel narratives, the essential matters of Christianity are necessary and eternal facts of nature or truths of reason, is henceforth the
key to the whole defence of Christianity" (X: 227). For the most part
the Coleridgean influence was early, and by way of Thomas Arnold,
and it simply became integrated with his line of thought. In the *Note-
Books* we find only two *pensées* from Coleridge, not directly but
through an article on Coleridge in the *North British Review* for 1865:
"Faith is allegiance of the moral nature to Universal Reason, or the
will of God," and, "An approving conscience is the sense of harmony
of the personal will of man with that impersonal light which is in him,
representative of the will of God" (*Note-Books* 40, 50, 72). One can
see how "Universal Reason" and the "impersonal light" are types of
Arnold's "force not ourselves," the "Eternal."

It appears from E. S. Shaffer's researches that Coleridge was versed
in the Germans both more deeply and earlier than has been thought.[5]
(It is her view that his plan to write the great epic *The Fall of Jerusalem* grew out of the study of this biblical criticism.) Coleridge had
learned German before going to Germany in 1798. He could have read
Eichhorn's Latin commentary on the Apocalypse of John (Göttingen,
1791) soon after it was published, and he would have known the
material of Eichhorn's *Einleitung in das Neue Testament* (1804 ff.)
before it was published, from lectures he heard in Germany. He
would, furthermore, have known the German school through Unitarian circles at Cambridge and through Thomas Beddoes in Bristol;
apparently he also knew Alexander Geddes. The artistic flowering of
all this comes out deviously in "Kubla Khan," Shaffer argues. But it
culminates more prosaically later in Coleridge's own contribution to
the Higher Criticism: *Confessions of an Inquiring Spirit*, published
posthumously in 1840. The year of his death, the work was apparently
circulating in manuscript as *Letters on the Inspiration of the Scriptures*: A. P. Stanley writes in 1834 from Hurstmonceaux, where he

4. Samuel Taylor Coleridge, *Confessions of an Inquiring Spirit*, ed. H. StJ. Hard
(London: Adam and Charles Black, 1956), pp. 42, 43; *Prose* III: 279, VIII: 41.

5. E. S. Shaffer, *Kubla Khan and the Fall of Jerusalem* (Cambridge: Cambridge
University Press, 1975), pp. 17–28.

was visiting Julius Hare, that John Sterling (who was Hare's curate at the time) had brought him the *Letters* to read before they were to be sent to Thomas Arnold. Stanley is much impressed with their insistence on "the exceeding value and beauty of the Bible, and the exceeding evil of Bibliolatry."[6] Then we find in Thomas Arnold's letter of January 1835 to J. T. Coleridge: "Your uncle's Letters on Inspiration" are "well fitted to break ground in the approaches to that momentous question"—of biblical interpretation. The shock must come, but will end in "the more sure establishing of Christian truth."[7]

Stanley reported its emphases correctly: the beauty of the Bible and the evil of bibliolatry. *Bibliolatry* is not a word coined by Coleridge, as Basil Willey believes, but had been used by Lessing and in English by John Byrom before 1763.[8] Coleridge starts the *Confessions* with a rather strained reference to "*The Confessions of a Fair Saint* in Mr. Carlyle's recent translation of the *Wilhelm Meister*,"[9] as though to suggest that he is writing a comparable spiritual autobiography, but he seems to define himself in contradistinction to the *schöne Seele*, and to the plenary-inspirationists, and, moreover, in contradistinction to Wordsworthian benign Naturism. His confessions are those of an *inquiring* spirit; this he feels to be his essence, the searching, interrogating mind, defining itself in relationship to the Bible. The inquiring spirit inclines to trust his "angel of light," his *reason* (and here Coleridge would understand *Vernunft* in its well-known differentiation from that lower capacity, *Verstand*), and his reason refuses to accept plenary inspiration. It is bibliolatry. It devalues the text; it "destroys the doctrine which it professes to interpret"; it "converts it into its own negative." Our religion sustains "positive harm . . . both historically and spiritually" from this doctrine. "A still greater evil . . . is the literal rendering of Scripture in passages, which the number and variety of images employed in different places, to express one and the same verity, plainly mark out for figurative." And in a pattern that Matthew Arnold was to adopt Coleridge contrasts the narrow illogic of some literal interpretations with the fullness of spiritual meaning of

6. Rowland E. Prothero, *The Life and Correspondence of Arthur Penrhyn Stanley*, 2 vols. (London: John Murray, 1893), vol. 1, pp. 111, 114.

7. Stanley, *Life*, p. 344.

8. Willey, *Nineteenth Century Studies*, p. 39. See Coleridge, *Confessions*, p. 7n.

9. Coleridge, *Confessions*, p. 39. This would be *Meister's Apprenticeship* (1824). Goethe's addition, *Meister's Travels*, Carlyle brings out in translation in 1839.

the figurative interpretations. He insists too on historical study. Examine "the circumstances of the Writer or Speaker, the dispensation under which he lived, the purpose of the particular passage, and the intent and object of the Scriptures at large. . . . Fear not the result. I venture to tell it you before hand." You will discover an ever-deepening richness of spiritual meaning.

This I believe by my own dear experience,—that the more an inquirer takes up the Bible as he would any other body of ancient writings, the livelier and steadier will be his impressions of its superiority to all other books, till at length all other books and all other knowledge will be valuable in his eyes in proportion as they help him to a better understanding of his Bible.[10]

Thomas and Matthew Arnold clearly follow Coleridge's line here. Thomas had a few reservations about Coleridge—he felt he was obscure at times. He wittily observes to J. T. Coleridge: "I often think I could have understood your Uncle better if he had written in Platonic Greek."[10] He writes to another friend of another larger reservation, associated, one supposes, with the opium—"the unsteadiness of his mind and purposes." Thomas Arnold believes passionately in the life of action; he thinks "the very power of contemplation becomes impaired or perverted when it is made the main employment of life." But Thomas Arnold appears to accept Coleridge's hermeneutics and writes, "I think, with all his faults, old Sam was more of a great man than any one who has lived within the four seas in my memory."[11]

Eichhorn in his *Einleitung ins Alte Testament* praises Ezekiel "as the greatest artist of the prophets—and therefore the least visionary." Coleridge demurs, in a marginal comment. As an experienced visionary-artist himself, Coleridge will not allow the distinction. The prophetic role *is* the poet's role. Both work by "Symbols," or "Images and Mental Sounds."[12] Notoriously the poet of the Romantic "fragment," he yearned for the whole, and in his religious thought did actually achieve much integration. John Tulloch, in his *Movements of Religious Thought* (1885), places him in the line of Richard Hooker and of Milton: "He has . . . the same love of wisdom, the same largeness—never despising nature, or art, or literature for the sake of re-

10. Coleridge, *Confessions*, pp. 44, 54, 58, 65, 75.
11. Stanley, *Life*, pp. 374, 424.
12. Shaffer, *Kubla Khan*, pp. 88–92.

ligion, still less ever despising religion for the sake of culture."[13]

For the prime formative element on Matthew Arnold we must center on Thomas Arnold himself, the great headmaster of Rugby who changed the face of education in England, pamphleteer and leader of the Broad Church Movement, editor of Thucydides, author of the *History of Rome*, Professor of Modern History at Oxford, clergyman and author of published sermons including those "On the Interpretation of the Scripture," spiritual father of a distinguished generation of statesmen, churchmen, teachers, and civil servants. Born like Carlyle in 1795, he died just when his career was developing well beyond the school, in 1842, when Matthew was twenty.

At Oriel he was one of the group called the Oxford "Noetics." The term implies Thomas Arnold's principles: unquestionable piety combined with a secure faith in the power of reason to determine the nature and operation of Christianity, and a refusal to consider that piety and reason could be at odds. He seems to have adopted from Coleridge the reason-understanding (*Vernunft-Verstand*) dichotomy, as Charles R. Sanders points out,[14] and to have applied it to Bible interpretation as Coleridge did. The *understanding* (*Verstand*) has its work to do in historical scholarship of the Bible, since it was written by human beings. But it cannot do all; in Thomas Arnold's own words: "Of human things the understanding can judge, of divine things it cannot," and so it must be supplemented by "reason [*Vernunft*], and reason's perfection, faith."[15] He is steadily confident in what he feels to be the truth of Christianity and is impatient with dogma and argument. The Scriptures are validated for us by "an ex-

13. John Tulloch, *Movements of Religious Thought in Britain During the Nineteenth Century* (London: Longmans, Green, 1885; reprint ed., with an introduction by A. C. Cheyne, New York: Humanities Press, 1971), pp. 7–8.

14. Charles R. Sanders, *Coleridge and the Broad Church Movement* (Durham, N.C.: Duke University Press, 1942), p. 98. The *Vernunft-Verstand* distinction, which causes such labor for students of the Romantics, was regarded with a fine irreverence by Carlyle: Coleridge brought over to England "the great ocean of German speculation," and Wordsworth and Coleridge "translated Teutonic thought into a poor disjointed whitey-brown sort of English," and he speaks of the "hocus-pocus of reason versus understanding." Quoted in ibid., pp. 156, 160.

15. Quoted from Thomas Arnold, *Miscellaneous Works* (New York: Appleton, 1845), pp. 268–70, in Sanders, *Coleridge and the Broad Church Movement*, pp. 98–99.

perimental knowledge of [their] power and living truth," and the result is right conduct.[16] Matthew Arnold's emphasis on, first, *experience*, and second, *conduct*, are clearly a paternal legacy. Thomas Arnold's version of Romantic transcendental unity showed practically in conduct—his administration of Rugby: he combined in himself the office of teacher and chaplain—and friend; all learning tended toward the learning of Christian ethics; Rugby men were to carry with them Arnold's sense of Christian sacrament into all spheres of life—domestic, political, military, professional. And his ideal of the Church of England was a kind of universal Christendom, coextensive with the state, not differentiating secular and clerical, and not excluding any protestant Christian sect.

His biblical hermeneutics are bound up with a passion for history that he had since his youth, and this again is one with his other concerns. As a Christian he could not believe there is no pattern of events on earth. What, then, *is* the pattern? What is the place of Christianity in this pattern? What is the nature of revelation? What is the nature of the Bible, in time, and in history? It was a driving need, a religious need, that implemented the passion for history. Of the classical historians it was Thucydides who most drew him, whose history of the Peleponnesian War is often considered to anticipate modern historical method, its reasoning upon cause and effect, its liveliness and accuracy, and for its moral concern. When Thomas Arnold encountered Vico's *La Scienza nuova* (in the French translation of Jules Michelet) he recognized a theory of history that met his driving concerns and his sense of Thucydides' value, "the study of the human past as a form of collective self-understanding."[17] Thomas Arnold found the *Scienza nuova* "so profound and striking" that he wondered it was not better known.[18] He appropriated the essential Viconian paradigm, the cycle that all societies go through: from the bestial age to the barbaric age, in which poetry and religion are merged (for poetry is the earliest form of utterance; man sings before he speaks, uses metaphors before technical terms); to the heroic, or aristocratic age, in which families

16. See Eugene L. Williamson, *The Liberalism of Thomas Arnold* (University: University of Alabama Press, 1964), pp. 92–93, and Thomas Arnold, *Sermons Chiefly on the Interpretation of Scripture* (London: B. Fellowes, 1851), passim.

17. Isaiah Berlin, *Vico and Herder: Two Studies in the History of Ideas* (London: The Hogarth Press, 1976), p. 98.

18. Quoted by Williamson, *Liberalism of Thomas Arnold*, p. 61.

unite into tribes and write their myths, their "poetic" wisdom (such was the Homeric age) ; to the age of "man," where all recognize themselves as equal—aristocracy becomes outworn, and as reason and intellect spread, philosophy conquers poetry and religion. For Thomas Arnold, Thucydides appeared to be writing at a crucial point where Greece was moving from the heroic age into the age of man, and he felt that England in the 1830s was at a similarly crucial point. This concept informs his view of the applicability of history and unquestionably shaped the teaching at Rugby. Volume 1 of his edition of Thucydides was published in 1830, with an essay on Vico's theory, "The Social Progress of States," as an appendix, and this book was used as a text at Rugby when Matthew Arnold was in the Upper School.[19]

Thomas Arnold planned a history of Rome, and in preparation for this his friends Julius Hare and Connop Thirlwall urged on him in 1825 the reading of the great German history of Rome (1811–32) by Barthold Niebuhr. This was an encounter momentous for consequent shaping of what Duncan Forbes has studied as *The Liberal Anglican Idea of History*, and for English Bible criticism. Thomas Arnold had had a certain mistrust of current German biblical-historical scholarship, so far as he knew it, as tending to unbelief: but here in Niebuhr he now finds implementation of his dearest ideas and intimations of his most pressing concerns.[20] As Duncan Forbes says, "The presupposition of Niebuhr's critical method . . . pointed to a possible science

19. R. H. Super supplies part of Thomas Arnold's writings on Vico, from the appendix to his *Thucydides* (XI: 519), as an additional note to I: 23. The question of Vico and Thomas Arnold is taken up by Duncan Forbes in *The Liberal Anglican Idea of History* (Cambridge: Cambridge University Press, 1952) ; by Williamson in *Liberalism of Thomas Arnold*; by Paul W. Day in *Matthew Arnold and The Philosophy of Vico*, University of Auckland bulletin no. 70, English series no. 12 (Auckland, N.Z.: The Pelorus Press, 1964) ; and now most recently by Peter Allan Dale in *The Victorian Critic and the Idea of History* (Cambridge: Harvard University Press, 1977). David DeLaura objects that when Day takes up Viconian elements in Matthew Arnold he commits the fallacy of the unique source (*Victorian Prose: A Guide* [New York: Modern Language Association, 1973]). No one in Arnold studies seems to have recognized that what appears to be Vico is often in fact Herder, in Thomas Arnold's case by way of Niebuhr and in Matthew Arnold's case by way of Niebuhr and Carlyle, as well as directly from Herder's *Ideen*.

20. Friedrich Meinecke links Thucydides and Niebuhr as both practicing a "spiritualized realism." *Historism* (*Die Entstehung des Historismus* [1959]), trans. J. E. Anderson (London: Routledge and Kegan Paul, 1972), p. 509.

which would render the application of history more certain, and make
the scientific historian a real force in practical thinking, and in the
solution of social and moral problems."²¹ Thomas Arnold rejoices to
recognize in Niebuhr a version of Viconian ideas—which are, in fact,
for the most part Herder's *Ideen*. And so the Herderian philosophy of
history, encompassing a whole worldview—or cosmos view—and a
developmental theory of history that provides for the development of
Christianity—enters English culture. It seemed to Hare, Thirlwall, and
Arnold that "Niebuhr's philological method provided the basis for a
proper study of the biblical narratives."²² According to J. B. Bury, it
was Wolf's *Prolegomena* above all that "gave historians the idea of a
systematic and minute method of analysing their sources."²³ By applying this philology to history, Niebuhr, to Thomas Arnold's mind,
has "done for ancient history what Bacon did for science."²⁴ Following the lead of Herder and Wolf, Niebuhr believes that myth and
legends have a kind of truth in them. Just as the philological school
assumes there was a body of myth in something like ballad form before Homer, on which Homer drew, so Niebuhr proposes there was a
body of ballad literature of the most ancient history of Rome, and historians like Livy in their prose histories drew on this body.²⁵ Arnold's
opening chapter in his *History of Rome* accordingly recounts the
venerable tales of Aeneas, Romulus and Remus, Numa Pompilius,
and the other old favorites of our first Latin books. (Thomas Macaulay's *Lays of Ancient Rome*, one remembers, are an attempt to re-
construct this Ur-history.) The implications of all this for biblical
scholarship are clear, as Thomas Arnold is perfectly aware. The
Viconian-Herderian developmental philosophy of history envisages
the childhood of a culture as a time when man sees events in mythic
terms, and there is a symbolic "truth" in the early myths of the nascent

21. Duncan Forbes, *The Liberal Anglican Idea of History* (Cambridge: Cambridge University Press, 1952), p. 15.

22. Robert Preyer, *Bentham, Coleridge and the Science of History* (Bochum-
Langendreer: Verlag Heinrich Pöppinghaus, 1958), p. 33.

23. J. B. Bury, *Selected Essays*, ed. Harold Temperly (Cambridge: Cambridge
University Press, 1930), pp. 5–6 (quoted by Preyer, *Bentham, Coleridge and the
Science of History*, p. 28).

24. Ibid., p. 28.

25. Matthew Arnold's own regard for Niebuhr shows in I: 14, where he brackets
him with Goethe. See also I: 26, 35, 43.

culture, the mythic and heroic age, "when history, law, and religion are alike poetry."[26]

The intellectual courage of Thomas Arnold seems to me impressive. He was uneasy about Niebuhr's orthodoxy, and yet these daring ideas make unquestionable sense, to this mind that reached out toward order, analogy, and integration. In 1827, he made a memorable European tour and in Rome met Christian Bunsen (whom we shall consider later), friend of Niebuhr, Niebuhr's successor as Prussian minister to the Vatican, and a man of signal Christian piety who was himself working to apply Niebuhr's principles in various historical projects—and the closest of friendships between Bunsen and Thomas Arnold ensued. On another European trip, in 1830, Thomas Arnold visited Niebuhr at Bonn, talked with him for three hours, and wrote, "I am satisfied from my own ears, if I had any doubts before, of the grossness of the slander which called him an unbeliever." Finally, then, the mythological school of criticism was welcomed by Thomas Arnold as not merely reconcilable with true Christianity but indeed a means to a new and firmer base for Christianity and a deeper piety. We find him in 1835 proposing a review to present this new biblical criticism in England.[27] He was, then, "advanced," and what is called in theological circles, liberal.[28] It was German biblical criticism that enfranchised and shaped his thought, specifically the "mediating" critics such as Christian Bunsen and Schleiermacher, who aimed to syncretise rationalism and piety. Schleiermacher called for

a thoroughgoing historical, linguistic, literary and scientific criticism to disengage the "kernel" from the "husk," the spiritual principle from the temporal

26. Henry Hart Milman, quoted by Forbes, *Liberal Anglican Idea of History*, p. 35.

27. Stanley, *Life*, pp. 40–41, 236, 344.

28. In a well-documented article Merton A. Christiansen takes up "Thomas Arnold's Debt to German Theologians: A Prelude to Matthew Arnold's *Literature and Dogma*," *Modern Philology* 55 (August 1957): 14–20, pointing out that earlier criticism neglects the German influence: Tulloch in his *Movements of Religious Thought* (1885) denies its importance, and so does Vernon F. Storr in his *Development of English Theology in the Nineteenth Century* (1913). And Christiansen notes that Sanders in his *Coleridge and the Broad Church Movement* (1942) never mentions Germany in connection with Thomas Arnold. One must protest that Sanders describes Thomas Arnold's principles justly, even though he may not indicate their sources.

expression of it; and thus . . . hoped to reinterpret the Bible for modern times on the basis of its spiritual truth.[29]

As Matthew Arnold himself says in a letter of 1867 to his mother:

Papa worked in the direction of these ideas of Bunsen and Schleiermacher, and was perhaps the only powerful Englishman of his day who did so. In fact, he was the only deeply religious man who had the necessary culture for it.

(*Letters* I: 442)

Thomas Arnold's *Fragment on the Church*, published posthumously in 1844, is wonderfully characteristic in its steamroller style: the distinction between spiritual and secular, he writes, is "utterly without foundation"—how unlike this is to the spirit *ondoyant et divers* that Matthew was to cultivate! But his substance anticipates Matthew's *Literature and Dogma* in some remarkable ways. He insists on the eucharist as a figurative act, a symbolic one. The Jewish sacraments are not *types* of the Christian, but, rather, Jewish sacraments and Christian alike are *types* of spiritual reality. He uses from the gospels the very texts Matthew Arnold makes much of later:

The memorable words of our Lord himself to Nicodemus, "Except a man be born of water and of the spirit, he cannot enter into the kingdom of God," contain, perhaps, the same figure in words that Baptism contains in action.[30]

He indicates just as Matthew Arnold is to do in the case of the woman of Samaria, the mistake of interpreting "water" literally, corrected by Jesus (VI: 274).

He presents a developmental theory of institutions: first, the church in its pristine state is not without forms but keeps forms subordinate; in the second phase, the existence of the spirit of the institution depends on adherence to the forms; and in a third phase, the forms "wither away, as the husk of the seed," and it is "a foolish zeal" that labors to hold the husk together.[31] It should be noted that Thomas Arnold does not extend his figurative interpretations to

29. Quoted in Christiansen, "Arnold's Debt," p. 16.

30. Thomas Arnold, *Fragment on the Church* (London: B. Fellowes, 1844), 132 pp. of text, p. 79 (John 3). The prefatory "Advertisement" is signed "M. A." R. H. Super believes this to be Matthew Arnold. It is more probably, as Park Honan claims, Mary Arnold, Matthew's mother (private communication).

31. Ibid., pp. 118–21.

Christ's resurrection—or to his own. This *Fragment* demonstrates what John O. Waller demonstrates from other texts, that the senior Arnold "entertained no doubts concerning the central supernatural claims of Christianity."[32] He had certainly an admirable courage of conviction, and he had also a kind of impatience. "What is revealed in Scripture is the will of God and the duty of man,"[33] and he felt sure he knew just what these were, and felt one must get on with the duty part.

It was left for Matthew Arnold to work out a sadder consistency in things.

> For rigorous teachers seized my youth,
> And purged its faith, and trimmed its fire,
> Showed me the high, white star of Truth,
> There bade me gaze, and there aspire.
>
> (304)

It was with the very method of the father that he, even when young, modified the father's thought. I think R. H. Super is right when he proposes that Arnold did not undergo the usual Victorian spiritual crisis of loss of faith, and that "precisely for that reason he became a sounder spiritual guide than almost any of his contemporaries."[34] I think that it is by virtue of his early contact, through his father, with Historicism, that he becomes the first poet of *Entwicklung* and its discontents, living in a Heraclitean fire (or "between two worlds") with the comfort of nothing more than a metaphorical resurrection. Thomas Arnold recognized Carlyle's Historicism, but missed the radicalism of his religious thought. But Matthew Arnold saw how the Historicism needed a retailored, nonsupernatural Christianity, and for him Carlyle's religious thought became a phase on his own way toward restabilization.

In the articulate home of the Arnolds, the working base of the father's activist career, it was inevitable that certain of the wide circle

32. John O. Waller, "Matthew and Thomas Arnold: Soteriology," *Anglican Theological Review* (January 1962), pp. 3–15. See especially p. 11.

33. From Basil Willey's landmark study of Thomas Arnold, in *Nineteenth Century Studies* (London: Chatto and Windus, 1949), p. 68.

34. R. H. Super, *The Time-Spirit of Matthew Arnold* (Ann Arbor: University of Michigan Press, 1970), p. 61.

of devoted friends would be agents in shaping Matthew Arnold's Bible criticism. John Keble was Matthew's godfather and gave him the Bible he refers to in the introduction to his Isaiah (VII: 55); party and faction made the association less close in later years, but as Stanley says, "It was not in [Thomas] Arnold's nature to forget how much he had owed to Keble,"[35] and both Thomas and Matthew Arnold venerated this saintly man.[36] Keble published his long life of Bishop Thomas Wilson in 1863 and may have first drawn Matthew's attention to Wilson, who figures so conspicuously in his prose.

Two of the "Oriel Noetics" have been revealed by William Blackburn as particularly important for *Literature and Dogma*: Richard Whately and R. D. Hampden.[37] Whately, probably Thomas Arnold's most intimate friend, Anglican Archbishop of Dublin and well-known opponent of the Tractarians, published in 1828 *Essays on Some of the Difficulties in the Writings of St. Paul*, where he declares it a source of error to treat the Bible as if it were a "Scientific system" and to extract from it "a complete technical vocabulary, with precise definition of the terms employed."[38] Hampden, the center of the doctrinal storms over the Tractarians, later appointed Bishop of Hereford despite High Church opposition, takes a similar position. In his Bampton Lectures of 1833 he contrasts the "popular . . . rhetorical, animated, energetic, glowing" language of the Bible with "that vast apparatus of technical terms which Christian theology now exhibits." The Bible presents the divine attributes "darkly, under the signs appropriate to the thought of the human mind." This is "altogether inadequate in point of science" but sufficient to teach us "both how to feel and act toward God."[39] Blackburn gives Whateley and Hampden too much weight as Matthew Arnold's only two sources; the distinction between the two languages is important in Vico, and in Herder, and almost ubiquitous in the Romantics in some form or other. But

35. Stanley, *Life*, p. 13.

36. Keble's views on poetry and religion, demonstrated by G. B. Tennyson, would make constructive contrast with Arnold's. Both see a close alliance, but— briefly—Keble sees poetry as serving religion, while Arnold sees religion as part of poetry ("Tractarian Poetics," in *Victorian Devotional Poetry* [Cambridge: Harvard University Press, 1981], pp. 12–71).

37. William Blackburn, "Matthew Arnold and the Oriel Noetics," *Philological Quarterly* 25 (October 1946): 70–78.

38. Blackburn cites Richard Whately.

39. Blackburn quotes from R. D. Hampden.

certainly the rhetoric of both Whately and Hampden contributes to Arnold's.

Two other Broad Church men who were close friends of the father's were deeply influential: Julius Hare and Connop Thirlwall. The breadth of Julius Hare must have been fostered by being born in Italy and left at the age of two in the care of the learned Clotilda Tambroni, female professor of Greek at the University of Bologna; at four he was brought to the family home at Hurstmonceaux, but he was abroad again at ten, living at Weimar with his parents and becoming adept in German. As the prodigiously learned and pious rector of Hurstmonceaux, he translated Niebuhr's *History of Rome* with Thirlwall—and recommended it to Thomas Arnold, who undertook to learn German in order to read it for himself in the original. Niebuhr was charged with infidelity, and Hare published in 1829 his "Vindication of Niebuhr," the first of a series of vindications—of Luther, of Bunsen, of Hampden, which in his later life he playfully said he should collect in a volume *Vindiciae Harianae*, or *The Hare with Many Friends*[40]— one of the most valued of whom was Thomas Arnold.

Connop Thirlwall was so precocious that his father published his poems when the little lad was only eleven. He had learned Latin at three and at four was also fluent in Greek. When he came to the age of discretion he made an effort to collect and burn the early *Poems*. Still discreet, we may judge, in 1825 he published his translation of Schleiermacher's "Critical Essay on the Gospel of St. Luke" with a critical introduction that showed him to be of Englishmen the most learned in German scholarship. Schleiermacher's insistence on the validity of experience, his understanding of religion as the "most highly and fully developed form of self-consciousness," and of the word *God* not as a concept of perfect being but "the felt relationship of absolute dependence"[41] are all concepts clearly contributory to those of Matthew Arnold. In 1840 Thirlwall was appointed Bishop of St. David's, and he learned Welsh with such effect that within a year he was reading prayers and preaching in Welsh. He was wonderfully effective as an administrator, as a clergyman, as a member of the House of Lords, and as a scholar. He embodied—as indeed all these

40. *Dictionary of National Biography*, s.v. Julius Charles Hare. The article is by his nephew, A. J. C. Hare.

41. Reinhold Niebuhr, in *The Macmillan Encyclopedia of Philosophy*, ed. Paul Edwards (New York: Collier and Macmillan, 1967), s.v. "Schleiermacher."

Broad Church men did—the Coleridgean ideal of the Clerisy: priest, teacher, and gentleman.

That curious foreign personage styled "Chevalier" or "Baron Bunsen," who had become Thomas Arnold's friend in Rome, helps, I think, to bring the whole English group into focus. There is an old and thorough study of him by Ralph Albert Dornfeld Owen,[42] and a recent short and stylish one in an essay by Robert O. Preyer.[43] Owen's thesis is that in Bunsen "the great religious movement of the last century in Germany, identified with the name of Schleiermacher, had an authoritative representative in England."[44] Preyer sees him as a superlative sort of public relations man for the whole German movement and notes he may be glimpsed by the English novel reader as the Ambassador in Charles Kingsley's *Alton Locke*.

Christian Bunsen, Prussian diplomatist and scholar, lived from 1791 to 1861, rising from humble beginnings through scholarship. Even as a child he had read Hebrew, and later besides the ordinary languages he studied Arabic, Persian, and Norse. He seems, like so many of this great German period, to have been possessed by the idea of *Bildung*, of developing his powers, his humanity, to the utmost. Niebuhr, when Prussian envoy to Rome, was impressed with his promise and devotion and made him his secretary in 1817. He married Frances Waddington, an English heiress of intellectual distinction. Among those who visited the Bunsens in Rome were Crabb Robinson, Wordsworth, Sir Walter Scott, Connop Thirlwall, Julius Hare, Richard Monckton Milnes, Gladstone, and—in 1827—Thomas Arnold, delighted with the Niebuhr association and keen to see all the places of his projected *History of Rome*. Bunsen seems to have helped both Hare and Thirlwall overcome scruples about taking orders, and Thirlwall years later still refers to Bunsen as a sort of oracle, whereas it was said of Julius Hare that he had five popes: Wordsworth, Niebuhr,

42. Ralph Albert Dornfeld Owen, *Christian Bunsen and Liberal English Theology* (Montpelier, Vt., 1924), 86 pp.

43. Robert O. Preyer, "The Dream of a Spiritualized Learning and Its Early Enthusiasts: German, British and American," *Geschichte und Gesellschaft in der amerikanischen Literatur*, Herausgegeben von Karl Schubard und Ursula Müller-Richter (Heidelberg: Quelle und Meyer, 1975), pp. 62–85.

44. Perhaps he had an influence in America also: he was for some time in his youth tutor to W. B. Astor, with what effect Owen does not say.

Frederick Maurice, Henry Manning, and Bunsen.[45] Bunsen very much admired the Anglican church, presumably for its breadth. He regarded Schleiermacher as a sort of older brother, and on reading the preface to his work on Luke exclaimed that it was written "with the wisdom of Christian freedom and fearlessness."[46] This epitomizes the attitude that so bound Thomas Arnold to the man—it might characterize the hermeneutics of both Arnold and Bunsen. When Thirlwall translated the Schleiermacher essay on Luke in 1825, his orthodoxy was questioned, and when Hare and Thirlwall brought out their first volume of the translation of Niebuhr's *Rome*, the evangelicals were further alarmed. It was a time of a particularly frenzied wave of evangelical enthusiasm, involving glossolalia and millenarianism. A letter of Thirlwall's to Bunsen indicates the climate of opinion and the Broad Church attitude in 1831:

In Germany, I hear, most persons were at a loss to conceive on what grounds Niebuhr could have been assailed in England as irreligious. But our religious atmosphere is a very peculiar one, as may be supposed when it is known that we are beginning to be very fluent in unknown tongues, which are now attracting crowds to one of our meeting houses [the church of Edward Irving, Carlyle's friend]. The millenarian persuasion is becoming so universal that any man who doubts the certainty of the Messiah's appearance on earth being now near at hand is denounced by—I am afraid I may say—a majority of the persons who claim the epithet *religious* by way of eminence, as a downright infidel. That persons of this description would be scandalized by Niebuhr's divergency from the book of Genesis I know to be an unavoidable misfortune.[47]

Bunsen labored to promote the rapprochement of the Lutheran and Calvinist churches in Prussia, much as Thomas Arnold labored to promote the inclusion of Dissenters in a broader Church of England.

45. See Augustus J. C. Hare's *The Story of My Life*, 6 vols. (London: George Allen, 1896), 1: 88. A. J. C. Hare is himself memorialized by W. Somerset Maugham in *The Vagrant Mood: Six Essays* (London: Heineman, 1952).

46. Owen, *Christian Bunsen*, p. 16. Christian Bunsen's *Memoirs*, English edition, vol. 1, p. 146.

47. Owen, *Christian Bunsen*, pp. 23–24; *Letters Literary and Theological of Connop Thirlwall*, ed. J. J. Stewart Perowne, 2 vols. (London: R. Bentley and Son, 1881), 1: 101.

Bunsen developed a liturgy and hymnbook that aimed to be acceptable to both parties, and like Thomas Arnold, Hare, and Thirlwall, he
pleaded for Catholic emancipation. In 1835 Bunsen writes to Arnold
to say

how he had been applying Niebuhr's critical method to the construction of a
chronology for the life of Christ, and how he was trying to take middle ground
between the unbelieving Neologists who can recognize no prophecy in the
Old Testament, and the stubborn conservatives who can recognize no historical facts where they scent a Messianic prophecy.[48]

Thomas Arnold writes back:

It is strange to see how much of ancient history consists apparently of patches
put together from various quarters without any *redaction*. Is this not largely
the case in the books of Samuel, Kings, and Chronicles?[49]

This exchange shows both Bunsen and Arnold *doing* Higher Criticism
and how well Arnold was coming along in it. Bunsen did not hold as
Arnold did that Church and State should be one; indeed one may
smile to see Bunsen blandly recommending the Episcopal church in
America as a model to Arnold—which would, I think, have set Arnold's
teeth a little on edge. For a time he is ambassador in Switzerland. The
stream of visitors continues: the F. D. Maurices and young Rugbeian
Arthur Stanley, Arnold's pupil. Of all the English, it seems that Maurice alone resisted Bunsen's charms—one detects only in him something less than the otherwise universal devotion, and he and his wife
were articulate in German.[50] We find Bunsen in England in 1839; Dr.
and Mrs. Arnold attended the Oxford ceremony at which both Bunsen and Wordsworth received honorary degrees (and Arthur Stanley
the prize for the Latin essay). This year in England he met Gladstone,

48. Owen's words, *Christian Bunsen*, p. 34.
49. Ibid., p. 34; Stanley, *Life*, 1: 372–74. Arnold's italics.
50. Maurice is often included among the Broad Church group and has lately received a great deal of attention and respect. Matthew Arnold, however, lavishes on
him twice such well-turned sentences as seem to be the result of closely considered
disrespect: Maurice, "that pure and devout spirit,—of whom, however, the truth
must at last be told, that in theology he passed his life beating the bush with deep
emotion and never starting the hare" (VI: 383); "Mr. Maurice . . . seems never
quite to have himself known what he himself meant, and perhaps never really quite
wished to know" (X: 226).

Hallam, Macaulay, John Gibson Lockhart, Lord Greville, Carlyle—
and Edward Pusey, John Henry Newman, and William Ward—of
these Tractarians he found the spectacle "admirable . . . but sad."
Bunsen and Thomas Arnold both felt that Protestant solidarity was
the best defense against Roman Catholicism.

The extraordinary affair of the Bishopric of Jerusalem was one effort toward this Protestant solidarity. There had been German official
correspondence with Gladstone and Lord Shaftesbury[51] about extending the influence of the Protestants in the Near East. Bunsen in
1841 came to London as a special envoy from the new king of Prussia
to negotiate the establishment of the joint English and Prussian bishopric of Jerusalem. Maurice and Stanley were involved, and the idea
was dear to Thomas Arnold, with his special love for Protestant unity.
The British Service for mission work among the Jews had already
bought land and built a school, hospital, and church at Jerusalem.
King Frederick William of Prussia proposed that the Anglicans take
this over and cooperate with Prussia in creating a bishopric for Pales-
tine, to protect German-speaking Jews and missionaries as well as
the English in this Turkish territory. The Prussian Church would have
to recognize the authority of the Anglican bishop, and the Anglicans
would have to recognize the validity of the Augsburg Confession. The
idea, says Owen, was really Bunsen's. It has certain anti-Roman
Catholic, anti-Greek Orthodox overtones, let alone anti-Jewish and
anti-Islamic, but Bunsen and Arnold would have thought it quite
ecumenical enough, and the whole operation casts light on the complacency and naïveté of these two holy connivers. It may also strike
us now—as it did *some*, then—as absolutely absurd—the wilder side
of the general learned interest in the Near East. Newman said it was
one of the events that drove him out of the Anglican fold. Perhaps
Thirlwall, the least naïve of the Broad group, if he had not been off at
St. David's learning Welsh, might have proposed restraint. However,
if there was to be such a bishop, it must be admitted the candidate
was perfect: a converted Anglican Jew who had been born in Prussia,
Dr. Michael Solomon Alexander, was made in 1841 the first Bishop of
the Church of St. James of Jerusalem, legal protector of all Protestants
to the Turkish government, with the power of ordination of both

51. For Shaftesbury's involvement, see G. F. A. Best, *Shaftesbury* (London:
Batsford, 1964; reprint ed., London: Mentor, 1975), pp. 73–75.

Prussians and Anglicans. He proceeded to the East, with his pregnant wife, on the steamship *Devastation*. Augustus J. C. Hare writes:

It must have been in 1841 that Bunsen innoculated my uncle [Julius Hare] and my mother [adoptive mother] with the most enthusiastic interest in the foundation of the Bishopric of Jerusalem, being himself perfectly convinced that it would be the Church thus founded which would meet the Saviour at his second coming. Esther Maurice, by a subscription among the ladies of Reading, provided the robes of the new Bishop.[52]

The joint bishopric was not a great success, and it did not outlive the second incumbent, Prussia's appointee, Dr. Gobat.

Dr. Arnold's sudden death in 1842 came as a heavy blow to all the Broad Church circle. The same year Bunsen, now a baron, was made ambassador to England, and he and his family (there were ten children) moved to Julius Hare's Hurstmonceaux for mutual support, Bunsen proposing that they complete some of Arnold's favorite projects, such as a critical edition of the Greek New Testament. It fell to Stanley to complete the *History of Rome* and to write the superb *Life*, done in 1844; it went through many editions and has been a classic of English pedagogy.

Bunsen's publications include *The Church of the Future* (1845) and *Egypt's Place in History* (1845), where he shakes up Bishop Ussher's biblical time-scheme and arouses enmity in both Evangelicals and High Church. At this point Julius Hare the Vindicator publishes his *Vindication of Bunsen*. In 1855 Bunsen publishes *God in History*, which his translator Susanna Winkworth says enables us to see the

gradual unfolding of God's revelations to man, and the unity of His teachings everywhere, and at the same time to see the enormous and generic superiority of the Jewish and Christian revelations. It makes infidelity appear so thoroughly unhistorical and unphilosophical.[53]

When Bunsen is engaged on revision of Luther's Bible in 1857 he writes to the duchess of Argyle a letter that reveals the state of Bible scholarship in England:

We in Germany may be said to have been at this work of revision for 87 years, say 100. For in 1770 Michaelis at Göttingen published his great translation

---

52. Hare, *Story of My Life*, 1: 129.
53. Owen, *Christian Bunsen*, p. 70, quoting Margaret Shaen, ed., *Memorials of Two Sisters* (London: Longmans, Green, 1908), p. 186.

and commentary of the Old Testament. And yet the German nation has still the least correct of all Bible translations, although it is marked by the greatest genius, and in spite of the fact that our men of learning have made unparalleled exertions to effect a revision. But as to England, it is more than a hundred years since you have given up all really exegetical study of the Bible. Jowett's and Stanley's and Alford's work are, however, excellent beginnings,—at least as far as the New Testament is concerned.[54]

Bunsen's health failed in 1858, and he died in 1860, the year of *Essays and Reviews*, which he never read. One of the articles in this notorious work was "Bunsen's Biblical Researches" by Rowland Williams, which was specifically castigated in the charges brought in the Ecclesiastical Court "as being contrary to, or inconsistent with, the doctrines of the Church of England." The feeling against the authors of the book, the *Septem Contra Christum*, was strangely virulent. The modern reader may dismiss Williams's crimes against Christ and castigate him rather for the most damnable obscurity.[55] Williams was one of the two tried for heresy, however, and found guilty. But the Privy Council reversed the decision. It found, in Stanley's words, "that the Church of England does not hold Verbal Inspiration, Imputed Righteousness, Eternity of Torment," and Stanley concludes, "I hope that all will now go smoothly and that the Bible may be read without these terrible nightmares. Thank God."[56]

The Bunsen that emerges from all this is a dynamo of piety, learning, and enthusiasm. Thomas Arnold was like this, the more for Bunsen's support. One pictures Bunsen as sharing the gleaming confidence that shines in Thomas Arnold's eye in the fine Phillips portrait, the frontispiece to Stanley's *Life*. Both were compact of quintessential Earnestness. Understanding this, one appreciates all the more the grace of Matthew's rebellious phase, his adorable flippancy and dandyism, and later the irony of the *esprit ondoyant et divers*. Bunsen and Thomas Arnold were unwavering—positive that reason would guide us right, all the way. Cardinal Newman sees, rather, the limits of reason and insists on the leap of faith. Matthew for all his coolness

54. Owen, *Christian Bunsen*, p. 69; Bunsen, *Memoirs*, p. 429.

55. Basil Willey clarifies the issues, *More Nineteenth Century Studies* (London: Chatto and Windus, 1956), pp. 142–45.

56. Owen, *Christian Bunsen*, p. 72; Prothero, *Life and Correspondence of Stanley*, vol. 2, p. 44.

and detachment and critical skepticism still retains the paternal faith
that reason and Christianity are not at odds, and he refuses to leap—
but he has to retailor Christianity to fit reason. Where Thomas Arnold
is somewhat naïve, and insouciant as to dogma, Matthew rationalizes
in a sophisticated way the father's dismissal of dogma. Meanwhile he
had seen in his father—and in Bunsen—something like an "Imitation,"
impressive examples of high principle and striving for right conduct.

In 1868 the Baroness Bunsen published the *Memoirs* of her husband, which are acclaimed by Stanley and the new generation he had
influenced. And Matthew Arnold takes from them in his note-book
some *pensées* of Bunsen for his meditation:

People have no conception of the one only solid basis: inward truth, rectitude,
and the fear of God.

                                  .   .   .

Let me ever feel that I can only perceive and know God in so far as mine is
a living soul, and lives, moves, and has its being in him.
                          (*Note-Books* 81, 82)

Requiescat in pace. In the same year Arnold writes to Grant Duff that
he has been reading Bunsen's life, and he comments in one of the few
unbuttoned moments that escaped the editor's scissors: "With a
certain obvious splay-footedness, he is yet very edifying" (*Letters*
I: 461). Two years later he writes to his mother:

I have just finished re-reading Bunsen's life, with great interest. The way he
vitally connected different great branches of knowledge and made them all
serve one object is truly German, but German of the best kind.
                          (*Letters* II: 47)

And he goes on to say it is what England needs. Arnold's knowledge
of German learning helps explain his idea that the English Romantic
poets *didn't know enough*. Bunsen was not titanic, but he was in the
line of the titans: Schiller, Goethe, Herder, Wilhelm von Humboldt,
all of whom knew a lot, whole encyclopedias' worths, and were all
the greater for their intimacies and interactions, and their prodigious
scholarship and insights shook the world.

Die Kette der Bildung, "the chain or links of culture," without which
the spectacle of history is unintelligible and insupportable, in the passage that Arnold marked with double emphasis in his copy of Herder's
Ideen, has a special meaning in English intellectual history. Max Mül-

ler, coming over from Germany in 1848, writes of England's "close intellectual organization":

The number of public schools is limited. Of the universities there there are, or there were till lately, two only. Most men of note are acquainted with each other . . . . Add to this the innumerable societies, clubs, charitable institutions, political associations, and last, not least, the central hearth in London, Parliament, where everybody appears from time to time . . . and you will understand that England hangs more closely together and knows itself better than any country in Europe.[57]

Elements of Matthew Arnold's intellectual inheritance are impressively linked. Bishop Robert Lowth had been Professor of Poetry at Oxford, 1741 to 1750, in the chair later to be held by Keble and then Matthew Arnold. In this position, he was in frequent intimate communion with certain old Hebrew poets, historians, and rabbinical editors, by virtue of a continuous series of linking impulses to preserve the written word. He was moreover in communion with the writers of Greece and Rome and all modern Europe. So too was Francis Hare, Bishop of Chichester, tutor to Robert Walpole, friend of William Warburton and Richard Bentley, complimented in the *Dunciad*. This Francis Hare published in 1736 an edition of the Psalms in Hebrew, with an essay presenting a theory of Hebrew meter. It was this that was the occasion of Lowth's *Confutation of Bishop Hare's System of Hebrew Metre*, which makes mincemeat of Hare with surprising acrimony, considering that the man had been dead for twenty-six years. Hare had married a cousin surnamed Naylor, heiress of Hurstmonceaux Castle; his son Robert learned Greek as a household language, took the surname Hare-Naylor, and was canon of Winchester. *His* son, Francis Hare-Naylor, distinguished himself by not taking orders—he merely wrote plays, histories, and a novel, and married the learned Georgiana Shipley, sister of the wife of Sir William Jones, forerunner of the German school in the study of Sanskrit and comparative philology. They lived in Germany and Italy, and it was in Italy that their four sons were born, of whom Augustus and Julius were to take orders and be warm friends of Thomas Arnold. By a second marriage Francis Hare-Naylor had a daughter who became

57. Quoted in Nirad C. Chaudhuri, *Scholar Extraordinary: The Life of . . . Friedrich Max Müller* (London: Chatto and Windus, 1974), p. 67.

the second wife of F. D. Maurice the Broad, close associate of the
Arnolds. On the other hand, it was one of F. D. Maurice's sisters who
married Julius Hare. Augustus Hare, the clerical brother of Julius,
was adopted by Sir William Jones's widow. Julius and Augustus published in 1827 *Guesses at Truth, by Two Brothers,* a much reprinted
work not uninfluenced by early German biblical researches. Lady
Jones piously wished that all Julius's German books (*he* was the ac-
quisitions librarian of the family) might be burned, but Julius roundly
asserted they enabled him "to believe in Christianity with a much
more implicit and intelligent faith." Augustus Hare married a clergyman's daughter, Maria Leycester, who was sister of the mother of
A. P. Stanley, pupil of Thomas Arnold and close friend of Matthew's,
biographer of Thomas Arnold, distinguished and learned Broad
Church clergyman and Dean of Westminster. Augustus died early and
was buried in the Protestant cemetery in Rome. His widow joined the
household of Julius Hare and was "Auntie" to young Stanley when he
visited Julius Hare when Hare's curate was John Sterling, the subject
of Carlyle's celebrated *Life,* who gave Coleridge's *Confessions* to
Stanley to read before sending it on to Thomas Arnold. Poet Coleridge's nephew was Thomas Arnold's close friend; his grandnephew
John Duke Coleridge, Lord Chief Justice of England, was Matthew
Arnold's close friend. Sterling's wife was a sister of F. D. Maurice's
first wife. Julius Hare was a schoolfellow at Charterhouse of Thirlwall's, later to be his friend and associate, and Thomas Arnold's, and
Bishop of St. David's in Wales where Lowth had once been bishop.
Another of his schoolfellows was George Waddington, traveler and
church historian, brother of the learned Frances Waddington who
married Christian Bunsen, later baron. The Waddingtons were connections of the Stanleys and of Lord Lansdowne. Julius Hare translated—and vindicated—Niebuhr, who was Wilhelm von Humboldt's
successor as Prussian legate at Rome, Niebuhr himself being succeeded in that post by Bunsen. A later Hare, Augustus Julius Charles,
had carried on the kind of jet-setting Anglican tradition by being born
in Rome, adopted by his godmother Maria, widow of his uncle Augustus; he was a prolific travel writer and memoirist—of the Baroness
Bunsen, of his adoptive mother (this went through eighteen editions),
and of himself (in six volumes), and he contributed to the *Dictionary
of National Biography* many articles on his relations and connections.
Connop Thirlwall and this last-mentioned Hare died bachelors—or

there might have been an infinite proliferation of clerical families and of the Higher Criticism. It all constitutes a chain, or web rather, of *Bildung* or Culture that is particularly Protestant: it depends on Bible-reading and on the sexual reproduction of the clergy. The web that succeeded Matthew Arnold is rather better known: the Humphry Ward-Huxley-Leslie Stephen-Virginia Woolf complex. Both illustrate, besides the sensationalism of the *Dictionary of National Biography*, the characteristic homogeneity of England's class culture: these people *were* a kind of Clerisy, and elitist too, if you will.[58] Perhaps we can look back on this now to see an enviable advantage in learning, for those who were part of this elite. But we cannot accept it for ourselves. Nor could Matthew Arnold. It was in his vision of democracy to extend the intimate communion with the "poets," ancient Hebrew and others, "clouds of witnesses," to those disadvantaged little philistines he saw in the schools. And even now, through an interest in his work, *die Kette der Bildung*, without which the spectacle of the world is insupportable, stretches down to us, philistines of a latter day.

58. See Ben Knights, *The Idea of the Clerisy in the Nineteenth Century* (Cambridge: Cambridge University Press, 1975), for a remarkably hostile evaluation.

IV

Education:
The Wisdom of the Race

THE first song of Callicles in *Empedocles on Etna*, the first of those songs that constitute as I believe a counter-movement to Empedocles' despair, describes the education of Achilles by Chiron the Centaur. After a rather Wordsworthian preamble, Callicles sings:

> In such a glen, on such a day,
> On Pelion, in the grassy ground
> Chiron, the aged Centaur lay,
> The young Achilles standing by.
>
> (166)

"In such a glen, on such a day" is a poetic locution which in fact links our place and time, and Empedocles' place and time, to old tradition.[1] Chiron teaches a kind of practical natural history, as he had to Peleus "in long distant years," and teaches also the religious myth.

> He told him of the Gods, the stars,
> The tides; and then of mortal wars,
> And of the life which heroes lead
> Before they reach the Elysian place
> And rest in the immortal mead;
> And all the wisdom of his race.
>
> (167)

1. It works in the same way as "In such a night . . ." in the Lorenzo-Jessica love-passage in *The Merchant of Venice*. Arnold refers to that passage as a prime example of "natural magic" in his essay on Celtic literature (III: 379).

This is a different wisdom from Empedocles', certainly. In this wisdom, there is a life close to nature, a poetic nostalgia, and an invocation of the mythic and heroic, a serene acceptance of the Gods and the cosmic order, and of something lasting, an element of immortality. Kenneth Allott suggests the significance of the traditional lore with an interesting citation from Edgar Quinet's *Le Génie des religions* (1842) (166), which describes the education of Achilles as the acquisition not only of survival skills but also of the tradition and "the mystery of the first days of the world." "'Tout peuple reçoit de même; en secret, les enseignements de Chiron" (All people receive this, in secret, the teachings of Chiron). The Maurice de Guérin poem *Le Centaure* helped to shape Callicles' songs, as Arnold's de Guérin essay will show. *Le Centaure*, for instance, includes a vision in the mountains of the choir of the mythic divine muses of Callicles' last song; in the essay he translates passages on the education by Chiron. Callicles' centaur song brings together Wordsworthian nature with the religious myth as the constituents of education itself. This chapter aims to trace Arnold's developing concept of education, which is not separate from his religious thought.

The question of myth is central to that curious preface to the *Poems* of 1853 (I: 1–5), which can stand as preface also to the next phase of his career. He explains why he does not reprint his own *Empedocles*: it is not because it is antique but rather because it is *modern*, oppressively so, *modern* in the historicist sense he has taken from Vico-Herder-Niebuhr-Thomas Arnold: for Empedocles, Vico I and II have passed—the mythic age and the heroic, aristocratic age—and Vico III, or a "modern" phase of the cycle, begins; hence the enervating "dialogue of the mind with itself," the "doubts," the "discouragement" as of Hamlet and of Faust. But Arnold insists the best poetry must "inspirit and rejoice." In "Obermann Once More," joy takes on a religious aspect; we must search out the "joy whose grounds are true" (572), but here in the 1853 preface, Arnold turns to art—and to Schiller:

All art is dedicated to Joy, and there is no higher and no more serious problem than how to make men happy. The right art is that alone, which creates the highest enjoyment.

(I: 2)

Art—which for Arnold is poetry—has a way of transcending time in achieving the needed joy; it appeals to "elementary feelings which subsist permanently" (I: 4), as even our greatest recent poets—Goethe, Byron, Lamartine, Wordsworth—do not. The greatest poets of the ancients, however, have "nothing local and casual" but are accessible to us now.

Their secret appears to be that they turned to *myth*, to their own prehistory, known to all. Arnold presents in a memorable metaphor the phenomenology of the *ficta nota*:

The terrible old mythic story on which the drama was founded stood, before [the spectator] entered the theatre . . . in his memory, as a group of statuary, faintly seen, at the end of a long and dark vista . . . until at last, when the final words were spoken, it stood before him in broad sunlight, a model of immortal beauty.

(I: 6)

The principle of this kind of art was brilliantly demonstrated in an essay Arnold would have known, "On the Irony of Sophocles" (1833), by Thomas Arnold's friend Connop Thirlwall.[2] Thirlwall explains "tragic irony," which depends on the audience's previous knowledge of the essential story and by which the dramatist achieves the perspective of "the invisible power who orders the destiny of man." If we follow Arnold's logic, it must seem that then as now it is the task of education to provide the memory with the outlines of those groups of statuary, to tell the children the old stories, uncommented, just as Achilles acquired "the wisdom of his race." Older, we return to recognize the outlines fulfilled and illuminated with meanings. For this most serious kind of poetry Arnold borrows the epithet *pragmatic* from Polybius—who was also, like Chiron, like Arnold, an educator—Scipio's tutor. Poetry is *pragmatic*, it does something for you, it works, it brings you closer to achievement of joy. He cannot yet understand its working and yet is so absolutely convinced of its efficacy that he must make it his prime concern.

2. Connop Thirlwall, *The Philological Museum*, ed. J. C. Hare, 2 vols. (Cambridge: J. Smith, 1832–33), 2: 483–537; reprinted in Thirlwall's *Remains: Essays, Speeches and Sermons*, ed. J. J. Stewart Perowne (London: Richard Bentley, 1880), pp. 1–57, especially p. 9.

I know not how it is, but their commerce with the ancients appears to me to produce, in those who constantly practise it, a steadying and composing effect upon their judgment, not of literary works only, but of men and events in general.

(I: 13)

Such literature has a "transfer" value, the education people would say now. These beneficiaries of the ancients "are like persons who have had a very weighty and impressive experience" (the idiom is that of religious experience). They are "more independent of the language current among those with whom they live. They wish neither to applaud nor revile their age; they wish to know what it is." Here I think we can recognize the Herderian principle of assessing a culture in its own terms. "What they want, they know very well; they want to educe and cultivate what is best and noblest in themselves." Arnold copied into his *Note-Books* a similar statement from Goethe:

Ich wünsche Glück denen, die ihre Augen nach dem Alterthum wenden, wo ganz allein für die höhere Menschheit und Menschlichkeit reine Bildung zu hoffen und zu erwarten ist.

(*Note-Books* 2)

I wish them well who turn back to antiquity, for from there alone may we hope and await an unalloyed education [*Bildung*] toward an ideal humanity and humaneness.

The preface of 1853 ends with a kind of dedication to what Herder called *die Kette der Bildung*, "the chain of culture."

Let us not bewilder our successors; let us transmit to them the practice of poetry, with its boundaries and wholesome regulative laws, under which excellent works may again, perhaps, at some future time, be produced, not yet fallen into oblivion through our neglect, not yet condemned and cancelled by the influence of their eternal enemy, caprice.

(I: 15)

Caprice is his word for the Victorian absurd; "We fluctuate idly without term or scope" (364), he writes elsewhere, of what has become our twentieth-century nightmare, now richly studied as contingency, randomness, *La Nausée*. Herder had recognized it in his "grausenvoller Anblick," "Trümmer auf Trümmern," and declared that only *die*

Kette der Bildung can give order to this chaos. Arnold will follow suit with *his* Culture, and *transmit* is the key word.

C. A. Runcie, in a perceptive study of the preface, argues that its central concept of myth leads on into Arnold's writings on religion.[3] Runcie connects the preface with Arnold's reading in the philological and anthropological study of myth—back from Max Müller and Bunsen, as Runcie sees it, through Georg Friedrich Creuzer, Humboldt, Herder, Berkeley, Ralph Cudworth, Edward Stillingfleet, Glanvill— and earlier, from which the view emerges of myth as "a trans-cultural primitive phenomenon, a form of knowledge, anthropomorphic . . . recording man's original significant experiences." One attitude contemporary to this accepted view is John Stuart Mill's, the skeptical empiricist attitude, that this anthropomorphic projection is the religion of "savages"—"personification and divinization of the occult causes of phenomena." For the other, Runcie cites Bunsen: mythology unites the finite and the infinite, the human and the divine; it is the poetry of the consciousness of God in the world; it is the record of the meaning of being, of the conditions of human existence. Arnold, he says, takes up a particular position of his own: "Unlike Mill, Arnold accepts the anthropomorphized predication of deity, not to refute its implications but to reinforce the notion of some power akin to God in the universe; and unlike Bunsen, he reinforces this notion not by some transcendental *a priori*, but by 'proof' that historical man actually felt the 'not ourselves' that makes for righteousness operative in his world."[4] Furthermore, writes Runcie,

When Arnold says to Clough in 1852 that the religion and poetry of the ancients are one, it is with full awareness that myth is the common factor to both.[5]

He cites a paper by Bunsen read at Oxford in 1847, which Arnold quite probably heard:

The power of mind which enables us to see the genus in the individual, the whole in the many, and to form a word by connecting a subject with a predi-

3. C. A. Runcie, "Matthew Arnold and Myth: A Reading of the Preface of *Poems, 1853*," *AUMLA: Journal of the Australasian Universities Language and Literature Association*, no. 37 (May 1972): 5–17.
4. Ibid., pp. 7, 8, 11.
5. Ibid., p. 12; *Clough* 124.

cate, is the same which leads man to find God in the universe, and the universe in God. Language and religion are the two poles of our consciousness, mutually presupposing each other.[6]

This may seem a little too intuitive, too loose—like Bunsen! Max Müller, Bunsen's protégé and Arnold's friend, claimed the dependency of religion on language rather more responsibly:

Mythology will enable us to see in the history of the ancient religions, more clearly than anywhere else the Divine education of the human race.[7]

And again:

Mythology is only a dialect, an ancient form of language.[8]

(Significantly, Carlyle, when he speaks of God, says he is speaking in "the ancient dialect.")[9]

As for Arnold's withdrawal of *Empedocles on Etna*, one can only join the general chorus to the effect that Arnold was simply wrong. Would he withdraw *Hamlet* too? and *Faust*? The dialogue of the mind with itself in *Hamlet*, *Faust*, and in *Empedocles* as well, seems pragmatic poetry to us, if not to Arnold during a mood of 1853. The odd thing is that *Empedocles* carries its own antidote, its own counterweight, in the songs of Callicles, as I argued above. They are the *saving* grace of this long poem, related to the whole as the Voice from the Whirlwind is related to the whole of the book of Job.[10]

This preface of 1853 is not a complete or well-argued statement; Arnold freely grants in his preface to the second edition of the *Poems* (1854) that there was much "incompletely stated" (I: 16). But the

6. Ibid., p. 15, n. 7; quoted from Christian Bunsen, in *Three Linguistic Dissertations* (London: British Association for the Advancement of Science, 1848), p. 287.

7. Runcie, "Arnold and Myth," p. 16; quoted from Max Müller, *Introduction to the Science of Religion* (London: Longmans, Green, 1893), pp. 150–51.

8. Runcie, "Arnold and Myth," p. 17; quoted from Max Müller, *Oxford Essays* (London, 1856), p. 87.

9. Thomas Carlyle, "Phenomena," in *Past and Present* (1843), vol. 3 of *Works* (London: Chapman and Hall, 1910), p. 117.

10. I make this case in "Waiting for Gödel: Some Literary Examples of Hierarchical Thinking," in *Language, Logic and Genre*, ed. Wallace Martin, (Lewisburg, Pa.: Bucknell University Press, 1974), pp. 28–43, especially pp. 37–40.

loose ends are also promises, to be picked up and worked out in future essays. I want to trace now some of the themes started here connecting education with Arnold's developing notion of religion: myth, history, poetry, language, and metaphor, in some of their weavings, up to the more evolved fabric of *Literature and Dogma.*

"On the Modern Element in Literature" is particularly connected to the 1853 preface. It was Arnold's first lecture as Professor of Poetry at Oxford in 1857; when he prints it in 1869 he introduces it from his post-*Culture and Anarchy* vantage point: this lecture, he says, may serve "to give some notion of the Hellenic spirit and its works, and of their significance in *the history of the evolution of the human spirit in general*" (I: 18). My italics indicate Herder's idiom, *Entwicklung, Humanität*—evolution, human spirit. It was in 1867–68 that he was reading Herder's *Ideen* with great engagement, and he reendorsed the broad comparativist point of view. Quite appropriately then, the lecture begins with a parable from outside the European tradition, a Buddhist parable borrowed from Eugène Burnouf, on the theme of "transmit" which ended the 1853 preface.

> Go then, O Pourna: having been delivered, deliver; having been consoled, console; being arrived thyself at the farther bank, enable others to arrive there also.
>
> (I: 19)

Arnold's leitmotiv words, *deliver* and *console*, appear then to derive from Burnouf's French.[11] In the parable it is a moral deliverance, Arnold notes, but parables are made for transference, and the transferred gist of this is that he, Arnold, through poetry (in some special sense) has been delivered intellectually, and so he is as an apostle (which has become a byword for Arnold, of course) with the gospel of poetry to spread. The baldness of this statement of mine helps to indicate in contrast the discretion of his parable-metaphor. He does not use a Christian parable, for that might offend, and the Buddhist story has the added advantage of opening his audience's consciousness to a remote mode of religion.

He develops rather specifically the Viconian-Herderian historicism broached in the preface. Cultures, like individuals, transform themselves. "Modern" phases—the age of Pericles in Greece, the age of

11. Super quotes Burnouf's French, and credits Kenneth Allott for discovering Arnold's French source (I: 226). See also XI: 518–19.

Virgil and Horace in Rome, and the present time in England—are compared, tested on the degree to which *Bildung* takes place, that is, "human nature developed in a number of directions, politically, socially, religiously, morally developed—in its completest and most harmonious development in all these directions" (I: 28). Literature is the best gauge of a civilization, Herder had said, and its most precious product. By this gauge, Arnold insists, the Greeks are far ahead. Of all "modern" periods, their "modern" period produced the "most adequate" literature, in that it affords man the most complete deliverance from the confusions of "modern" epochs, "the spectacle of a vast multitude of facts awaiting and inviting his comprehension"—or order out of chaos, we might say.

The deliverance consists in man's comprehension of this present and past. It begins when our mind begins to enter into possession of the general ideas which are the law of this vast multitude of facts. It is perfect when we have acquired that harmonious acquiescence of mind which we feel in contemplating a grand spectacle that is intelligible to us.

The goal is—

the intellectual maturity of man himself; the tendency to observe facts with a critical spirit; to search for their law, not to wander among them at random; to judge by the rule of reason, not by the impulse of prejudice or caprice.

(I: 20, 24)

In our own twentieth-century "modern" age (if we have not indeed relapsed into the naïve and bloody barbarism of a pre-Vico I phase) we are rather more familiar with the random and have become connoisseurs of the absurd and of caprice—not even, at times, without some relish—and we doubt whether there can be general ideas or laws, though we may know of logotherapy and hope it works.[12] And yet I suppose the confidence of Arnold's statement is part of his argument, the result of his own deliverance by the values he claims for Greek literature. It is a kind of logotherapy not tried these days on any very extensive scale. He includes in his argument Thucydides' history of the Peloponnesian War as a flower of "modern" culture, and for him

12. Viktor Emil Frankl, *Man's Search for Meaning: An Introduction to Logotherapy* (published in 1959 under the title of *From Death-camp to Existentialism*; New York: Pocket Books, 1973). Frankl is a post-Freudian psychotherapist whose "logotherapy" involves the curative power of meaning systems, religious or artistic.

Burke and Niebuhr are not unworthy analogues, as his father Thomas
Arnold would have claimed. But the greatest achievements are the
works of Pindar, Aeschylus, Sophocles, and Aristophanes—more adequate for us moderns than Homer, even.
The rather offensive devaluation of the Romans—Lucretius, Virgil,
Horace, as *inadequate*—can be explained in part, I think, by his German predilections. The Germans took Greek art for their standard and
ideal, from Winckelmann on through Lessing, Herder, Humboldt, and
Goethe, and *paideia* prefigures *Bildung*.[13] Moreover, Arnold tended
to join in the moral disapproval of the Romans so common in Victorian thought, the idea that the Roman Empire collapsed of its own
evil weight, giving place to the better world of Christianity. But what
is notable in this essay is the opening of a large comparative view, and
a comparative method.

The intellectual history of our race[14] cannot be clearly understood without
applying to other ages, nations, and literatures the same method of inquiry
which we have been here imperfectly applying to what is called classical
antiquity.

(I: 37)

In "On Translating Homer," he turns to a vital issue, urgent in the
cause of *Bildung* and of democratic education. For if the mission is to
transmit, translation itself is of prime importance. Furthermore, the
issue of Homer translation implies the yet greater issue of Bible translation. It was not till 1870 that the actual work of Bible revision was
undertaken, but the question was much in the air, and scholars had accumulated a library of *corrigenda*. I do not mean to say that Arnold
in this Homer essay is particularly conscious of Bible translation, but
he simply takes up the practical problems (the essay is consistently,
avowedly, wittily practical throughout), which naturally are the same
as problems of Bible translation, especially in the poetic parts. He
does say that the translator should not trouble himself with "whether

13. See, for instance, R. T. Clark, *Herder* (Berkeley: University of California
Press, 1955), especially pp. 36–38. But in other moods, he was much interested in
Lucretius, planned a work on him, and felt rather undercut by Tennyson's "Lucre-
tius." *Letters* I: 575.

14. The concept of "race" has been definitively treated in the invaluable *Matthew Arnold, Ethnologist* by F. E. Faverty (Evanston: Northwestern University
Press, 1951; reprint ed., New York: AMS, 1968). In cases such as this, "culture" in
its present anthropological sense makes a good substitute.

the poet of the Iliad be one poet or many," and this seems to have certain implications for the Bible. Even if the translator could solve such problems, he says, the solution "could be of no benefit to his translation" (I: 100). It is only incidentally that he mentions the Authorized Version as a masterpiece; one of the circumstances that made it so was the devout respect of the translators for their text; "they did not dare to give the rein to their own fancies in dealing with it" (I: 113) — as Homer translators have all too often done.

Arnold's missions on the continent, March through August 1859 and April through November 1865, for two separate Royal Commissions on Education, brought him into an increased intimacy with intellectual affairs in both France and Germany. For in France and Germany the best minds had played a part in shaping the systems of public education—a situation very unlike that of England, Arnold does not fail to observe. In France, the aged historian François Guizot, when Arnold knew him, retained his interest and power in the Academy and was still a leader in education as well as in intellectual affairs in general. In Germany, Arnold encounters in the schools the concrete results of the work of the sages: Herder, Goethe, and above all Wilhelm von Humboldt, and notes how most of the intelligentsia worked in common public education: Humboldt, Schleiermacher, Wolf, for instance (IV: 223). So Arnold's reports on continental education are not cut off from the mainstream of his political, literary, and religious thought. The school inspectorship seems to have been undertaken as a meal ticket and felt as drudgery, and indeed the work was staggeringly heavy and very far from the elegant world he fancied. The fifties were for him a time of dissatisfaction, at least. But Fred G. Walcott, who best knows Arnold's work in education, goes so far as to say: "His official journey to the Continent [in 1859] marked the end of this dark interval and the moment of a great spiritual rebirth; . . . he beheld at once the larger vision of his own calling as a servant of the benevolent and enlightened state in disseminating culture . . . . The labor begun in drudgery became the grand mission."[15]

Arnold's devotion to popular education is the best confutation of the charge of elitism, even lately voiced by Ben Knights. For Knights, the ideas of Culture, the remnant, and the best self are bound to be

15. Fred G. Walcott, *The Origins of Culture and Anarchy: Matthew Arnold and Popular Education in England* (Toronto: University of Toronto Press, 1970), pp. 143–44.

undemocratic, and Arnold's demurrers are hypocritical.[16] But Arnold's sense of risks in democracy is warranted: one sees often enough the frequent triumph of mediocrity. Nevertheless Arnold's moral base is unquestionably in the simple humaneness of the democratic ideal. It is as an introduction to *The Popular Education of France* (1861) that his essay "Democracy" takes shape.

Can it be denied, that to live in a society of equals tends in general to make a man's spirits expand, and his faculties work easily and actively; while, to live in a society of superiors, although it may occasionally be a very good discipline, yet in general tends to tame the spirits and to make the play of the faculties less secure and active?

(II: 8–9)

The example of France demonstrates that education *can* be for all, but England need not, like France, go in for extreme state control, nor go the American way of "the misfortune of having to grow up without ideals"! (II: 16, 160). In England the state can shape a public education that harmonizes with what is good in English traditions and tastes. Let it be a state that "really represents its best self," but it must be by the state.

Undoubtedly we are drawing on toward great changes; and for every nation the thing most needful is to discern clearly its own condition, in order to know in what particular way it may best meet them.

(II: 29)

The changes here are Viconian-Herderian changes, and the "condition" of a nation is the Herderian uniqueness of cultural context, in which the uniquely English *Bildung* is to be pursued. "Openness and flexibility of mind are at such a time the first of virtues," he continues, again in the Herderian mode.

Be ye perfect, said the Founder of Christianity; *I count not myself to have apprehended*, said its greatest Apostle.

(II: 29)

I think it is one of Arnold's distinctions to have related the German ideal as specifically as this to the New Testament, to have recognized in the example of Christ the goal of *Bildung* and to have recognized

16. Ben Knights, *The Idea of the Clerisy in the Nineteenth Century* (London: Cambridge University Press, 1978).

in Paul's acceptance of human limitations the never-ending process toward perfection, "reaching forth unto those things which are before" (the Philippians 3: 13 text continues). The "quest" of Arnold's pastoral poems has a Pauline sanction. And so "Democracy" concludes:

Perfection will never be reached; but to recognize a period of transformation when it comes, and to adapt themselves honestly and rationally to its laws, is perhaps the nearest approach to perfection of which men and nations are capable. No habits or attachments should prevent their trying to do this; nor indeed, in the long run, can they. Human thought, which made all institutions, inevitably saps them, resting only in that which is absolute and eternal.

(II: 29)

This introduction to a school inspector's commission report on the educational system of France thus ends with no less than "the absolute and eternal," the *Dauerndes*, in which even commissions live and move and have their being.

The great obstacle to public education in England was, of course, "The Religious Question": if state education is to be established, should, then, the religious part of that education be that of the Established Church, or not? And so to deal with state education commits the writer to deal with the religious issue. Arnold shoulders the burden of the history of French education and description of its present state and marshals a mass of detail in a form that is still readable, all welded by his developing sense of *Bildung*. He describes the French solution to the religious problem, shaped by the "tolerant disposition" of Guizot, to show that the problem can be solved, and he is ever careful to insist that the English need not solve it in the French way. In France, schools are either Protestant, or Catholic, or Jewish—or common—and, where common, separate religious instruction for the different groups is provided according to the will of the parents. Arnold assumes the passionately warring sects of England will not be satisfied by so few as three kinds of religious instruction. Guizot guarded against an unspecific religiosity in the common schools: "He wished the religious instruction to be, above all things, real; not 'a series of lessons and practices apparently capable of being used by all denominations in common'" (II: 83). Obviously, Arnold would deplore the "vague abstractions" of some sort of common "religion"; religion, it seems, to be religion, must be specific.

The French system . . . inculcates the doctrines of morality in the only way in which the masses of mankind ever admit them, in their connection with the doctrines of religion. I believe that the French system is right.

(II: 142)

Arnold's first mission was officially confined to primary education in France, and his report, published as a book, is *The Popular Education of France* (1861) ;[17] his second mission concerned secondary education and resulted in the book *Schools and Universities on the Continent* (1868),[18] but from the first his interest extended to secondary education, and in 1863–64 he published the essay "A French Eton" (II: 262–325). It is probably the most anthologized and most read of Arnold's writings on education, but, even so, it is possibly not enough read. The center of it is this: England congratulates itself on its great "public schools," but while the education at these schools may well be better than anything on the continent and has produced statesmen and citizens of high caliber, it is very expensive, and it is for the few. In fact, it educates only about some 5,000 youths, while the comparable institutions in France, the *lycées*, educate some 65,000—to a comparable pitch.[19] Another moving set of statistics is the proportion of illiterate army recruits in the country: in Prussia 2 percent; in France 27 percent; in England 57 percent (IV: 20).

He presents in the essay two alternatives to the English schools, one which he felt to be a pretty typical state *lycée* in Toulouse, and the other, the private school headed by the distinguished Dominican Père Lacordaire at Sorèze.

In the writing of this essay Arnold found himself beset with some difficulties of delay (II: 369–73). At the time, he was regularly reading the French journals, a habit no doubt strengthened by his recent travels. Besides the *Revue des deux mondes*, there was also the notable *Revue germanique et française*. The published *Note-Books* record this reading, but in the unpublished "General Note-Book" Arnold made such extensive transcripts from the *Revue germanique* that it must be given special notice.[20] It was founded and directed

17. Contained in *Prose*, volume II.

18. Constituting nearly all of *Prose*, volume IV.

19. These statistics are in fact from *Prose* IV: 329 but represent the situation in "A French Eton."

20. Matthew Arnold, "General Note-Book," Tinker, no. 24, Beinecke Library; Yale University, New Haven, Conn. William Bell Guthrie's University of Virginia

through its whole course from 1857 to 1868 by Charles Dollfus, a French philosopher and man of letters, who, Larousse tells us, "declared himself incapable of living without religion or with religion in its traditional forms, and he addressed himself to those in a like situation."[21] Arnold refers to him in "A French Eton" as an able critic of education, citing his "Le Lycée et la liberté d'enseignement," printed in this *Revue*.[22] Dollfus translated (with a certain M. Nefftzer) D. F. Strauss's *Leben Jesu*, the only French translation sanctioned by the author. It is this translation from which Arnold copied a short passage in the *Note-Books* in 1874 (p. 222), but in 1864 Dollfus had published a long essay on Strauss's *Leben Jesu*,[23] from which Arnold transcribed in this unpublished note-book upwards of 3,000 words in his careful and deliberate hand. This postdates, of course, "A French Eton" and is related to *Literature and Dogma*. But another enormously lengthy transcript from Dollfus's *Revue* appears to have delayed the completion of "A French Eton" and, I believe, affected its shape. This is about 2,000 words copied from a series of essays on Wilhelm von Humboldt by Paul-Armand Challemel-Lacour, published in December 1863, February 1864, and April 1864.[24] Part 3 of "A French Eton" Arnold had promised for February 1864; he did not deliver it until May. It was Challemel-Lacour who was later to review *La Crise religieuse*,[25] the French translation of *Literature and Dogma*; when

thesis, "Matthew Arnold's Diaries, the Unpublished Items: A Transcription and Commentary," (Ann Arbor, Mich.: University Microfilms, 1957), covers "The Diaries" only, not the "General Note-Books" 1 and 2 in Lowry, Young, and Dunn's *Note-Books*. The "General Note-Books" 1 and 2 are Tinker 22 and 23. Tinker 24, the "General Note-Book," with lengthy transcriptions I refer to here, appears to be ignored by Guthrie as well as by Lowry, et al. See Richard Tobias, "On Dating Matthew Arnold's 'General Note-Books,'" *Philological Quarterly* 39 (July 1960): 426–34.

21. Pierre Larousse, *Grand Dictionnaire universel du XIX*[e] *siècle* (Paris: Larousse Boyer, 1866–[90]), s.v. Charles Dollfus.

22. II: 298, 377; *Revue germanique et française* 16 (August 1863): 385–404.

23. Charles Dollfus, "À propos de la nouvelle vie de Jésus par David Strauss," *Revue germanique et française* 31 (November 1864): 358–64.

24. Paul-Armand Challemel-Lacour, "Guillaume de Humboldt," *Revue germanique et française* 27 (December 1863): 650–79; 28 (February 1864): 346–74; 29 (April 1864): 65–105. In book form, *La philosophie individualiste: Étude sur Guillaume de Humboldt* (Paris, 1864).

25. Paul-Armand Challemel-Lacour, in *La République française* (November 14, 1876), pp. 3–4. *Prose* VIII: 415.

Arnold refers to this review in 1877 he writes of Challemel-Lacour as "one of the best, gravest, most deeply interesting and instructive of French writers. His admirable series of articles on Wilhelm von Humboldt, which I read a good many years ago . . . still live as fresh in my memory as if I had read them yesterday."[26]

I quote from Arnold's transcriptions some passages which reinforced the seminal *Bildung* idea.

C'est donc [writes Challemel-Lacour, paraphrasing Humboldt's thought] uniquement par l'antiquité qu'il est possible d'acquérir l'idée concrète de toutes les puissances intellectuelles et actives de la nature humaine . . . l'expansion harmonieuse de l'individualité.

It is then uniquely through antiquity that it is possible to acquire the concrete idea of all the intellectual and active powers of human nature . . . the harmonious expansion of the individuality.

It is men's duty to develop themselves to the utmost; Humboldt "ne songe que subsidiairement à l'action qu'ils peuvent exercer sur la civilisation générale" (thought only subsidiarily of the effect they could have on general civilization). Language conditions culture:

Les langues expriment chacune *le monde aperçu, conçu, et senti différemment.*

Each language expresses *the world perceived, conceived, and felt, differently.* [Arnold's emphasis].[27]

Humboldt et Goethe étaient de la même religion, avaient la même foi, apercevaient partout le doigt de l'incompréhensible ouvrier, le sentirent, comme Spinoza, travailler dans le monde, dans la nature et dans leur coeur.

Humboldt and Goethe were of the same religion, had the same faith, perceived everywhere the finger of the incomprehensible maker, like Spinoza felt him at work in the world, in nature, and in their hearts.

La langue que, dans cet ordre d'idées et de sentiments, Humboldt parlait le plus volontiers, était celle du paganisme et des livres de l'Inde. L'effort de

26. His memory on their location was less fresh—he mentions the *Revue des deux mondes* (VIII: 150). "On the Study of Celtic Literature" (1866) refers to a passage he had transcribed on Humboldt's attitude to Semitism (III: 301, 501).

27. The underlining here is in ink the same as from Arnold's pen. Miss Marjorie Wynne of the Beinecke Library believes the pencil markings in this "Note-Book" are from another hand.

la Grèce pour tout intellectualiser, pour absorber dans l'art la morale, la religion, l'État, la vie privée de la nature, lui semble un oeuvre divine par excellence. Le beau avait, à un haut degré, la puissance d'élever sa pensée au-dessus
de la realité passagère et incomplète; et qu'est-ce que la religion, même la
plus haute, sinon le détachement du fini? [Here, Arnold puts an X in ink in
the margin.]

In this order of ideas and feelings, the language that Humboldt spoke most
readily was that of paganism and the books of India. The Greek effort to in-
tellectualize everything, to absorb into art—ethics, religion, the State, the intimate life of nature—seemed to him the supreme divine achievement. The
beautiful had to a great degree the power to raise his thought above fleeting
and incomplete reality; and what is religion, even the highest, if not the detachment from the finite?

One can see Arnold here embracing Humboldt's thought on Greek
paideia and on that *livre de l'Jnde*, the *Bhagavad-Gita* (Clough 69, 70,
75).

Another passage in his transcription he marked with an X, his *nota
bene*:

Humboldt se maintenait à cet hauteur, où la moralité, la religion, l'art, l'amour,
manifestations si diverses de la vie humaine, s'identifient comme expressions
de la force éternelle, qui est immanente dans l'humanité.

Humboldt maintained himself at that level where morality, religion, art, love—
such diverse manifestations of human life—identify themselves as expressions
of the eternal force which is immanent in humanity.

Herder had a certain idea of vitalism, maintained by Humboldt; perhaps it contributes to Arnold's ideas of God-the-force.

H's patience

Cette douloureuse impatience de savoir le comment et le pourquoi des choses,
ce tremblement de l'esprit à la pensée de l'éternité, qui a parfois tourmenté
les sceptiques—cette maladie de l'intelligence, toute moderne, ne l'atteignit
jamais. [Sometimes Arnold puts English headings in his transcripts.]

H's patience

That painful impatience to know the how and why of things, that trembling of
the spirit at the thought of eternity which has sometimes tormented skeptics,
that altogether modern malady of the intelligence, never touched him.

Here one imagines Arnold recognizing Challemel-Lacour's version of Empedocles' complaint, and Humboldt's way out, by *Bildung*. Challemel-Lacour goes on to acclaim the faculty of the Germans for the conception of general ideas:

On peut réduire toutes les idées élaborées en Allemagne depuis un demi-siècle à une seule, l'idée du *développement* (entwickelung [*sic*]) [Arnold's emphasis] qui consiste à représenter toutes les parties d'un groupe comme solidaires et complémentaires, en sorte que chacune d'elles nécessite le reste. . . .

All the ideas elaborated in Germany in the last half-century can be reduced to a single one, the idea of development, which consists in representing all elements of a set as unified and complementary, so that each part necessitates the rest. . . .

Humboldt embodies the Arnoldian paradigm: retirement, withdrawal into oneself or the region of ideas, and return to man, to society with something of value, the paradigm of "The Scholar-Gipsy," of the Obermann poems, of "Palladium." The paradigm is not merely an ideal, it was the fact of Humboldt's life: the long retirement and *Bildung* before the prodigious career—as Arnold would have known. And again:

The same in Humboldt and Goethe

Nous trouvons dans Humboldt un des exemples les plus parfaits de ce besoin d'accroître sans cesse sa valeur intime et ses richesses intérieures qui fut aussi pour un homme tel que Goethe, la préoccupation de toute la vie. . . . Aux yeux de Humboldt le premier devoir est de cultiver, de perfectionner sans cesse en soi cette nature humaine si digne de soin et de respect. Après cela, on l'a vu préoccupé de créer, par l'instruction, une aristocratie, la plus nombreuse possible, d'intelligences et de caractères. [The heading is Arnold's.]

The same in Humboldt and Goethe

We find in Humboldt one of the most perfect examples of this need to enlarge unceasingly one's inner worth and interior resources which was also for such a man as Goethe the preoccupation of his whole life. . . . In the eyes of Humboldt the first duty is to cultivate, to perfect unceasingly in oneself that human nature which is so worthy of care and of respect. After that, he is seen to be preoccupied with creating, by education, an aristocracy as numerous as possible, of intelligence and character.

Walcott finds that in "A French Eton," "the humanistic principles that underlay Arnold's educational philosophy . . . received their first clear and sympathetic enunciation,"[28] and in this connection he refers to the one passage in the essay that mentions Humboldt. We can now recognize the great influence of this *schöne Seele* (as Arnold calls him later [V: 161]) in the actual process of the writing of "A French Eton."[29]

Goethe supports the idea of perpetual *Bildung*, as the *Note-Books* show:

Man muss sich immerfort verändern, erneuen, verjüngen um nicht zu verstocken.[30]

(*Note-Books* 313)

One must continually change oneself, renew, become young, in order not to stultify.

And how vividly the record of Goethe's life endorses this maxim Arnold well knew, from, for instance, the picture we have of the old man in the *Conversations with Eckermann*, still welcoming new experience, new art, new light. Arnold records in the *Note-Books* a remarkably similar maxim from Johann Comenius, two hundred years earlier anticipating this developmental democratic education:

Ich beabsichtige eine allgemeine Bildung aller, welche als Menschen geboren sind, zu allem, was menschlich ist.[31]

(*Note-Books* 350)

The aim is to train generally all who are born men to all which is human. [Arnold's translation]

Arnold's careful meditation on Humboldt—for so it must be called, such long passages, so carefully and, one may say, lovingly transcribed, read and reread as the headings and markings indicate—

28. Walcott, *Origins of Culture and Anarchy*, p. 53.
29. For other readings of Humboldt see *Note-Books* 573, 575.
30. See also *Note-Books* 385, 401, 424, 493.
31. No source given in *Note-Books*. But see *Prose* XI: 29, 390, where Arnold translates the passage. It is ironic that Comenius visited England in 1641, invited in order to advise Parliament in establishing a reformed educational system, and it was politics, then as in Arnold's time, that aborted the plan. He lived on to make the first picture book for teaching children, however, the *Orbis Sensualum Pictus* (1658), which was among the delights of the child Goethe.

signifies a period of particular dynamic intellectual development, the shaping of the Arnoldian idea of Culture in a context of thought on education, and it was this that delayed the last section of "A French Eton." Just as Humboldt, prime apostle of Herder's *Humanität*, turned from self-development to his work in the state, so does Arnold now turn to a more public career. Part 3 of "A French Eton" holds the promise of *Culture and Anarchy*, an idea of human nature, its dignity and potential, first to move in progress toward perfection of itself and then to turn outward to create a more extensive "aristocracy" than hitherto dreamed, by the education of the middle class, who will eventually bring the lower classes up with themselves.[32]

The great end of society is the perfecting of the individual, the fullest, freest, and worthiest development of the individual's activity. . . . It was said, and truly said [by Challemel-Lacour, we now know],[33] of one of the most unwearied and successful strivers after human perfection that have ever lived—Wilhelm von Humboldt—that it was a joy to him to feel himself modified by a foreign influence. And this may well be a joy to a man whose centre of character and whose moral force are once securely established. Through this he makes growth in perfection. Through this he enlarges his being and fills up gaps in it; he unlearns old prejudices and learns new excellences; he makes advance towards inward light and freedom. Societies may use this means of perfection as well as individuals.

(II: 312, 313)

And he proceeds with a very German passage on *Humanität*:

It is in making endless additions to itself, in the endless expansion of its powers, in endless growth in wisdom and beauty, that the spirit of the human race finds its ideal.

(II: 318)

He concludes with a metaphor of his own, the metaphor of the Children's Crusade:

Long before Asia was reached, long before even Europe was half traversed, the little children in that travelling multitude began to fancy, with a natural

32. René Wellek pointed out as central to Arnold's thought "the ideal of *Bildung* as it was formulated by Goethe and Wilhelm von Humboldt," but no one seems to have followed this up. *A History of Modern Criticism, 1750–1950* (New Haven: Yale University Press, 1965), p. 155.

33. As transcribed by Arnold in "General Note-Book," Tinker 24.

impatience, that their journey must surely be drawing to an end; and every evening . . . they cried out eagerly to those who were with them, "Is this Jerusalem?" No, poor children, not this town, nor the next, nor yet the next.

(II: 320)

With such figures Arnold remains the poet even in a treatise on education, addressed to government and the public.

The truth is the English spirit has to accomplish an intense evolution [or *Entwicklung*] . . . ; in a middle class raised to a higher and more genial culture, we may find, not perhaps Jerusalem, but, I am sure, a notable stage towards it.

(II: 322)

And the means is a state system of education.

The old bugbear which scares us all away from the great confessed means of best promoting this culture—the religious difficulty, as it is called—is potent only so long as these gentlemen [our leaders] please.

(II: 323)

"Children of the future," the essays ends,

whose day has not yet dawned, you will hardly believe what obstructions were long suffered to prevent its coming! You . . . will not comprehend how progress towards man's best perfection—the adorning and ennobling of his spirit—should have been reluctantly undertaken. . . . But you, in your turn, with difficulties of your own, will then be mounting some new step in the arduous ladder whereby man climbs towards his perfection.

(II: 324–25)

Arnold was right enough about difficulties of our own.

In *Schools and Universities on the Continent* (1868), the book that came out of Arnold's research of 1865, he again marshaled a large amount of historical material and descriptive detail, this time freely exploring the secondary education that he had really wanted to include in his first survey, and the universities in France, Italy, Prussia, and Switzerland. His mission and its importance seem to become increasingly clear to him in the course of the work. "There is no doubt," writes R. H. Super, "that 'A French Eton' helped give impetus to the new investigation" (IV: 344). In a letter Super quotes, we find Arnold wishing that the Commission was more open-minded, but dedicating himself not to practical political action but to fixing "all my care upon a spiritual action, to tell upon people's minds" (IV: 345).

At the beginning of the book he puts a motto from Wilhelm von Humboldt:

The thing is *not*, to let the schools and universities go on in a drowsy and impotent routine; the thing is, to raise the culture of the nation ever higher and higher by their means.

(IV: 14)

When he comes in his text to "the great epoch of reform, . . . von Humboldt's year and a half at the head of the Education Department," he quotes the German original of this motto, which was, he tells us, the opening of a mere memorandum but might "be taken as a motto for his whole administration of public instruction." It is not far from a commonplace in itself, yet of course it would be far from commonplace if applied.

Occasionally, even when he is tracing educational history, his literary-religious interests shine through, as when he cannot forbear noting that a fourteenth-century bishop of Paris "publicly condemned as current in the University, such propositions as these: *Quod sermones theologi sunt fundati in fabulis; . . . Quod fabulae et falsa sunt in lege christiana sicut et in aliis; . . . Quod sapientes mundi sunt philosophi tantum*" (IV: 42) (That theological discourse is founded on fables; . . . That there are fables and false things in Christian law just as in others; . . . That secular wise men are sufficient philosophers). I think this instance of medieval fermenting free thought interested him, and he passes it on as an item to enlarge the temporal provincialism of his readers: some of the daring new propositions current in the nineteenth century are not so new but were alive even in the "Dark Ages."

In general, it would seem that Arnold knows his business—one gets from these books the sense of him as a humane investigator, just as one does where he talks of the schoolchildren in his *Letters*. He has a marked tenderness for the little boys: let us not be too hard on them in their studies, and let them develop freely in play. He knows good teaching. Wolf (of the *Prolegomena ad Homerum*) was famous as a teacher; Arnold says that his

great rule in all these lessons was that rule which masters in the art of teaching have followed,—to take as little part as possible in the lesson himself;

merely to start it, guide it, and sum it up, and to let quite the main part in it
be borne by the learners.

(IV: 223)

Arnold's own knowledge of and interest in the sciences was somewhat
defective, and he acknowledges this, perhaps not quite heartily
enough. But he does recognize that the English system neglects the
sciences unduly and acclaims the German system for its

Lehrfreiheit and *Lernfreiheit,* liberty for the teacher and liberty for the
learner; and *Wissenschaft,* science, knowledge systematically pursued and
prized in and for itself. . . . The French university has no liberty, and the
English universities have no science; the German universities have both.

(IV: 263–64)

The German system puts less pressure on examinations than the English, and:

The paramount university aim in Germany is to encourage a love of study and
science for their own sakes; and the professors, very unlike our college tutors,
are constantly warning their pupils against *Brodstudien* ["bread-studies," or
training for a job, as we say].

(IV: 262)

His considered philosophy of education comes out most clearly
toward the end of the book, with some glances, I think, toward Newman on the University:

The aim and office of instruction, say many people, is to make a man a good
citizen, or a good Christian, or a gentleman; or it is to fit him to get on in
the world, or it is to enable him to do his duty in that state of life to which
he is called. It is none of these; . . . its prime aim is to enable a man *to know
himself and the world.* Such knowledge is the only sure basis for action, and
this basis it is the true aim and office of instruction to supply. To know himself, a man must know the capabilities and performances of the human spirit;
and the value of the humanities, of *Alterthumswissenschaft,* the science of
antiquity, is, that it affords for this purpose an unsurpassed source of light and
stimulus.[34]

(IV: 290)

34. This is as Super notes the basis of his 1882 lecture on "Literature and
Science."

And he acclaims the "great and complete spirits" who are developed both in the humanities and in the sciences, and hopes that education can more and more present the "entire circle." But if our institutions make out of this circle two separate parts, Arnold—and he grants his own prejudices—opts for the humanities, in an argument that echoes Vico:

The study of letters is the study of the operation of human force, of human freedom and activity; the study of nature is the study of the operation of non-human forces, of human limitation and passivity. The contemplation of human force and activity tends naturally to heighten our own force and activity; the contemplation of human limits and passivity tends rather to check it.

(IV: 292)

It is men with humanistic training who have played the prominent roles,

because their training has powerfully fomented the human force in them. And in this way letters are indeed runes, like those magic runes taught by the Valkyrie Brynhild to Sigurd, the Scandinavian Achilles, which put the crown to his endowment and made him invincible.

(IV: 292)

This is a large claim for letters—no less than freedom itself. Freedom is traditionally the condition of the Western religious consciousness, and of morality. By claiming freedom for the condition of the humanities, Arnold would seem to be anticipating that displacement of spiritual authority that Northrop Frye considers in a classic essay, a displacement of authority from the Church toward education, toward the University.[35]

R. H. Super includes in his edition of Arnold's prose his own recent find of a *Pall Mall Gazette* piece, "German and English Universities," from Arnold's hand soon after the publication of *Schools and Universities on the Continent*. It is a ripe and witty piece of writing on the occasion of a pamphlet by a German comparing university systems. The German, Dr. Von Sybel, envies the English universities for one thing and one thing only—their endowments! And Arnold leaves the last word to his German friend:

35. Northrop Frye, "The Problem of Spiritual Authority in the Nineteenth Century," *Backgrounds to Victorian Literature*, ed. Richard Levine (San Francisco: Chandler, 1967), pp. 120–36.

At least one moment in his life every educated man on German soil is to have, when the organs of authority, when nation, State, and teachers themselves, as the first and foremost of their injunctions to him, lay upon him this command —to be spiritually free. . . . The individual may . . . follow this line or that . . . : *for us, the essential thing is only, that whatever he be, he be it not out of youthful habit, vague disposition, traditional obedience, but that he be it, from this time forward, upon scientific appreciation, critical verification, independent decision.* [Arnold's emphasis]

(IV: 334)

That, for Arnold, is the way to see the "freedom" of the University. Education is the exercise of one's distinctive humanity. Education is the *most* "practical poetry": without it, literature or poetry—and the myth and religion that accrete to them—cannot happen. *Bildung*, the Germans say, *macht frei*.

V

Essays in Criticism:
A Religious Book

A R N O L D ' S *Note-Books*, which he kept from 1852 to the year of his death, were published in 1952 in a beautifully annotated edition.[1] In 1952, what impressed and surprised even those who knew Arnold's work well was the high percentage, among the thousands of entries, of texts from documents that must be considered primarily religious. First in frequency comes the Bible: from the Old Testament, mostly Psalms, Proverbs, and the prophets, especially Isaiah; from the New Testament, all four gospels about equally represented, Acts, virtually all the Epistles, and Revelation; and from the Apocrypha, Ecclesiasticus, Baruch, and the Wisdom of Solomon. Second to the Bible in frequency, well ahead of Goethe, is the famous old manual of devotion *The Imitation of Christ*, ascribed to Thomas à Kempis (c. 1380–1471). Next in frequency come the secular figures of Goethe and Sainte-Beuve, then Bishop Thomas Wilson, whose *Maxims* and *Sacra Privata* are classically devotional. A good proportion of these transcriptions are repeated again and again through the years. They call to mind Arnold's use of the word *dwell* when he speaks of the way we use poetry: we *dwell* on certain texts. One cannot but infer from the *Note-Books* something like a sustained discipline of spiritual exer-

1. *The Note-Books of Matthew Arnold*, ed. Lowry, Young, and Dunn, uses less than half of the manuscript material. See William Bell Guthrie, *Matthew Arnold's Diaries, the Unpublished Items: A Transcription and Commentary* (Ph.D. diss., University of Virginia, 1957; Ann Arbor, Mich.: University Microfilms, 1959). Guthrie does not include the "General Note-Books," Tinker 22, 23, and 24, Beinecke Library, Yale University, New Haven, Conn. Lowry, et al., uses some of Tinker 22 and 23, but none of Tinker 24.

cises. The editors note that Paul Elmer More had called them "the critic's breviary"; John Livingstone Lowes was reminded of Keats's letter: "When Man has arrived at a certain ripeness in intellect, any one grand and spiritual passage serves him as a starting-point towards all 'the two-and-thirty Palaces.' "[2]

The worldly, dandiacal Matthew Arnold is to be remembered and cherished; he retained, it seems, always something of his flair for elegance and the *beau monde* and cultivated the amiable pretense of superciliousness. But he was nonetheless a man—I think it is clear in the Honan *Life*[3]—who strove for virtue both public and domestic. While Thomas Arnold was perhaps oppressively consistent, Matthew was complicated. A poem of about 1864 shows him interested in a case of the doubleness of secret piety: the beautiful, bejeweled young wife of Giacopone di Todi was mortally injured when a platform at a public celebration collapsed:

> Shuddering, they drew her garments off—and found
> A robe of sackcloth next the smooth, white skin.
> Such, poets, is your bride, the Muse! young, gay,
> Radiant, adorned outside; a hidden ground
> Of thought and of austerity within.
>
> (532)

Arnold's own hidden ground of thought and of austerity may be best seen in the *Note-Books*, but it appears at times in the letters, where we learn how he aimed every day to read regularly in "the best," to rise early, to read the school papers at set hours.

The romance of medieval Christianity and of asceticism appealed to him as it did to many of his contemporaries. He did not *join* medieval Christianity by a leap of faith as Newman did, but he did not dismiss it as the positivists did. The Giacopone poem, and the "Stanzas from the Grande Chartreuse," are part of the work of relating himself as a nineteenth-century rationalist to the mystical tradition. He is one of those who have done much to further the humane understanding of religious phenomena in rationalist terms. Where William James makes a clinical study of the "Varieties of Religious Experience,"

2. *Note-Books* ix. Keats to Reynolds, February 19, 1818, in *The Letters of John Keats*, ed. Hyder Edward Rollins (Cambridge, Mass.: Harvard University Press, 1958).

3. Park Honan, *Matthew Arnold: A Life* (New York: McGraw-Hill, 1981).

Arnold makes a literary study. The secret hair shirt of the worldly young woman he uses as a metaphor for the devotion to poetry, and some of the aura of sanctification carries over with it to the secular life. Arnold was much too worldly to castigate the flesh, but ordinary life can with appalling convenience supply the hair shirts. In Arnold's case, much of the school inspecting served the purpose; but worse, there was the sickness of his ailing children, anxiety for them and for his much-tried wife; in 1868 the infant son Basil died, then Tommy the eldest son died at sixteen in the same year; and in 1872 his son William, or "Budge," was to die at age eighteen. One may follow in the *Note-Books* the way in which he made of these trials stages of *Bildung*.

In what sense can we call him religious? The *Note-Books*, observe the editors,

mark Arnold's consecration to a life larger than that of the poet and essayist. Whatever one thinks of his studies in religious subjects, few men have tried harder to attend to the great language of faith and to make it the word of their daily lives. The note-books can rightly take their place, we feel, among the best of the books of devotion—the more so because the devotional parts are so rightly and naturally blended with so much else. The quest for piety is mixed with fine Attic salt and the bright things of the secular world. But the piety is there.

(*Note-Books* xiii)

Piety? The editors were as aware as we are of Arnold's thoroughly rationalist turn of mind. He simply did not believe in any miracles, resurrection, afterlife—or any form of the supernatural. In what, then, can piety consist? His writings become increasingly devoted to this subject. What is the phenomenon called religion? How are we to understand the term *God*?

After 1865, the number of entries for each year increases, and we may assume from this that the meditative habit grew on him. But even before 1865 there are many entries that indicate the quality of his piety. We find interest in Eastern religious discipline,[4] with some lines from R. Spence Hardy's *A Manual of Budhism* [sic] (*Note-Books* 9) and from Sir William Jones's translation of *Mānava Dharma Sāstra* (*Note-Books* 10–11). Wilhelm von Humboldt had been one of the first in Europe to take up the Eastern wisdom, and Arnold's interest in

4. For his early interest in the *Bhagavad-Gita* see *Clough* 69, 70n., 71, 75.

it is like Humboldt's.[5] Marianne Cowan remarks how Humboldt was by no means a "sectarian" or "prayerful" man and yet was marked by "an essentially religious turn of mind."[6] The name of God is invoked in both Eastern and Western traditions; what Arnold means by it becomes increasingly clear through the years, although of course from the beginning God is for him something other than a literal personage. In the *Note-Books* we find a mix of the Vulgate New Testament,

Vitam aeternam dedit nobis Deus, et haec vita in Filio ejus est.

(1 John 5 : 11; *Note-Books* 9)

God hath given to us eternal life, and this life is in his Son.

(King James Version)

a Buddhist text,

By meditating on the divine essence, let a man extinguish all qualities repugnant to God.

(*Note-Books* 12)

and a passage from Confucius on the *Jao* (*Note-Books* 38). I think the mere fact of the eclecticism indicates Arnold is himself working toward definition of the common nonsectarian ground of religious thought.

Already in 1856 we find the saying of Spinoza's that will be much repeated:

Vera hominis felicitas et beatitudo in solâ sapientiâ et veri cognitione constitit.

(*Note-Books* 2 et passim)

The true felicity and beatitude of man consists in wisdom alone, and in true knowledge.

We find a rationalist definition of prayer from George Sand:

Je n'appelle pas prière un choix et un arrangement de paroles lancées vers le ciel, mais un entretien de la pensée avec l'idéal de lumière et de perfections infinies.

(*Note-Books* 2)

5. He read it in the translation of Charles Wilkins (1785) but used Humboldt's German commentary and the comments of Victor Cousin.

6. Marianne Cowan, *Humanist Without Portfolio: An Anthology of the Writings of Wilhelm von Humboldt*, trans. with an introduction by Marianne Cowan (Detroit: Wayne State University Press, 1963), pp. 23–24.

I do not call prayer a choice and arrangement of words aimed at the sky, but [rather] a communion of thought with the ideal of light and of infinite perfections.

He reveres St. Francis and his love of sorrow and poverty (*Note-Books* 22). He quotes the Père Lacordaire he had met at the school described in "A French Eton":

En général, les grands hommes de l'antiquité ont été pauvres. Aujourd'hui, tout le monde échoue là; on ne sait plus vivre de peu.
(Note-Books 22)

In general, the great men of antiquity were poor. Today, everyone fails in this respect; one no longer knows how to live abstemiously.

Se retirer en soi et en Dieu est la plus grande force qui soit au monde!
(Note-Books 16)

To withdraw into oneself and into God constitutes the greatest power in the world!

He quotes Heine on the Bible, in French:

Les propagateurs de la Bible fondent le règne du pur sentiment religieux, de l'amour du prochain, de la vraie moralité enfin, qui ne peut être enseignée par des formules scolastico-dogmatiques, mais seulement par des images et des exemples, tels qu'il s'en trouve dans ce saint et beau livre d'éducation écrit pour des enfants de tout âge, et que nous appelons la Bible.
(Note-Books 19)

The propagators of the Bible founded the reign of pure religious sentiment, of love for one's neighbor, of, in short, the true morality, which cannot be taught by scholastico-dogmatic formulas, but only by images and examples, such as are found in this holy and beautiful book of education written for children of all ages, which we call the Bible.

Images and *examples*, these are what affect us morally—"Literature," that is, not "Dogma." And we encounter again and again the injunction from the *Imitation*: *Semper aliquid certi proponendum est* (*Note-Books* 8 et passim; Always there is something definite that [shall we say?] one must be getting on with). This favorite motto is of course but another version of Carlyle's exhortation to *work*, but Carlyle—interestingly—is never quoted in the *Note-Books*. Goethe is, on the same theme:

Es ist besser das geringste Ding von der Welt zu tun, als eine halbe Stunde
für gering halten.

(Note-Books 17)

It is better to do the slightest thing in the world than to slight the value of a
half hour.

And Dante:

Omai convien che tu cosi ti spoltre,
Disse 'l Maestro.

(Note-Books 5)

Now it behooves you to cast off sloth, said my master. [Singleton translation]

And, most intimately, Arnold's own words to himself:

At least one case reported daily till finished.
One canto of Dante daily.
One ½ chapter of Guizot's Memoirs daily.

(Note-Books 13)

The overriding frequency of the *Imitation* is one of the most impressive aspects of the *Note-Books*, perhaps because Thomas à Kempis's
temper is as indicated by his title: he does not go in for dogma but
rather a *way*, a behavior, which is at best an imitation of Christ.
Arnold's attitude to the *Imitation* varies, but the *Note-Books* seem to
show how much he *used* this manual of devotion, like a man with a
vocation.

The great metaphorical language of the Psalms graces his meditations, early and late. Here in 1865:

My days are gone like a shadow: and I am withered like grass.
But thou, O Lord, shalt endure forever; and thy remembrance throughout all
  generations.

(Psalm 102: 11–12, Prayer Book version; Note-Books 30)

He muses on Johann Tauler, the fourteenth-century German mystic
(in a French translation):

L'homme est véritablement un composé d'éternité et de temps; plus il
s'attache aux choses temporelles et s'y repose, plus il s'éloigne des choses
éternelles.

(Note-Books 13)

Man is truly a combination of eternity and time; the more he attaches himself
to temporal things and reposes there, the farther he moves from eternal things.

Late in life, Arnold wrote: "Let me be candid. I love the mystics, but what I find best in them is their golden single sentences, not the whole conduct of their argument and result of their work" (XI: 186). But of course. Here as everywhere in Arnold, dogma and doctrine cede in favor of "poetry," the great successes in the deployment of language.

The "golden sentences" are mixed in the *Note-Books* with mundane newspaper lists and school details, but one can see why Paul Elmer More called it the critic's breviary. It should also be the Arnoldian's breviary. David DeLaura deplores the fact that so few studies have exploited the riches of the *Note-Books*.[7] This present study, I hasten to say, will not, or cannot, make full use of this inexhaustible treasury. Arnold's daughter tells us that he

used often to say, half jokingly, that if anyone would ever take the trouble to collect all the extracts from various writers which he had copied in his notebooks, there would be found a volume of priceless worth.[8]

Altogether aside from joking, they *are* that, in themselves, and doubly so for the light they throw on Arnold's career and his works. They indicate a kind of ground of being, and course of *Bildung*, intimate and yet distanced by the insights of the "poetry-religion" concept. The note-book for 1864 has the statement from Ernest Renan that the aim of art, broadly interpreted, is religious:

Le but essentiel de l'art est d'élever l'homme au-dessus de la vie vulgaire, et de réveiller en lui le sentiment de son origine céleste . . . L'homme qui prend la vie au sérieux et emploie son activité à la poursuite d'une fin généreuse, voilà l'homme religieux.

(*Note-Books* 29)

The essential end of art is to raise man above vulgar life, and awaken in him the feeling of his celestial origin . . . . The man who takes life seriously and uses his activity in the pursuit of a generous end—there is the religious man.

Such, then, is the temper of mind of the author of *Essays in Criticism, First Series*.[9] Having recognized this, one recognizes in the

7. David DeLaura, *Victorian Prose: A Guide* (New York: Modern Language Association, 1973), p. 254.
8. Quoted in *Note-Books* ix. The Viscountess Sandhurst, Arnold's younger daughter, published a small selection in 1902.
9. This study is chronological, and so Super's arrangement is what I follow. I

critical essays the remarkably high proportion of concern with religious matter. The point of the "Dante and Beatrice" piece, for instance, is to insist on Dante's religious essence; his poem is not the Victorian genre of the sentimental novel which the all too Victorian translator makes it out to be. Arnold explains that with Dante, the world becomes metaphor for spirit; Beatrice is one "whom he could divinize into a fit object for the spiritual longing which filled him" (III: 9). Almost all the rest of the volume has some religious aspect.

The essays on the two de Guérins are studies of two essentially religious spirits. Maurice de Guérin is one in whose career religious experience seems significantly interchangeable with the poetic experience. In his youth he had felt the possibility of a vocation and had joined the community of the Abbé Lamennais at La Chênaie—where Lacordaire (of "A French Eton") and other dedicated souls had been drawn, but in the communal discipline he found himself less than free to follow his bent toward "Nature," and he departed for Paris and the literary life and deserted, for a time, the Church. As Arnold explains it, it is poetry that takes the place of religion in his career. He quotes de Guérin, translating,

I owe everything to poetry, for there is no other name to give to the sum total of my thoughts; I owe to it whatever I now have of pure, lofty, and solid in my soul; I owe to it all my consolations in the past; I shall probably owe to it my future.

(III: 30)

"Poetry," Arnold goes on, "is the interpretress of the natural world, and she is the interpretress of the moral world." It was in her first aspect that de Guérin's gift lay: "To make magically near and real the life of Nature, and man's life only so far as it is part of that Nature, was his faculty" (III: 30). In de Guérin as in Keats, "the natural magic is perfect." "Poetry is interpretive," Arnold goes on, "both by having *natural magic* in it, and by having *moral profundity*. In both ways it illuminates man; it gives him a satisfying sense of reality; it reconciles him with himself and the universe" (III: 33).

The peculiar term *natural magic* (which he returns to in the essay on Celtic literature) can, I think, be understood as a literary analogue

---

take up here, then, *Prose*, volume III, which consists of *Essays in Criticism, First Series*, augmented by the short "Dante and Beatrice" and the long "On the Study of Celtic Literature."

to Carlyle's *natural supernaturalism*. Carlyle would say that biblical miracles, besides being against reason, are altogether negligible anyway in the light of what is marvelous and mysterious in ourselves and in the cosmos; our sense of wonder at the *natural* marvelous is our best religion. In a parallel way, Arnold suggests that as we do not have the science to explain how the great literary texts have the power to move us, we can call it, in a figure, *magic*; but it is *natural magic*. De Guérin's *Centaure* had "bewitched" the young Arnold. *Natural magic* even without moral profundity helps "to reconcile [man] with himself and the universe." "He goes into religion and out of religion" (III: 31), with no great convulsive stress, because the element —which I would call poetry-religion—is all one.

The religious overtones of de Guérin's *Centaure* have recently been demonstrated by the distinguished Indian scholar, Nirad C. Chaudhuri. He uses a passage from the *Centaure*, which includes what Arnold quotes, to define "The Quest of Hinduism":[10]

Me dit un jour le grand Chiron—

> Cherchez-vous les dieux, ô Macarée! et d'où sont issus les hommes, les animaux et les principes du feu universel?

> Mais le vieil Océan, père de toutes choses, retient en lui-même ces secrets, et les nymphes qui l'entourent décrivent en chantant un choeur éternel devant lui, pour couvrir ce qui pourrait s'évader de ses lèvres entr'ouvertes par le sommeil.

> Les mortels qui touchèrent les dieux par leur vertu ont reçu de leurs mains des lyres pour charmer les peuples, ou des semences nouvelles pour les enrichir, mais rien de leur bouche inexorable.

. . . .

> Les dieux jaloux ont enfoui quelque part les témoignages de la descendance des choses; mais au bord de quel océan ont-ils roulé la pierre qui les couvre, ô Macarée!

One day the great Chiron said to me:

> Do you search for the gods, O Macarée! and the origin of men, animals and the principles of universal fire?

> But the old Ocean, father of all things, keeps these secrets in himself, and the nymphs who surround him, perform in singing an eternal chorus

before him, to obscure whatever might escape from his lips half-open in sleep.

The mortals who have through their virtue touched the gods have received from their hands lyres to charm the peoples, or new sowings to enrich them, but from their inexorable mouths—nothing.

. . . .

The jealous gods have confounded the evidences of the origin of things; but on the shore of what ocean have they rolled the obscuring stone, O Macarée!

This *vieil Océan*, Chaudhuri notes, is *Ouranos* (Uranus, equivalent to *Varuna*, the god of the waters in the vedic myth. Considering the intimacy of the de Guérin influence on Arnold, I think this sense of ocean contributes to the "wide-glimmering sea" part of the Arnold paradigm as Dwight Culler presents it (the *forest glade*, the *burning plain*, the *sea*) and contributes to the awesome mystery of the "luminous home of waters" in the end of "Sohrab and Rustum."[11] The "Quest of Hinduism," to search out the gods, is another type of the Arnoldian quest.

In the essay on Eugénie de Guérin, Arnold deals with an almost purely religious spirit, *une religieuse*, although not in orders, calling her a "beautiful soul" (III: 83) in allusion to the German idea of the *schöne Seele*, one of those whose inclinations are as by nature in accord with virtue. Her readings include the letters of Saint Theresa, the *Imitation*, Bossuet, Fénelon, and the *Lives of the Saints*, as well as secular things, and the life of reading, thinking, and writing was sufficient to her. She does not have the power of poetry that her brother has, but "she was penetrated by the power of religion" (III: 90). Arnold comments, ever the comparativist, "The religious life is at bottom everywhere alike" (III: 96), but he goes on to compare the "setting and outward circumstance" of Eugénie's Catholicism with those of English Protestantism. Protestantism, he says, has the greater future (he will write more of its projected development), while Catholicism "appears . . . to be fatally losing itself in the multiplication of dogmas, Mariolatry, and miracle-mongering. But the style and circumstance of actual Catholicism is grander than its present tendency, and the style and circumstance of Protestantism is meaner than its tendency" (III:

11. A. Dwight Culler, *Imaginative Reason: The Poetry of Matthew Arnold* (New Haven: Yale University Press, 1966).

97). Here is an early instance of Arnold's devaluation of dogma in favor of style and conduct. One imagines that in these sympathetic studies of the two Roman Catholic de Guérins, Arnold takes some pleasure of the *épater-les-bourgeois* sort, jolting the complacency of the anti-Papists.

The essay on Heinrich Heine is a rather uncomfortable piece of work in some respects: it has some of Arnold's flagrantly unfair condescension to Carlyle, who "mistook," he says, the mainstream of German culture after Goethe, neglecting Heine.[12] And it shows Arnold's discomfort about Heine's morals. But some significant Arnoldian themes are developing in this essay, the theme of freedom, for instance. Heine wishes to be known not as the servant of poetry in a narrow sense but as "a brave soldier in the Liberation War of humanity" (III: 107 ,132). Arnold hails Goethe as the supreme "liberator" of his time, by way of his "profound, imperturbable *naturalism*" —we might call this, I think, non-supernaturalism, or *empiricism*. "He puts the standard, once for all, inside every man instead of outside him." Goethe asks "with Olympian politeness, 'But *is* it so? is it so to *me?*' Nothing could be really more subversive" (III: 110). This experiential principle is central to Arnold's thought and accounts for his greatest critical successes as well as for the honesty of his *misevaluations*. The subversive enfranchisement from dogma owes something to Arnold's developing notion of freedom through the humanities in his education books; in the Heine essay he first refers to the "Prison of Puritanism" (III: 121), the negation of freedom. Heine's love for France consists essentially in this "new religion" of freedom. Arnold quotes:

The French are the chosen people of the new religion, its first gospels and dogmas have been drawn up in their language; Paris is the new Jerusalem, and the Rhine is the Jordan which divides the consecrated land of freedom from the land of the Philistines.[13]

(III: 112)

12. When I discover that Heine supplied Wagner with the story of *The Flying Dutchman*, Nietzsche with the theme of the "death of God," and Marx with the figure of religion as the "opium of the people," I think Arnold may have been *right* about Heine being the main line.

13. Super notes the source in Heine as *Reisebilder*, vol. 4: "Englische Fragmente," chap. 11, "Die Befreiung," last paragraph, and comments: "The 'new religion' is 'die Freiheit, . . . die Religion unserer Zeit' " (III: 436).

The essay does capture some of Heine's quality,[14] and includes like the other *Essays in Criticism* a set of samples. One Arnold takes pleasure in translating (from a French version) is the *Lied* "Berg-Idylle" that happens to be a playful enactment of the *Entwicklung* of the religious consciousness.

While I was yet a little boy . . . I believed in God the Father. . . . When I got bigger I comprehended a great deal more than this, . . . and grew intelligent . . . and I believe on the Son also. . . . Now, when I am grown up, have read much, have travelled much, my heart swells within me, and with my whole heart I believe on the Holy Ghost. . . . A thousand knights, well harnessed, has the Holy Ghost chosen out to fulfill his will . . . . one of those Knights of the Holy Ghost am I.

(III: 124–25)

It would appear, though Arnold does not say so, that the least anthropomorphic member of the Trinity (or the ornithomorphic one) is the more *developed* and might even have some of the character of Arnold's force-not-ourselves.

One of the things Heine did for Arnold was to foster his way of using the Old Testament as a quarry for metaphors, and above all, this essay is a kind of developing ground for the great metaphors of *Culture and Anarchy*. As all the world must know by now, Carlyle had already used the term "Philistine" in Arnold's sense, but it is Heine who seems to suggest the possibility of exploiting it in a grand cultural diagnosis as a term for the enemies of *Bildung*. And the Hebrew-Hellene theory takes shape here: Heine

himself had in him both the spirit of Greece and the spirit of Judaea; both these spirits reach the infinite, which is the true goal of all poetry and all art, —the Greek spirit by beauty, the Hebrew spirit by sublimity.

(III: 127–28)

Arnold is interested in Heine's Jewishness, which is a rather new element in the English consciousness. He notes the particularly Jewish humor in the story of Moses Lump and is moved by Jehuda ben Halevy's romantic devotion to his lady, "a woe-begone poor darling,

14. It connects with Arnold's poem on "Heine's Grave" (507), which is to my mind one of Arnold's worst poems, perhaps because of his doubts about Heine's morality.

a mourning picture of desolation . . . and her name was Jerusalem"
(III: 129).

The beautiful essay on Marcus Aurelius brings Arnold into the
main line of his religious thinking, associated here as typically with
analysis of language: the occasion is a new translation of the *Meditations* (not particularly distinguished, Arnold says). Here emerges his
principle of the two languages, that of morality and that of religion.
He first defines *morality* in the terms he is to maintain in his later
writings.

The object of systems of morality is to take possession of human life, to save
it from being abandoned to passion or allowed to drift at hazard, to give it
happiness by establishing it in the practice of virtue; . . . by prescribing . . .
fixed principles of action, fixed rules of conduct. . . . Human life has thus always a clue to follow, and may always be making way towards its goal.

(III: 133)

The characteristically Arnoldian points are, first, "happiness," not as
a reward in the afterlife but here and now in the practice of virtue;
the organizing or anti-random power of virtue; and the progressive-
ness of "always be making way"—this is the becoming, the *Bildung*.

Literal statements of these principles or rules, Arnold says, exist in
the work of the "great masters of morals"—Epictetus or Marcus Aurelius—and likewise in the Christian *Jmitation*, and he quotes from these
several maxims including ones he inscribed for himself in his *Note-
Book*, such as from the *Jmitation*, "*Semper aliquid certi proponendum
est*," which he translates here as "Always place a definite purpose before thee" (III: 133–34). But moral rules are, and must be, for the
sage only. "The mass of mankind have neither force of intellect
enough to apprehend them clearly as ideas, nor force of character
enough to follow them strictly as laws." Humankind needs a mode
other than the abstract, one which is easier for the intellect and at the
same time powerful enough to affect behavior. There must be, says
Arnold, "a joyful and bounding emotion." "The noblest souls of whatever creed, the pagan Empedocles as well as the Christian Paul" (III:
134) have insisted on this. And it is religion that supplies this emotion:
"The paramount virtue of religion is, that it has *lighted up* morality"
(III: 134), and then he uses the contrasting pairs of statements that
will be essential to the demonstration in *Literature and Dogma*. The
first element of the pair is the maxim, the second is the more figurative

statement: Epictetus, "Lead me, Zeus and Destiny! whithersoever I am appointed to go; I will follow without wavering," is here contrasted with the Old Testament, "Let thy loving spirit lead me forth into the land of righteousness" (Psalm 143: 10, Book of Common Prayer), or with the New Testament, "Except a man be born again, he cannot see the Kingdom of God" (III: 135). It is perfectly clear that the potent statements are the metaphorical ones: easier to understand, stronger to affect.

He tells us—and Arnold is generally kindly informative in his essays—of Marcus Aurelius' life and times, explaining for the broadening of the more parochial Christians among his readers how it came about that so excellent a man was a persecutor of the Christians and the sad circumstance of his having a son so evil as Commodus. And then he gives us some of the *Meditations,* first some prudential ones, worthy, as Arnold says, of Benjamin Franklin. "But it is when he enters the region where Franklin cannot follow him . . . that he becomes the unique, the incomparable Marcus Aurelius" (III: 148). Christianity tends to lean on the reward as a motive for virtue, but Marcus Aurelius has a better idea: when a man does a virtuous act he is *conforming to his nature;* "he is like a vine which has produced grapes, and seeks for nothing more after it has once produced its proper fruit. . . . What more dost thou want when thou hast done a man a service? Art thou not content that thou hast done something conformable to thy nature, and dost thou seek to be paid for it, just as if the eye demanded a recompense for seeing, or the feet for walking?" (III: 148). The particular passage from Marcus Aurelius is remarkable I think for its consonance with Herderian *Humanität.* Man is separate from that indifferent and bloody "Nature" of the Darwinian vision: he alone of all creation has the power to perform the virtuous act, and he fulfills his being, his *Humanität,* when he does so.

Arnold claims that Marcus Aurelius in this mode achieves something close to the religious emotion: "The emotion of Marcus Aurelius does not quite light up his morality, but it suffuses it" (III: 149). He has "a delicate and tender sentiment, which is less than joy, and more than resignation." It enables him to observe nature with "a sympathetic tenderness, worthy of Wordsworth," and there follows the lovely passage on figs and their ways and "the ears of corn bending down, and the lion's eyebrows" (III: 149), which *we* might call worthy of Hopkins. He speaks for Arnold especially when he counsels man to "retire into thyself. For nowhere either with more quiet or more freedom from trouble does a man retire than into his own soul" (III: 151).

"What an affinity for Christianity had this persecutor of the Christians!" (II: 156), Arnold exclaims in his conclusion, and he has led up to this by frequent analogies to Christian thought in his citations. There is a strain of melancholy in this man, who "remains the especial friend and comforter of all clear-headed and scrupulous, yet pure-hearted and upward striving men . . . because he too yearns as they do for something unattained by him" (III: 156). Arnold ends with the very *locus classicus* of *yearning*, from Marcus Aurelius' countryman, Virgil—*tendentemque manus ripae ulterioris amore*— who has something like this melancholy, over the "doubtful doom of humankind." It is here that one realizes how much Pater drew on Arnold for *Marius the Epicurean*.[15] For Arnold calls Marcus Aurelius' time a "modern" period, in the Viconian-Thomas Arnoldian sense, a period analogous to his own time, that is. So it is that Pater can allegorize the stages of his own Victorian life in a tale of Marcus Aurelius' contemporary.

With the Joseph Joubert essay, Arnold comes to grips with a theory of religion itself. The essay shows connections with his research into French education—Joubert went to school at Toulouse, where Arnold had inspected, and was the associate of Louis de Fontanes, the Grand Master of the University under the Empire. We are told of Joubert's life, how he is like our Coleridge,

both of them desultory and incomplete writers . . . , both of them ardent students and critics of old literature, poetry, and the metaphysics of religion; both of them curious explorers of words, and of the latent significance hidden under the popular use of them; both of them, in a certain sense, conservative in religion and politics, by antipathy to the narrow and shallow foolishness of vulgar modern literalism.

(III: 189)

What will last of Coleridge is "the stimulus of his continual effort,— not a moral effort, for he had no morals,—but of his continual instructive effort . . . to get at and lay bare the real truth of the matter in

15. See Kenneth Allott, "Pater and Arnold," *Essays in Criticism* 2 (April 1952): 219–21, referred to by Super, *Prose* III: 441. See also David DeLaura, *Hebrew and Hellene* (Austin: University of Texas Press, 1969), p. 267.

hand" (III: 189). But—those hard words on Coleridge say it—Joubert's effort was a moral effort, associated with a devoted care for style: "He thought the truth was never really and worthily said, so long as the least cloud, clumsiness, and repulsiveness hung about the expression of it" (III: 194). Throughout this essay, Arnold's translations from the French have particular distinction, as a contemporary in the *Spectator* observed, saying they are "not merely equal, but in some respects superior . . . , [perhaps now and then] a little too good" (III: 452). When he translates Joubert, then, Arnold gives more of himself than might first appear.

Joubert is thoroughly sympathetic to Arnold for his acuity, his wit, and his rejection of religious theory in favor of experience.

May I say it? It is not hard to know God, provided one will not force oneself to define him.

Do not bring into the domain of reasoning that which belongs to our innermost feeling. State truths of sentiment, and do not try to prove them. . . .

"Fear God," has made many men pious; the proofs of the existence of God have made many men atheists. . . . The only happy people in the world are the good man, the sage, and the saint; but the saint is happier than either of the others, so much is man by his nature formed for sanctity.

(III: 197–98)

How stunningly this accords with Herderian ideas of *Humanität*: it is quite true anyway that animals can hardly be good; how much less can they be *sages*, and still less *saints*! It just may be the best way to think about mankind, that man alone is uniquely capable of both moral and intellectual development and best realizes himself in pursuing it.

Arnold turns from Joubert on the "inward essence of religion" to its "outward form," anticipating the idea of *conduct* as the main issue. "Religion," says Joubert, "is neither a theology nor a theosophy; it is more than all this; it is a discipline, a law, a yoke, an indissoluble engagement" (III: 199). When he takes up Joubert on the Jansenists, that severe sect so like the Calvinists, he finds the argument he is to develop on the erroneous Puritan interpretation of Paul, the interpretation of a figurative term as though it was literal. Here is Joubert:

Instead of "grace," say help, succour, a divine influence, a dew of heaven; then one can come to right understanding. The word "grace" is a sort of talisman, all the baneful spell of which can be broken by translating it. *The trick of personifying words is a fatal source of mischief in theology.* [My emphasis]

(III: 200–201)

We must know our metaphors for what they are, metaphors; must know our fictions for fictions, or they cease to be useful and make mischief. Joubert describes the Jansenists as constricted by doctrine, while the Jesuits, whose doctrine is far from unassailable, are "the better directors of souls." The Jesuits take account, practically, of how human nature works. "In their books of devotion you find joy, because with the Jesuits nature and religion go hand in hand" (III: 201).

When he takes up Joubert on literary matters, he himself brings the Bible into the field of literary discourse: Priam to Achilles, "And I have endured," is compared with Joseph, "I am Joseph your brother, whom ye sold into Egypt," both being great moments where one recognizes the author as "a born man of genius" (III: 191). Arnold's way of referring to the human "author" of a biblical text is calculated; it is part of a program of chipping away at the doctrine of Plenary Inspiration. And he says the Bible is admirable "because of the miscellaneous character of the contents" (III: 203); this impugns the Puritan doctrine of the one author.

Joubert on politics anticipates Arnold on the vanity of liberal "machinery":

Let your cry be for free souls rather even than for free men. Moral liberty is the one vitally important liberty, the one liberty which is indispensable; the other liberty is good and salutary only so far as it favours this. . . . Liberty! liberty! . . . in all things let us have *justice*, and then we shall have enough liberty!

(III: 207)

In short, Joubert brings the moral test both to literature and to politics, and his distinction, says Arnold, is "in the union of *soul* with intellect."

He is the most prepossessing and convincing of witnesses to the good of loving light. Because he sincerely loved light, and did not prefer to it any little private darkness of his own, he found light. . . . He loved and sought light till he became so habituated to it, so accustomed to the joyful testimony of a good

conscience, that, to use his own words, "he could no longer exist without this, and was obliged to live without reproach if he would live without misery."
(III: 208–9)

This "literary" essay is taking on the character of a saint's Life.

Great writers, and lesser ones, Arnold concludes in this essay, all have the same work: *a criticism of life*. The great are available to all generations, their "criticism of life is a source of illumination and joy to the whole human race forever. . . . These are the sacred personages" (III: 209). The second class are the "forerunners" of the new generation, oracles for a later time. These recognize the sacred personages that they may be handed on in safety and are themselves valued in the generation after them. Joubert "lived in the Philistine's day, . . . [yet] kept aloof from the reigning superstitions, never bowed the knee to the gods of Canaan" (III: 211).

The important series of essays on Spinoza begins in controversy, the occasion being Bishop John Colenso's *The Pentateuch and the Book of Joshua Critically Examined* (first volume, 1862) ; *Essays and Reviews* had appeared in 1860, and the brouhaha over problems of biblical criticism involved an astonishingly broad range of the English public. It must be emphasized that most of Arnold's prose is highly *engaged*, and the occasions of his writings are part of their meaning.[16] As an epigraph for *Essays in Criticism, First Series*, Arnold takes a passage from Burke:

Our antagonist is our helper. This amicable conflict with difficulty obliges us to an intimate acquaintance with our object, and compels us to consider it in all its relations. It will not suffer us to be superficial.
(III: 2)

In this case Bishop Colenso was a *help* in launching Arnold's writings on Spinoza. Colenso, once a teacher of arithmetic, had worked out certain sums implied in Old Testament history, and when they didn't make literal sense, he felt he had invalidated the whole of Christian theology. The seven writers of *Essays and Reviews*, although more

---

16. Scholarship owes a debt to two excellent books on these "occasions": William E. Buckler's *Matthew Arnold's Books: Toward a Publishing Diary* (Geneva: E. Droz, 1958), and Sidney Coulling's *Matthew Arnold and His Critics: A Study of Arnold's Controversies* (Athens: Ohio University Press, 1974).

sophisticated than Colenso, had perpetrated some similar naïvetés. Arnold holds that Spinoza can be the best corrective to these misleading naïvetés. Spinoza was in the air in these exegetically troubled times, generally ill-understood, sometimes considered an atheist. Arnold is instigated to make plain his real drift, making him freshly available to Arnold's own time—and to ours.[17] In the process, Arnold's own thought becomes more finely articulated.

Spinoza, whose *Tractatus Theologico-Politicus* was published in Holland in 1670, figures recurrently as an influence in the history of the higher biblical criticism from that date, sometimes, as with Pierre Bayle (*Dictionnaire historique et critique*, 1702), reviled at the same time as used. The Germans had rehabilitated him: it was Novalis who called him lovingly the *gottbetrunkener Mensch*; Lessing, Herder, Goethe, and Schleiermacher were all in various respects neo-Spinozists, and in France he was accepted by Cousin, Quinet, Lamartine, Michelet, George Sand, Renan, and the Saint-Simonians—through all of whom his doctrine came to Arnold. To Coleridge, Spinoza was of course very well known—and problematical. Arnold knew Spinoza directly from early years, at least from 1850 on. Super quotes Arnold writing in a letter late in life:

It makes me rather angry to be affiliated to German biblical critics; I have had to read masses of them, and they would have drowned me if it had not been for the corks I had brought from the study of Spinoza. To him I owe more than I can say.[18]

In "The Bishop and the Philosopher" (1863) Arnold ironically presents his own point of view as that of "a humble citizen of the Republic of Letters." For "religious books come within the jurisdiction of literary criticism so far as they affect general culture" (III: 41). If

17. Super's introductions and notes to the Spinoza essays constitute an authoritative commentary. He considers that Arnold's précis of Spinoza's thought is a "masterful synthesis" (III: 447). In chapter 3 of his *The Time-Spirit of Matthew Arnold* (Ann Arbor: University of Michigan Press, 1970), the discussion of the Spinoza essays is particularly illuminating (pp. 64–70, 74–76). William Robbins gives a fuller and most helpful discussion of Spinoza in *The Ethical Idealism of Matthew Arnold* (London: Heineman, 1959), see especially pp. 63–69 and 99–102. The question of Spinoza and Coleridge is treated exhaustively by Thomas McFarland in *Coleridge and the Pantheist Tradition* (Oxford: Clarendon Press, 1969). McFarland, however, is not familiar with Arnold.

18. Quoted in Super, *Time-Spirit of Matthew Arnold*, p. 65.

a religious book claims to intellectual argument, it is the literary critic's concern, and if it is edifying and at the same time shows the mark of a "gifted nature" (III: 42)—like the *Imitation*, or Bunyan's *Pilgrim's Progress*, or Keble's *The Christian Year*—then again it is the concern of the literary critic. But Colenso's book is neither sound intellectually nor edifying, and so it serves neither the "instructed few" nor the "scantily instructed many" (III: 44) and in fact shakes the religious convictions of many. Arnold supports this elitism-in-religion concept with dicta from Ecclesiasticus, Jesus, Pindar, Plato, Spinoza, and Newman—just about everybody who should know. The instructed few of England and Europe have been perfectly aware of the Old Testament discrepancies Colenso has just discovered. As for Spinoza's *Tractatus*, previously it would not have unsettled the multitude, for it was written in Latin, but now speculation is open. Spinoza is not more unorthodox than Colenso, and he is far more edifying.

The next Spinoza essay is a rather short review of the *Tractatus Theologico-Politicus* as translated into English by Robert Willis, *A Critical Inquiry into the History, Purpose, and Authenticity of the Hebrew Scriptures* (1862). Arnold recounts Spinoza's life: his rabbinical training, his dissatisfaction, his espousal of Cartesian philosophy, his excommunication by the Portuguese synagogue at Amsterdam, and his exemplary life. His work has not heretofore been translated into English, because there has hung over him

the cloud of heterodoxy, bold, boundless, uncompromising; so bold, so boundless, and so uncompromising that his enemies have not hesitated to give to it the terrible name of Atheism. . . . Whatever Spinoza was, he was not an Atheist: "the more we know God, the more do we become masters of ourselves, and find in this knowledge our rest and our salvation." This is his doctrine from the first line of his works to the last.

(III: 57)

It is well to have the *Tractatus* translated now—but—and the rest of the essay is a demonstration of the miserable failure of this translation, which simply gives a false idea of Spinoza.

Arnold made his review of A. P. Stanley's *Lectures on the History of the Jewish Church* the occasion to return to Spinoza.[19] Stanley was,

19. Volume 1 (1862) covers from Abraham to the death of Samuel, volume 2 (1865) from Saul to the fall of Jerusalem.

of course, an old Rugbeian and a friend of the Arnold family; as an historian he follows his revered teacher's method, using the new German historicism. In the years 1843–55 Heinrich Ewald had published the *Geschichte des Volkes Israel*, following Schleiermacher's line of combining free scholarly investigation with reverence. What Niebuhr was to Thomas Arnold's Roman history, Ewald was to Stanley's Jewish history.[20] "Here is a clergyman, who, looking at the Bible, sees its contents in their right proportion. . . . Here is an inquirer, who, treating Scripture history with a perfectly free spirit, . . . treats it so that his freedom leaves the sacred power of that history inviolate" (III: 65). Here, that is, is a book which, unlike Colenso's or *Essays and Reviews*, both edifies and informs. F. D. Maurice had attacked Arnold's elitism, and Arnold redefines. There are "a few" who seek the ideal life—"the *summum bonum* for a born thinker . . . like Parmenides, or Spinoza, or Hegel—is an eternal series of intellectual acts."[21] Criticism justifies this freedom of intellect for the few. Religious life, however, is the life of the many, and it is not a matter of intellectual acts, but *feeling*.

The religious life of Christendom has thus attached itself to the acts, and words, and death of Christ, as recorded in the Gospels and expounded in the Epistles of the New Testament; and to the main histories, the prophecies and the hymns of the Old Testament. In relation to these objects, it has adopted certain intellectual ideas: such are, ideas respecting the being of God, the laws of nature, the freedom of human will, the character of prophecy, the character of inspiration. But its essence . . . consists in the ardour, the love, the self-renouncement, the ineffable aspiration . . . , not in the intellectual ideas.

(III: 67)

Whenever the ideas are given prominence, the religious life is violated, and there is confusion and falsehood.

Now Arnold recognizes the challenge of his time: "It is one of the hardest tasks in the world to make new intellectual ideas harmonize truly with the religious life." The men who do this are the great religious reformers. "No such religious reformer for the present age has

20. See Rowland E. Prothero and G. G. Bradley, *The Life and Correspondence of Arthur Penrhyn Stanley* (London: John Murray, 1893), 2: 110.
21. III: 65–66. Arnold seems not to have been very familiar with Hegel. See DeLaura, *Hebrew and Hellene*, pp. 190–91, 191n. But in this "series of intellectual acts" he seems to me to catch a principle of the Hegelian dialectic.

yet shown himself" (III: 69). Meanwhile, the good teachers will put that first which is first; Stanley, for instance, might have embroiled himself in controversy but finds a better way. He does not go into the difficulty of how the Israelites literally got out of Egypt but points out how they are "the only nation in ancient or modern times, which, throwing off the yoke of slavery, claims no merit, no victory of its own. . . . All is from above, nothing from themselves" (III: 70).

Ideas, Arnold says, "are liable to development [*Entwicklung*]" (III: 77); they are in the domain of the *Zeitgeist*, the Time-Spirit. The letter belongs to the *Zeitgeist*, the spirit transcends it.

So divine, so indestructible is the power of Christianity—so immense the power of transformation afforded to it by its sublime maxim, "The letter killeth, but the spirit giveth life," that it will assuredly ever be able to adapt itself to new conditions, and, in connexion with intellectual ideas changed or developed, to enter upon successive stages of progress.

(III: 78)

At this point I think we encounter the solid Herderian base of Arnold's vision of Christianity developing, transforming itself into "higher" modes, through which the essence prevails.

Protestantism has formed the notion [of literal inspiration]. The critical ideas of our century are forcing Protestantism away from this proposition, untrue like the proposition that the Pope is infallible . . . [Arnold's strategy is to align the literalists' principle with the Roman superstition which they often hated more than sin!] but the religious reformer is not he who rivets our minds upon the untruth of this proposition . . . ; he is the man who makes us feel the future which undoubtedly exists for the religious life in the absence of it.

(III. 79)

Some day the religious life will have harmonized all the new thought with itself, will be able to use it freely: but it cannot use it yet. And who has not rejoiced to be able, between the old idea, tenable no longer, which once connected itself with certain religious words, and the new idea, which has not yet connected itself with them, to rest for awhile in the healing virtue and beauty of the words themselves?

(III: 81)

So our position "between two worlds" can have a kind of joy, after all. The theory of Providence we think erroneous, but the words of Isaiah are nevertheless "adequate":

In all their affliction he was afflicted, and the angel of his presence saved them;
and he bare them and carried them all the days of old.

(Isaiah 63 : 9; III: 81)

This is a curious and challenging fact. Arnold was unquestionably a
rationalist, but this poetry does seem to work; it seems a kind of
pragmatic poetry. The Bible transcriptions in the *Note-Books* demonstrate that he felt its power. Similarly with the Liturgy. He asks:

What intellectual definition of the death of Christ has yet succeeded in plac-
ing it, for the religious life, in so true an aspect as . . . "O Lamb of God, that
takest away the sins of the world, have mercy on us!"

(III: 82)

And this review of Stanley ends with a marvelous rhetorical flourish,
exclaiming over how it has taken a mere literary critic to proclaim
these truths that the clergy, "the masters in Israel," should know (III:
82).

It is in "Spinoza and the Bible" that Arnold sets forth his fully developed and eloquent statement on the significance of the *Tractatus
Theologico-Politicus*. He starts dramatically by quoting the horrify-
ing anathema with which the Portuguese synagogue expelled Spinoza:
"With these amenities" they took their leave—"they remained children of Israel, and he became a child of modern Europe" (III: 158).
Spinoza has observed the practice of Christian nations to fall something short of the religion of the Bible, and he ascribes this to a misreading. He, Spinoza, will show what it really does say, will show gov-
ernments that they should remodel the national churches to conform
with the true spirit of the Bible.[22]

To understand Scripture we should know the life and character of
the writer and his circumstances and place in history—this we cannot
know completely, and yet we can apprehend the main sense. All
knowledge is divine Revelation, but prophecy is a special case. The
prophets are not like Christ in immediate communion with the mind
of God, neither are they men of philosophical intellect: they excel in
representing and imagining, by means of *figures*. Moses imagined

22. The paragraph that follows is a condensation for convenience of Arnold's
pages 161–69; it would be really much better for the reader to turn to those pages
for their wonderfully succinct plainness and accuracy. It is a polished résumé of a
text that Arnold knew intimately, as Super says, a "masterful synthesis."

God could be seen and could be capable of anger and jealousy; Micaiah imagines him on a throne surrounded by hosts of heaven; Daniel sees him as a white-haired old man in a white garment, Ezekiel as a fire, the disciples as a dove, the apostles in the form of fiery tongues. The validity of their vision cannot be proved by intellectual process but is guaranteed by a "sign"—chiefly a good conscience and a good life. The sum of prophetic revelation is: believe in God, and lead a good life. Abraham and Moses were not metaphysicians, and Joshua was not a natural scientist; in their speculative opinions they are varied and speak as mere men; Revelation has nothing to do with these opinions. To know and love God is the highest blessedness of man and of all men alike. The "election" of the Jews was a temporal thing; when the Jewish state fell the election was over, and Christ proclaims the universal law. With insight, one knows eternal truth and has liberty and self-knowledge, but for the ignorant multitude one makes *commands*: love God and thy neighbor. The apostles like all prophets took their essentials from Revelation; where the Old Testament prophets had made their announcement in a dogmatic form, the apostles used a reasoning and argumentative form, each as he could best commend the message to his hearers—they claimed no divine authority for their reasonings. The assertive style of the Old Testament, and the Hellenized rationalizing style of the New, both the rabbinical and Christian theologizing, all these are of the *Zeitgeist* and of secondary importance. In each of these cases, essential religion is built on a nonessential foundation. Human churches seize on these nonessentials as the essentials. Hence unprofitable disputes and endless schism, "religion turned into a science, or rather a wrangling." Essential religion according to both Old Testament and New Testament is simple: to love God and our neighbor. These precepts are also the precepts of the universal divine law written in our hearts, and it is only by this that Scripture is established as the Word of God. This law was in the world, as St. John says, before the doctrine of Moses or the doctrine of Christ. To the multitude, religion seems imposing only when it is subversive of reason, confirmed by miracles, conveyed in documents materially sacred and infallible, and dooming to damnation all outside its pale. But reason tells us miracles are impossible, and to think them possible is to dishonor God. As Jeremiah declares, Nature follows order; the laws of Nature are the laws of God. Scripture, like Nature herself, does not lay down speculative propositions but presents matters in a human mode. To know Scripture we must study the tropes and the phrases of the Hebrew language, along with the historical circumstances and the preconceived opinions of the writers. This method is fatal to the notion of verbal inspiration—which vulgar notion is, indeed, a palpable error. One need only instance what we know of the human councils whose thoroughly human judgment determined the Canon of both Old and New Testaments.

This then (reduced even more than Arnold reduces it) is the work that is of great importance for "the general culture of Europe." What then? "If the old theory of Scripture inspiration is to be abandoned, what place is the Bible henceforth to hold among books? What is the new Christianity to be like?" (III: 170). These are the questions that lead to *Literature and Dogma.*

Spinoza's ideal is the intellectual life, not the religious life, and yet, by

crowning the intellectual life with a sacred transport, by thus retaining in philosophy, amid the discontented murmurs of all the army of atheism, the name of God, Spinoza maintains a profound affinity with that which is truest in religion. . . . His whole soul was filled with the desire of the love and knowledge of God, and of that only.

(III: 178–79)

Arnold describes how Spinoza turns on the "worshippers of the letter" with the famous apostrophe:

"What! our knowledge of God to depend upon these perishable things . . . ! It is you who are impious, to believe that God would commit the treasure of the true record of himself to any substance less enduring than the heart!"

(III: 180)

The development of Arnold's own thinking comes out of an effort to resolve these Spinozist terms—the Spinozist understanding of God yields Arnold's subsequent God-definitions, and the Spinozist insistence on "the heart" leads Arnold to define the essence of inwardness, of one's experience of one's self.

He concludes the essay with a meditation on Spinoza's exemplary life. He is one of the great figures in philosophy—in a line with Plato, with Hegel. His ideas stimulate the thought and imagination of his times and after times. "So Hegel seized a single pregnant sentence of Heracleitus, and cast it, with a thousand striking applications, into the world of modern thought" (III: 181). Although Arnold may not have studied Hegel deeply, he seems to me here to seize, in his turn, on a single pregnant concept of Hegel's, his use of Heraclitean flux as the constitution of things, connecting with the Herderian *Entwicklung* to yield the dynamic process of dialectic. For a comparison of Spinoza with Hegel, Arnold turns to Heine:

"I have seen Hegel," he cries, "seated with his doleful air of a hatching hen upon his unhappy eggs. . . .—How easily one can cheat oneself into thinking that one understands everything, when one has learnt only how to construct dialectical formulas!" But of Spinoza, Heine said, "His life was a copy of the life of his divine kinsman, Jesus Christ."

(III: 182)

Here is the Arnoldian scale of values: the limits of intellection, and the supremacy of "behavior"—of the "Imitation."

The essay "Pagan and Mediaeval Religious Sentiment" could be taken as a study in comparative hymnology, if it were not that the term suggests such dreary music and the hymns Arnold takes up are—heavenly. But that is part of his argument. He starts out with a little explanation of Roman Catholicism—it is not just a superstition for the poor Irish, as English Protestants tend to think. Look at the shelves of the British Museum reading room, he invites us, and the largest block of works is the "Catholic Leviathan," a monument, embracing all phases of life for a long period. In history it is "eminently *the Church*" (III: 213), he says, making the same point that Gary Wills makes recently when he says the Catholic Church is the only *The* Church. Having given this jolt, in some elegantly witty paragraphs, to Protestant parochialism, he invites us to consider some poems of paganism and of Christianity, without, if we can manage it, sectarian interestedness. And he presents to us the lovely hymn to Adonis as it is imbedded in Theocritus' fifteenth idyll, the whole in his own grace-ful translation. The hymn is adapted "to the tone and temper of a gay and pleasure-loving multitude." It has, it is true, a symbolism "capable of noble and touching application": Adonis is a sun god, and becomes "an emblem of the power of life and the bloom of beauty" (III: 222) in its inevitable decay and yet recurrent renovation. But this symbolism is unconscious in the popular religious use of the hymn. Arnold implies here, I think, that a religious text in its use may be taken literally even when at the same time the true symbolic import is functioning. Then he gives us the thirteenth-century St. Francis's *Canticle of the Sun*, again beautifully translated:

Praised be my Lord God with all his creatures; and specially our brother the sun . . . our sister the moon . . . our brother the wind, our sister water . . .

and finally

Praised be my Lord for our sister, the death of the body.
(III: 224–25)

This is in a tradition of spiritual poetry that leads up to Dante, Arnold says. The *Canticle*'s meaning, or the functions of its bold images, Arnold does not go into; we might observe that they serve to answer the prayer of the Psalm: "I am a stranger here on earth: O hide not thy commandments from me" (119: 19, Book of Common Prayer). St. Francis's sibling-images make us the less strange to our earthly mortal condition. Arnold delights in both the Adonis-hymn and the *Canticle*, but his point here is the contrast: "The poetry of Theocritus' hymn is poetry treating the world according to the demand of the senses; the poetry of St. Francis' hymn is poetry treating the world according to the demand of the heart and imagination" (III: 225). Both modes may be taken to injurious extreme: the poetry of the senses may overdo sensualism, and St. Francis receiving the stigmata is rather too much for the Protestant Arnold—that *underdoes* the sensual, perhaps.

Heine is still running in his mind and is taken here to be in the line of the sensual mode. Arnold, anthropologizing like Herder, will not blame or reject either mode, but in characterizing each he sees in Heine's own career the defect of the sensual, when Heine is stricken with his wasting mortal disease (understood to be venereal) and the religion of pleasure no longer suffices. Heine writes:

The great author of the universe, the Aristophanes of Heaven, has determined to make the petty earthly author, the so-called Aristophanes of Germany, feel to his heart's core what pitiful needle-pricks his cleverest sarcasms have been, compared with the ‘thunderbolts which his divine humour can launch against feeble mortals!
(III: 228)

But this religion of the senses is a failure. "One man in many millions, a Heine, may console himself . . . by a colossal irony of this sort, by covering himself and the universe with the red fire of this sinister mockery; but the many millions cannot" (III: 229). Christianity, though, succeeds in effecting joy for the many, even actual joy in the things of this world, the joy St. Francis takes in the simple elements of earth.

But in the last section of the essay Arnold says he has neglected one period of paganism, the great age, which was a "modern" age in the Viconian sense, when Greece produced a poetry of the highest beauty and value. No other poetry than the Greek, he says, has so well satisfied both intellect and the religious sense, and he quotes the great ending of *Oepidus Rex*:

Oh! that my lot may lead me in the path of Holy innocence of word and deed, the path which august laws ordain. . . . The power of God is mighty in them, and groweth not old.

And Arnold adds:

Let St. Francis,—nay, or Luther either,—beat that!
(III: 231)

The gauntlet is thrown down to both brands of Christianity, to the medieval saint and the Reformation hero, both great literary men as well as holy men. And the *preux chevalier* Matthew Arnold undertakes to champion the cause of poetry without regard to sect. The cause of poetry seems to be the cause of a religion that transcends sects.

The next essay, "The Literary Influence of Academies," is the most remote from religious interests, and yet Arnold would not have thought it unconnected, for the issue is a matter of style, which applies in institutions both secular and religious, and in writers both secular and religious. He acclaims here Newman's *urbanity* as a rare thing in English writers; I think in fact Newman valued urbane grace very highly yet would have counted it as but dross compared to the soul's health. For Arnold, it is an important part of the soul's health. Moreover, Arnold's idea of an Academy might be thought of as the literary tradition institutionalized, a sort of secular established church, of Culture, manned by the "Clerisy" in one of its aspects.

With "The Function of Criticism at the Present Time" we are back in the mainstream of Arnold's poetry-religion line of thought. We have already seen in the peroration of the essay on Stanley, underneath the gorgeous biblical rhetoric, the plain statement that you the clergy have to have a literary critic explain to you the function of figurative speech (III: 82). This essay on criticism has been much studied because literary criticism has been a major interest of the universities; to look at it from the interest of religious issues yields a little different light. Its key ideas are well known: the principle of "disinterestedness," "the free play of mind," "the endeavour to learn the best that is known and thought in the world" and to "propagate it," to "establish a current of fresh and true ideas," and the virtues recommended—all indeed are virtues one might plead for now, and F. W. Bateson did,[23] for one. But as Super remarks in surveying the scholarship, "the apparently divided current of the essay has led such very opposed schools as the 'art for art's sake' critics and the social reformers to claim it as an ancestor" (III: 473). Disinterestedness, that is, leads into the art-for-art's-sake school, while the propagation idea is very much socially engaged and moral. Furthermore his theory of "epochs of concentration and expansion" is, after all, doubtful, and of course "seeing the object as in itself it really is" and complete "disinterestedness" seem to us today vain impossibilities, here rather arrogantly laid down. As critical theory, the essay is strained.

But of course his castigation of jingoistic liberalism and party interests both in politics and religion is simply grand. He restates the issue he had seen in the Colenso case: the public will mix up science and religion, "but happily that is of no real importance, for while the multitude imagines itself to live by its false science, it does really live by its true religion" (III: 277). Colenso is a grave cultural symptom, however. "It is really the strongest possible proof of the low ebb at which, in England, the critical spirit is, that while the critical hit in the religious literature of Germany is Dr. Strauss's book, in that of France M. Renan's book, the book of Bishop Colenso is the critical hit in the religious literature of England" (III: 278). Strauss and Renan in their two biographies of Jesus made attempts at careful historical scholarship. Whether they are successful or not, the work is a legitimate one for criticism. It is better to reexamine Christianity than

23. F. W. Bateson, "The Function of Criticism at the Present Time," Essays in Criticism 3 (January 1953): 1–27.

to dismiss it. The non-Christian "religion of the future" of Francis Power Cobbe may be revealed by criticism as neither noble nor beautiful. The historic religions, with all their faults, were at least noble and beautiful. Protestantism must not claim intellectual superiority over Roman Catholicism: "The Reformation was a moral rather than an intellectual event" (III: 281).

Religious concepts keep emerging as part of culture: the view of an ideal "European" culture is something like medieval "Christendom." The attitude owes much to Newman, as DeLaura has shown;[24] Arnold is concerned, like Newman in the *Idea of a University*, to "raise the tone" of society, but while Newman offers his idea as a purely secular one, Arnold connects secular culture with religion. The attitude owes something to Renan also, who was like Arnold both a literary critic and scholar of religions and who asserted that "the extinction of the critical spirit marks the end of all serious morality,"[25] and everywhere Arnold might be writing under Renan's banner, *Essais de morale et de critique*. If religion has a proprietary interest in morality, and Arnold says it has, then criticism has a religious function.

"The Function of Criticism" was written last but placed first in *Essays in Criticism, First Series*; there is something in it of an overview from an advanced position back on the series: the de Guérin essays, the Spinoza essays, those on Heine, Marcus Aurelius, Joubert, pagan and medieval religious sentiment, academies—a strikingly high proportion of these is indeed taken up with religion—and hence it is that Bush can call it Arnold's "first religious book."[26] Every one of the personages is a kind of saint except Heine—and Arnold is positively troubled about Heine's lack of sanctity. One might even say that Arnold is not quite *disinterested*. The whole book has a strong bias toward morality and its relation to religion. Later yet Arnold wrote the "Preface" (1865) to *Essays in Criticism* that was placed in front of all. And it is a marvelously playful answer to some objections, a defense of vivacity, "the last sparkle of flame before we all go into the dark . . . , the drab of the earnest, prosaic, practical, austerely literal future" (III: 287), the Benthamite future, an avowal that although he is Professor of Poetry at Oxford, he alone and not Oxford is responsi-

24. DeLaura, *Hebrew and Hellene*, pp. 43–45.
25. Super cites this from Renan as relevant here (III: 473).
26. Douglas Bush, *Matthew Arnold* (New York: Macmillan, 1971), p. 93.

ble for his opinions, he alone, "a plain citizen in the republic of letters." But it ends with the prose-poem apostrophe to Oxford:

We are all seekers still! . . . Beautiful city! so venerable, so lovely, so un-ravaged by the fierce intellectual life of our century, so serene! . . . And yet, steeped in sentiment as she lies, spreading her gardens to the moonlight, and whispering from her towers the last enchantments of the Middle Ages, who will deny that Oxford, by her ineffable charm, keeps ever calling us nearer to the true goal of all of us, to the ideal, to perfection,—to beauty, in a word, which is only truth seen from another side—nearer, perhaps than all the science of Tübingen. Adorable dreamer whose heart has been so romantic! who hast given thyself so prodigally, given thyself to sides and to heroes not mine, only never to the Philistines! home of lost causes, and forsaken beliefs, and unpopular names and impossible loyalties!

(III: 289–90)

This Oxford is the Oxford of "The Scholar-Gipsy" and "Thyrsis," where we are seekers, where the quest is for "the light from heaven, shy to illumine." In fact, the early promise of the Oriel Noetics went largely unfulfilled, and Oxford was left "unravaged" by the intellectual issues of the continent, or even of London or Hurstmonceaux. The Oxford movement turned Oxford back to the last enchantments of the Middle Ages, but is nevertheless to be venerated for its anti-materialism and its "sentiment." Oxford itself, stronghold of the Anglican Church and of the education of its clergy, is to be venerated for what she has been, what that church has been. One thinks of the subjects of Izaak Walton's *Lives* and of the great translators of the Authorized Version, and of Glanvill, and of all the figures in the canon of "English Literature" that were clergymen—and of how many nameless ones who were yet "gentlemen" in Newman's sense, and humanists. *Sentiment* invokes the essential of *feeling* as opposed to intellect. By her connections with the Middle Ages, she whispers still of the "Old Religion" and its "enchantment"—and the thing that *en-chants* is natural magic. In all this she directs us to that goal of per-fection, here defined perilously broadly as *beauty*, but narrowed by a qualification, "which is *truth* seen from another side." I think this is not so much Keatsian as Arnoldian, and it is parallel to Arnold's other dichotomies: beauty : truth :: poetry : science :: religion : morality. The science of "Tübingen" is the rationalist, materialistic, reductive strain of the Higher Criticism. Arnold refuses to reduce what Oxford symbolizes: religious *sentiment,* ecclesiastical tradition, the Authorized Version and the Book of Common Prayer, and the classics, which were the gentleman's education. These have a value which German scholarship has not invalidated; they may save us yet. "The lost causes, the forsaken beliefs, unpopular names and impossible loyalties" are Plenary Inspiration, literal miracles, Moses narrating his own death, Newman's belated nineteenth-century return to a medieval church. But "the cause in which I fight is, after all, hers" because it is for the Christian religion (redefined) and for tradition; it is against the philistines.

One fortuitous advantage of Super's chronological arrangement of the prose is that the beginning page of "On the Study of Celtic Literature," which its half-comic motto from Ossian—"They went forth to the war, but they always fell"—faces the last page of the preface to *Essays in Criticism* (III: 290–91), and we see a wry link between it and Arnold's "cause in which I fight," the "queen of romance" and her "lost causes, forsaken beliefs, impossible loyalties." Let them, the philistines, "find my body by the wall" (587)—along with Ossian's Celtic warriors.

"On the Study of Celtic Literature" opens up to the English consciousness yet another great body of mythic material—other than Germanic, Norse, classical, and Judaeo-Christian. It came out of Oxford lectures delivered in 1866 and was published as a book in 1867—which in all probability, it has been said, provided impetus for the Irish Renaissance. Among other things, it constitutes a delightful Celtic florilegium. It is the first work of Arnold that makes massive use of Renan, often even the same citations Renan uses,[27] but it is

27. Almost enough to classify as "Hazard and *Almost* Random Choices from the *Mabinogion*," e.g.:
Je choisis au hasard un de ces récits qui me semble propre à donner une idée de la composition toute entière. Il s'agit de retrouver Mabon, fils de Modron, qui fut enlevé à sa mère trois jours après sa naissance.
(Ernest Renan, "La Poésie des races celtiques,"
Essais de morale et de critique [Paris, 1859], p. 398)
To get a full sense . . . take, almost at random, a passage. . . . Search is made for Mabon, the son of Modron, who was taken when three nights old from his mother.
(III: 319)

nevertheless very much his own.[28] It connects with some of Arnold's own poems, with his "Tristram and Iseult" insofar as Renan's thesis holds, that the chivalric *matière* is "une création réellement celtique." Arnold's own sense of kinship with the Celts, through his Cornish mother, was fostered by his reading of Renan: his feeling for Celtic Brittany appears earlier in his "Stanzas from Carnac" (1492–95), which anticipate Celtic "natural magic" in the "weird and still" prospect of Mont-Saint-Michel, the sense of the "wizard Merlin's will" among the great Druid menhirs. As Dwight Culler writes, he gives us in this poem "the sense of a continuous religious tradition—paganism, medieval magic, Christian faith."[29] His most Celtic poem, however, is "Saint Brandan" (1501–04), where he tells a medieval saint's legend he got from Renan—catching at its best some of the *frisson* of the Irish poems. The nineteenth-century rationalist Arnold performs rather well in this medieval genre of the miracle story; it is not as brilliant as Tennyson's "Voyage of Maeldune," but it stands with it in historic importance for the Victorian literary use of the *matière* of Ireland.

This essay on Celtic literature is posited on two Herderian axioms: "By the forms of its language a nation expresses its very self" (III: 334), this *expressing* being understood in the sense of *making*; and "To know the Celtic . . . one must know that by which a people best express themselves,—their literature" (III: 321). And so it is by the new science of philology that we will be able to reach the Celts. Two kinds of unserviceable scholarship Arnold deplores: first, that kind of interpretation by which anything can mean anything, where anything can be a key to all the mythologies—Ceridwen is not only Rhea and Ceres but also the ark, and "O Brithi, O Brithoi" is Heliodaemonic and can be written in Hebrew characters. Arnold contrasts two translations of a passage from two different wildly interpretive schools, with hilarious effect. The other kind of evil in scholarship is —in short—what we call reductive, and he cites those who have said this material is "nothing but"—barbarism, late medieval invention, or purest nonsense. But there is external evidence that the Celtic matter has something historical: Lucan, Caesar, Gildas, Nennius are witnesses. And there is moreover, an invaluable "mythological import" (III: 321). The poet Tom Moore appreciated it: "Petrie, these huge

---

28. Super calls it a "spectacular achievement" (III: 495, 496).
29. Culler, *Imaginative Reason*, p. 248.

tomes could not have been written by fools or for any foolish purpose" (III: 315). Arnold, quoting some of Taliesin's beautiful songs, imagines a religion: "Have they not an inwardness, a severity of form, a solemnity of tone, which indicates the still reverberating echo of a profound doctrine and discipline, such as was Druidism?" (III: 326). And in the *Mabinogion* the medieval storyteller, we feel sure, is using very old material, which he may know "by a glimmering tradition merely"; we glimpse "an older architecture, greater, cunninger, more majestical" (III: 322). In short, to disprove literal historicity does not negate the value of the writings. The principles involved, although Arnold does not say so here, are just the principles involved in Bible criticism. Here, a character called Nash plays the part of Colenso: he negates the literal historical truth and therefore dismisses the poems as worthless. But Celtic literature is characterized, in the grand phrase of Henri Martin, by the rebellion against the "despotism of fact" (III: 344, 507). Finally he counsels action, to acquire this Celtic resource for the spiritual, and to counteract a political mistake:

Let us reunite ourselves with our better mind and with the world through science; and let it be one of our angelic revenges on the Philistines, who among their other sins are the guilty authors of Fenianism, to found at Oxford a chair of Celtic, and to send, through the gentle ministrations of science, a message of peace to Ireland.

(III: 386)

VI

Bildung or Anarchy

*C*U *L* T *U* R *E* *and Anarchy* draws together Arnold's main strands of thought into a direct disquisition on the great theme of *Bildung*, and the element of religion is one of the factors. The motto of *Culture and Anarchy* is *Estote ergo vos perfecti!* (V: 86), "Be ye therefore perfect!" in the sense that Arnold has already established by connecting the Pauline injunction to German developmental theory. Culture—or *Bildung*—is "a study of perfection," and where Arnold first defines it in "Sweetness and Light" he says it combines "the scientific passion for pure knowledge" with "the moral and social passion for doing good," citing Montesquieu for the scientific aim: "To render an intelligent being yet more intelligent," and Bishop Wilson (in his first appearance) for the moral aim: "To make reason and the will of God prevail" (V: 91). And lo, here is God in the beginning as part of Culture.

Arnold's friendly adversary Thomas Huxley claimed that this Bishop Wilson was an invention of Arnold's, a fictive offstage authority to sanction his own ideas, like Sairy Gamp's Mrs. 'Arris.[1] Bishop Wilson, although somewhat off the beaten path of conventional authority, is nevertheless perfectly real. I think it is true, however, that Arnold uses him with some sense of play, disarming criticism by referring to an authority of provenance uncertain to his audience, with such assured confidence that a reader less canny than Huxley might

---

1. See *Prose* V: 231 and VI: 10. The origin of the Mrs. 'Arris comment is obscure. Douglas Bush refers to it but gives no reference (*Matthew Arnold* [New York: Macmillan, 1971], p. 150).

feel it his own grave fault to fail to recognize this obviously illustrious moralist.

Thomas Wilson, Bishop of Sodor and Man, 1663–1775, a contemporary of Swift's at Trinity College, Dublin, was singularly virtuous, active, and practical: planting, building, doctoring, establishing schools and libraries, directing the translation of the Gospels and Catechism into Manx, reforming Church discipline, and even being imprisoned for his principles. In the Isle of Man he had a diocese that was in some respects untouched by the Reformation, and he seems to have maintained its old style. Arnold's godfather, John Keble, devoted sixteen years to writing Wilson's life, published in 1863; a review of this *Life* in 1866 caught Arnold's attention, and Wilson's devotional manuals, the *Sacra Privata* and the *Maxims of Piety and Christianity*, became some of Arnold's favorite reading. Bishop Wilson is frequently invoked by Arnold, and he presides as a kind of muse over *Culture and Anarchy* and *Literature and Dogma*. He fills a peculiarly Anglican place in Arnold's book of saints: indeed, Arnold calls him "that survivor of the saints" (VIII: 16), notes his connection with the "rational theology" of the Cambridge Platonists (VIII: 122), recognizes him as an Anglican "worthy" in the line of George Herbert and Thomas Ken (VI: 104), and finds him, though not a mystic, in a deeply practical and influential way a "Friend of God" (XI: 185). The *Maxims* are organized alphabetically under headings; hence it was that Huxley, in the interest of getting back his own umbrella, advised Arnold in a charming note to look up Wilson on *Covetousness* (V: 447). On this head, as on others, Wilson evinces the intense practicality that attracted Arnold, who was to emphasize *conduct* as three-fourths of life (VI: 175). In his *Maxims*, Wilson calls Christ "Our Pattern," just as Arnold emphasizes the "Imitation" at the expense of the supernatural and mystical. The *Maxims* may often seem commonplace, but Arnold's very use of them indicates, I think, his cultivation of the meditative habit, and, in Keats's terms, he had arrived where "any one grand and spiritual passage serves him as a starting point toward all 'the two-and-thirty Palaces.'" Wilson serves Arnold rhetorically, as a starting point toward the best two-and-thirty insights of *Culture and Anarchy*.

The overlap of secular culture with religion that marks *Culture and Anarchy* had its first important English treatment in Carlyle: "Literature is but a branch of Religion and always participates in its character; however, in our time, it is the only branch that still shows any greenness; and, as some think, must one day become the main stem."[2] The "some" Carlyle refers to are obviously the Germans, and the *participation* of literature in the character of *religion* is Herderian—and all this Carlylean new wine Arnold had certainly imbibed. As early as 1852 we find him at home with the idea, in the "magister vitae" letter to Clough: poetry can only "subsist" by including religion (*Clough* 124). Some of Arnold's contemporaries objected that he aimed to substitute Culture for religion, and T. S. Eliot was still objecting years later on those same grounds. Such objections oversimplify the drift of Arnold's thought, which a review of his German studies helps to illuminate.

Charles Taylor in his survey of the German "New Epoch" explains how the Pietist movement in Germany was not separate from the Enlightenment, and even "helped shape the thought of some of Germany's greatest *Aufklärer*, e.g., Lessing and Kant."[3] Enlightenment reason and Pietist spirituality are combined in Herder, who, in reacting against the rationalist objectification of human nature, offers "an alternative anthropology" that Taylor, following Isaiah Berlin, denominates "expressionism."[4] This is the idea that by self-expression we define and make the self; the "message" cannot be known before it is expressed. What makes man capable of expression is chiefly language, and so his very being is dependent on language, or poetry. For Herder, this linguistic consciousness is the central question. Berlin writes:

What is it which makes it possible for us to have this distinct, focused awareness of things, where animals remain caught in the dream-like, melodic flow of experience? It is language that makes this possible . . . . It . . . is the necessary vehicle of a certain form of consciousness, which is characteristically human, the distinct grasp of things which Herder calls "reflection" (*Besonnenheit*). In other terms, words do not just refer, they are also precipitates of

2. Thomas Carlyle, "Characteristics" (1831), in *Works, Critical and Miscellaneous Essays*, vol. 4, (London: Chapman and Hall, 1910), p. 20.
3. Charles Taylor, *Hegel* (Cambridge: Cambridge University Press, 1975), p. 12.
4. He takes the term from Isaiah Berlin, who later published his own important study of expressionism in *Vico and Herder: Two Studies in the History of Ideas* (London: Hogarth Press, 1976), p. 13.

an activity in which the human form of consciousness comes to be. . . . This is one of Herder's great seminal ideas.[5]

Language is essential to thought; each of the different languages constitutes a unique way in which a people realizes the human essence. The most adequate language unites description of the world and expression of feeling and hence is continuous with art. While the standard Enlightenment view is that art teaches or pleases by imitation, the new expressionist view is that art externalizes profound feelings and thereby completes and extends human existence. The artist is now seen as creator; *logos* shifts to *poesis*[6] (compare Arnold's insistence on the need for "making something" in poetry), and art is the most authentic expression of man.

Hence the 1770's in Germany saw a new philosophy of language and a new theory of art which formed part of a new developing theory of man. As a result of this art was given a central part to play in the realization of human nature, in the fulfilment of man. It is from this time that art begins to take on a function analogous to religion.[7]

The role of feeling becomes important, "inseparable from thought, just as thought, if it truly engage with reality, is inseparable from feeling."[8] Our life is a unity and cannot be artificially divided as in the old faculty psychology. The feeling of self is also a vision of self created in language and art, and through it we achieve freedom. For Herder, this vision was strongly religious. Isaiah Berlin quotes Herder:

"See the whole of nature, behold the great analogy of creation. Everything feels itself and its like, life reverberates to life." Man, as the image of God, "an epitome and steward of creation," is called to this, "that he become the organ of sense of his God in all the living things of creation, according to the measure of their relation to him."[9]

Language and art are the modes of communion with nature, with one's fellow man, with God. Religion and poetry, then, become, as in

5. Ibid., p. 19.
6. Ibid., p.18.
7. Ibid., p. 21.
8. Ibid., p. 21.
9. Ibid., p. 25; Herder, *Vom Erkennen und Empfinden der menschlichen Seele*, vol. 8 of *Herders sämmtliche Werke*, ed. Bernhard Suphan (Berlin: Weidmann, 1877–1913), p. 200.

Arnold, inseparable. Even Arnold's reverence for the signal "adequacy" of Greek poetry is German, from Winckelmann through Schiller and Goethe. The Greeks, as Taylor puts it, represent

an era of unity and harmony within man, in which thought and feeling, morality and sensibility were one, in which the form which man stamped on his life whether moral, political or spiritual flowed from his own natural being.[10]

For Schiller, "man recovers his unity in the aesthetic dimension"[11]— hence the doctrine of the *schöne Seele*, hence the *joy* of Beethoven's Ninth Symphony, that *joy* that Arnold feels man is entitled to by the urgency of his need.

Robert T. Clark further explains Herder's idea of poetry: "Corollary to the proposition of the ultimate value of poetry is that of the identity of poetry with religion and *vice versa*. Religion and poetry . . . are in the last analysis coextensive."[12] The Bible, for Herder, contains the highest poetry of the human race, and the rationale for this has nothing to do with "Inspiration" but rather with the expressionist view of language and art, which reveres the poetry of the *"Volk"*— myth, folk song, or Bible—as the *making* of the human consciousness in all its varieties. Carlyle had cautiously made Literature a *branch* of Religion; Arnold, taking fuller possession of the Herderian thought, really assumes their codeterminacy, using the word *Culture* to indicate the whole.

He had been freshly reviewing the idea of *Bildung* in his study of Wilhelm von Humboldt and education, and finding again and again in the literary essays that this idea served and confirmed his interests. Now, sometime in 1867–69 he read (or reread) Herder's *Ideen*, with the greatest devotion, marking in his own copy those passages which particularly struck him. The ideas had long been familiar to him, through Carlyle at first and then, even more sympathetically, through Goethe, but here in Herder he finds the fount and text of the *Humanität-Entwicklung-Bildung* line of thought. He grasps the vision of the coextensiveness of language, literature, and religion under the rubric

10. Taylor, *Hegel*, p. 26.
11. Ibid., p. 38.
12. Robert T. Clark, *Herder* (Berkeley: University of California Press, 1955), p. 278.

of *Bildung*-Culture, and this becomes the controlling idea of *Culture and Anarchy*.

The making of *Culture and Anarchy* has been studied and well documented in its relationship to contemporary affairs.[13] The first essay, "Sweetness and Light," is really Arnold's last lecture as Professor of Poetry at Oxford, "Culture and Its Enemies"; it is tied to Oxford itself and related to the two Oxford elegies and the prose essay-peroration "Beautiful city! so venerable, so lovely!" (III: 290). Ideally, Oxford should embody in one both sides of the study of perfection, the intellectual and the moral. To direct the moral effort, "to make reason and the will of God prevail," we need intelligence, precisely in order to determine what *are* reason and the will of God. In Wilson's idiom, reason and the will of God are much the same thing, reason being an aspect of God, or at least what cannot be contrary to God. In Arnold's evolving thought, "God" is rather a figurative way of speaking of reason, of something like Milton's "Right Reason" or German *Vernunft*, and so he finds Wilson's doublet to his purpose. The cultivated intelligence "demands worthy notions of reason and the will of God" (V: 92). Religion, in turn, "enjoins and sanctions" the great aim of Culture, "to ascertain what perfection is and make it prevail."

Religion says: *The Kingdom of God is within you;* and culture in like manner, places human perfection in an *internal* condition, in the growth and predominance of our humanity proper, as distinguished from our animality. It places it in the ever-increasing efficacy and in the general harmonious expansion of those gifts of thought and feeling, which make the peculiar dignity, wealth, and happiness of human nature.

(V: 94)

This is purely Herderian; it is followed by the passage from "A French Eton" that describes the Herder-Humboldt idea of *Bildung* in its infiniteness (II: 318). And then he adds:

Not a having and a resting, but a growing and a becoming, is the character of perfection as culture conceives it; and here, too, it coincides with religion.

(V: 94)

13. See Super's introduction to *Culture and Anarchy* (V: 408 ff.) and his reference to the work of William Buckler, Sidney M. B. Coulling, Martha S. Vogeler, and Patrick J. McCarthy.

The expansion of humanity, moreover, must be a *general* expansion, must be social. "The individual is required . . . to carry others along with him in his march toward perfection" (compare the children's crusade toward "Jerusalem" in "A French Eton" and the march toward the "City of God" in "Rugby Chapel").

The commonly sought after goals—freedom, railroads, wealth, health—are but *machinery* (*means*, that is, not *ends*), of no profit except insofar as they can contribute to *euphuia*, the Greek ideal of the finely tempered nature. The idea of beauty and intelligence (Sweetness and Light), "which is the dominant idea of poetry," is destined to transform and govern the other moral, religious idea—as in the best poetry of the Greeks, where religion and poetry are one. Our religious organizations need to be tested "by the ideal of a human perfection complete on all sides" (V: 102). In Oxford, we have seized one truth, "that beauty and sweetness are essential characters of a complete human perfection" (not *light*, that is—Oxford has not been strong on intelligence), but the faith and tradition of Oxford, its *beauty*, "have been at the bottom of our attachment to so many beaten causes [the old religion, Plenary Inspiration], of our opposition to so many triumphant movements [science, German criticism]." A tradition of beauty must be valid; it is this which "keeps up our communication with the future" (V: 106). Newman and the Oxford Movement attacked Liberalism, and Liberalism prevailed. But Newman's movement, being devoted to the faith and tradition of Oxford, its beauty, has contributed to the tide of self-criticism—intelligence, or light. Loyalty to Oxford will help to reveal the inadequacy of mere Liberalism. The love of beauty, that is, will lead us back to intelligence and the harmoniously developing whole.

Culture rejects machinery and rejects system—Benthamism, Comtism, Jacobinism—and works toward an ideal of perfection for all: "It seeks to do away with classes; to make the best that has been thought and known in the world current everywhere"; it aspires to a stage at which men may use ideas, "nourished, and not bound by them." Intellectual freedom connects with political freedom. The great men of Culture are "the true apostles of equality . . ." for they have "a passion for diffusing . . . the best knowledge. . . ." (V: 113) ("Go then, O Pourna: having been delivered, deliver!")

As examples of the great men of Culture for our time he cites Lessing

and Herder—Herder, of course, and Lessing, who had played a role
in the beginnings of the Higher Criticism: he was one of the first of
the neo-Spinozists, one of the first to question conventional Bible interpretation and to apply historical scholarship to the gospels. He had
edited the controversial *Wolfenbüttel Fragments* of Reimarus (1774),
an early document in the Higher Criticism. His deeply influential play,
Nathan the Wise (1779), presents an idea of religion transcending
Judaism, Christianity, and Islam. Furthermore, we find in Arnold's
"General Note-Books" of uncertain date[14] some careful, captioned
transcriptions from Lessing's *Die Erziehung des Menschengeschlechts*
(1780) (The Education of the Human Race) even the title of which
indicates Lessing's espousal of a developmental theory. One of these
six short extracts is as follows, with Arnold's title:

The Everlasting Gospel

Sie wird kommen, sie wird gewiss kommen, die Zeit der Vollendung, da der
Mensch, je überzeugter sein Verstand einer immer bessern Zukunft sich fühlet,
von dieser Zukunft gleichwohl Bewegungsgründe zu seinen Handlungen zu
erborgen, nicht nöthig haben wird; da er das Gute thun wird, weil es das
Gute ist, nicht weil willkührliche Belohnungen darauf gesetzt sind, die seinen
flatterhaften Blick ehedem blos heften und stärken sollten, die innern bessern
Belohnungen desselben zu erkennen.

(*Note-Books* 521–22)

The Everlasting Gospel

It will come, it will certainly come, the time of Perfection, when man, the
more convinced his mind feels of an ever-improving future, will not find it
necessary to borrow motivating reasons for his actions from this future, since
he will do what is good because it is good, and not because arbitrary rewards
are placed upon it, which previously were only to capture and strengthen his
wavering eye in order to better recognize the inner, better rewards.

This passage answers to Arnold's sense of the shabbiness of the literal
afterlife and his sense of a new possibility for Christianity. The great
men of Culture, he says, *humanize knowledge.* And in closing the
essay he cites Saint Augustine, who is revealed here as another developmental thinker, even what is now called a "process theologian":

14. See Richard Tobias, "On Dating Matthew Arnold's 'General Note-Books,'"
Philological Quarterly 39 (July 1960): 426–34.

"Let the children of thy spirit . . . make their light shine on earth . . . and announce the revolution of the times. . . . Thou shalt send forth new labourers to new seed times, whereof the harvest shall be not yet."[15] And so the opening essay of *Culture and Anarchy* is stamped as a challenge to renew religion.

In the second essay, "Doing as One Likes," Arnold returns to modify and define the concept of freedom that was broached in the books on education. Freedom is hardly to be worshipped in itself (as we tend to do), for it is in itself only *machinery;* in its current sense, as "the assertion of personal liberty" (V: 117), it leads to anarchy. Arnold modifies Viconian cyclic Historicism into a two-phase concept of systole and diastole: the systole is the period of contraction, the aristocratic; the diastole is the period of expansion, the democratic. A "modern" age like ours (Arnold's) stands in between, developing toward democracy, and in the instability of the change, we risk a speedy reversion to anarchic bestiality instead of a harmonious expansion, through Culture, of democracy (V: 124). We need the notion of "the State," which can help us toward "enlightening ourselves and qualifying ourselves to act less at random" (V: 116). For Arnold, the stabilizing principle in all the threatening randomness is Culture and the hopes of education; one does not oppose a *state of being* to randomness but a *direction of becoming.* Arnold proposes that "we rise above the idea of class to the idea of whole community, *the State,* to find our centre of light and authority there." As members of a class we are "separate, personal, at war": from this comes anarchy. "But by our *best* self we are united, impersonal, at harmony." And "this is the very self which culture, or the study of perfection, seeks to develop in us" (V: 134).

The famous chapter "Barbarians, Philistines, Populace" presents the possibility of that "something" better in each class uniting to constitute the State, our collective "best self." In each class there are those who transcend class in their "humane spirit," and we must determine how to foster and unite these elements in a cultivated *humanity.* Just as now in the absence of an Academy, literary taste maintains itself at a low level of bathos, each literary entity pursuing its own interests, or ordinary self, in the absence of any transcending "authoritative centres," so does religion maintain a low style. The warring sects, he

15. V: 113–14. Augustine *Confessions* 13. 18 (Super's note).

says, put their trust in ignominious interested leaders, just as though they carried "the weight and significance of Plato and Saint Paul," and put their faith in numbers of adherents or (as with the Mormons) — rifles! (V: 148). The parallel suggests that an Established Church is as desirable in the sphere of religion as an Academy in the sphere of literature, but the idea of the Church here must be very Broad indeed, for it includes Plato with Saint Paul. Political institutions as they are seem to support our ordinary selves in all their divisiveness. Even royalty, "a sort of constituted witness to its best mind" (he recognizes the public usefulness of the symbol), gets turned into "a kind of grand advertising van" for our ordinary selves (V: 153–54). In Prussia, he remembers, the sovereign patronized certain schools as types or examples, taking advice from men like Wilhelm von Humboldt and Schleiermacher. Nothing like this obtains in England. Licensed Victuallers' Schools and Commercial Travellers' Schools set the tone.

Where nothing can function except our ordinary selves we have a situation (if I may paraphrase Arnold with a figure from American politics) where there is nothing but *lobbyists*: "Every force in the world, evidently, except the one reconciling force, right reason!" (V: 157). He ends the essay with a tribute to Wilhelm von Humboldt and his work on *The Sphere and Duties of Government*, granting that in Germany the people are liable to rely too much on the government. But Humboldt, "one of the most beautiful souls that have ever existed, used to say that one's business in life was first to perfect one's self by all the means in one's power, and, secondly, to try and create in the world around one an aristocracy, the most numerous that one possibly could, of talents."[16] But he saw, and Renan in France sees, that government has a great work to do yet: government, as the best self, transcending classes, must above all enact and support disinterested legislation for schools.

In the next essay, "Hebraism and Hellenism," Arnold's diagnosis of nineteenth-century England, even the term "Hebraism" teases the Puritans of England into remembering the Jewish base of their religion and at the same time invites the larger view of Christianity. Hebraism, as we all know, is concerned with conduct and obedience, Hellenism with "seeing things as they really are" in the light of intelligence;

16. V: 161. This translates part of Challemel-Lacour's article on Humboldt in the *Revue germanique et française*; see above, p. 96.

"C'est le bonheur des hommes," according to Hellenism, "quand ils pensent juste."[17] Yet profoundly different as these elements are, the final aim of both, he insists, is the same: man's perfection or salvation. "At the bottom of both the Greek and the Hebrew notion is the desire, native in man, for reason and the will of God, the feeling after the universal order,—in a word, the love of God" (V: 165). Here man's *Humanität* is connected with a very broadened emergent definition of God. God equals reason, universal order, as opposed to randomness, anarchy; and it is man's nature to seek reason and order. Behind all this lies Herder's vision of the immensity and infinity of human potential: "The human spirit," Arnold says, "is wider than the most priceless of the forces which bear it onward." On the idea of immortality, he declares Paul's argument confused and inconclusive and the Greeks over-subtle and sterile: "Above and beyond the inadequate solutions which Hebraism and Hellenism here attempt, extends the immense and august problem itself, and the human spirit which gave birth to it" (V: 171). Both Puritan literalism and Roman Catholic superstition are outmoded, and our present ideas of religion will become so likewise, and we will develop on into new modes of religion. With the help of light from Herder, Humboldt, and Goethe we may see Arnold's vision of the new religion to be an inclusive and holistic *Culture*. Malaise comes about because our two main social impulses are at odds: since the Renaissance "the main stream of man's advance" has been with Hellenism, but England's main impulse has been Hebraism—hence, "a certain confusion and false movement" (V: 175). *The time is out of joint!* as the young Arnold-Hamlet had felt so poignantly, but now he has a program to offer toward setting it right. We can work to reestablish the harmony proper to *Bildung* by "enlarging our whole view and rule of life."[18]

The chapter "Porro Unum Est Necessarium" is Arnold's denial that our problems can be solved by any "one thing" or any one party; the tendency to look at the simple single solution is positively injurious. Even Paul himself asks, "Who hath known the mind of the lord?"; "Who hath known, that is, the true and divine order of things in its entirety?" (V: 181). *All* writings are "but contributions to

17. V: 165. This memorable definition of human bliss is from Frederick the Great, as quoted by Sainte-Beuve.

18. Park Honan has discerned the Hamlet phase. *Matthew Arnold: A Life* (New York: McGraw-Hill, 1981), pp. 146–47.

human thought and human development, which extend wider than
they do." Arnold presumably knew Goethe's admirable paradox:
"He who knows one language knows none"; Arnold's friend Max
Müller applied it to the study of religions: "He who knows one,
knows none."[19] Arnold turns it against the bibliolators: "No man,
who knows nothing else, knows even his Bible" (V: 184). While
Hebraism tends to narrowness, "Essential in Hellenism is the impulse
to the development of the whole man, to connecting and harmonizing
all parts of him, leaving none to take their chance" (V: 184). However sound the doctrine may be, the mean or vulgar or hideous, as in
many English hymns, destroys the harmony.

"Our Liberal Practitioners" exhibits the various inadequate nos-
trums in contemporary English life; in it Arnold again incidentally
reveals the drift of his developing religious philosophy. Reaching back
to one of the education books, he catches up a statement used there
tentatively and presents it here with more confidence as an ideal:
"The State is of the religion of all of its citizens, without the fanaticism of any of them" (II: 198, V: 193), and he goes on to defend what
was his father's idea of the "Broad" Established Church with arguments of his own. It saves society from the excesses of sectarian
thought and speculation by uniting it in a common worship and
devotion. "The consecration of common consent, antiquity, public
establishment, long-used rites, national edifices, is everything for religious worship" (V: 197), and he quotes Joubert: "The same devotion unites men far more than the same thought and knowledge."
Arnold concludes: "Man worships best, therefore, with the community; he philosophizes best alone" (V: 197).

Even to national social problems, Arnold brings the idea of the
study of perfection, which must be a general perfection. "Such is the
sympathy which binds humanity together, that we are indeed, as our
religion says, members of one body, and if one member suffer, all
the members suffer with it" (V: 215). And so even on the problem
of free trade he brings in Bishop Wilson, who "Hellenized much within the very limits of Hebraism" (V: 208), and Thomas à Kempis's
Imitation (V: 216). He reveals the canting narrowness of "the one
thing needful" in an elegant paragraph that in structure and rhetoric

19. I suppose the paradox is well known to Goethe scholars. I only came across
it in Max Müller's *Lectures on the Science of Religion*, delivered as lectures in
1870 (London: Longmans, Green, 1893), pp. 12, 13.

is like one of his social sonnets ("East London" [486]) : while he stood with a clergyman regarding the destitute children of the London slums, the clergyman declared, "The one thing really needful is to teach these little ones to succour one another . . . but . . . one hears nothing but the cry for knowledge, knowledge, knowledge!" (V: 217). And yet, Arnold declares, the *first* thing necessary would be the knowledge of how to prevent this misery. "The poor shall never cease out of the land" is a premise we had better not accept. The stock notions of the Hebraizers can be perfectly vicious (V: 219). Knowledge is needed, even the historical criticism of the Bible: the text praising philoprogenitivity, for example, was composed when many children were an economic and military advantage; they may not be so now. Ultimately Culture is necessary not only to perfection but to actual safety, to the survival of our present civilization. We need something like the Socratic "disinterested play of consciousness upon stock notions and habits" (V: 228). We might pursue, with Culture, the high destiny of the human race, the way of "development," but our politicians eddy about, disestablishing the Irish Church for the wrong reasons or pluming themselves on having enabled a man to marry his deceased wife's sister.

The preface to *Culture and Anarchy*, being written in 1869, is in reality retrospective, and after some circumstantial evidence that Bishop Wilson does indeed exist Arnold reaffirms his argument that Culture speaks to the present difficulties and turns to the vision of the "Broad" Established Church, Hooker's vision, showing how the Church in its beginnings included what are now the Nonconformists, arguing that they could be brought back into the Establishment with mutual benefit, dissipating provincialism and bringing all together in their common interests for the national life. "Not that the forms in which the human spirit tries to express the inexpressible, or the forms by which man tries to worship, have or can have . . . anything necessary or eternal. . . . What is alone and always sacred and binding for man is the making progress toward his total perfection" (V: 250–51). Early Christianity had sustaining roots both Jewish and Greek; in later phases it might have "lost itself in a multitude of hole-and-corner churches like the churches of English Nonconformity," but Constantine at the critical moment "established" Christianity, or, "let us rather say, placed the human spirit, whose totality was endangered,— in contact with the main current of human life" (V: 251). Development could then proceed in harmony, Arnold would say, as it cannot now in the nineteenth-century dislocation, where science and faith pull in different directions. Constantine's act "was justified by its fruits, in men like Augustine and Dante, and indeed in all great men of Christianity, Catholics or Protestants, ever since" (V: 251).

"The days of Israel are innumerable," he concludes, and I take this to mean that the possible transformations of Christianity extend into the future in more ways than we can envisage; for he goes on to say that "culture must not fail to keep its flexibility, and to give to its judgments that passing and provisional character" (V: 255) that is proper to it. Arnold prophesied here more than he knew, it seems to me, recommending a stance that even in science we now know is necessary: our best theories must be understood only as provisional hypotheses. And he recommends the discipline of Culture, "by which alone man is enabled to rescue his life from thralldom to the passing moment and to his bodily senses, to ennoble it, and to make it eternal" (V: 255). The nature of this "eternity" he will explicate in his ensuing writings; for now he insists that though Hebraism is badly in need of its balancing Hellenism, we will yet return to it, and the Bible will remain, as Goethe said it would, "not only a national book, but the Book of the Nations" (V: 256). And he ends with Baruch, "Lo, thy sons come, whom thou sentest away; they come gathered from the west unto the east by the word of the Holy One, rejoicing in the remembrance of God."

For a secular and topical book, *Culture and Anarchy* has a great deal of religious talk. Biblical images shape the whole of it (Philistines, the children of light, the will of God, the return), and allusions to and quotations from the Bible and Christian apologists are legion. It is true that all this dialect of religion might be understood as a sort of patina to lend dignity and authority, but it is deployed with art and power and somehow seems central to the urgency of the message. It might appear to be used only as metaphor—and yet it carries tremendous weight. This is a mystery of rhetoric, one to which Arnold himself will direct his attention. And in the meantime, the "Preface," the last part written of *Culture and Anarchy*, anticipates in various specific ways *St. Paul and Protestantism*, which is soon to take shape.

Super's chronological arrangement, his volume V, called *Culture and Anarchy*, finds *Culture and Anarchy* itself enveloped in between the two parts of *Friendship's Garland*, those high-spirited periodical letters that constitute Arnold's closest approach to the novel. *Friendship's Garland* is like *Sartor Resartus* in its fiction of a German perspective on England; by this ironic device, Arnold's Arminius in his ostensible attempts to defend England invariably makes it look worse. The subject matter is the subject matter of *Culture and Anarchy* but without the religious idiom. Arnold cavorts in his ironic game and exposes "a religion, narrow, unintelligent, repulsive" (V: 19), implying a criterion for religion that is not of doctrine but of *breadth*, of *intellect*, and of *beauty*.

In this period Sainte-Beuve died, and Arnold published in 1869 the short essay that commemorates his death. Sainte-Beuve, modest as he is as to the value of his own role as critic, nevertheless sets a precedent for Arnold's vision of criticism and consequently shapes "Literary Criticism" in our Anglo-American society. Sainte-Beuve is the ideal, for he is consistently a *scientist*, a *naturalist*: "Man, as he is, and as his history and the productions of his spirit show him, was the object of his study and interest; he strove to find the real data with which, in dealing with man and his affairs, we have to do" (V: 306). I think there is an implied parallel here with biblical criticism: just as biblical criticism must cleanse itself of superstition and literalism, all literary criticism must eschew the fanciful, the visionary, the fictitious, and the conventional.

Again in the same period, Arnold's short magazine piece on Theodore Parker, the American Unitarian preacher, recognizes a sympathetic liberalism. Parker knew the Germans and imbibed Herderian developmentalism—"Man advances continually. No man is fullgrown"—and the Goethean activist ethic—"In human action there is always more of virtue of every kind than vice" (V: 79, 80). But, Arnold objects, it is all stamped with the American new world, its virtues certainly, but also its limitations. What we now need in spiritual leadership is neither an American voice, nor an English voice, nor a French voice, but something broader: Arnold calls it a "European" voice. And Parker is, moreover, inadequate in his literary taste and in his theism, positively out of date in his contempt for popular unscientific theology. The language of the Deists is now as unscientific as "the idea of a God who turns himself into a sacrificial wafer or who foredooms a large proportion of the human race to hell" (V: 83). And then Arnold in a memorable sentence presents again his conception of the way things are in religion:

The idea that the world is in a course of development, of *becoming*, toward
a perfection infinitely greater than we now can even conceive, the idea of a
tendance à l'ordre present in the universe . . . , this the scientific intellect may
accept, and may willingly let the religious instincts and the language of religion
gather around it.

(V: 83)

The important phrase "tendance à l'ordre" is from Etienne de Senancour's *Obermann*,[20] from a passage which Arnold is to use as an
epigraph for *Literature and Dogma*.

In these years when Arnold was marking Herder's *Ideen*, he was
freshly engaged with Senancour:[21] his poem "Obermann Once More"
belongs to 1865–67, and his essay on Senancour to 1869 (Super includes it in the *Culture and Anarchy* volume), twenty years after the
time of writing the "Stanzas in Memory of the Author of 'Obermann' " (130–38). The "Obermann" essay in effect explicates from
a retrospective position his own early Obermann poem. Senancour's
distinguishing characteristics are his "profound inwardness, his aus-
tere and sad sincerity, and his delicate feeling for nature," and his "un-
remitting occupation with that question which haunted St. Bernard—
Bernarde, ad quid venisti?" (V: 296)—the urgent problem of vocation, that is. Goethe and Wordsworth are in comparison diffuse;
Rousseau, Chateaubriand, Byron all attitudinize. A man who was,
"from the very profoundness and meditativeness of his nature, religious, Senancour felt to the uttermost the bare and bleak spiritual
atmosphere into which he was born" (V: 296). He is a victim of the
Zeitgeist, that disjunction of the times Arnold describes in "Hebraism
and Hellenism." The religious need was in Senancour (as it is in humankind, it is suggested) "a passion for order and harmony," and
Arnold quotes here in his own translation that passage so much on his
mind that he refers to it in the Theodore Parker essay and uses it later
as a headnote to *Literature and Dogma*.

20. V: 83n., 407. See also V: 297.

21. Iris Sells considers Senancour to be the main French influence on Arnold's
thought, and I think this part of her book is hardly to be dismissed. *Matthew Arnold
and France* (Cambridge: Cambridge University Press, 1935; reprint ed., New
York: Octagon Books, 1970), pp. 38 ff. and 252–53. Tinker and Lowry's explication of "Obermann Once More" is especially illuminating (*The Poetry of Matthew
Arnold: A Commentary* [London: Oxford University Press, 1940]), pp. 261–74.

May we not say that the tendency to order forms an essential part of our propensities, our *instinct*, just like the tendency to self-preservation, or to the
reproduction of the species? . . . Inasmuch as man had this feeling of order
planted in him, inasmuch as it was in his nature, the right course would have
been to try and make every individual man sensible of it and obedient to it.
(V: 297)

But, Arnold now paraphrases, leaders have "sought to control human
conduct by means of supernatural hopes, supernatural terrors, thus
misleading man's intelligence and debasing his soul." "Depuis trente
siècles, les résultats sont dignes de la sagesse des moyens" (For thirty
centuries, the results are what you might expect from the "wisdom"
of the means). Paganism and Christianity alike "have tampered with
man's mind and heart, and wrought confusion in them" (V: 297).
Then Arnold quotes an interesting paragraph which sees the sin of
priestcraft as literalism—

explaining allegories and making nonsense of them. . . . The principle of life—
that which was intelligence, light, the eternal—became nothing more than the
husband of Juno; . . . the great ideas of immortality and retribution consisted
in the fear of a turning wheel, and the hope of strolling in a green wood.
(V: 297–98)

Christianity, at a time when intelligence was spreading more and
more, offered not the needed profound spirituality but dogmas which
were more absurd than the fables. Christianity was constructed on a
base that is radically faulty—and it has failed to establish social justice.
Senancour was a Hamlet, Arnold says: "But as deep as his sense that
the time was out of joint, was the feeling of this Hamlet that he had no
power to set it right. *Vos douleurs ont flétri mon âme*, he says—your
miseries have worn out my soul" (V: 300). Behind Arnold's own
Hamlet-attitudinizing lay, I think, a sense of the well-nigh intolerable
burden of the duty to a time out of joint, to work toward setting it
right. And yet, in all the desolation there are still moments, tenuous
sensations of some consolation, a recurrent theme of Arnold's poems
—those nights of the nightingales in "To Marguerite—Continued"
when the impossible communion becomes possible, or the rare moments of lull when "a man becomes aware of his life's flow" in "The
Buried Life." These moments came for Senancour in the communion
with nature; Arnold quotes:

I stand still, and marvel; I listen to what subsists yet, I would fain hear what will go on subsisting; in the movement of the forest, in the murmur of the pines, I seek to catch some of the accents of the eternal tongue.

(V: 301)

"What subsists" becomes for Arnold the best definition of God; he will explain it as Moses' *J am*, and it becomes his favorite term for deity, the "Eternal."

The Obermann essay concludes with a tribute to Senancour's "bleak frankness," as though to a sort of Samuel Beckett of his time, but the poem "Obermann Once More" (559–76), though not a good poem, goes farther and is a sort of revisionary piece, of all Arnold's poems the most explicit on his religious views and purpose. It is a kind of essay in the form of versified dream-vision. In the well-remembered Alpine setting, he reencounters Obermann, who explains that the situation has changed, and this is now a time for new beginnings and new hope. In about thirty four-line stanzas, Obermann then gives a considered versified history of Christianity: the corrupt, sensation-seeking Roman world into which comes the gospel of Christ like a draught to slake a thirst (compare "all religions fall on the dry heart like rain" in "Progress"); the message is of inwardness, the word is to be found in one's own soul (where Spinoza finds the word of God); imperial Rome gives way to repentance, the joy of the new religion, the monastic movement, and the many cultural gifts of Christianity, such as the myriad of indispensable icons, art whose power indicates the saving vigor of the religion itself. But, "Now he is dead!" cries Obermann, anticipating Nietzsche by a good decade or so, and from the sacred places comes a clear message:

> *Unduped of fancy, henceforth man*
> *Must labour!—must resign*
> *His all too human creeds, and scan*
> *Simply the way divine!*

Man must, that is, recognize his fables and anthropomorphisms for what they are, resign the dogma constructed by theologians, and turn to the imitation of Christ. In spite of the great cleansing storm of the French Revolution, the old religion dies slowly, like the habits of men surviving on icebergs cut off from the main. Nature tarries yet, though promising in the words of Revelation, "See, I make all things new" (Arnold has a gift for connecting Herderian development with biblical texts) :

> The millions suffer still, and grieve
> And what can helpers heal
> With old-world cures men half believe
> For woes they wholly feel?
>
> And yet men have such need of joy!
> But joy whose grounds are true. . . .

Obermann lived out his life in a time when there was no cure. His tomb (like Senancour's actual tomb in Paris) bears the inscription *Eternité, deviens mon asile*—"Eternity, be thou my refuge!" (words which would have suited the dying Empedocles, which reverberate with ties to Arnold's "Eternal"). But thou, Obermann addresses the poet, livest on in a time of sunrise; it is announced with a Shelleyan overtone:

> The world's great order dawns in sheen. . . .

Even thou that art in some ways "marred, / Shorn of the joy, the bloom, the power" that belong to those born in a harmonious time, nevertheless now thou must bring a message of "Hope to a world new made!" The poet wakes, to nature still consolingly beautiful, speaking still, it is implied, the language of eternity, and the dawn breaks, as though to validate the mission imposed by Senancour. Senancour cannot be accounted a minor interest of Arnold's, for his Obermann not only articulates the intensity of spiritual need, expressing and creating the Arnoldian self, but also supplies a ground by which to articulate the vocation. The whole poem stands as preface to Arnold's religious books, his great effort to determine *order*, the alternative to anarchy.

VII

The Parable of the Three Rings:
Victorian Comparative
Religion

A R N O L D ' S prose work is always tied to contemporary controversy, as has been well illustrated,[1] even though for us the
works may transcend the controversy. I propose now to consider
some aspects of the general climate of religious thought that set some
of Arnold's assumptions in the religious books. It must be remembered
that in taking up religious topics he was not pursuing some private
frowsty interest of his own, but he was, rather, coming to the center
of contemporary concerns. The great British public, it has been said,
followed religious controversy with the enthusiasm of present-day
football fans.[2] Mere literary criticism and sociology have never, then
or now, been so exciting. There was unquestionably the most enormous bulk of print on religious topics ever, in all history.

I propose that Arnold's writings on religion are his most carefully
argued, his most *guarded*, and his most substantial. Neglected for
many years, moreover, they may now appear to be central to his oeuvre. Such a view may seem to slight the vital message of *Culture and
Anarchy*, but I think rather, when the nature of his religious theory is
determined, the social criticism and the literary criticism as well can be
better understood as directed by the lodestone of the religious idea.
The still rather gnomic statement that "the strongest part of our religion today is its unconscious poetry" (IX: 63, 161) will appear to be
central and thematic. *St. Paul and Protestantism* develops directly out

1. Especially in Sidney Coulling's *Matthew Arnold and His Critics* (Athens:
Ohio University Press, 1974), and in Super's introductions in *Prose*.
2. *Times Literary Supplement*, February 4, 1971, p. 41.

of the "Preface" (the last part written) of *Culture and Anarchy*. That *St. Paul and Protestantism* and *Literature and Dogma* follow so close on the heels of *Culture and Anarchy*, chronologically and logically, illustrates in itself the connection of poetry with religion.

Arnold's very broad sense of the word "religion" is in part an inheritance from his father and from Coleridge. Anglican "breadth" implies a negligence of doctrinal differences in the light of a Christianity defined by its activism, the practice of the virtues traditionally called Christian. Thomas Arnold had taken over a good deal of the new German theory in a loose sort of way: he was not concerned with philosophical discrepancies, having a very sure sense of what right conduct is and how our main business is to get on with it. On biblical criticism, he was so sure of his rightness that he was not aware of how inconsistently he mixed new Higher Criticism with old supernaturalism. Matthew Arnold inherited, then, a set of discrepancies, in religious theory and in Bible criticism. It was for him to set things straight. He saw that the "breadth" implied by Coleridge and Thomas Arnold should logically not be limited to Protestantism, nor even to Christianity. In Herder's *Ideen* he met the new anthropological view, that what distinguishes the whole human species is the capacity for religion. "Zur Humanität und Religion ist der Mensch gebildet" (Man is formed for humanity and religion) is the heading of a chapter liberally marked in Arnold's own copy.[3] Being above all social, man needs a protracted childhood to learn language and tradition, and it is his characteristic to inquire after the causes of things. "In a sense," writes Herder, in a passage Arnold marks:

all the phenomena around us are but a dream . . . , though we regard it as reality if and when we observe the same effects linked with the same occasioning circumstances, often and constantly enough. This is how philosophy proceeds, and the first and last philosophy has always been religion. . . . Thou [O, God] hast exalted man, so that, even without his knowing or intending it, he inquires after the causes of things, divines their connection, and thus discovers thee, thou great bond of all things, being of beings! Thy inmost nature he knows not . . . , for thou art without form, though the first cause of all forms. . . . The law of nature will not change on thy [man's] account; but the more thou discoverest its beauty, goodness and perfection, the more will this living

3. See above, chapter 2. Book 4, chapter 6 of Herder's *Ideen zur Philosophie der Geschichte der Menschheit*, 2 vols. (Leipzig, 1828), 1: 146.

model form thee to the image of God in thy earthly life: True religion is therefore a filial service of God, an imitation of the most high and beautiful in human
form [the best man can imagine, I take it] with the extreme of inward satisfaction [*Zufriedenheit*], active goodness, and love of mankind. . . . Nothing
has so much ennobled our form and nature as religion.[4]

The new German philosophy of religion respects the religious impulse as essentially human, grants legitimacy to all religions, and still
in its developmentalism sanctions the Old Testament and other bodies
of myth as poetry, a literature of metaphor or symbol concerning the
most significant human experience of the world; it supports the claim
of Christianity as superior because it is later, more *developed*; and it
refuses to accept present Christianity as complete and absolute; it is
but a stage on the way to developing an ever more perfect religion, a
more perfect humanity. According to Ludwig Feuerbach, for instance,
as translated by George Eliot (1854) and therefore current even in
English, "all the moral relationships are *per se* religious."[5] Feuerbach
deprecates theology and reveres religion, looking to its roots in human
psychological need.[6] German philosophy shaped French religious
theory more dynamically than English. Edgar Quinet translated Herder's *Ideen* into French (1825) and himself wrote on *Le Génie des
religions* (1842) and "De l'avenir des religions."[7] He studied religion
as a social phenomenon, the *Grande Encyclopédie* tells us, and refused to consider the religious impulse an error of the mind (as the
Enlightenment tended to) and refused to confound it with ecclesiastical institutions or dogma. Arnold transcribes a passage from
Quinet in his *Note-Books*:

Ne dîtes pas que la poésie finit; dîtes plutôt, telle qu'elle est, qu'elle seule
reste vivante. Il n'est pas une tradition, pas une autorité, pas une lettre écrite
qui ne tombe en cendre si vous la touchez de la main. Dans ce bouleversement
du réel, l'idée seule subsiste. On remplace la foi par la poésie.

4. Ibid., pp. 153–54.
5. Ludwig Feuerbach, *Essence of Christianity*, trans. Mary Ann Evans (George
Eliot) (New York: Harper, 1957), p. 271. I owe this reference to my student Dale
Flynn.
6. Lionel Trilling explains this point in *Matthew Arnold* (New York: Norton,
1939), pp. 333–34.
7. Edgar Quinet, "De l'avenir des religions," *Revue des deux mondes*, 1st ser.,
vol. 3 (June 1831), pp. 213–20.

Chaque peuple se dépouille aussi de son art indigène. Mais de ses ruines particulières se forme la personnalité du genre humain. Un même génie cosmopolite se met à la place des génies différens [sic] d'idiomes et de races. De là la mission réelle du poète commence. Sa vocation religieuse est d'être le médiateur des peuples à venir.[8]

(Note-Books 501–2)

Do not say poetry is finished; say rather that such as it is, it alone remains alive. There is not a tradition, not an authority, not a letter written that does not fall to ashes if you touch it. In this overthrow of reality, the idea alone subsists. Faith is replaced by poetry.

Each people divests itself also of its own indigenous art [having grown out of it]. But from the particular ruins of it is formed the personality of the human genre [the remnants of a religion, I interpret, constitute the culture, as Christianity does ours]. A single cosmopolitan spirit takes the place of the different spirits of idioms and races. It is in this that the real mission of the poet commences. His religious vocation is to be the mediator to the people of the future.

The reader will recognize the very rhetoric of Quinet in a key passage of Arnold's own:

The future of poetry is immense, because in poetry, where it is worthy of its high destinies, our race, as time goes on, will find an ever surer and surer stay. There is not a creed which is not shaken, not an accredited dogma which is not shown to be questionable, not a received tradition which does not threaten to dissolve. Our religion has materialized itself in the fact, in the supposed fact; it has attached its emotion to the fact, and now the fact is failing it. But for poetry the idea is everything; the rest is a world of illusion, of divine illusion. Poetry attaches its emotion to the idea; the idea *is* the fact. The strongest part of our religion to-day is its unconscious poetry.

(IX: 63, 161)

When this passage is considered in conjunction with the Herderian Quinet's, I think Arnold's own "religious" vocation as poet-critic becomes admirably clear. As school official, as social critic, as literary

8. From Edgar Quinet, "Poètes allemands—Henri Heine," *Revue des deux mondes*, 3rd ser., vol. 1 (January 1, 1834) : 367–68. This is in the "General Note-Books" and therefore hard to date, but it follows a transcription from the same journal for 1863 and therefore cannot, I suppose, have been transcribed earlier than 1863.

critic, he feels called to mediate to the people of the future their cultural heritage of the art-religion continuum and the cultural processes that maintain and develop their humanity, and these processes must now become less provincial and more cosmopolitan. Arnold had called for a "European" voice rather than an American one (V: 81), or English, or French, and this "Europeanness" can be interpreted as a stage in moving toward something yet larger.

All Arnold's literary experience pressed on him this vocation to the service of a culture that combines a variety of literatures with a variety of religions into one continuum: Homer, the Bible, the *Bhagavad Gita*, the *Imitation*, Marcus Aurelius, Plato, Sophocles, Dante, St. Francis, Spinoza, Wordsworth, the Celts.

The new learning of the nineteenth century, beginning in Historicism and developing into comparative philology and comparative anthropology, turned quite naturally to the study of comparative religion, making an effort to be objective, impartial—disinterested. Arnold, like Max Müller, attacks Emile Burnouf's *La Science des religions* (Paris, 1872) as unscientific:[9] it aims to demonstrate the superiority of Hinduism and is therefore just as culpable as demonstrations of the superiority of Christianity. And Max Müller in his own *Science of Religion* (1870) goes to the heart of the matter: "Language is the necessary condition of every other mental activity, religion not excluded."[10] He envisages the science of religion as parallel to the science of language, now in 1870 legitimized and accepted, even in England—witness the university chairs of Sanskrit and comparative philology. The subject of religion is for some too holy to approach scientifically, for others too superstitious, and yet to study it comparatively will yield results as enlightening as the results of comparative philology. *He who knows only one, knows none.* Müller recognizes a religious faculty in man and calls it the "faculty of the Infinite, which is at the root of all religions." This is how he defines the German *Vernunft*, as opposed to *Verstand*, reason, and *Sinn*, sense; and Arnold-like he tries out a definition of the Infinite as "something with-

9. VI: 239–40; Max Müller, *Introduction to the Science of Religion: Four Lectures Delivered at the Royal Institution . . . 1870*, printed in *Fraser's Magazine* in the same year (London: Longmans, Green, 1893), pp. 27, 28.

10. Quoted in Nirad C. Chaudhuri, *Scholar Extraordinary: The Life of Professor the Right Honourable Friedrich Max Müller P.C.* (London: Chatto and Windus, 1974), p. 193.

out us which we cannot resist."[11] He recalls the Emperor Akbar (1542–1605), who invited to his court Jews, Christians, Moham- medans, Brahmans, and Zoroastrians and studied all their sacred books, and he describes the present advantages for such a study, the comparative wealth of texts now available. (His own monumental edition of the *Rig-Veda* was one of the notable contributions.) And now, as a further great advantage, "we have been taught the rules of critical scholarship." The study of Judaism and Christianity as com- pared with the religions of Greece and Rome, long carried on by some of our most learned divines, has been an excellent preparation. And no one now believes the pagan religions are corruptions of the religion of the Old Testament[12] any more than that the Greek and Latin lan- guages are corruptions of Hebrew, traditionally the original, "re- vealed" language. He observes that the Hebrew language did not ar- rive at a level of abstraction but worked in metaphors—a mode that "lives on in the language of every true poet."[13] His first lecture has a Herderian-Spinozan conclusion: we shall be the gainers in this new science; it will reveal "the ancient religion"

in all its purity and brightness: and the image which it discloses will be the image of the Father, the Father of all the nations upon earth; and the super- scription, when we can read it again, will be, not in Judaea only, but in the languages of all the races of the world, the Word of God, revealed—where alone it can be revealed,—revealed in the heart of man.[14]

This Spinozist "heart of man" is, in Arnold's terms, *experience* and presages the scientific consideration of religion in terms of psychologi- cal phenomena. Arnold is firmly set in the same line as William James, as Lionel Trilling recognizes:

"God is real since he produces real effects" was the doctrine of William James. It is also the doctrine of Arnold, and had James not read Arnold, we might have said that Arnold had read James, for the earlier writer argued the pragmatic position.[15]

11. Ibid., pp. 14–15. My friend Günther Rimbach points out that Max Müller is at times practically quoting Schleiermacher, *Über die Religion* (1799).

12. This is the line of research followed by the notoriously dated Casaubon in *Middlemarch*.

13. Chaudhuri, *Scholar Extraordinary*, p. 32.

14. Ibid., pp. 50–51.

15. Trilling, *Matthew Arnold*, p. 319. William Robbins kindly calls my attention

James's *The Varieties of Religious Experience* (1902) indicates even in his title his psychological objectivity, and his text is of course the landmark in the field. The new science of religion has flourished as Müller predicted, both as comparative religion and as a field of psychology.

"The rules of critical scholarship" bound investigation of that most supremely important of documents, the Bible, to the study of Hebrew and hence to a new kind of linguistic and historical study of Judaism. The inheritors of the Judaic tradition, the present Jews of Europe, elicited accordingly a certain curiosity. And in the nineteenth century there grew up a new and fervent interest in the Jews, both scholarly and romantic. Simple people are not aware of the old allegations that God speaks in Hebrew, the *lingua Adamica*, and that the angels speak in Greek; they hear both God and the angels speaking in their own tongue. The more naive circles of Protestant Bible-reading cultures even forget that the Bible is a translation; one encounters from time to time variants of the story of the school principal in America's Bible Belt who would have no truck with foreign languages: "If English was good enough for Jesus Christ, it is good enough for me." The Higher Criticism at its most elementary level reminded the world that the Bible is a translation, of the Hebrew in the Old Testament, and that Jesus and his associates were Jews who spoke Aramaic, a language closely related to Hebrew, although the New Testament record, for certain historical reasons, is in Greek.

At the same time, there had developed a fresh cultural self-consciousness in Judaism itself, led chiefly by the great Moses Mendelssohn (1729–86). Having made his name first as one of the leading lights of the *Aufklärung* with deistical proofs of the existence of God and the immortality of the soul, he acclaimed the principles of Jesus but rejected miracles as religious proof; the Mosaic revelation on Sinai he considered not miraculous since it was public and historic.

---

to this passage, but he himself thinks Arnold is too persistently transcendental to be called pragmatist in his belief in the "power not ourselves" (*The Arnoldian Principle of Flexibility*, English Literary Studies [Victoria, B.C.: University of Victoria, 1979], p. 20). See also William Robbins, *The Ethical Idealism of Matthew Arnold* (London: William Heinemann, Ltd., 1959), pp. 87–88. I think, however, Arnold is pretty well guarded and scientific on the *power*. Whether it makes for righteousness is the most difficult and possibly transcendental point.

He seemed in fact to embody the view that Judaism sorted better
with reason than did Christianity. The combination of Jewish orthodoxy with intellect, sobriety, charity, and charm was too much for
some of the narrower Christians: the Swiss evangelical Johann Caspar
Lavater delivered him an ultimatum to either refute Christianity or
convert. Mendelssohn graciously sidestepped the challenge and continued to practice and recommend tolerance, which he pointed out
was more a Jewish virtue than a Christian one. He made a translation
of the Pentateuch into German, to serve Jews in the study of Hebrew
as well as to bring them into the European mainstream. He labored
tirelessly for civil rights for Jews and for peaceful coexistence. Once,
to speak to a "religious difficulty" in the German state schools, he
offered his own German translation of the Psalms to draw attention
to the joint legacy of synagogue and church.[16] (It was under somewhat
parallel circumstances of a "religious difficulty" that Matthew Arnold
was to offer his English version of the Book of Isaiah for a school text.)
Mendelssohn's devoted friend Lessing took him for a model of a
moral ideal in his influential play *Nathan the Wise* (1779), which declares the common moral ground of the great religions. In the play
the Jew Nathan tells the story of the man who had a wonderful ring,
which made its owner beloved of God and man. As he became old,
he was distressed to decide which one of his three beloved sons should
inherit the ring. He called in a jeweler, who made two exact replicas,
and when in due course the man died, each son received a ring and no
one knew who had the original. The point of this is that whether you
are Moslem or Jew or Christian you had better respect your two
brothers, for one of them may have the *real* thing. *Nathan the Wise*
did much to foster the new romantic Judaeophilia, such as that of
George Eliot. Mendelssohn's daughters Henriette and Dorothea were
among the influential Jewish hostesses of the Humboldt-Schleier-
macher circle shaping the new German humanism, and indeed the
Mendelssohnian principle of respect for Jewish culture made itself
part of the German movement. His own descendants exercised religious freedom so far as to be Christian, his grandson the composer
himself devoutly so. Isaac D'Israeli in England quarreled with his
synagogue about money and turned Anglican.

16. Alexander Altmann, *Moses Mendelssohn: A Biographical Study* (University: University of Alabama Press, 1973), p. 501. This book is thorough and authoritative.

Mendelssohn's movement for the study of Jewish culture, not yet in political or Zionist form, was supported by the wealthy Jews of Europe, notably Sir Moses Montefiore and the Rothschilds. Montefiore's father was an Italian Jewish merchant of London, and his mother one of a distinguished old family of Spanish Jews. He himself was devoutly orthodox, and he made tremendous contributions—financial, diplomatic, and spiritual—to the recovery of the Holy Land, and he lived to over a hundred, an example of piety and intellectual culture, well known throughout Europe and the Near East. The Montefiores were connected by marriages to the Rothschilds: Sir Moses had married a Rothschild kinswoman, and his niece Louisa Montefiore married Sir Anthony Rothschild. The Rothschilds were likewise orthodox and devout, and of course their wealth and power were famous throughout Christendom. In England, Sir Anthony's elder brother Lionel was elected M.P. in 1847 and was reelected repeatedly, but he was not permitted as a Jew to take his seat until in 1858 the enabling laws were passed. (Disraeli being Anglican had no such problem.)

There was a tradition of learning and piety among the Rothschilds and the Montefiores, particularly in the women. Louisa Montefiore, Lady de Rothschild, was learned, pious, and charming. While not a great Hebraist herself, she saw to it that her daughters Constance and Anne acquired Hebrew and grew up in humane learning and virtue. Their tutor and beloved friend was the distinguished Hebraist, biblical and talmudic scholar Marcus Kalisch (1825–85).[17] He was a rationalist, thoroughly familiar with continental scholarship, and had published a biblical commentary and a Hebrew grammar. This man, also tutor to Lionel's children, as lovable as he was learned, was an habitué of the Rothschild homes. Constance and Anne flourished in their scholarly regime and published jointly in 1870 *The History and Literature of the Israelites*. One of their Frankfurt cousins, Clementina de Rothschild, had composed *Letters to a Christian Friend on the Fundamental Truths of Judaism*, which was translated from the German and published in London in 1869.[18] Arnold met her in England in 1863, along with another female cousin from Vienna, and he writes: "What women these Jewesses are! with a *force* which seems to triple

17. *Dictionary of National Biography*, s.v. Marcus Kalisch.
18. Clementina de Rothschild, *Letters to a Christian Friend on the Fundamental Truths of Judaism*, (London: Simkin, Marshall, 1869), 93 pp.

that of the women of our Western and Northern races" (*Letters* I: 234, 243, 292). She lived but to the age of twenty (1845–65), and these "Dear Ellen" letters by this young saint represent devoted Jewish piety in sympathy if not in communion with Christianity. And the English Rothschilds remained devoutly orthodox while sympathetic and friendly to Anglicanism; they would on occasion attend Anglican services. The sublime example of this friendship is the recorded fact that the Bishop of Oxford, on a mission to perform confirmations in the neighborhood, was accommodated with his retinue at Aston Clinton, Sir Anthony's country estate.[19]

Sir Anthony's daughter Constance, being asked at her sixteenth birthday what she would like for a present, requested that she might have a school for her own. A school was accordingly built on the estate at Aston Clinton, and Constance and her sister Anne conscientiously ministered there to the village children. The government of England, though woefully laggard in establishing a state education, nevertheless administered a system of school inspection, and it was the assignment of Matthew Arnold to inspect the nonconformist schools, including this one at Aston Clinton, and the big Jewish Free School in Bell Lane in London, largely supported by the Rothschilds. Constance and Anne later contributed to the teaching in this school too. Arnold was much interested and impressed; he writes Lady de Rothschild once expressing "gratitude for the *ideas* your great Bell Lane Schools have awakened in me."[20] And we see him in later years making a warm and witty speech at a ceremonial dinner there (X: 245–26). Meantime, the intimacy with the Rothschilds was one of his greatest pleasures.

He enjoyed the domestic circle, and he enjoyed the *beau monde* at the Rothschild town houses, the house parties at Aston Clinton or at Gunnersbury, Lionel's estate, and at the more gorgeous if less tasteful Mentmore Towers, the Mayer Amschel Rothschild estate. The company included from time to time everybody who was anybody— Disraeli or Gladstone, Thackeray, Browning, Tennyson; when Lady de Rothschild was reading Stanley's *Lectures on the Jewish Church*, Arnold arranged for Stanley to be introduced. But his relationship

19. Frederic Morton, *The Rothschilds: A Family Portrait* (New York: Athenaeum, 1962), p. 156.
20. Letter quoted in *Prose* X: 538.

with Lady de Rothschild was more than the pleasure of society in general. Park Honan calls it love—of the chaste sort, and one feels he is right.[21] She was beautiful, elegant, and charming, and she was philanthropic and well read. Like Arnold, she made lists of books to be read, and mostly read them, and she kept notebooks of extracts from her reading, with her own comments, was deeply interested in the philosophy of religion, studied the New Testament sympathetically, and was steadfastly pious in Jewish religious observance. A leader in intellectual society and a distinguished hostess, she was at the same time something of a contemplative. Her daughter Constance writes: "She hated the fanaticism of extreme dogmatic belief, and she welcomed liberal thought in religion as in politics."[22] Her Quaker friends told her she could well be one of them in her habits and turn of mind. And the devoted Dr. Kalisch said of her: "She was in the world but not of it."[23] Such was Arnold's dear friend from about 1860 on. Disposed anyway to a sympathetic interest in Judaism, as was most of cultivated Europe, he had close to him this gracious example of Jewish liberal culture. When Arnold writes in the "Preface" to *Culture and Anarchy* that "the conception which cultivated and philosophical Jews now entertain of Christianity and its Founder, is probably destined to become the conception which Christians themselves will entertain,"[24] I think it is clear that this friendship had an effect on his religious thought.[25]

In his youth the world of Europe had been won by a great Jewish actress, Rachel; having seen her in London, Arnold was smitten, and his travels in France seem to be not unrelated to her theatrical itinerary. The experience is recorded in the three retrospective Rachel sonnets (1863) (521–24)—Rachel had died in 1858 at thirty-six. The

21. Park Honan, *Matthew Arnold: A Life* (New York: McGraw-Hill, 1981), p. 362.

22. Constance Battersea, *Lady de Rothschild: Extracts from Her Notebooks with a Preface by Her Daughter* (London: Arthur L. Humphries, 1912), p. 18.

23. Battersea, *Lady de Rothschild*, p. 19. See also Lucy Cohen, *Lady de Rothschild and Her Daughters* (London: John Murray, 1935).

24. V: 251. Arnold paraphrases a statement by Albert Réville.

25. Leslie Brisman makes a very interesting study of the way in which, on the other hand, a great modern Jewish thinker, Mordecai Kaplan, feels himself indebted to Arnold's *Literature and Dogma* ("The Romantic Faith and the Primitive Logia," *Arnoldian* 5 [Winter 1978]: 2–14).

third sonnet, flawed but interesting, best expresses his romantic feeling for her and her Jewishness, a Jewishness that permits an interest in his beloved à Kempis's *Imitation*!

> Sprung from the blood of Israel's scattered race,
>
> · · · · · · · · · · · · · · · · · ·
>
> · · · soothing with thy Christian strain forlorn,
> A-Kempis! her departing soul outworn,
> While by her bedside Hebrew rites have place—
>
> · · · · · · · · · · · · · · · · · ·
>
> In her, like us, there clashed contending powers,
> Germany, France, Christ, Moses, Athens, Rome.
> The strife, the mixture in her soul, are ours;
> Her genius and her glory are her own.

Jews and Judaism were becoming more conspicuous culturally. Felix Mendelssohn, friend of Queen Victoria and the Prince Consort, much beloved in England, carried the famous Jewish name although he was Christian; Arnold jots some passages in his *Note-Books* from an edition of his brilliant and charming letters translated into English and published in London in 1862 (*Note-Books* 16, 17, 476). Arnold's essay on Heine and his extensive work on Spinoza show him much interested in their Jewishness. Dickens's Fagin (*Oliver Twist*, 1837) and the stereotype of the Jewish old-clothes man and moneylender was being modified by sympathetic portrayals of Jews: Dickens's Riah in *Our Mutual Friend* (1864), Trollope's Brehgert in *The Way We Live Now* (1875), and in due course the idealized Judaism of George Eliot's *Daniel Deronda* (1876). The stream of travelers to the Near East increased steadily: Lady Hester Stanhope, Byron, Alexander Kinglake, Disraeli, Holman Hunt, Edward Lear, Trollope's George Bertram, Melville's Clarel. A knowledge of Hebrew became progressively more obviously essential to philological study, not merely to theologians. Arnold owned Gesenius's Hebrew Grammar and acquired in 1871 a polyglot Bible—Hebrew, Greek, Vulgate, Luther's German—and worked away at Hebrew from time to time (*Letters* II: 85–88). Constance Rothschild is recorded as having helped Gladstone with his Hebrew studies;[26] it is hard to imagine that

---

26. Cohen, *Lady de Rothschild and Her Daughters*, p. 252. Constance continued to educate English religionists: at age eighty-one she wrote of the Bishop of

Arnold in his familiar and affectionate association with the girls and their mother would not have been similarly helped. He mentions a debt to their teacher, Kalisch, for his Old Testament *Commentary* (VII: 186).

Besides Marcus Kalisch, there was another distinguished Jewish Hebraist in England: Emanuel Deutsch (1829–73),[27] born in Silesia, underwent a rigorous early rabbinical training from his uncle and then became proficient in the classics and theology at the University of Berlin. In 1855 he came to England as assistant in the library of the British Museum. He taught George Eliot Hebrew while she was preparing for *Daniel Deronda*, and he was himself the model for Mordecai in that book. The elegiac elements represent in part Deutsch's tragically early death from cancer. The *Quarterly Review* published a lengthy essay of his in 1867, "The Talmud,"[28] where he describes in an attractive and accessible way the origin and nature of this great collection of Hebrew lore. He graciously forestalls the charge of proselytizing with the Herderian statement that all literature, religious or otherwise, is part of humanity, and he takes a reverent but ecumenical attitude, just the attitude characteristic of Louisa de Rothschild. The Talmud, he explains, is a *corpus juris*, civil and penal, ecclesiastical and international, human and divine, and like the Bible it is a microcosm of heaven and earth. On the relationship of Christianity to the Talmud, he notes the striking parallels then coming into notice between the doctrines of Hillel and of Jesus, for instance, and he observes: "It is the glory of Christianity to have carried these golden germs [from Judaism] into the market of humanity."

It was just these "golden germs" of Judaism and how they shaped Christianity that was part of the new wave of historical study. How *Jewish* is Jesus? and how *Jewish* is Paul? were new concerns shaped by the new Historicism—and of supreme interest to Arnold. Arnold writes to Lady de Rothschild in 1867:

You will have read with pleasure the article on the Talmud in the *Quarterly*. I daresay you know the author, who is in the British Museum. The English

Norwich, "I think I have broadened the Bishop's mind and taught him a great deal about Judaism" (Cohen, p. 339).

27. See *Dictionary of National Biography*, s.v. Emanuel Deutsch, and *Literary Remains of E. Deutsch* (London: J. Murray, 1874).

28. Emanuel Deutsch, "The Talmud," *Quarterly Review* 123 (October 1867): 417–64.

religious world is reading the article with extraordinary avidity and interest. What most interests them, the abundance of Christian doctrine and dispositions present in Judaism toward the time of the Christian era, and such phenomena as Hallet's [editor's misreading of Hillel's] ownership of the Golden Rule, for instance—I knew already . . . . But the long extracts from the Talmud itself were quite fresh to me, and gave me huge satisfaction. It is curious that, though Indo-European, the English people is so constituted and trained that there is a thousand times more chance of bringing it to a more philosophical conception of religion than its present conception of Christianity as something utterly unique, isolated, and self-subsistent, through Judaism and its phenomena, than through Hellenism and its phenomena.

(*Letters* I: 434)

In "The Bishop and the Philosopher" he had referred to some Talmudic lore, which Super indicates is from a section of the Talmud translated into English and published in 1852 (III: 42–43, 417–18). Writing again to Lady de Rothschild in August 1868:

I met Mr. Deutsch the other day, and had a long talk with him about Hebraism and Hellenism. I was greatly interested in seeing him, and any diffidence I felt in talking about my crude speculations to such a *savant* was set at rest by his telling me that he was distinctly conscious, while writing his article on the Talmud, that if it had not been for what I had done he could not have written that article in the *Quarterly*, and the British public could not have read it.

(*Letters* I: 458–59)

One imagines Arnold's pleasure at the compliment and gathers, Deutsch's generosity aside, that Arnold was being felt as a force in the literary world.[29] And he was well disposed to consider Judaic elements in religious philosophy by reason of contemporary movements in philology and Bible scholarship, his whole disposition *touched with emotion*, we might say, the emotion of his affection for Louisa, Lady de Rothschild. Thomas Arnold had believed Jews should be barred from citizenship.[30]

29. Another reference to Deutsch occurs in the *Letters* (II: 59) when Arnold writes to his mother in 1871 that he had written to Deutsch to ask his opinion on the meaning of *Jerusalem*. The answer is presumably incorporated into *Literature and Dogma* (V: 180). See also V: 448, 471, 499.

30. A. P. Stanley, *Life of Thomas Arnold* (London: John Murray, 1904), p. 402.

England's consciousness of Judaism was extended perhaps most notably by the extraordinary and flamboyant Disraeli. It was early in his political career that he published the trilogy *Coningsby* (1844), *Sybil* (1845), and *Tancred* (1847), a curious amalgam of delightful wit, absurd romanticism, purple passages, and frequent distinguished insight. The phrases "Young England" and "The Two Nations," from *Coningsby* and *Sybil*, became household words. *Tancred*, though, which was not quite so successful, was the author's own favorite,[31] and it demonstrates a kind of thinking about religion not irrelevant to Arnold's. In writing *Tancred, or the New Crusade*, Disraeli turns away from immediate political involvement to a consideration of the springs of action and the basis of moral judgments, at the same time indulging himself in romantic atavistic daydreams of the Near East that he had loved so in his travels as a young man. In Robert Blake's biography of Disraeli, *Tancred* is not valued much except for the witty first part, about English society; the rest is considered rather pointless fantasy.[32] But even though the longer "Crusade" part reads like a script for a De Mille spectacular-musical comedy, it is nevertheless, as Richard Levine argues, to be explained by, and valued for, its religious philosophy. The essential idea is, as Levine puts it, that political and social problems multiply because English life is not motivated by any great principle rooted in the religion of the past; politics is stalemated for lack of a culture in tune with the Hebraeo-Christian church as Disraeli imagined it.[33]

Disraeli's hero, Tancred, Lord Montacute, on coming of age refuses to take his seat in parliament and, after some diverting delaying actions in English society, departs on his crusade to the Holy Land to elucidate "The Great Asian Mystery" and to gain divine direction for Europe. The wise Jew Sidonia supplies him with a knowledgeable courier, Baroni, and advises him that now with modern means of travel it is not hard to get to Jerusalem; the problem with such a pilgrimage is *what you are to do once you get there*. Tancred gets there in style, with his yacht and entourage. (Our old friend the Bishop of Jerusalem, creation of the Chevalier Bunsen as abetted by

31. Richard Levine, "Disraeli's *Tancred* and 'The Great Asian Mystery,' " *Nineteenth-Century Fiction* 22 (June 1967) : 71–85.
32. Robert Blake, *Disraeli* (New York: St. Martin's Press, 1967), pp. 214–20.
33. Levine, "Disraeli's *Tancred*," p. 71.

Thomas Arnold, is just offstage: Baroni reports that the chaplain of the party is well entertained in Jerusalem—"Mr. Bernard is with the English bishop, who is delighted to have an addition to his congregation, which is not much, consisting of his own family, the English and Prussian consuls, and five Jews, whom they have converted at twenty piastres a week; but I know they are going to strike for more wages" [bk. 3, chap. 3].) Tancred visits all the noteworthy places, meditates and prays, and the great problem of *what to do* is solved for him when he is kidnapped by a Bedouin sheik. This puts him in a convenient position for a subpilgrimage to Sinai, where he is vouchsafed a vision, monitored by the "Angel of Arabia" who, palm tree in hand, represents a kind of ecumenicism, "Arabia" being understood broadly as the land where the Divine deigned to commune with mankind, the land that saw the origin of Judaism, Christianity, and Islam, the former two of which have shaped the culture of the "flatnosed" Franks, or Europeans. Even "the life and property of England are protected by the laws of Sinai." The vision announces the "expiring attributes" of Christendom and Europe "in the throes of a great birth." (This is Disraeli's version of Carlyle's Phoenix and Arnold's "two worlds.") The new social and political world will be one of "theocratic equality." "The equality of man can only be accomplished by the sovereignity of God. The longing for fraternity can never be satisfied but under the sway of a common father" (bk. 4, chap. 3). Tancred ponders this oracle during the rest of his astonishing adventures here in "Arabia," where there once flourished—

the lawgiver of the time of the Pharaohs, whose laws are still obeyed; the monarch, whose reign has ceased for three thousand years, but whose wisdom is a proverb in all nations of the earth;[34] the teacher whose doctrines have modelled civilized Europe; the greatest of legislators, the greatest of administrators, and the greatest of reformers; what race, extinct or living can produce such men as these.

(bk. 3, chap. 1)

Moses, Solomon, Jesus—we can be sure Disraeli felt the blood of all of them in his veins, and their capacities likewise, for law, for administration, and for reform.

34. Disraeli, like most of his contemporaries, dismisses China. Remember Tennyson, "Better fifty years of Europe than a cycle of Cathay." Arnold was perhaps a little more guarded on this point, having read Herder's *Ideen*.

Disraeli may have felt *Tancred* to be a propagandist book or, rather, a *teaching* one; it popularizes just those areas of learning that concerned Arnold: the "Orientalism" of the Germans, comparative religion, the way in which intertestamentary Judaism had anticipated much of Christianity (one Jewish character is named for his great ancestor Hillel, as a sort of reminder). The religious concept of "Arabia" in *Tancred* is analogous to the field of the new philology, the Semitic languages—Hebrew, Aramaic, Arabic. Even the new idea of the Indo-European language group has a religious aspect: Sanskrit is the mother of our languages, just as India is the mother of religions. Both languages and religions, by their transformations (*Entwicklungen*) evolve into more and more refined and spiritualized forms. The Anglican Disraeli would not have objected to the modern term, "fulfilled Jew." In a wildly funny part of *Tancred*, the ebullient arch-intriguer Fakredeen proposes a political model of the Indo-European idea: England's game is up, for Ireland threatens, and the world grows weary of cottons, naturally preferring silk because it is more beautiful; Louis Philippe will take Windsor Castle; "Let the Queen of England collect a great fleet . . . and transfer the seat of her empire from London to Delhi. . . . Aberdeen and Sir Peel will never give her this advice; their habits are formed," but you, Tancred, must persuade her. It is all "quite practicable; for the only difficult part, the conquest of India which baffled Alexander, is all done!"[35]

In this "Arabia" where God has deigned to speak to man, Tancred encounters Eva, the daughter of the great Jewish banker in Jerusalem, an absolute paragon of a woman, young, supreme in beauty, intelligence, and learning, pious in her orthodox faith, but with Islamic and Christian connections. Their eventual union is nothing if not symbolic. It is Eva who enlarges Tancred's views of religion, in discourses in her own Arabian-Nights palace-garden in Bethany, or in Bedouin tents of great splendor, under Arabian stars. She discourses on the Eastern varieties of Christianity (till now conveniently ignored by European Christendom)—the Armenian, Abyssinian, Greek, Maronite, and Coptic; knowledge of the varieties in their practices, dogmas, and appreciation of Judaic elements is bound to put European Christianity in a somewhat new and objective light. From Eva's colorful kinsman, the Emir Fakredeen, who is a Maronite Christian but quite

35. Bk. 4, chap. 3. It is delightful to remember that some thirty years later Disraeli made the Queen "Empress of India."

as willing to turn Moslem, Jew, or pagan for his whim or his interest, as is his contemporary Bertie Stanhope in Barchester (Bertie had tried being a Jew for a while, as he tells Bishop Proudie), Tancred learns a zany kind of strongarm politics and a dream of a political unification of all the Eastern religious groups. There is even a "Young Syria," analogous to the Young England movement and the new feudalism. There figure also the volatile Druses (among whom Lady Hester Stanhope had so delighted to foment rebellion)—not quite Moslem, perhaps crypto-Christian. We even encounter, in the most extraordinary adventure of all, the Ansaray, a people who in an isolated part of Asia Minor have maintained the cult of the pagan gods, of Phoebus Apollo of Antioch, and of the still more ancient goddess the Syrian Venus (Robert Graves's "White Goddess"). The ruling queen of this people is Astarte, another absolute knockout of a girl. Fakredeen is smitten and is ready to turn pagan. Tancred finds himself quite at home, for as an aristocratic Englishman he has had, of course, a classical education. His cultural purview takes in Mount Sinai and Mount Calvary, and Mount Olympus as well. This too is absorbed into Tancred's emergent syncretic theocratic vision. The idea is not altogether alien to Arnold's concept of the common ground of Homer and the Bible.

The accomplished courier Baroni (who makes the famous observation: "The Arabs are only Jews upon horseback" [bk. 4, chap. 3]), in a rare slow place in the novel, takes an opportunity to tell his own story (bk. 3, chap. 11). He is Italian-Jewish, and his family represents a range of accomplishment that is reminiscent of the Italian Renaissance: one sister is an actress (this suggests Rachel), one a musician, a brother is a dancer, and so on. It appears to be suggested that the Jewish element promises well for the arts, for learning, and for general acuity. Throughout the novel Disraeli is as though preening himself on the contributions of his people to European culture. The Anglo-Saxon body-servants of Tancred, Freeman and Trueman, exhibit all through the crusade their true English dogged loyalty as well as a wonderfully funny degree of insular philistinism.

Bunsen had represented serious German "Orientalism"; "My purpose," he wrote, and Arnold copied this in his *Note-Book* for 1868, has been "to bring over into my own knowledge and into my own fatherland, the language and spirit of the solemn and distant East"

(*Note-Books* 83). *Tancred* is popular "Orientalism";[36] it is a *vulgarisation*, more or less *haute*, of the comparative approach to religion, the new appreciation of the Judaic elements in Christianity, the idea of the regeneration of Europe by Asia,[37] the extended cultural vision. Of course Arnold read it. Everyone read Disraeli. And Arnold would have been delighted with his wit and amused at his flamboyance (they were both of them *dandies* in their own different styles), and for the most part he approved his politics. He writes in French in 1878 recommending to Ernest Fontanes that he do an article on "Lord Beaconsfield homme de lettres"; he would find a rich, amusing and timely subject. Our liberals, adds Arnold, misunderstand and detest him, but— "je ne l'ai détesté, moi; il n'appartient pas à la famille de Périclès, bien sûr, mais je le préfère à la plupart de ses rivaux" (I have not detested him; he doesn't exactly belong to the family of Pericles, but I prefer him to most of his rivals). Arnold had sent Disraeli a copy of *Culture and Anarchy* and had been pleased with Disraeli's compliments (*Letters* II: 1, 26; *Note-Books* 25). The introduction to *Literature and Dogma* opens with a playful reference to Disraeli's latest novel, *Lothair* (1870) (VI: 164, 464), in which the hero is engaged in a comparative study of the religions of three attractive young English women—evangelical, High Anglican, and Roman Catholic, respectively—in order to make up his mind on marriage.

Religion is the great Victorian subject. The new German learning had occasioned innumerable traumatic crises of faith, and it also made for a ferment of interest at both the popular and learned level, an exhilarating new perspective and a new objectivity.

36. Edward Said's *Orientalism* is a curious study of this phenomenon (New York: Pantheon Books, 1978). He deplores its legacy of racism, but is overhard on nineteenth-century "Orientalists"; surely theirs was a necessary stage in understanding, and a stage considerably ahead of ignorance.
37. See Said, *Orientalism*, especially p. 115.

_____VIII _____

St. Paul and
_____ Protestantism _____

IN 1869, when Arnold turned to his specifically religious writings, he was forty-six years old, the age at which his father had died from a heart weakness understood to be hereditary. In January of the preceding year Arnold's infant son Basil had died, and then in November, his frail eldest son, Tommy. The *Note-Books* keep a touching record of the deaths, in among the injunctions from the *Imitation*, Psalms, and Bishop Wilson. He writes to his sister "K":

So much other "suffering in the flesh,"—the departure of youth, cares of many kinds, an almost painful anxiety about public matters,—to remind me that *the time past of our life may suffice us!* . . . and that we "should no longer live the rest of our time in the flesh to the lusts of man, but to the will of God." However different the interpretation we put on much of the facts and history of Christianity, we may unite in the bond of this call, which is true for all of us, and for me, above all, how full of meaning and warning.[1]

This year he writes to his mother on the anniversary of his father's birthday:

I think of the main part of what I have done, and am doing, as work which he would have approved and seen to be indispensable.

(*Letters* I: 455)

And again:

Tommy's death in particular was associated with several awakening and epoch-

_____

1. Letters I: 444. It was also in a letter to "K" that he had early described his sense of a kind of truth in common religious idiom: the pure in heart will "in some sense or other, see God" (*Letters* I: 38).

176

making things. The chapter for the day of his death was that great chapter, the 1st of Isaiah; the first Sunday after his death was Advent Sunday, with its glorious collect, and in the Epistle the passage which converted St. Augustine. All these things point to a new beginning, yet it may well be that I am near my end, as papa was at my age.

(Letters I: 433)

One should reread Isaiah 1 to recapture here what Arnold felt: the vision of the prophetic office, the passionate lament for religion misunderstood, and the idea of the saving "remnant." The epistle is from Romans 13, and the passage that converted St. Augustine is "Owe no man anything but to love one another: for he that loveth another hath fulfilled the law" (13:8). The collect echoes a line from the same epistle, to mark the beginning of Advent: "Put upon us the armour of light, now in the time of this mortal life." On the day of Tommy's death Arnold writes in his note-book, from the *Imitation*: *Leva igitur faciem tuam in caelum*—"Lift up your face to heaven!" and writes it again on the first anniversary of Tommy's death (*Note-Books* 87, 113). It is a time, it would seem, of dedication to that imperious "call," whatever might be—as he writes to "K"—the interpretation one puts on Christianity. A new beginning, then. This is not to say that Arnold puts aside his urbanity, his wit, and his zest for the world, but there is an aspect of him that must be called *devout*. Unquestionably the language of Christianity is full of powerful meaning for him. He will put on the armor of light as he sees it in a time of great darkness—as in Isaiah 1, or as according to Hosea, copied out in another note-book item of 1868, "My people are destroyed for lack of knowledge" (4:6). His mission is to supply the saving knowledge.

And yet this newly envisaged mission is a fulfillment at the same time of his immediately previous writings. The late written "Preface" (1869) to *Culture and Anarchy* is an impassioned and carefully argued plea for a cause dear to Thomas Arnold—the return of the Dissenters into a broadened Established Church. In this preface, Arnold insists on the original principle of breadth as set down by Hooker in the shaping of the Church of England, and he cites historical examples of the actual inclusiveness of the Church before the revolution. And *St. Paul and Protestantism* grows directly out of *Culture and Anarchy*.[2]

2. See R. H. Super, *The Time-Spirit of Matthew Arnold* (Ann Arbor: University of Michigan Press, 1970), p. 80.

Dissent is divisive and debilitating in the spiritual life of the nation, and Arnold now undertakes to show that the doctrinal differences that separate the Dissenters from the Church are in fact founded on a misreading of Scripture, especially of St. Paul. Renan has said Paul is now coming to the end of his reign of power, and Arnold denies this; it is rather that "the Protestantism which has so used and abused St. Paul is coming to an end" (VI: 5), and the real St. Paul is only beginning to come into power. Puritanism's very reason for existing, its dissent from the Established Church, is a certain interpretation of election and justification in Paul's writings, and this interpretation is misconceived. "What in St. Paul is secondary and subordinate, Puritanism has made primary and essential; what in St. Paul is figure and belongs to the sphere of feeling, Puritanism has transported into the sphere of intellect and made thesis and formula" (VI: 8). Calvinism and Methodism both err in this, Calvinism by exploiting man's fears, Methodism man's hopes.

He lays out his arguments strategically. The Calvinist idea of a personal God, in which the Calvinists would hold themselves much more holy than the liberals, Arnold undermines by quoting doctrine detailing His arrangements as "a machinery of convenants, conditions, bargains, and parties-contractors, such as could have proceeded from no one but the born Anglo-Saxon man of business" (VI: 14) — a God who makes deals, we would say now. This cannot be a God to compel devotion. For are not these Dissenters "talking about God just as if he were a man in the next street, whose proceedings Calvinism intimately knew and could give account of, could verify that account at any moment and enable us to verify it also?" (VI: 9). The language of doctrine is scientific language, and scientific language must be verifiable or nothing. And the doctrine, the creedal formularies, are quite unverifiable. Can we then as scientists, dealing only in the verifiable, talk about God at all? Science may admit the name of God

as a point in which the religious and the scientific sense may meet, as the least inadequate name for that universal order which the intellect feels after as a law and the heart feels after as a benefit. "We too" might the men of science say to the men of religion, . . . "would gladly say *God*, if only, the moment one says God, you would not pester one with your pretensions of knowing all about him." That *stream of tendency by which all things seek to fulfill the law of their being;* . . . science alone might willingly own for the fountain of all goodness, and call God.[3]

Since the errors are due to misinterpretation of texts: in this case, a mistaking of a subsidiary point for a main one, missing the logic and proportions of an argument, and mistaking of figurative language for scientific language, the whole matter of religion would seem to depend on linguistic skill, literary and scholarly skill. "No man, then, who knows nothing else, knows even his Bible." To know the Bible one needs to know history—the time, the place, the writer, the audience; one needs to know language and its conventions: Hebrew, Greek, and English. One must be able to recognize figurative language. The word *God* is not to the scientist nonsense but rather (in line with verifiable experience of our own and of a myriad other experiences recorded in the annals of humankind) a convenient short term, a fictive personification, of the processes in the universe. *God* is not exclusively a Christian entity, nor even a Judaeo-Christian one; this is quietly implied in these essays on St. Paul by mixing in evidence from old pagans, such as Epictetus, Ovid, and Socrates, along with evidence from the rabbis, Thomas à Kempis, and Bishop Wilson. Much of the Bible is poetry like Aeschylus, not science like Aristotle. The principle of Scripture is as the rabbis explained: *the Law speaks with the tongue of the children of men.*[4] Arnold cites this maxim as "the basis of all sane Biblical criticism" (VI: 21); he would understand it to mean that *figure* is the distinctive human mode, as Herder would have it. Things otherwise inexpressible, when they are presented in figures, become understandable to human beings, even vivid and irresistible, or "true." Paul, like Semitic people in general, "has a much juster sense of the true scope and limits of diction in religious

3. VI: 9–10. In the *Note-Books* for 1869, Arnold is as though trying out a sentence for this context: "However much more than this the heart may with propriety put into its language respecting God, this is as much as science can in strictness put there" (p. 108).

4. VI: 21. This maxim, I am told, is ubiquitous in the Talmud. Arnold might have got it from Deutsch (though it is not part of Deutsch's Talmud article in the *Quarterly*), from the Rothschilds, or from some German critic. My learned informant David Rosenberg tells me it is often used as an "out" in commentary, so as to say: you can't argue from this particular text because here God puts the ineffable in human terms which are inadequate to the subject.

deliverances than we have" (VI: 20); he *orientalizes* (this term comes, of course, out of the German Higher Criticism), which is to say he speaks in figures. Prosaic and obtuse Western readers may not have "enough tact for style" to comprehend. Paul also at times *judaizes*, using Jewish scriptures in a talismanic way, arbitrarily and uncritically, shaping his rhetoric to touch on the experience of his contemporary Jewish hearers; in our interpretation we must allow for this. And so Paul needs to be read critically; we need to determine at which points he orientalizes or judaizes—or just plain hellenizes. Throughout, Arnold insinuates the idea that Paul is human; he is a *writer*, an *author*, rather than an apostle or saint; he can be right at times, that is, wrong at other times. "The object of this treatise is not religious edification, but the true [or *literary*] criticism of a great and misunderstood author" (VI: 46). The implications for the importance of literary criticism in matters of religion are far-reaching.

Paul, read aright, reveals an essential message of *righteousness*. Right conduct is conformity to "the will of God," and the problem is "how to find the energy and power" to pursue righteousness in the face of all the imperious impulses of the flesh. Whatever it is that does have the force and power, Arnold defines as *Religion*—"Religion is that which binds and holds us to the practice of righteousness" (VI: 33). As Arnold traces Paul's argument in the Epistle to the Romans, he hews out a line which can in his terms be called *scientific*, or experiential; again and again what in experience exhibits the *binding* force and power is—a metaphorical injunction. When Paul speaks of the Messianic coming and the Kingdom, he intends them literally, and later Christianity has interpreted them to mean a life beyond the grave. But this

by no means spiritualised them. Paul, as his spiritual growth advanced, spiritualised them more and more; he came to think, in using them, more and more of a gradual inward transformation of the world by a conformity like Christ's to the will of God, than of a Messianic advent. Yet even then they are always second with him, and not first; the essence of saving grace is always to make us righteous.

(VI: 42–43)

The *spiritualizing* process, as Arnold calls it, is essentially the same thing that Rudolf Bultmann has called *demythologizing*;[5] Arnold's

5. Rudolf Bultmann, *Offenbarung und Heilsgeschehen* (Munich: A. Lempp,

term and strategy may be considered more precise and useful, at least in English. *Demythologize* is simply ambiguous: to reject or ignore the myth? To literalize it? But "spiritualization" of a myth can be grasped by anyone immediately, and according to the nature of our language recommends itself as an advance over those things less in virtue—the material, the mechanical, the literal. It even makes sense: an idea of a material literal kingdom in the sky after death is something the civilized mind rejects; a "spiritualized" idea of the Kingdom of God as a psychological state we might attain through exercise of the Christian virtues—*that* could have its attractions. That certain psychological states can indeed transform the world for us, Arnold argues, we all know, from our simple familiarity with being in love.

Paul's doctrine of necrosis is the main case in point. The miracle of the resurrection Paul believed in literally and also understood spiritually; the literal belief in it is not important, but the spiritual understanding is everything.[6] It means, spiritually, that we can "die to sin" on this earth and be as "reborn" to a new way of life on this earth, so different in quality that we sense a different relationship to time, indicated by feeling one with the *eternal*, a state so full of joy it needs the New Testament metaphors of heaven and the Kingdom of God to do it justice. "To popular religion the real Kingdom of God is the New Jerusalem with its jaspers and emeralds; righteousness and peace and joy are only the Kingdom of God figuratively. . . . *Science* [literary criticism] *exactly reverses this process* [my emphasis]. For science, the spiritual notion is the real one, the material the figurative." What is remarkable about Paul is that in spite of his time and place,

---

1941). The word in German is *Entmythologisierung*. For Bultmann's own treatment of the subject in English, see *Jesus Christ and Mythology* (New York: Scribners, 1958).

6. The *Note-Books* record a similar idea in Albert Réville that seems to have helped Arnold toward articulating his own: "L'enseignement mystique de S. Paul, d'après lequel en vertu de sa communion de vie morale avec le Christ, le fidèle souffrait, mourait, et ressuscitait spirituellement pour devenir en lui une nouvelle créature, fut de bonne heure incompris (Albert Réville, "Le Procès de Lucifer contre Jésus de Nazareth," *Revue moderne* 39 [December 1, 1866]: 460; *Notebooks* 48). (The mystic teaching of Paul, according to which the faithful, by virtue of his communion in the moral life of Christ, would suffer, die, and come to life spiritually, to become in himself a new creature, was from early times not understood.)

"he yet grasped the spiritual notion, if not exclusively and fully, yet firmly and predominantly" (VI: 55).

Throughout, Arnold returns to Paul's theme of experiential results: "righteousness, and peace, and joy in the holy spirit" (VI: 55 et passim), and we recognize in this joy and abundant life the answer to man's supreme need so poignantly expressed in Arnold's poetry. The *Note-Books* afford a gloss to this theme of joy—it was much in his meditations in the time of writing *St. Paul and Protestantism*, in the form of Old Testament passages.

He that keepeth the law, happy is he.

(Prov. 29: 18)

It is a joy to the just to do judgment.

(Prov. 21: 15)

The fruit of the righteous is a tree of life.

(Prov. 11: 30)

To the counsellors of peace is joy.

(Prov. 12: 20)

Let the heart of them rejoice that seek the Lord.

(Ps. 105: 3)

And he takes from Bishop Wilson:

To love God above all things is the sure principle of holiness, and the greatest happiness of a human soul.

and from the *Imitation*:

Habe bonam conscientiam et semper habebis laetitiam.

Have a good conscience and you will always have joy.

(*Note-Books* 67–70, 72, 77, 119)

The *Note-Books* endorse the earnest motivation of these prose writings—to mediate the Pauline joy to a new generation. Understanding this, we can understand Arnold's rejection of the Carlylean doctrine that man has no rights: "What Act of Legislature was there that thou shouldst be happy?" For Arnold, man's need of joy constitutes his right.

On all this interpretation of Paul, one may perhaps stand back a little and question whether literalism was as secondary to Paul as

Arnold argues. There is some strain, I think. Paul is probably more "fundamentalist" than Arnold would have him. It is hard to see, for instance, that the famous passage in the burial service, "the dead shall be raised incorruptible" (I Cor. 15–52), is not intended literally, and to call such a focal passage "secondary" seems pointless. Arnold rather high-handedly *cancels* certain aspects of Paul for the convenience of his argument. At times we can hear a tone of Thomas Arnold in the Chapel, taking advantage of a captive audience: if Paul's language "is to be turned into positive language, then it is the language into which we have translated it that translates it truly." I am right, in short. Occasionally the argument lapses: "This is Calvinism, and St. Paul undoubtedly falls into it!" Surely it verges on the absurd to consider the first-century apostle *guilty* of a sixteenth-century doctrine, and anyway the statement otherwise implies that the Calvinists read Paul *aright*—hardly Arnold's case! And somehow we cannot be very confident in Arnold when he declares, "Back rolled over the human soul the mist which the fires of Paul's spiritual genius had dispersed for a few short years" (VI: 70); it is hard to accept the rehabilitation of a man who copes with this mist with such limited success, for only "a few short years"! What is finally most impressive is Arnold's extreme anxiety to rehabilitate St. Paul; his heroic labor, the elaborateness of his argument, and what we must call his overingenuity, all witness the urgency of his desire to reconcile the Dissidents with the Church of England.

I do not think anyone could confidently claim that the Arnoldian prophecy has been fulfilled, that "the doctrine of Paul will arise out of the tomb where for centuries it has lain buried; it will edify the church of the future." But granting the overconfidence, and the overingenuity of *St. Paul and Protestantism*, there are certain ways in which Arnold's work anticipates the main lines of modern scholarship. First of all, there is now an enormous amount of Pauline scholarship and criticism in many schools and sects: Paul is a key figure, one way or another. Arnold's bent to consider Paul's Judaic elements is now central. It becomes a matter of discriminating among Judaisms. W. D. Davies traces how C. J. G. Montefiore interpreted Paul as part of Hellenistic or Diaspora Judaism, while Schweitzer takes him as Semitic or Palestinian Judaism; Davies himself explains that, with the new light on first-century Judaism that we have from the Dead Sea Scrolls and from the work of Gershom Sholem, Hellenistic Judaism and Palestinian Judaism can hardly be sharply differentiated.[7] Even rabbinical exegesis, which seems so "Semitic," was most probably inspired by Greek models: "Aristotle begat Akiba."[8] Wayne A. Meeks observes that "some Jews are discovering that, if they wish to understand what was going on in first-century Judaism, one of the authors they must read is Paul, while Christians are finding that, if they want to understand Paul, they must learn about Judaism."[9] Furthermore, Weeks writes,

There is a singular irony in the fact that the great system builders of Christian doctrine quarried their choicest propositions from Paul's letters, only to have later generations discover that they had thus built time-bombs into the structure that would, in a moment of crisis, bring the whole tower of syllogisms crashing down.[10]

This is precisely Arnold's argument, which Meeks has arrived at independently.

Arnold ends his Paul essays with an overview:

Of those who care for religion, the multitude of us want the materialism of the Apocalypse; the few want a vague religiosity. Science . . . will gradually serve to conquer the materialism of popular religion. The friends of vague religiosity, on the other hand, will be more and more taught by experience that a theology, a scientific appreciation of the facts of religion, is wanted for religion.

(V: 71)

Popular religion, it may seem now in 1983, depends as much as ever on the materialism of the Apocalypse; *science* has not reached as many as Arnold might have expected. But there has been, on the other hand, certainly a flourishing of the scientific study of religion, in psychology since William James, in anthropology with comparative religions, in literary scholarship with the close consideration of the

7. W. D. Davies, *Paul and Rabbinic Judaism* (London: Society for the Propagation of Christian Knowledge, 1948), pp. vii–ix. A reprint by Harper and Row (New York, 1967) has a new introduction, "Paul and Judaism Since Schweitzer," pp. vii–xv, which surveys the scholarship.

8. Davies, *Paul and Rabbinic Judaism*, p. viii.

9. Wayne A. Meeks, "The Christian Proteus," in *The Writings of St. Paul*, ed. Meeks (New York: Norton, 1972), p. 435.

10. Ibid., p. 437.

great religious texts. Most of what now professes to be "literary criticism" of the Bible, however, does in fact turn out to be, after all, sectarian and "interested" still. The Arnoldian invitation to literary study of the Old Testament and the New Testament still stands, largely unaccepted.[11]

For its own time, *St. Paul and Protestantism* is a rather heroic achievement, if only in that it is a literary analysis of Scripture. In the context of Arnold's own career, it is in this work that his theory of religion becomes articulated, and it is a theory that has to do with literature. I find its most interesting aspect to be the spectacle of Arnold drawing close to a theory of the centrality of figure or metaphor in matters of religion. He sums up: "Paul's figures our Puritans have taken literally, while for his central figure [necrosis] they have substituted another which is not his [jasper-and-emeralds heaven]. And his central idea [righteousness] they have turned into a figure [justification] and have let it almost disappear out of their mind" (VI: 69). This misreading all started early, when the philosophical turn of the Greeks and Romans was brought to bear on Paul's writings; Augustine, even, found "in Paul's eastern speech . . . the formal proposition of western dialectics," and so on until the time of the Protestant philistine "in whose slowly relaxing grasp we still lie" (VI: 70).

The ensuing sections of *St. Paul and Protestantism*, "Puritanism and the Church of England" and "Modern Dissent" (VI: 72–127), show Arnold's insistence on a developmental theory of church and religion, where his reading of Herder is once again conspicuous. Newman indeed had in his *Essay on the Development of Christian Doctrine* (1845) already asserted that a church, to be great, must have changed

11. For a statement of the poverty of real literary analysis of the Bible, see Robert Alter, "A Literary Approach to the Bible," *Commentary* 60 (December 1975) : 70–77. At present some distinguished scholars have broached the field auspiciously: Northrop Frye's *The Secular Scripture* (Cambridge: Harvard University Press, 1978) and his *Great Code: The Bible and Literature* (New York: Harcourt Brace Jovanovich, 1982); and Frank Kermode's *The Genesis of Secrecy* (Cambridge: Harvard University Press, 1979). Jean Starobinski supplies a brilliant structuralist analysis of the narrative of the Gadarene swine, "The Struggle with Legion: A Literary Analysis of Mark 5: 1–20," *New Literary History* 4 (1973) : 331–56. This was also published in French, in Starobinski, *Trois fureurs* (Paris: Gallimard, 1974), pp. 73–126, a longer version of an essay "Le Démoniaque de Gérasa . . ." previously published in *Analyse structurale et exégèse biblique*, ed. François Bovon (Neuchâtel: Delachaux et Niestlé, 1971), pp. 63–94.

much. But Newman, Arnold says, in turning this principle to support the claims of Rome, is using it "in a manner which, though ingenious, seems to us arbitrary and condemned by the idea itself" (VI: 88). Newman, that is, cannot really defend infallibility and other absolute claims with the relativistic idea of development. Bishop Butler's developmental insight is more just: "The Bible contains many truths as yet undiscovered" (VI: 88). The Anglican Church, is, of all churches, the one that has best adapted to the reality of historical process. "The historic Church of England, not existing for special opinions but proceeding by development" (VI: 85), has shown freedom of mind as regards doctrines, while the Puritans claim to have the true gospel for once and all, perfect and absolute. Hooker was well aware that Church doctrines are but "developments," and he laid down the principle of "providing room for growth and further change" (VI: 103) within the Church. Separation on points of doctrine is harmful to all parties, leading to the primacy of doctrine over morality, and tends to "a spirit of watchful jealousy" (VI: 116) rather than the Pauline fruits of the spirit: love and joy and peace. "The moral corruptions of Rome" were the real and valid ground for the separation of the Reformation. There is no real reason against an ultimate "general union of Christendom" (VI: 107). John Tillotson's proposals for comprehension, laid out in 1689, follow the broad principles of the English Reformation, as the liturgy itself does, avowedly being "such a liturgy as neither Romanist nor Protestant could justly except against" (VI: 80). The Evangelical party within the Church of England has a great advantage in not separating, and by conforming it does "homage to an ideal of Christianity which is larger, higher, and better" than that of any party within or without the Establishment (VI: 109). Finally it is as though Arnold sees the Church of England as a saving *Kette der Bildung*: "It is the one Protestant Church which maintained connexion with the past" (*Letters* II:151), and for this reason it holds the best promise for the future.

These essays are absolutely peppered with the word *development*, a clue to their Herderian base. His own interpretation of Paul, Arnold says, is also only a stage of development, belonging to the *Zeitgeist*. This *Zeitgeist* of Arnold's, the "time-spirit," is a concept that grows out of Herderian Historicism to represent the uniqueness of particular phases of history. Early, in the *Letters to Clough*, Arnold feels the particular *Zeitgeist* as something malign—"These are damned times"

(*Clough* 111). Here, in the religious books, it has come to be simply the way of things in one's own time and place, and one accepts it and acts in accord with it.[12] And so Arnold says his present interpretation of Paul is "a product of nature, which has grown to be what it is and which will grow more . . . ; which will be *developed* [Arnold's emphasis], in short, farther, just in like manner as it has reached its present stage by development." Ostensibly the Puritans do not accept such a principle, but in truth, "the better minds among Puritans try instinctively to give some fresh turn or development" to their absolute dogmas; they "begin to feel the irresistible breath of the Zeit-Geist" (VI: 111–12, 113). The essence of Christianity, which survives the *Zeitgeist*, he defines as "grace and peace by the annulment of our ordinary self through the mildness and sweet reasonableness of Jesus Christ" (VI: 121), and the German idea of *Bildung*, which he recurs to here (VI: 125), seems to connect naturally with the Christian idea of "perfection" toward which our new or un-ordinary self progresses. One of his footnotes to *St. Paul and Protestantism* concludes with Goethe: "Religion itself, like time, like life and knowledge, is engaged in a constant process of advance and evolution."[13]

12. It is Fraser Neiman who points out the change in Arnold's attitude to the *Zeitgeist* ("The Zeitgeist of Matthew Arnold," *Publications of the Modern Language Association* 72 [December 1957]: 977–96). Neiman is one of the first to note Arnold's concern with history, and his essay is very fresh and suggestive. Neiman doubts the consistency of Arnold's historical thought, however, and therefore misreads the later sense of *Zeitgeist* as an "aspect of the eternal." The *Zeitgeist* is precisely what is *variable*.

13. "Endowments," VI: 138. The passage is in the *Note-Books*, p. 85.

_____ *Literature and Dogma* _____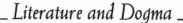

IN considering *Literature and Dogma: An Essay Towards a Better Apprehension of the Bible*, we do well to keep in mind Arnold's own epigraphs for the work—banners, as it were, to hold aloft as the investigation, the *essay*, proceeds. First he sets down Psalm 32: 19 in the Vulgate: "O quam magna multitudo dulcedinis Tuae, Domine, quam abscondisti timentibus Te!" (Oh, how great is thy goodness, which thou hast laid up for them that fear thee! [King James Version]). Then he puts a favorite passage from Senancour, in French, followed by his own translation with a peculiar variant:

La tendance à l'ordre ne peut-elle faire une partie essentielle de nos inclinations, de notre instinct, comme la tendance à la conservation, à la reproduction?

May not the tendency to *conduct* [Arnold's emphasis] form an essential part of our inclinations, of our instinct, like the tendency to self-preservation, to the reproduction of the species?

This passage, frequent in the *Note-Books*, he used twice before in his prose,[1] where he translates *ordre* in the usual way as *order*. I think it is not too much to say that now in his thinking *conduct* has become the great principle of *order* in human affairs; it is *conduct*—always understood as *controlled* conduct—that reduces chaos, that rescues us from a capricious universe, *conduct* that represents in the Psalm above the fear of the Lord. In this way Senancour, amended as it

1. As Super notes, in 1866, 1867, 1868, 1869, 1873, 1875, and 1877. VI: 459n. and V: 83, 297.

were by Arnold's new insight, his new "translation," endorses this central work. Next is a passage from Bishop Butler's *Analogy of Religion* that anticipates German developmentalism and the principles of the Higher Criticism:

And as it is owned the whole scheme of Scripture is not yet understood, so, if it ever comes to be understood, it must be in the same way as natural knowledge is come at: by the continuance and progress of learning and liberty, and by particular persons attending to, comparing, and pursuing intimations scattered up and down it.

(VI: 140)

We recognize Arnold here as one of the many "particular persons," by scholarship developing the understanding of the Bible. Then comes Edmund Burke, in an arresting statement which also anticipates German developmentalism, most specifically the concept of the *Zeitgeist*.

If a great change is to be made, the minds of men will be fitted to it, the general opinions and feelings will draw that way. Every fear, every hope, will forward it; and then they, who persist in opposing this mighty current, will appear rather to resist the decrees of Providence itself, than the mere designs of men. They will not be resolute and firm, but perverse and obstinate.

(VI: 140)

The implication is that Arnold moves with the Time-Spirit as with Providence, and how pleased he must have been to find just the right terms for his enemies: perverse and obstinate! And so Arnold proceeds, with the Psalm to suggest the rewards of the undertaking, with Obermann as a memento of the desolation and wistfulness of his youth, and then—ingeniously—two great insights from Englishmen which happen to epitomize a whole movement of German thought. We must recognize Arnold's own insight in discovering English anticipations of German theory, and his tact in calling on comfortably English witnesses rather than the distrusted, heterodox Germans.

In his study of Paul, Arnold had claimed the misreading of Scripture as the reason for the grave error of the Dissenters; now he is ready to apply the idea on a larger scale, to the Bible as a whole and to religion in general. Accordingly, "Religion Given," the first chapter of *Literature and Dogma*, starts with a reference to *St. Paul and Protestantism* and moves immediately to the largest issue, the "supreme term"—*God*. The term, associated with *morality* and *perfection*, is "by no means a term of science or exact knowledge, but a term of poetry and eloquence, a term *thrown out,* so to speak, at a not fully grasped object of the speaker's consciousness, a *literary* term, in short; and mankind mean different things by it as their consciousness differs" (VI: 171). He then moves carefully to try to determine "the common substratum of idea" in the varied uses of the word. Etymologically it seems to suggest something "shining" or "brilliant"; Luther took it to mean "good." There is also the abstract theological sense,

which has all the outward appearances, at any rate, of great precision,— God is an infinite and eternal substance, and at the same time a person, the great first cause, the moral and intelligent governor of the universe; Jesus Christ consubstantial with him; and the Holy Ghost a person proceeding from the other two.

(VI: 172)

It is very hard to see, he goes on, how this sense proceeds, as is claimed, from the Bible, and he says there are many now who feel that if this does proceed from the Bible, and if our religion proceeds from the Bible, then we shall have to give up the Bible.

But it cannot be hard, he argues, to think about religion; "plain" men do it. "For the object of religion is *conduct,*" and it is easy for everyone to grasp the idea of it—although it may be very hard to follow the right line of conduct.

And certainly we need not go far about to prove that conduct, or "righteousness," which is the object of religion [the field of concern of religion, we might say] is in a special manner the object of Bible-religion. The word "righteousness" is the master word of the Old Testament. *Keep judgment and do righteousness! Cease to do evil, learn to do well!* . . . Offer the sacrifice, not of victims and ceremonies, . . . but: Offer the sacrifice of *righteousness!* The great concern of the New Testament is likewise righteousness, . . . by the means of Jesus Christ. . . . *Let every one that nameth the name of Christ depart from iniquity!*[2]

It will be objected, Arnold says, that this is morality, not religion; religion is supposed to be connected with propositions about the Godhead of the Eternal Son, and so on.

Religion, however, means simply either a binding to righteousness, or else a

2. VI: 175; Isaiah 56: 1, 1: 16–17; Psalms 4: 5; 2 Timothy 2: 19.

serious attending to righteousness and dwelling upon it. . . . And the antithesis between *ethical* and *religious* is thus quite a false one.

(VI: 176)

The words *ethical* and *religious* both mean practical, *religious* meaning it in a higher degree, and the right antithesis to both is *theoretical*. Propositions about the Godhead of the Eternal Son, and so on, are theoretical, and need not necessarily concern us. The difference of degree between *morality* and *religion*, "if we follow the intention of human thought and human language in the use of the word," is that religion is "ethics heightened, enkindled, lit up by feeling . . . , *morality touched by emotion*" (VI: 176).

This often quoted definition of Arnold's may, I propose, be taken with a little grace. Since he himself had so early and so clearly recognized the fictive and provisional quality of language, of such terms as "Affections, Instincts, Principles, and Powers, Impulse and Reason, Freedom and Control," having grown impatient with Butler for taking terms as realities, and since he had then posited "man's one nature" that "queen-like sits alone / Centred in majestic unity" (42), we may I think reassociate *morality* and *emotion*. We may dismiss the objectionable overtones of *emotion* as of something soft and undisciplined, implying the surrender of intellect, and think rather of morality *moved, motivated*, or *put into action* and take religion to be morality engaging us at a great depth of being. This matter of degree then becomes, in the case of religion, a greater degree of engagement.

The term *religion*, he notes, is often used very broadly indeed, for "all high thought and feeling . . . such as in that saying of Goethe: 'He who has art and science, has also religion' " (VI: 176–77). But the word *religion* is just not ordinarily used in Goethe's way, and meanings evaporate (he implies) if we do not "use words as mankind generally use them" (VI: 177). To isolate, as it were, *religion*, let us set out examples of texts. Arnold puts all these in paragraphs, but I would like, in his experimental spirit, to set forth the exhibit in columns.[3]

By the dispensation of Providence to mankind, goodness gives men most satisfaction.	The path of the just is as a shining light which shineth more and more unto the perfect day.
(Quintilian)	(Prov. 4: 18)

3. All these pairs are to be found in *Prose*, VI: 177–78, 189–90, 183–95, 203–4.

Hold off from sensuality, for if you
    have given yourself up to it, you
    will find yourself unable to think
    of anything else.
               (Cicero)

Blessed are the pure in heart, for
    they shall see God.
           (Matt. 5: 8)

We all want to live honestly, but
    cannot.
          (Greek proverb)

O wretched man that I am, who
    shall deliver me from the body of
    death!
           (Rom. 7: 24)

The earth is an oblate spheroid.
           (Science)

Earth, the mighty mother of mankind.
         (Wordsworth)

The power that makes for . . .
    righteousness.

God.

Trust in the law of conduct.

Trust in God.

Happiness comes from conduct.

Delight in the Eternal.

To depart from Evil.

The fear of the Eternal.

Whoso keepeth the commandment
    keepeth his own soul.
         (Prov. 19: 16)

My soul, wait thou only upon God,
    for of him cometh salvation!
         (Ps. 57: 5,1)

Bind them [the laws of righteous-
    ness] continually upon thine heart,
    and tie them about thy neck!⁴
         (Prov. 6: 21)

Have I not remembered Thee on
    my bed, and thought of Thee when
    I was waking?
         (Ps. 58: 6)

Take thought for your permanent,
    not your momentary, well-being.
       (Commonplace adage)

Honor the Eternal, not doing thy
    own ways, nor finding thine own
    pleasure, nor speaking thine
    own words.
         (Isa. 58: 13)

Conduct brings happiness.

Sion heard of it and rejoiced,
    and the daughters of Judah were
    glad, because of thy judgments,
    O Eternal!
         (Ps. 97: 8)

4. This is in the literal column because of those orthodox Jews who take it
literally and bind phylacteries to themselves.

Righteousness tendeth to life.	Blessed is the man whose delight is in the law of the Eternal; his leaf shall not wither, and whatsoever he doeth, it shall prosper. (Ps. 1:3)
The more a man walks in this way of righteousness, the more he feels himself borne by a power not his own. (Arnold)	Not by might and not by power, but by my spirit, saith the Eternal. (Zech. 4:6)
Man feels he is far from fulfilling or even perceiving the law of his being. (Arnold)	I am a stranger upon earth, Oh, hide not thy commandments from me. (Ps. 119:19, Book of Common Prayer)

This is a small sampling of Arnold's immense and to my mind eloquent exhibit, to which may be added pairs from earlier essays and from later. Any of us in the least degree used to literary analysis will recognize in the morality column the more-or-less literal mode and in the religion column the metaphorical. Such a table neglects the art of Arnold's strategy: he starts, for instance, with old pagan wisdom for the literal, and the poetry of the Old Testament and New Testament for the metaphorical—this will carry the religionists along in sympathy. Then he takes a prosy Old Testament Proverb for the literal, and a poetic passage from a Psalm for the metaphorical—this breaks the pattern that all the Bible is religious. Then he takes a scientific statement (earth an oblate spheroid) and sets it against Wordsworth's metaphor (earth the mighty mother), implying that metaphor is the element common to religion and poetry. And then further he will take metaphorical passages from Homer or from Sophocles that now, if you have followed his argument, present themselves as religion itself. But the baldness of my table exposes, I think, his method as scientific, experimental. He invites us to test on our psyches the effects of group A as compared to the effects of group B. And I think we are obliged to recognize the emotive power of B, in the latinate sense of *emoveo*, having the power to *dislodge*, to *move*, to *change* men; to recognize that all group B items are metaphorical;

to analyze them as metaphor; to consider that the pretense or approximation of metaphor carries more meaning than the literal; to realize that these expressions do not lose in power when we realize they are "not true," but they gain in power rather, and that to misunderstand these metaphors as literal or scientific statement is to miss the power and the point; to speculate that it is the metaphor itself that is the *motor*, the functional element; to speculate that metaphor is of the essence in this religious mode, which differs in intensity from the scientific mode to such an enormous extent that it is not a difference in degree but in kind.

In broaching thus the phenomenology of metaphor, Arnold demonstrates what he has claimed to be the relevance of literary criticism in matters of religion. He continues here to consider just how these "religious" statements work; "How does one get to feel much about any matter whatsoever?"

By dwelling upon it, by staying our thoughts upon it, by having it perpetually in our mind.

(VI: 179)

Then he indulges himself in some speculative etymology, that *mind*, *memory*, *remain*, perhaps *man* all come from the notion of attention span, which the animals do not have. It has been speculated, in our time, that it is language itself that gives man his power of attention; Arnold's etymologies may be questionable, but his notion is perfectly respectable. He continues:

The idea of humanity, of intelligence, of looking before and after, of raising oneself out of the flux of things, rest[s] upon the idea of steadying oneself, concentrating oneself, making order in the chaos of one's impressions, by attending to one impression rather than the other. . . . [Hence has come the idea] of a whole self as opposed to a partial self, a best self to an inferior self, to a momentary self a permanent self requiring the restraint of impulses a man would naturally have indulged;—because by *attending* to his life, man found it had a scope beyond the wants of the present moment. Suppose it was so; then the first man who, as "a being," comparatively, "of a large discourse, looking before and after," controlled the native, instantaneous, mechanical impulses . . . , had morality revealed to him.

(VI: 179)

The more men attend to the momentary self the more they are distracted from morality.

The Hebrew culture that produced the Bible, Arnold argues, was a culture not much occupied with that one-fourth of our being which is not conduct, that one-fourth which embraces theory, or dogma. The Hebrews were wrapped up, rather, with experience.

The Old Testament . . . is filled with the word and thought of righteousness. "In the way of righteousness is life. . . . He that keepeth the law, happy is he; its ways are ways of pleasantness, and all its paths are peace."[5]

Such a people, so long and deeply engaged with righteousness, less distracted from it than the generality of mankind, could not have failed to be struck by "the very great part in righteousness which belongs, we may say, to *not ourselves*" (VI: 181). It was not we who made our constitutions as they are, or provided that happiness follows moral conduct, or that right conduct should give such satisfaction to the doer, as good art to the poet or painter, or food to the hungry. Nor do we have complete power to deal with the nature of things and of ourselves. We frequently cannot understand our own motivations or do what we intend to do. This *not ourselves* impressed the Hebrews with awe, as we (Wordsworthians as we are) are impressed with some mighty natural object. This *"not ourselves* which weighed upon the mind of Israel, and engaged its awe, was the *not ourselves* by which we get the sense for *righteousness*, and whence we find the help to do right" (VI: 182).

Hence the Mosaic denomination of God: the Eternal. Arnold has in mind here the Hebrew tetragrammaton that we spell out as *Jehovah*, or *Jahve*, and the Jews pronounce "Adonai." In the famous passage in Exodus (3: 14) where Moses asks the name of God, the answer is the untranslatable peculiar progressive nontemporal first-person-singular form of the verb *to be*, which can be glossed: I am what has been being, what is being, and what will be being. Jerome translates it as *ero quid ero*, Coleridge as the "Infinite I AM," Martin Buber as "I will be as I will be"; Arnold takes it as something like "I am what continues to go on," or "I am what endures"—and so the "Eternal" is Arnold's preferred name of God. Super notes Arnold had observed its use in the Jewish schools he visited; it is also standard

5. VI: 180; Proverbs 29: 18, 3: 17; Baruch 3: 13.

in the French Protestant Bibles.[6] This *I am*, as it is usually referred to in English, would in fact be an abstract or scientific term, then, like the force-not-ourselves, or the stream-of-tendency. Interestingly, it comes from the mouth of God himself in one of his most anthropoid phases, when he has to argue with the reluctant Moses about his vocation. In the history of thought, it represents, we may say, a tremendous Mosaic insight, even at that time helping man to discover how anthropomorphic he is. For the rest, "Israel personified . . . his Eternal, for he was strongly moved, he was an orator and a poet" (VI: 184); and God is a father, a shepherd, a personage who walks in the cool of the evening, who submits to Moses' complaints and is susceptible to Moses' flattery; he is also a pillar of fire, a voice from a whirlwind, a fortress, a reaper, a winnower, a plumb-line, a refiner's fire. Arnold's refrain, "Israel was a poet," embodies the Herderian principle of *Das Volk dichtet*: the common people, the folk, make poetry. According to Goethe's maxim, frequently quoted throughout *Literature and Dogma*, like a leitmotiv, *Man never knows how anthropomorphic he is* (VI: 184 et passim), the Hebrew poet tends to "represent everything under his own figure" without stopping to think whether it is a figure. The figure of Abraham as the "friend of God" represents a stage in this developing idea of the Eternal, and the Hebrews, by dwelling on the idea of righteousness and the not-ourselves, conceive of the Eternal as an unchangeable power that makes for righteousness. This did not come out of metaphysical speculation, or ratiocination, but out of feeling and experience.

Even Goethe, who understood better than anyone else the anthropomorphosizing impulse as a fiction-making or a symbol-making function—Goethe whom Arnold recognized far back in his first Obermann poem as very *nice* in his own anthropomorphs—

> Neither made man too much a God,
> Nor God too much a man.
> (138)

Goethe tells us, Arnold says, "that the words which rose naturally to his lips, when he stood on the top of the Brocken," awed by the grandeur of the world and

---

6. VI: 472; and Arnold's "Preface to Isaiah," VII: 59.

the grandeur of the sense of its all being *not ourselves*, were the words of the Psalmist: "Lord, what is man, that thou mindest him, or the son of man, that thou makest account of him?" [7]

Arnold appears to be saying that even so sophisticated a mind as Goethe's has *use* for the anthropomorphic fiction.

For Israel, Arnold says, the need to praise the *not ourselves* came from gratitude for righteousness, and so Israel posited the *Eternal*. "Righteousness, order, conduct, is for Israel at once the source of all man's happiness, and at the same time the very essence of *The Eternal*" (VI: 185). The figures Israel uses, Arnold goes on, all represent aspects of his experience of God. God is a father, for that figure presents graphically "this authoritative but yet tender and protecting relation" (VI: 185). "The Lord our God is one Lord," the monotheistic idea, is simply *seriousness*, the singleness (I add) of the standard of righteousness. And because Israel had no talent for abstract reasoning (to lead him astray) he consistently speaks of God with great propriety: "The high and lofty One that inhabiteth eternity, whose name is holy," instead of theology's "license of affirmation" (*insane* license of affirmation, he had said earlier) that God is "the moral and intelligent Governor of the universe" (VI: 187; VI: 152). The arrogance of theologians contrasts with the propriety of Job: "Lo, these are fringes of his ways; but how little a portion is heard of him." Israel "knew from thankful experience the *not ourselves* which makes for righteousness, and knew how little we know about God besides" (VI: 189). If the object of consciousness is not one to be fully grasped, the language of figure will work better than the language of literal fact and science. The language of science will fall short.

In popular religion, we find definitions that pretend to be scientific but are not: "A Personal First Cause, the moral and intelligent Governor of the Universe," and so on. They are clearly not scientific in that they are not verifiable. The *not ourselves* has been shown to be verifiable in the experience of us all; just so with "the stream of tendency." "That all things seem to us to have what we call a law of their being, and tend to fulfil it, is certain and admitted" (VI: 190).

7. VI: 184; Psalms 144: 3. This version is neither the King James Version nor the Book of Common Prayer.

If we call this "stream of tendency" God we can agree we are talking about an admitted reality.

The elements of this second of Arnold's definitions of God are various. "Stream of tendency" seems to come from Wordsworth, as Helen Darbishire points out. In The $Excursion$, one receives

> Fresh power to commune with the invisible world,
> And hear the mighty stream of tendency.[8]

Yet this expression seems so much the idiom of the German romantics that one wonders whether Wordsworth retained it from his German sojourn, or from Coleridge, and someone may yet find its prototype in Herder or Goethe. The "law of being" recalls Thomistic quiddity. But the idea may have come to Arnold through Herder's $Ideen$. "Man is organized toward" certain capacities, toward reason, art, and language, and "man is developed toward" humanity and religion—these are Herder's vision of the law of man's being, his $Humanität$, which he tends to fulfill. In fact Arnold's fondness for the verb $tend$ suggests the idea of process, the $becoming$, which distinguishes $Bildung$ itself. "The law of being" recalls also a passage from Marcus Aurelius that Arnold had quoted: the man who does a service to another is properly fulfilling the law of his being, "like a vine which has produced grapes, and seeks for nothing more after it has once produced its proper fruit." One is then only doing something "conformable to [one's] nature" and seeks no reward, no more than "if the eye demanded a recompense for seeing, or the feet for walking" (III: 148).

The notion of this stream of tendency, Arnold says, does come into the common understanding of the term God:

> To please God, to serve God, to obey God's will, means to follow a law of things which is found in conscience. . . . When St. Paul says, that our business is "to serve the spirit of God," . . . and when Epictetus says: "What do I want? —to acquaint myself with the natural order of things and comply with it," they both mean . . . we should obey a tendency, which is not $ourselves$, but which appears in our consciousness, by which things fulfil the real law of their being.
>
> (VI: 190–91)

And this gives joy. Hence, the Psalmist exclaims: "The statutes of the Eternal rejoice the heart" (19: 8). "God or $Eternal$ is here, at bottom

8. Quoted by Super, $Prose$ VI: 423.

but a deeply moved way of saying, 'the power that makes for . . . righteousness.' " *God,* insofar as it is a personification, an anthropomorph, we may adjudge a metaphor, a *moved* and *moving* locution. Arnold likes *Eternal* as a variant because it expresses *qualities* and calls to mind Moses' *J am.* But both are personification of something that is not a person. "With Israel, *religion* replaced *morality*" (VI: 194), and Israel functioned in *religion;* for, once one moves in the sphere of those joyful metaphors, one does not need literal moral injunctions.

It must be emphasized that Arnold's own definitions of God come out of ratiocination. They are arrived at by close linguistic and psychological considerations. Tennyson was repulsed: "Matthew Arnold —'Something outside of us that makes for righteousness'—ugh!"[9] But the point about them is precisely that—ugh. The language of science is a barren thing for "a not fully grasped object of consciousness." It is the metaphor that enables us to grasp the object to some extent, that has the power to "bind" us to morality. The value of the Arnold definitions is that they are articles to which a man of science can subscribe, and Arnold says they are all in literal fact the religious man need subscribe to, and there is no discrepancy between these minimal scientific statements on the nature of God and either the religious life or the devout reading of the Bible. This book is not addressed to mystics like Newman, it is addressed to rationalists. The definitions, by their effort to eschew figure, help us moreover to recognize figure when we see it and to assess its great function.

Arnold dismisses the old deist distinction between *natural* religion and *revealed* religion. For the two, he has labored to show, are the same; the real antithesis to *natural/revealed* is *invented/artificial—* theory, that is, theology, dogma. That "real germ of religious consciousness . . . out of which sprang Israel's name for God, . . . which came to be clothed upon, in time, with a mighty growth of poetry and tradition, was a consciousness of the *not ourselves which makes for righteousness.*" One discovers this by studying the Bible "with the tact which letters, surely, alone can give. For the thing turns upon

9. William Allingham, *A Diary* (London: Macmillan, 1907), August 8, 1880, p. 288. Quoted by Christopher Ricks, *Tennyson* (New York: Macmillan, 1972), p. 277. Tennyson's own witty definition of God should be better known: "The general English view of God is as of an immeasurable clergyman" (quoted by Douglas Bush, *Matthew Arnold* [New York: Macmillan, 1971], p. 174).

understanding the manner in which men have thought, their way of using words and what they mean by them" (VI: 196). This is the key passage in *Literature and Dogma;* it reveals the connections between Arnold's wide interests: social, literary critical, and religious. He is revalidating the Bible by means of literary criticism for a society in danger of losing it, taking into account "the manner in which men have thought" (his past tense here bears out the principle that customs *do* change) —history, psychology—and "their way of using words and what they mean by them"—language, its conventions and multiple translations. *Literature and Dogma* is an extensive piece of literary criticism, perhaps, after all, his finest. The first chapter of *Literature and Dogma* is, in short, a statement of principles for reading the Bible, principles that are thoroughly and consistently *humanist* in the sense of *nonsupernaturalist.*

In the very small body of criticism of *Literature and Dogma,* the concern seems to have been to determine the degree or kind of Arnold's Christianity as if it were somehow debatable. Newman had blandly asked concerning Thomas Arnold, "But is he a Christian?" thereby arousing Thomas Arnold to anger.[10] But it was a question to be asked. Newman could see the inconsistencies in Thomas Arnold's position. If he would have asked the question concerning Matthew Arnold, assuming that Christianity must be supernaturalist, the answer would have been simply no. The best criticisms of *Literature and Dogma*—Basil Willey's, Dorothea Krook's, A. O. J. Cockshut's, and R. H. Super's—make this abundantly clear;[11] Arnold can be called Christian only insofar as one allows nonsupernatural Christianity as possible. He calls for, in this first chapter, "Religion Given," a nonsupernaturalist reading of the Bible. Here is the challenge:

to take their fact of experience [the experiential religion of Israel as he has described it], to keep it steadily for our basis in using their language [the

10. See Arnold Whitridge, *Dr. Arnold of Rugby* (New York: Henry Holt and Co., 1928), p. 170.

11. Basil Willey, "Matthew Arnold," chap. 10 of *Nineteenth Century Studies* (London: Chatto and Windus, 1949), pp. 451–85; Dorothea Krook, *Three Traditions of Moral Thought* (Cambridge: Cambridge University Press, 1959), pp. 202–25; A. O. J. Cockshut, *The Unbelievers: English Agnostic Thought, 1840–1890* (New York: New York University Press, 1966), p. 63; R. H. Super, *The Time-Spirit of Matthew Arnold* (Ann Arbor: University of Michigan Press, 1970), especially pp. 81–88.

Bible], and to see whether from using their language with the ground of this real and firm sense to it, as they themselves did, somewhat of their feeling, too, may not grow upon us. At least we shall know what we are saying; and that what we are saying is true, however inadequate.

(VI: 200)

We will proceed, that is, with the most scrupulous humanistic, naturalistic principles, careful always to take cognizance of the limits of our experiential knowledge, as the Hebrews themselves did: "It is more high than heaven, what canst thou do? deeper than hell, what canst thou know?" (VI: 207; Job 11: 8).

"*Aberglaube* Invading," chapter 2, explains that in the last centuries before Christ, when Israel suffered poverty and deprivation, and the Persian overlord, when resources were slight and taxes heavy, the priesthood in decline, it was very hard to remember the joyous rewards of righteousness; and the book of Ecclesiastes, written in this period, "has been said, and with justice, to breathe resignation at the grave of Israel" (VI: 208)—with its poetry of desolation and pointlessness (we would now call it absurdist). "The earth is given unto the hand of the wicked!"[12] "Wherefore I praised the dead which are already dead more than the living which are yet alive" (Eccles. 4: 1–2). There were the voices of the prophets nevertheless asserting that " 'the Eternal's arm is not shortened,' that 'righteousness shall be for ever,' and that the future would prove this, even if the present did not" (VI: 210; Isa. 59: 1, 51: 8). Hence arises the *Aberglaube*, the superstructure of belief in an afterlife. And of course Arnold refers to this as phantasm and fairy-tale. But such phantasm does not cancel out the original experiential principle, that *righteousness tendeth to life*; in fact it is a sort of tribute to the great power of it. It is part of Arnold's discretion to call these fantasies *Aberglaube* rather than superstition, to protect the feelings of those who have leanings toward them; he claims that *Aberglaube* means "extra-belief" and is not so denigratory as our English *superstition*. But in fact, *Aberglaube* is better said to mean "but-belief," or "belief-in-spite-of," in spite of reason or knowledge, that is; and it is really a pretty close equivalent to English *superstition*. The Germans have no other common word for it. Goethe has

12. This particular line is from Job, again (9: 24)—which is also late, like Ecclesiastes.

said, and Arnold quotes approvingly, "Aberglaube ist die Poesie des Lebens" (VI: 212) (*Aberglaube* is the poetry of life). Since Arnold in the context of this book takes *poetry* most often to mean figurative language, we might conclude that he is saying the superstition of the afterlife is a metaphor—for the sense of the Eternal.

In chapter 3, "Religion New Given," he presents Jesus' great insight in taking hold of elements of current thought and connecting them to himself. Jesus appropriates the later prophets' "inwardness" as opposed to superficial law-keeping and mechanical ritual; he appropriates the image of the "suffering servant" in Isaiah, and other strains of Messianic thought flourishing in the period, all in a renewal of the message of righteousness, with the thoroughly practical effect of a change in the conduct of his followers.

The motive of Christianity,—which was, in truth, that pure souls "know the voice" of Jesus as sheep know the voice of their shepherd, and felt, after seeing and hearing him, that his doctrine and ideal was what they wanted, that he was "indeed the saviour of the world,"—this simple motive became a mixed motive, adding to its first contents a vast *extra-belief* of a phantasmagorical advent of Jesus Christ, a resurrection and judgment, Christ's adherents glorified, his rejectors punished everlastingly.

(VI: 230–31)

When this did not in fact happen, the generation of the disciples discovered, according to a process by which in Bishop Butler's phrase "anything can be made out of anything," that this great event was to come in the future (VI: 231). The *Aberglaube* came to surpass the original insight, and more and more the proof of Christianity came to rest "not on its internal evidence" but on prophecy and miracle (VI: 232).

"The Proof from Prophecy" and "The Proof from Miracles" (chapters 4 and 5) are more or less tactful dismissals of the significance of biblical prediction and of miracles. First, it is natural and not blamable for men to answer to the *desire* for an afterlife by telling themselves fairy-tales; the *desire* exists nonetheless, and hope and presentiment are valid though their objects are not demonstrable. And there is an advantage to be gained in conduct, if a man takes (and this is important) "an object of hope and presentiment *as if* [my emphasis] it were an object of certainty" (VI: 232). But he explains man had better remember his as-if's for as-if's, his fictions for fictions. If he does not, *"he pays for it* [Arnold's emphasis]." The time comes when he discovers it *is* a fiction, or metaphor, "and then the whole certainty of religion seems discredited, and the basis of conduct gone" (VI: 236). But in truth, "religion is the solidest of realities, and Christianity the greatest and happiest stroke ever yet made for human perfection." With that *yet* Arnold maintains his developmental theory of religion. Christianity is capable of improvement. Prediction and miracles *were* useful fictions, and now no longer are.

On the matter of prediction, Arnold notes the innocent use, by pious translators, of the future tense for the nontemporal Hebrew verbs; the translators simply believed the Old Testament predicted the ministry of Jesus. This is a matter of literary history and criticism, and knowledge of mistranslations is becoming current. "What will be *their* case, who have been so long and sedulously taught to rely on supernatural predictions as a mainstay?" (VI: 236).

Arnold glances at the wild theory of Emile Burnouf, who holds that the original Christian religion came from India through to the Aryans, and that therefore Aryan Christians need not feel indebted to the inferior Semites, with their "frizzled hair, thick lips, small calves, flat feet," and a brain that cannot grow above the age of sixteen, "whereas the brain of a theological Arya, such as one of our bishops, may go on growing all his life"—this is part of Arnold's calculated and hilarious campaign against the "clap-trap" of the Bishops of Winchester and Gloucester and their expressed desire to "do something for the honour of our Lord's Godhead" (VI: 240), like a businessman anxious to do a little favor in return for some profit thrown his way.

But we, who think that the Old Testament leads surely up to the New, who believe that, indeed, "Salvation is of the Jews,"

(VI: 240; John 4: 22)

we turn to the Jews as guides to righteousness just as one turns to the Greeks for art or to Newton for physics. The Jews' lack of talent for metaphysics constitutes their greatness in religion: they founded religion not on metaphysics but on experience. To those whose faith rested on prediction and miracle, who now cast the Bible aside because they know miracles do not happen, "to these persons we restore the use of the Bible" if we show them the true metaphysical nature of Bible language, which "deals with facts of positive experience, momentous and real" (VI: 244). It is the *Zeitgeist* itself that saps the proof from miracles; the human mind is turning away from them, because it can see how in the course of history the report of them arises. Arnold presents the New Testament miracles as quite in a class with the modern Roman Catholic miracles, like liquefaction of saints' blood, that the complacent Protestant so despises. And he takes a text that even "the veriest literalist" will cry out must not be taken literally, Psalm 18, with the fire coming out of the mouth of God, to light coals by (VI: 249). Moreover the reporters of the New Testament "could err and did err" (VI: 250). The clear case is their mistake in thinking Jesus would return in their own lifetimes. Even they failed in literary criticism! for they took the Psalmist's couplet—

> They parted my garments among them,
> And for my vesture did they cast lots—
> (Ps. 22: 18; VI: 252)

to represent two contrasted events, when in fact by the literary rules of parallelism in Hebrew prosody there is but one event. (The common knowledge of this literary convention of parallelism is thought, in fact, to have diminished in Jesus' time.) And yet we need lose no respect for these reporters, but must do them all reverence, for they "chose the better part" and all helped to keep the record. But as with all documents in history, we must read with knowledge of their authors' capacity and their place in history. What Jesus said is recorded, and that is what is invaluable. Jesus himself seems often to insist on just that sense of figurative language that we need to have: "What does it matter whether I say, Thy sins are forgiven thee! or whether I say, Arise and walk!" (VI: 255; Matt. 9: 5). It seems to be suggested that these alternative statements are logical equivalents: one, presumably, is a figure for the other. But the reporters longed for the substance of the miraculous, and, as it were, made it grow. One hardly knows which is the more evident, "the perfect simplicity and good faith of the narrators or the plainness with which they themselves really say to us: *Behold a legend growing under your eyes!*" (VI: 257).

For the disciples, miracles validated Jesus' message, and yet they reported so faithfully as to record the very cautions Jesus himself makes against miracles. Here are three *topoi* of Jesus against miracles, followed by Arnold's exegeses:

Except ye see signs and wonders, ye will not believe!
(John 4: 48)

is as much as to say

Believe on right grounds you cannot, and you must needs believe on wrong!
(VI: 261)

And:

Believe me that I am in the Father and the Father in me; or else believe for
the very works' sake!
(John 14: 11)

is as much as to say

Acknowledge me on the ground of my healing and restoring acts being miraculous if you must; but it is not the right ground.
(VI: 261)

And when Nicodemus puts conversion on the ground of miracles:

"We know that thou art a teacher come from God, for no one can do these
miracles that thou doest except God be with him," Jesus rejoins, "Verily,
verily I say unto thee, except a man be born from above, he cannot see the
Kingdom of God!" thus tacitly changing his disciple's ground and correcting
him.
(VI: 261; John 3: 2–3)

Arnold omits here out of delicacy, I think, the next exchange:

Nicodemus saith unto him, How can a man be born when he is old? can he
enter the second time into his mother's womb, and be born? Jesus answered,
verily, verily, I say unto thee, Except a man be born of water and of the Spirit,
he cannot enter into the Kingdom of God.
(John 3: 4–5)

In the Arnoldian line of argument, one would say that Nicodemus by
literal interpretation proposes a "miracle" of new birth, and in so doing reduces it to absurdity. Jesus corrects him by proclaiming the
metaphor of new birth as functional, new birth symbolized by baptism (water) and spiritual in essence, a new capacity for virtue in this
life. The hunger for miracles and the degrading literalism explain, for
Arnold, why "Jesus *groaned in his spirit* and said, why doth this generation ask for a sign?" (VI: 262; Mark 8: 12), altogether like

Empedocles in disgust at the crowd's taking his cure of Pantheia for a miracle.

Where the naive take Jesus to be fulfilling Old Testament prophecy miraculously, we understand him to be making "the popular familiarity with prophecy serve him; as when he rides into Jerusalem on an ass, or clears the Temple of buyers and sellers." The reporters, in short, Arnold says, "are the servants of the Scripture-letter, Jesus is its master" (VI: 263). We must comment, though it may seem to trivialize Jesus, that Arnold is saying Jesus is master of language, he is the right kind of literary critic. I think it must be put in these terms so that we can see Arnold's sense of the vital role of literary criticism.

Orthodox divinity has been "an immense literary misapprehension," even (in a strikingly twentieth-century epithet) a "mess" (VI: 276–77)! The interpretation of the Bible "calls into play the highest requisites for the study of letters; great and wide acquaintance with the history of the human mind, knowledge of the manner in which men have thought, of their way of using words and of what they mean by them, delicacy of perception and quick tact, and besides all these, a favorable moment and the 'Zeit-Geist' " (VI: 276).

It was the mission of Jesus, *Aberglaube* having invaded, "to restore the intuition" (VI: 284) of righteousness as the essential Kingdom of God. And in this he had a method, a method of repentance, and a secret, a secret of *inwardness*. The method of Jesus is

the setting up of a great unceasing inward movement of attention and verification in matters [of conduct], where to see true and to verify is not difficult, the difficult thing is to care and attend. And the inducement to attend was because joy and peace, missed on every other line, were to be reached on this.

(VI: 288)

The thought and the idiom here—unceasing *movement*, and *inwardness*—are strikingly reminiscent of the vocabulary of German *Bildung*.[13] In fact the method and secret of Jesus appear to be the very method and secret of *Bildung* itself; by a perpetual inward movement toward *Humanität*, we fulfill the law of our beings. Repentance, Arnold explains, is not to be taken in our ordinary sense of groaning and lamenting over our sins but rather in the sense of the Greek *metanoia*,

---

13. *Inwardness* sounds like a translation of *Innerlichkeit*. See W. H. Bruford, *The German Tradition of Self-Cultivation: "Bildung" from Humboldt to Thomas Mann* (Cambridge: Cambridge University Press, 1975), p. vii et passim.

"a change of the inner man," by which we are put on the way to perfection. In this connection he glosses, demythologizing, Jesus' words to the woman of Samaria, "Except a man be born of water and of the Spirit, he cannot enter the Kingdom of God," to read, "Except a man be born of *cleansing* and of *a new influence* he cannot enter into the Kingdom of God" (VI: 290, John 3: 5). The rule of Jesus' method is *necrosis*, or dying to the things of this world:

Christ's *method* directed his disciple's eye inward, and set his consciousness to work; and the first thing his consciousness told him was, that he had two selves pulling him different ways. Till we attend, till the *method* is set at work . . . , it seems as if an impulse to do a thing must mean that we should do it.

(VI: 291–92)

But an impulse, we find, is really in itself no reason. For impulses are of two kinds, coming, in Paul's terms, either from the mind of the flesh or from the spiritual mind; in Jesus' terms from life *in this world* or from life proper. And we see that impulses from one source are to overrule those from the other. The mere negative morality of constraint, Jesus changed into religion (lighting up morality) by the figure of two lives—one the higher and permanent self, one the lower and transient self. "The first kind of life was already a cherished ideal with Israel ('Thou wilt show me the path of life!') ; and a man might be placed in it, Jesus said, by dying to the second" (VI: 292; Ps. 16: 11).

I think here we have the fruition of Arnold's sense of levels of consciousness, so often a theme in the poetry, and we have moreover the religious side of his political thought, perfectly consistent with it, the idea of the State as our collective best selves.

The figure of two selves is borne out, Arnold says, by science proper. Scientists, psychophysiologists, recognize it in *their* terms as Egoism and Altruism. And he recounts analogues to this in Aristotle, in Horace, in Goethe ("Alles ruft uns zu, dass wir entsagen sollen"; Everything cries out to us that we must *renounce*), in Plato, in Wordsworth (the "Ode to Duty"), and finally in Bishop Wilson: "They that deny themselves will be sure to find their strength increased, their affections raised, and their inward peace continually augmented." He climaxes all by returning to Goethe: "*Stirb und werde!* Die and come to life! for so long as this is not accomplished thou art but a troubled guest upon an earth of gloom" (VI: 295). By referring to the pagans, Arnold insists that this great secret is not exclusive to Christianity, and by returning to Goethe, the avowed nonsupernaturalist, he insists that it is a natural, nonsupernatural phenomenon, confirmed by science.

"A method of *inwardness*, a secret of *self-renouncement*;—but can any statement of what Jesus brought be complete, which does not include that temper of *mildness* and *sweetness* in which both of these worked[?]" (VI: 299–300). We remember Arnold implying that *style* is of the essence in religion,[14] and here he insists on Jesus' *style*: "Learn of me that I am mild and lowly of heart, and ye shall find rest unto your souls!" (VI: 300; Matt. 11: 29) ; "Sweet reasonableness!" (VI: 300). *Reasonableness*, the old word of the Deists,[15] and Arnold has cleaved throughout his argument to this, faithful in his way to the Enlightenment. But there is also the *sweetness*, all those characteristics of Jesus that attract us and invite us to an Imitation. "To believe in him" seems to be a way of doing it *meekly*.

Arnold then goes on to examine some of Jesus' characteristic figures, which are the characteristic figures of the Jewish tradition, in Daniel, in Isaiah, in the Psalms. Jesus himself, he says, spiritualizes, deliteralizes the figures. He *used*, that is, the popular Jewish *Aberglaube* and identified it with his own message. "He was forever translating it into the sense of the higher ideal, the only sense in which it had truth and grandeur" (VI: 305). To put it into our terms, he was forever demythologizing the Jewish superstition. "The Kingdom of God is the reign of righteousness, God's will done by all mankind. Well, then, seek the Kingdom of God! the Kingdom of God is within you!" (VI: 306; Luke 17: 21). Jesus' mode is the concrete figurative language of Israel understood by him as figurative, but, Arnold notes, "whereas Jesus spoke in Aramaic, the most concrete and unmetaphysical of languages, he is reported in the Greek, the most metaphysical" (VI: 308). The translation itself, he is saying, would skew the meaning toward metaphysics—as it did most notably with John. And we must try to reinvent the simple concreteness of the lost Aramaic, Hebrew-like original.

14. In the essay on Eugénie de Cuérin, III: 96–97, and in "Theodore Parker," V: 81–82.

15. Remember Locke, *The Reasonableness of Christianity*, 1695.

The usual assumption that between faith and reason there is an opposition, the assumption whose modern spokesman, Newman, Arnold cites with his usual reverence while he is differing from him, comes from the sense of faith, or religion, that has been falsely sophisticated by theologians. And the idea that one should "become as a little child" to accept the Kingdom of God is misunderstood by evangelicals as a reason for cultivating stupidity and leads to the disdain with which they dismiss art, literature, and science. "Faith is neither the submission of the reason, nor is it the acceptance . . . of what reason cannot reach. Faith is: *the being able to cleave to a power of goodness appealing to our higher and real self, not to our lower and apparent self*" (VI: 315).

In reading the Bible, theology is a hindrance. The Bible is literature (VI: 316), it is in words, and it needs then a *literary* understanding. "Three days," for instance, turns out to be a Hebrew idiom, for "a short time"—and therefore cannot sanction literal third-day theology (VI: 318). And Arnold takes up "The Early Witnesses" (chapter 8) to explain in each case the right discrimination of their language: Peter, Paul (briefly, here, for he has previously treated him), the author of the First Epistle of John, James, the author of the Epistle to the Hebrews (not Paul, as is generally known), and the early martyrs. He traces how the *Aberglaube*, from which Jesus had cleansed the Jews, "reinvades," and all the miraculous legends are developed and become the basis for the theory embodied in the Creeds. Aryan metaphysics takes over from Semitic poetry, and Christianity still suffers. "What the science of Bible-criticism, like all other science, needs, is a very wide experience from comparative observation in many directions, and a very slowly acquired habit of mind" (VI: 345). And Arnold gives examples of absurd rabbinical exegeses, and patristic-medieval and Reformation, Luther's and Newman's, too—all as invalidated as the belief that the world is flat, invalidated by the light of our *Zeitgeist*.

In "Our 'Masses' and the Bible," Arnold explains that *Aberglaube* is not necessarily degrading; it puts many into touch with religion who might otherwise miss it. But now, he insists (with a perhaps misplaced developmental faith), scientific attitudes are becoming more and more widespread, and so we must be ready with the new scientific literary interpretation of the Bible.

Throughout, Arnold's argument is supported by his own literary sense of the Bible. Face to face with the aridity of theology, he brings great texts like draughts of water (to borrow the biblical metaphor):

The statutes of the Eternal rejoice the heart; more desirable are they than gold, sweeter than honey; in keeping of them there is great reward. . . . The Eternal is my strength, my heart hath trusted in him and I am helped; therefore my heart danceth for joy, and in my song will I praise him.[16]

Isaiah and Psalms are the most used, both greatly bold and rich in metaphor. To deploy these texts so aptly argues his own experience in having long "dwelt" on their source, and they make an eloquence aside from their own: Arnold's eloquence, in that he, a nonsupernaturalist, has such a deep sense of meaning in this poetry; the metaphors *function* for him, according to his own theory. The Bible, he writes, is "not as other books that inculcate righteousness"; it is more than they, for it is more greatly *poetic*, more greatly metaphorical. Homer was the Bible of the Greeks, and the notion of an arcane theology in Homer proved to be a dream. So, too, will the patristic theology educed from the Bible prove to be a dream. Arnold is careful to say that in matters of literary criticism, final demonstration is impossible, and yet as experience and knowledge grow, the nonsupernaturalist reading of the Bible, "though it cannot command assent, . . . will be found to win assent more and more" (VI: 378). The analogy to Homer is delicately set in the reader's mind: it suggests the greatness of the literary value of the Bible better than any other analogue.

One hopes that in our time we need no longer defend Arnold's religious writings from the charges made by F. H. Bradley and T. S. Eliot. But it may be as well to refer to Dorothea Krook's conclusive defense. Where Bradley's reinterpretation of Christianity—she points out—is general and abstract, Arnold's is concrete and specific;[17] since Arnold, we might add, insists on the essential dependence of religion on language, his concreteness and specificity is altogether proper, as well as "scientific" in the only way we can be "scientific" about language (or religion). Krook writes, moreover:

In view of the quality of religious sensibility and insight [in *Literature and Dogma*], it is instructive to recall T. S. Eliot's remark about Matthew Arnold,

16. VI: 367–68; Psalms 19: 8, 10, 11; Psalms 28: 7.
17. Krook, *Three Traditions*, p. 249.

that "in philosophy and theology he was an undergraduate; in religion a Philistine" (*The Use of Poetry and the Use of Criticism*). One feels that bigotry can hardly go further than this in impairing true judgment.[18]

And she remarks how Arnold treats the statements on the efficacy of the mass in the *Imitation* "with obvious tenderness of feeling." "A man who can talk in this strain about a doctrine and a ritual in which he himself does not believe cannot, one feels, be fairly described as 'a Philistine in religion.' "[19]

Arnold, writes W. H. Auden in his poem, "thrust his gift in prison till it died."[20] It might be argued, rather, that he remained a poet. "Miracles," he says now in *Literature and Dogma*, "the mainstay of popular religion, are touched by Ithuriel's spear" (VI: 379). The figure is from *Paradise Lost*, where Satan squatting in the shape of a toad at the ear of Eve is stripped of his disguise by the touch of the spear of the angel Ithuriel and is revealed as the principle of evil.[21] That is, at least, a masterly use of figure, invoking in small space a powerful set of meanings and overtones. Perhaps he is never more the poet than in this revalidation of biblical poetry.

Meantime, the invalidation of miracles, Arnold predicts, will make a period of confusion and distress. With many religious people there will be "a recrudescence of superstition; the passionate resolve to keep hold on what is slipping away" (VI: 379), and the Church of Rome, upholding as it does authority against reason, will see a gain in numbers. In general, religion will simply decrease, because it has been set on the wrong grounds, a *thaumaturgy*. And this will be a great loss, for even "those who make the Bible a thaumaturgy get hold of the religion because they read the Bible" (VI: 350). Again, poetlike, he borrows the great metaphorical language of the prophet Amos, a passage where Amos himself demythologizes:

Behold, the days come, saith the Eternal, that I will send a famine in the land, not a famine of bread, nor a thirst for water, but of hearing the words of the Eternal.

(VI: 380; Amos 8: 11–12)

18. Ibid., p. 216n.
19. Ibid., p. 217.
20. W. H. Auden, "Matthew Arnold."
21. John Milton, *Paradise Lost*, 4: 810–14, as Super notes, *Prose* VI: 497.

It is a text that seems to retain meaning, even in later periods of cultural malnutrition. Nevertheless, still in the words of Amos, there is a future promise of return:

There shall yet not the least grain of Israel fall to the ground!
(VI: 380; Amos 9: 9)

And then such a reading as Arnold now offers he himself predicts will come into its own.

Meanwhile, we must indulge popular Christianity, for it has in good part got hold of the "method" and "secret" of Jesus. And even the naive missionary, confronting in ignorance the dignity and worth of Mohammedanism or Brahmanism or Buddhism, merely by making the Bible known may be doing some good. (Some sophisticated East Indians have sometimes charitably said as much.) However, the "pseudo-science of dogmatic theology merits no such indulgence."[22]

Arnold's own reading of the prophets suggests again and again the richness of this field for the study of metaphor. And the literary establishment has failed to exploit it. Again and again, even in so-called *literary* approaches to the Bible, one runs up against in the first few pages the disheartening discovery of the sectarian interest of the "critic." Since Bishop Lowth's delicate and discriminating considerations of metaphor in Isaiah, the record of literary criticism of the prophets is poor indeed. Arnold himself is its chief proponent and virtually its only glory. Dorothea Krook dissociates Arnold from that "vulgar modern notion" of the Bible-as-Literature, "the Bible read, that is, exclusively for its fine images and plangent rhythms, and the

22. VI: 382. In his attack on the dogmatists' foolishness here he includes F. D. Maurice and the paternal friend Bunsen, along with the Bishop of Exeter and his like. As though to restore filial piety, he then quotes a fine insight from another paternal friend, John Davison—"not the least memorable of that Oriel group, whose reputation I, above most people, am bound to cherish"; Davison has said, "Conscience and the present constitution of things are not corresponding terms; it is conscience and *the issue of things* which go together" [Arnold's emphasis]. This is simply true, Arnold comments; "Give time enough for the experience, and experimentally and demonstrably it is true, that 'the path of the just is as the shining light which shineth more and more unto the perfect day.' . . . One strain runs through it all: nations and men, whoever is shipwrecked, is shipwrecked on *conduct*. It is the God of Israel steadily and irresistibly asserting himself; *The Eternal that loveth righteousness*" (VI: 386; VI: 384; John Davison, *Discourses in Prophecy* [1824], p. 81; Super's note, *Prose* VI: 498).

emotional luxury of a small safe quantity of uplift that in no way commits me to the Bible's embarrassing doctrinal content." Arnold is thinking, she says, "precisely of the doctrinal content and how we may best possess ourselves of its saving truths."[23] And he has given us some very close and precise analysis of metaphor as the energizing force of this poetry-religion, analysis that has largely gone unregarded, because of the nervousness of literary academicians in approaching the Bible and because of the nervousness of the theological establishment in dealing with nonsupernaturalists like Arnold. If, as I suppose, Arnold's biblical criticism may be his best *literary* criticism, the literary establishment has much to gain from his work on these great poetic texts.

Arnold wonders if there has stayed with Israel any remembrance of the simple primitive intuition of *the Eternal that loveth righteousness,* and he supposes that the Talmudists have done to Judaism what the Christian theorists have done to Christianity. The Judaism that Arnold knew was the Judaism of the Enlightenment, the Mendelssohnian line, and the sort of reform orthodox piety well represented by Lady de Rothschild. One wonders what he would have made of the revival of Hasidism, and the Hasidic joy that has made itself felt in our society in general, in the ecstatic playing of the great violinists of our time, or what he would have made of the ecstatic dancing of the Hasidic rabbi with the Torah: *Thy testimonies are the very joy of my heart!* Here are people *possessed* with the power of righteousness. Although this Jeremiah in kid gloves, as Arnold was called, would not be much in personal sympathy with ecstatics, I think nevertheless he would have been much interested, for his own sense of the real power of religion—or poetry—is so acute. With his Herderian feeling for poetry as the most typical and most potentially valuable product of a culture, and with his literary apprehension of this Old Testament poetry as supreme, he endorses Isaiah's great metaphor, that Israel is to be "a light unto the Gentiles." Old Testament poetry constitutes a treasure for the world, and when it is dismissed as mere supernaturalist religion, there is a great loss.

In the New Testament, in Christianity, the vitality is not in "certain tenets about One God in Trinity and Trinity in Unity." It is in being "renewed in the spirit of your mind, and [in putting] on the new

23. Krook, *Three Traditions,* p. 208.

man which after God is created in righteousness and true holiness"
(VI: 395; Ephes. 4: 23–24). The dogmatists are rampant now, Arnold says, just as in Jesus' day.

The chief priests and elders of the people, and the scribes, are our bishops and dogmatists, with their pseudo-science of learned theology blinding their eyes. . . . The Pharisees, with their genuine concern for religion, but total want of perception of what religion really is, and by their temper, attitude, and aims doing their best to make religion impossible, are the Protestant Dissenters. The Sadducees are our friends the philosophical Liberals, who believe neither in angel nor spirit but in Mr. Herbert Spencer. Even the Roman governor has its close parallel in our celebrated aristocracy, with its superficial good sense and good nature, its complete inaptitude for ideas, its profound helplessness in presence of all great spiritual movements.

(VI: 399)

And so Jesus' *method,* his *secret,* and his *temper* are perfectly adapted for us, still.

"The True Greatness of Christianity" (chapter 12) lies in "the immense experimental proof of the necessity of it. Walking on the water, multiplying loaves, raising corpses, . . . what is this compared to the real experience" (VI: 400). The *motor* (Arnold's word) is "the conscious ardent sensation of personal love" to Jesus. Conscience and renouncement *are* righteousness. All religious aspiration after immortality is negligible in the face of the sense of life that righteousness affords; this sense of *life* is open to infinite development. The Bible record is imperfect, but only in it can we get at the *epieikeia* of Jesus, his temper of sweet reasonableness. "The *infinite* of the religion of Jesus,—its immense capacity for ceaseless progress and farther development,—lies principally, perhaps, in the line of disengaging and keeping before our minds, more and more, his temper, and applying it to our use of his method and secret" (VI: 405). Here converge the lines of Arnold's thought that have been evident in various ways in all his previous writing: the great shaping idea of Historicism—development, that is; the ideal of *Bildung* with its inwardness and never-ending process toward perfection; his fine sense of the power of literature in our lives; all this is rationally reconciled with Christianity—rationally, nonsupernaturally, experientially. It is a world away from Deism, for it brings together all the new learning, the higher criticism, and negates dryness. It discovers, instead, a new kind of spirituality. It is a great achievement in its time, in a way like that of Aquinas's for *his* time: the reconciliation of Christianity with Aristotle. It is a kind of Victorian *Summa*.

The stylish little poem-in-prose that is the "Conclusion" of *Literature and Dogma* reconnects the three-quarters of life that is conduct back to the one-quarter that is not conduct but intellect; reconnects art and science to man's singleness of being, his "one nature," as though the fractionalizing, which F. H. Bradley took too seriously (or literally), was only what we call now a heuristic fiction, a provisional idea by which we might arrive at a further stage of thought. Culture, intellect, science, and art are perfectly necessary. The whole misapprehension of the Bible comes in fact from the want of science and culture. Lacking these, our theologians in their literary inexperience confuse the figurative with the literal and create a great puzzling *fog*. "Culture, then, and science and literature, are requisite, in the interest of religion itself" (VI: 409). That part of ourselves that demands beauty and exact knowledge is imperious, and its demands must accord with the principles of conduct. "For the total man, therefore, the truer conception of God is as 'the Eternal Power, not ourselves, by which all things fulfil the law of their being'; by which, therefore, we fulfil the law of our being so far as our being is aesthetic and intellective, as well as so far as it is moral" (VI: 409).

———————— Metaphor ————————

FROM the perspective of Arnold's *Summa*, metaphor—broadly understood—takes on a central role in human affairs.[1] Arnold's theory of metaphor is never flatly articulated; perhaps if it were it would be blighted with dogma. He characteristically exhibits metaphor in action, and, in action, in great texts, metaphor can ravish the mind, it can remake the world, it can quite possibly affect conduct. What I call his theory of metaphor is clearly implied by his concept of the two languages, the paradigm of the literal mode contrasted with the poetic mode. The literal mode is that of science, moral maxims, creeds, dogmatic statements, newspaper reports; the metaphorical mode is the language of poetry (or art) and religion. If we extend this paradigm to larger units, the literal or discursive mode gives us theories, treatises, theology, dogma full-blown; the metaphorical mode gives us myth, ritual, epic, all the "stories" of all cultures. Myths or stories we call *fictions*, because they are recognizably "made up." Since the expressionist theory of culture has become more generally prevalent—the idea that man *makes* himself by his culture—we recognize more and more elements of culture to be, in fact, fictive. Language itself, the stuff of which culture is made, is various, relative, provisional, changing, by no means absolute. Metaphors are granted as fictive, of course —no one *believes* his love is a red rose, or really very *like* a red rose. Stories and parables fictive? yes, certainly; stories of gods and goddesses—yes; stories of God and patriarchs—yes, those too. Even the

1. I take *metaphor* to overlap with *symbol*, and to subsume *simile* and *metaphor* proper, and *synecdoche* and *metonymy*.

historian must, at best, select his details, and indeed must present them in a perspective skewed by his own time, and place, and self, even when he tries to be most conscientious, so that now we hardly speak of History but only of histories—all with degrees of fictiveness. And even science, which seemed so "pure," the ultimate best conscientious true account of things, is by now generally felt to consist of a series of provisional hypotheses, each in its turn the best we can adjust to the state of things as perceived at the time. The physical paradox of light has been a humbling experience: in some conditions the behavior of light can be explained only by a wave theory, in other conditions only by a particle theory; obviously both cannot be "true" or "right." Each then is a fiction, we must conclude, each useful in certain circumstances, *heuristic*, that is, in that it can help lead on to further discoveries. To face the paradox is a necessary stage, for the time, and this implies we must *always* face paradox. So it is said that the world turns out to be a lot queerer than we think, and queerer than we *can* think. We arrive more and more frequently at "limitation results" and have to shuffle by with makeshift ideas. Perhaps only mathematics is certain and absolute, as Pythagoras supposed; Bertrand Russell tells us it sustained him in the vertiginous modern sea of solipsism. At any rate, the realm of the "literal" part of Arnold's paradigm has very much shrunk. One result of this is a new respect for *fictions* in general. If even scientists must resort to them, they acquire a new dignity. They are just about all we have, whether they are theories or novels— which are macro-fictions—or metaphors—which are micro-fictions. More and more it is recognized that even scientific "descriptions" have to be metaphorical, and even the most rigorous philosophers do not feel so superior to metaphor as they used to.

One reason Matthew Arnold remains satisfactory to us now is that he anticipates all this: he recognizes the great thundering arrogance of dogma and the terrible constriction of the literal. Although he pretends to naïveté, and ironically declares himself incapable of "system," there is in fact a grand consistency lying behind all his writings that can be best appreciated, I think, if we apply our modern critical concept of *fictions*. If we put together his sense of the shifting provisional quality of language, his brilliant use of metaphor and his explication of it as engaging the whole personality and energizing it, and all his appreciations of both secular and religious myth, as stories that are not true but yet have a kind of "truth" in them—*He fables yet speaks truth!* exclaims Empedocles on hearing Callicles' song—the underlying consistency appears. Norse myth, Celtic lore, the stories of Homer, of the Bible, of all our great poets are "pragmatic"; they *make* ourselves and our culture, giving meaning and stability of life. To recognize them as fictive is by no means to depreciate them. As children, we can take possession of them and understand them literally. As we advance, we recognize their fictiveness and so understand more of man's condition, his need, and the powers he has to fulfill that need, by his *makings*, his poetry.

In accordance with the historicist view, certain myths function at certain stages of development and will give way to others in other stages. With Arnold, everything is in process; our myths are provisional and of their time, not absolute or final. Metaphor, considered as the smallest element of myth, the myth-eme, stands in a similar case, provisional and frankly fictive. Our love is not a red red rose, the Kingdom of God is not really a mustard seed, Jesus is not really a shepherd, nor do the floods clap their hands and the hills be joyful together. But we can all recognize that by these metaphors something is said—or made—that could not be said or made otherwise. If we attempt it, the result is so wordy and flaccid that it loses the characteristic energy and becomes different in kind. Certain cultural forces had induced a misreading of both metaphors and myths as literal, with absurd results. Hence, the labor of *Literature and Dogma* to reclassify the literal jasper-and-emeralds afterlife and the rest as metaphors. Arnold's understanding of these things is patterned after Lessing's in a passage he copied into his note-books:

The source of moral evil, too abstract a truth for a sensual people to understand, is bodied forth in the story of the forbidden tree.[2]

This pattern of exegesis, to discover the psychological need that the metaphor or myth answers to, is part of the new self-consciousness of the nineteenth century. When Arnold insists that the anthropomorphic God is a metaphor, a term "thrown out at an object of our consciousness," something approximate, provisional, not absolute or final, he educates the literalist, inviting him out of that "Prison of Puritanism" into a more adequate sense of man and God so that he can profit by the God metaphor as he does by the rose or the mustard-

2. *Note-Books*, p. 521. Arnold quotes the German, from *Die Erziehung des Menschengeschlechts*.

seed or the floods and hills rejoicing. In another part of the forest, Ivan Karamazov, demythologizing, explains:

What is strange, what is marvellous, is not that God really exists, the marvel is that such an idea, the idea of the necessity of God, could have entered the head of such a savage and vicious beast as man; so holy it is, so moving, so wise, and such a great honor it does man.

Arnold proposes, through this new self-consciousness, through the experiential scientific way of considering our own psychological processes, to exploit the fictiveness of both myth and metaphor, into new possibilities for a greater culture that embraces all art as well as religion.

"These are good times for the friends of metaphor," writes Ted Cohen in a recent book.[3] It was not always so. Aristotle granted that to deal with metaphor was a mark of genius, for by it one perceives similarity in dissimilarity, and by it we learn; but he speaks also of it as a sort of literary decoration to be used with restraint and kept in line by principles of decorum. Medieval culture developed a grander role for metaphor and used metaphors on a grand scale: the world is a book written by God; the poet's task is to discover God's meanings through his metaphors. This medieval idea was updated into Enlightenment terms by Bishop Butler's influential *Analogy of Religion* (1736), which was felt to be both orthodox and responsible intellectually, and which was the textbook for all Establishment theology. It was the book against which one defined one's own religious opinions. We have seen how Arnold took exception to Butler's faculty psychology (*Poems* 42), but he tells us in *God and the Bible* that he took the design for *Literature and Dogma* from Butler's treatment of *Nature* in connection with religion—in *analogy* (VII: 233). *Analogy* itself is a form of metaphor.[4]

Arnold's mentor Glanvill, in adopting the Renaissance experimental science of Descartes and Bacon, embraces provisionalism especially. *The Vanity of Dogmatizing or Confidence in Opinions* (1661) is sub-

3. Ted Cohen, "Metaphor and the Cultivation of Intimacy," in *Critical Inquiry,* Special Issue on Metaphor, vol. 5 (Autumn 1978), republished as *On Metaphor,* ed. Sheldon Sacks (Chicago: University of Chicago Press, 1979), pp. 1–10. The book form includes two extra short pieces by Nelson Goodman and Max Black.

4. See Wayne Booth, "Metaphor as Rhetoric," *Critical Inquiry* 5 (Autumn 1978): 51.

titled *A Discourse on the Shortness and Uncertainty of Our Knowledge and Its Causes*, and a good deal of the book is taken up with explaining what we call limitation theory—the deceptiveness of the senses and the distortions of solipsism; Glanvill acclaims the modesty of Descartes, the "Grand Secretary of Nature": "He intends his principles but for Hypotheses, and never pretends that things are really or necessarily, as he hath supposed them: but that they may be admitted pertinently to solve the Phaenomena, and are convenient supposals for the use of life."[5] When Arnold may seem very modern in his ideas of process and the provisional, he may be only following in Glanvill's way. *Convenient supposals* happens to be a good term for the way science now considers its theories. Glanvill's cheerful attacks on Aristotelian theorizing invigorate still: "A schoolman is the Ghost of the Stagirite, in a Body of condensed air: and Thomas but Aristotle sainted."[6] He castigates dogma with Arnoldian zest: "(1) 'Tis the effect of Ignorance. (2) It argues untamed passions. (3) It disturbs the world. (4) It is ill manners, and immodesty. (5) It holds man captive in Errour. (6) It betrays a narrowness of spirit."[7] Let us rather be like the Scholar-Gipsy, "seekers, still," not claiming to have *found* for once and all. Capacity is infinite. The new German learning Arnold was to appropriate did not clash with the scientific provisionalism of Glanvill.

Lowth extends the experimental method into literary criticism, in his *Lectures on the Sacred Poetry of the Hebrews* and in his annotated edition of Isaiah, and certainly contributes to Arnold's sense of metaphor. For Lowth, the two languages are the "Sententious" and the "Parabolic";[8] Lowth sets aside the complicated classification of figures of "parabolic" language and puts them all under "metaphor, and its extension, allegory";[9] he notes that the Hebrew word for poem, *maschal*, is in its first meaning "resemblance," hence a *figurative* thing. The word equals "he likened," "he compared," "he spoke in para-

5. Joseph Glanvill, *The Vanity of Dogmatizing* (1661; facsimile ed., New York: Columbia University Press, 1931), pp. 211–12.

6. Ibid., p. 152.

7. Ibid., p. 224.

8. Robert Lowth, *Lectures on the Sacred Poetry of the Hebrews*, ed. Vincent Freimarck, trans. from the Latin by G. Gregory, 2 vols. (1787; Hildesheim, W. Ger.: Georg Olms Verlag, 1969), lecture 4.

9. Ibid., lecture 5.

bles."[10] This Old Testament poetry, he says, depicts "the obscure by the more manifest; the subtile by the more substantial,"[11] using familiar objects from nature and from common life. When the Lord says by his prophet, "I will wipe Jerusalem as a man wipeth a dish, wiping it, and turning it upside down" (2 Kings 21 : 13), Lowth does "not scruple to call it sublime."[12] But above all, Lowth proposes that "the mind should . . . exert itself to discover, if possible, the connexion between the literal and figurative meanings."[13] It is precisely this fruitful method that Arnold exploits in *Literature and Dogma*.

In the new expressionist mode, Vico is the pioneer, in *La Scienza nuova* (1725) envisaging man *making* his world by symbol, myth, and fable. It is quite likely that Arnold by his early privileged exposure to Vico acquired this expressionist perspective, which by resting weight on symbol, myth, and fable rests on metaphor (subsuming all three) as the distinctively human response to the world. *Poesis* in this context replaces *mimesis*. We remember Arnold's early letter against "using poetry as a channel for thinking aloud, instead of making anything."[14] Following Hamann, Herder connects metaphor with the beginning of speech itself;[15] symbols, or metaphor, are for him the distinctively human mode. These ideas were appearing among the English Romantics. "Language is vitally metaphorical" avers Shelley in the "Defence of Poetry." Coleridge sees "the primary imagination . . . as a repetition in the finite mind of the eternal act of creation in the Infinite I AM"; symbols he sees as "living educts of the imagination, of that reconciling and mediatory power . . . incorporating the reason in images of the sense, and organizing (as it were) the flux of the senses by the permanence and self-encircling energies of the reason."

Historicism and developmentalism pose a question: If I am but one part in one phase of evolving cycles of societies, how is it with *me*? I

10. Ibid., lecture 4, p. 77.
11. Ibid., lecture 5, p. 117.
12. Ibid., lecture 7, p. 155.
13. Ibid.
14. *Unpublished Letters of Matthew Arnold*, ed. Arnold Whitridge (New Haven: Yale University Press, 1923), pp. 15–16.
15. See Herder, *Abhandlung über die Ursprung der Sprache* (1772), *Herders sämmtliche Werke*, ed. Bernard Suphan, 30 vols. (Berlin: Weidmann, 1877–1913), vol. 5.

seem a product of my time and place; how do I feel—or make—my own identity? It has been noted that "the nineteenth century" was the first to refer to itself with the temporal label, and it does so repeatedly. "Subjectivism," the convenient new term Coleridge imported from Germany, is well known as a mark of Romantics, with Wordsworth the supreme searcher and recorder of his own consciousness. Of the Victorians, I think Arnold most of all develops this subjectivism—striving to be objective about his own subjective experience. If Wordsworth is self-conscious, Arnold is conscious of being self-conscious. Between the well-known two worlds,

> We shut our eyes, and muse
> How our own minds are made.
>
> (179)

We may picture in Germany in the 1780s, Herder and Goethe together bending their own prodigious skulls over the skulls Goethe collected of various animals, including apes and even one elephant, both concerned with the similarities to human skulls, and their differences as well, both speculating on consciousness progressing from the simple to the more complex, just as the bony structures do. They thought in a kind of pre-Darwinian way of an evolution (without natural selection) by which once man arrives on the scene he goes on developing into a more complicated, superior kind of human being.[16] Herder's *Ideen* traces cosmological and biological history in a way strikingly parallel to Carl Sagan's in *Dragons of Eden: Speculations on the Evolution of Human Intelligence*.[17] Like Herder, Sagan uses the metaphor of history, the idea of the "childhood" of our species, when we were hunter-gatherers, and he speaks, like Herder, of the variety of societies, some of which more than others enable the "characteristically human components of our nature to flourish."[18] In his appreciation of "culture," he even gives us a convenient new term: "extra-somatic knowledge: information stored outside our bodies, of which writing is the most notable example."[19] Like Herder, Sagan an-

16. See, for instance, W. H. Bruford, *Culture and Society in Classical Weimar* (Cambridge: Cambridge University Press, 1962), pp. 145–46.

17. Carl Sagan, *Dragons of Eden: Speculations on the Evolution of Human Intelligence* (New York: Ballantine Books, 1977).

18. Ibid., pp. 202, 204.

19. Ibid., p. 4.

ticipates new more complicated forms of consciousness in the future. This anticipation is fairly common generally today; structuralists speak of increasingly complicated levels of consciousness as "pleats" in consciousness.[20] Irony may be considered such a "pleat," and perhaps also laughter, in its reflexivity. Most recently, Freeman Dyson proposes an open universe on a Gödelian model and "a constantly expanding domain of life, consciousness and memory."[21]

Carlyle in his early "Characteristics" is perfectly cognizant of the new self-consciousness, but has misgivings: it must be a kind of disease. The healthy mind like the healthy body is unaware of its own workings. But yet it is through this very cognizance that he finally effects from the sickly moultings of his Phoenix the new birth, the *Palingenesia* in "Wonder" and "Natural Supernaturalism," a religion that in no way offends our rational powers. This is effected through introspection and consideration of the nature of language and figure. "Prodigious influence of metaphors!" he writes in his notebook; "never saw into it until lately!"[22] It is not the pain-pleasure machinery of the foolish utilitarians that moves man. *They* cannot account for "Christianities and Chivalries, and Reformations, and Marseillese Hymns, and Reigns of Terror. . . . Nay, has not perhaps the Motive-grinder himself been in *Love*? Did he never stand so much as a contested Election?"[23] Here is Carlyle's prototype of Arnold's "morality touched with emotion"; discourse turned into powerful motivating force by means of *symbol* (or of metaphor). "It is in and through *Symbols* that man, consciously or unconsciously, lives, works, and has his being."[24] (Symbols daringly *replace* God here, in the allusion to Paul. "For in Him we live, and move, and have our being" [Acts 17: 28]). "Highest of all Symbols are those wherein the Artist or Poet has risen into a prophet, and all men can recognise a present God, and

20. The idea is Michel Foucault's. For one reference to it, see Jean Piaget, *Le Structuralisme*, "Que Sais-je" series, no. 1311 (Paris: Presses Universitaires de France), p. 45.

21. Freeman Dyson, "Time Without End: Physics and Biology in an Open Universe," *Reviews of Modern Physics* 51 (July 1979): 447–60, especially p. 449. I owe this reference to my daughter Alison apRoberts.

22. Quoted in John Holloway, *The Victorian Sage* (London: Macmillan, 1953), p. 14.

23. Thomas Carlyle, *Sartor Resartus*, ed. C. F. Harrold (New York: Odyssey Press, 1937), pp. 221–22.

24. Ibid., p. 222.

worship the same: I mean religious Symbols." Religions have been various, and our highest "divinest Symbol" has been "Jesus of Nazareth, and his Life, and his Biography, and what followed therefrom. . . . a Symbol of quite perennial infinite character; whose significance will ever demand to be anew inquired into, and anew made manifest." But "Symbols, like all terrestrial Garments, wax old." "A Hierarch, therefore, and Pontiff of the world will we call him, the Poet and inspired Maker; who Prometheus-like, can shape new Symbols, and bring new Fire from Heaven to fix it there."[25] Just as Carlyle has said that in symbols "there is concealment and yet revelation," so does his own highly metaphorical mode conceal or disguise the real shocking new unorthodoxy, that man *makes* his religion, while at the same time it reveals or communicates Carlyle's own Wonder, his Natural Supernaturalism. And all this Carlylean stuff, we remember, was what Arnold took in if not with his mother's milk, at least with his adolescent beer. Here is the Carlylean version of *development*—religions must change; here is the Carlylean version of the common ground of religion and art as consisting in the symbol. Israel, he is saying here in his way, was a poet, *Das Volk dichtet*, when Judaism and Christianity made the infinite manifest to *sense*, by metaphor.

The "Symbols" chapter is essential background to *Literature and Dogma*, and so is Carlyle's "Hero as Divinity." It is here that Carlyle defines religion broadly: "A man's religion is the chief fact with regard to him"[26]—not his creed, profession, or assertion, for these come "from the mere argumentative [dogmatic, prosaic] region of him, if even so deep as that . . . but the thing a man does practically believe . . . concerning his vital relations to this mysterious Universe, and his duty and destiny there, [which] creatively determines all the rest."[27] "What man feels intensely, he struggles to speak-out for him, to see represented before him in visual shape."[28] "Pagan Religion is indeed an Allegory, a Symbol of what man felt and knew about the Universe; and all Religions are symbols of that, altering always as that alters."[29] But Carlyle remarks that the allegorizing cannot be the origin and

25. Ibid., p. 224.
26. Thomas Carlyle, *Heroes and Hero-Worship*, in *Works*, 30 vols. (London: Chapman and Hall, 1910), 2:2.
27. Ibid., pp. 2–3.
28. Ibid., p. 24.
29. Ibid., p. 6.

cause; it is, rather, the result and termination. Carlyle in his vestigial Calvinism cannot quite join the expressionist school: men, he says, do not risk their soul's life on allegories. Man first, before he allegorizes, senses (and this Arnold remembered particularly well) in this universe, "a Force which is not *we*. That is all; it is not we, it is altogether different from *us*."[30] From this start, Carlyle traces the deification of the hero Odin. Along the way he recognizes culture-conditioning, even solipsism: "Curious to think how, for every man, any [*sic*] the truest fact is modelled by the nature of man!"[31] He speaks too of religious *development*: "Man first puts himself in relation with Nature and her Powers, wonders and worships over those; not till a later epoch does he discern that all Power is Moral" (that the force makes for righteousness). Carlyle's discreet tracing of Odin's deification is a rough model for Arnold's tracing of Jesus' deification, and his tracing of the development of the old Norse religion is a rough model of Arnold's tracing of the development of Christianity. Carlyle ends with the element of *good*, in this old religion of valor, that is still a *good* for us now.

For the whole Past, as I keep repeating, is the possession of the Present; the Past had always something true [Arnold's Eternal], and is a precious possession. In a different time, in a different place, it is always some other *side* of our common Human Nature that has been developing itself. The actual true is the sum of all these; not any one of them by itself constitutes what of Human Nature is hitherto developed. Better to know them all than misknow them. "To which of these Three Religions do you specially adhere," asks Meister of his Teacher. "To all the Three!" answers the other: "To all the Three; for they by their union first constitute the True Religion."[32]

This, from the last part of *Wilhelm Meister*, glowing with the late light of Goethe's *gebildet* old age, was something Arnold most probably first appropriated here, in Carlyle.

Max Müller, Arnold's learned friend at Oxford, a protégé of Bunsen's when he first came over into England, brought with him the whole complex of Herderian language theory and anthropology. He writes:

It is impossible to express abstract ideas except by metaphor, and it is not too

30. Ibid., p. 8.
31. Ibid., p. 24.
32. Ibid., p. 37.

much to say that the whole dictionary of ancient religions is made up of metaphors.[33]

We can see this process at work in religions both ancient and modern; if we understand it we can interpret our own more reasonably.

We shall no longer try to force a literal sense on words which, if interpreted literally, must lose their true and original purport, we shall no longer interpret the Law and the Prophets as if they had been written in the English of our own century, but read them in a truly historical spirit, prepared for the many difficulties, undismayed by many contradictions, which, so far from disproving the authenticity, become . . . the strongest confirmatory evidence of the age, the genuineness, and the real truth of ancient sacred books.[34]

Philology reveals the fictiveness of language. When we know more than one language we must recognize the word as provisional and relative, only one way of many possible ways to organize variable sets of experience, and the "thing" appears to be an invention of language. The common biblical example is *word* itself in John 1: 1, which in English means something like *name*. But here it is a translation of Greek *logos*, which combines our sense of *word* with our sense of *reason*, which together imply language as a sense-making principle. So we can understand *word* in John 1: 1 to be Christ-as-the-sense-making-principle, the opposite to *random* or *caprice*. And this fact itself suggests the power of language: in spite of all the shifting provisional impermanence, it is nevertheless man's best and most characteristic capacity. In the beginning of man, there is language, his power to make himself by the metaphorical word. Arnold proceeds toward the discovery of religious phenomenology by his searching analysis of literary phenomenology: how figures work.

If, as Ted Cohen says, "these are good times for the friends of metaphor," they are also very difficult times: the subject becomes more protean and paradoxical the more one looks into it. Middleton Murry said some time ago of metaphor and language, "If we try to penetrate them beyond a certain point, we find ourselves questioning the very faculty and instrument with which we are trying to penetrate them."[35]

33. Max Müller, *Introduction to the Science of Religion* (London: Longmans, Green, 1893), pp. 196–97.

34. Ibid., pp. 206–7.

35. Middleton Murry, *Countries of the Mind, Second Series* (London: Oxford

In linguistic analysis, we can proceed with some confidence up to a certain point, but when we encounter irony and metaphor, the investigation tends to lose stability. Noam Chomsky has declared in this connection that he thinks probably the mind cannot understand how it itself works.[36] In fact, the whole matter of metaphor is quite probably liable to "limitations" in the Gödelian sense.[37] Meantime, perhaps we can cautiously agree that metaphor is a phenomenon of vital importance, and of a larger importance than was thought even by the best friends of metaphor in the nineteenth century. Carlyle and Emerson I take to be two of the best friends: their insistence that language is metaphorical *in origin* is well known. And Arnold follows in this. His labors in "The God of Metaphysics" are his most elaborate in this regard, where he works out *being* to be essentially *breathing*, with certain reductive effects for Anselm on God and Descartes on *cogito ergo sum* (VII: 173–202). We find these etymologies doubtful, but generally share the idea of Herder, Carlyle, and Arnold that early or "folk" literature is highly metaphorical, and probably naively so. That is, the "folk" are not aware that their metaphors are metaphors. But the wiser ones make it their office to insist on the fictive quality of metaphor. Jesus repeatedly, as Arnold explains, must demonstrate the error of literalism. For the Old Testament, Hosea describes the poetic mode in a splendid quatrain:

> I have also spoken by the prophets
> and I have multiplied visions
> and used similitudes
> by the ministry of the prophets—[38]
> (Hos. 12: 10)

University Press, 1931), p. 1; quoted in George Whalley, "Metaphor," *Princeton Encyclopedia of Poetry and Poetics* (Princeton: Princeton University Press, 1965), p. 492.

36. Noam Chomsky, *Language and Mind* (New York: Harcourt Brace, 1968), pp. 82–84.

37. See my "Waiting for Gödel," *Language, Logic, and Genre,* ed. Wallace Martin (Lewisburg, Pa.: Bucknell University Press, 1974), pp. 28–43.

38. The New English Bible has "parables" for *similitudes.* I have proposed elsewhere that this passage refers to the parallel structure of Hebrew verse form as well as its metaphorical mode ("Old Testament Poetry: The Translatable Structure," *Publications of the Modern Language Association* 92 [October 1977]: 987–1004, see p. 997).

Arnold characteristically explains the vision or similitude—or metaphor. The idea of the love for the law of God, for instance, represents our experience that acting in accord with what we think right rather than with the impulse of the moment gives a certain joy. Jesus as "Son of God" (or Apollo as the Son of Zeus) represents our sense of the "offspring or outcome" of acting in accord with this natural law of experience (VII: 208).

Language, metaphor, and myth are bound to man's sociality—they are nothing if not shared. All are means by which we express or create ourselves as members of a culture. Arnold's theory is antireductive: we do not speak of *mere* metaphor, or *mere* myths, for they are our most precious possessions (as Herder held), by which we survive, and we do not regret our existence. Because metaphor has always been recognized as useful at least to some degree, a means of learning something new, or understanding something otherwise inapprehensible, to see metaphor as myth-eme illuminates the value of myth. The theory is of importance for Bible criticism, for literary criticism, for aesthetics, and for theory of religion. It leads into Susanne K. Langer's theory of man as a symbolizing animal: the making and use of symbols in art, music, literature, and in religion as well is a satisfactory end in itself, fulfilling man's humanness.[39]

Possibly Arnold has at some points some misgivings about developing his underlying theory: God as a metaphor is a concept even the broadest of the Broad might balk at—in its theory. But in its application, in Arnold's criticism of the Psalms, Isaiah, and the Gospel of John, and of Pindar, Sophocles, and Homer, it does not seem limiting. It was arrived at just because he is, as he says, against rigid system; he is *for*, in fact, fictions. By his pretense at naïveté, he consistently questions convention in theology and in criticism, holding experience as the sole validity. And he has had experience of literature, including the great translations of the Bible—Jerome's, Luther's, and the King James Committee's—and experience of ritual, with a great Prayer Book, and he knew the Roman Catholic mass, and the mystics, and the great medieval doctors of the church. He was born into the admirable Anglican tradition—of Hooker, Walton, Herbert, the Cam-

39. Susanne K. Langer, *Philosophy in a New Key* (Cambridge: Harvard University Press, 1942). Howard Gardner notes how she helps us appreciate symbols as functioning "to *make things conceivable* rather than store up propositions" ("Reconsiderations," *Human Nature* 1 [November 1978]: 92–96).

bridge Platonists, Bishop Wilson, Bishop Lowth, Bishop Butler, and of Thomas Arnold and his circle. In considering this broad literary, ritual, and social experience, he finds the common strong activating element to be figure of speech, and he is faithful to that insight. It is Arnold's refusal to systematize, to dogmatize, that makes for the splendidly British-empirical loose ends in his argument, grand inconsistencies that leave room for modern aesthetics. It is hardly to be expected of him that he should exploit his discovery in theory and proceed to invent William James, Susanne Langer, Wittgenstein, Logical Positivism, Vaihinger, Stevens, and the Supreme Fiction. But it is from data like Arnold's, and from attitudes like his, that all these have developed. And perhaps none of these has been so securely based as he in a broad experience of literature, secular and religious.

One may see how the main lines of Arnold's thought lead directly into principles of the Logical Positivists: the impulse to eliminate metaphysics, for instance, and the insistence on verifiability. Arnold's verifiability, an experiential one, might not meet the standards of some Logical Positivists; for him, it comes out of introspection, "common sense," and that very broad vicarious knowledge of human experience as recorded in literature that Arnold has at his fingertips. Furthermore, just as with Arnold, a large part of the Logical Positivists' effort is negative: Arnold exposes the vanity of dogma, they expose "nonsense" statements. The idea of the two languages, one of science, one of figure, by no means original with Arnold yet one he made particularly his own, has stayed current in modern criticism, endorsed by I. A. Richards: "No system of abstractions can affect man's behavior. . . . Myth is the element that activates ideas."[40] And it is paralleled in the Logical Positivists' classification of ethical and aesthetic "propositions" as forms of emotive as opposed to referential language. To determine the meaning of a proposition, says Wittgenstein, one must determine its use. And that "use" could be to make a place for ourselves in the world by means of figures. "Unsayable things do indeed exist," again says Wittgenstein, adding his stern and famous admonition, "Whereof one cannot speak, thereof one must be silent." But Wittgenstein actually interested himself in the language of art and

40. I. A. Richards, *Science and Poetry*, quoted in the excellent essay by Epifanio San Juan, Jr., "Matthew Arnold and the Poetics of Belief: Some Implications of *Literature and Dogma*," *Harvard Theological Review* 37 (April 1964): 97–118, especially p. 115.

religion, the efforts to say the unsayable.[41] His stern admonition would be suitably directed at Arnold's dogmatists, but the language of metaphor and myth is protected by its provisional nature, just as Sir Philip Sidney saw long ago: "The poet never lieth because he nothing affirmeth."[42] The poet tries out—words, figures, stories, hypotheses—fictions. The way of the poet is a tentative way, relative, progressive, a becoming-not-being sort of way. If there is a theory of art that is consonant with *Bildung*, it is certainly this theory of fictions. Arnold, who had a good nose for analogues to *Bildung*, fastened on Keats's "Negative Capability" in his *Note-Books*:

At once it struck me what quality went to form a man of achievement, especially in literature, and which Shakespeare possessed so uncommonly—I mean *negative capability*, that is, when man is capable of being in uncertainties, mysteries, doubts, without any irritable reaching after fact and reason.[43]

"Negative Capability" is to make do with our splendid fictive uncertainties and to eschew "fact and reason"—or dogma. Because poetry is provisional, its task is never done, and there is always new poetry to be written. That insight is presented in the Psalmist's "Sing a new song unto the Lord!" Hebrew poetry, by its particularly bold cultivation of metaphor, and its peculiar parallel structure (a form that also can be considered an "idea of order," a fiction), its high degree of translatability, not to mention great translators, has "said" so often what one might have thought "unsayable" that it has given to Western culture, as I believe, a sense of unlimited possibilities for art. It is no small part of Arnold's claim to greatness as a critic that he exercises his powers on the Bible in an age when it had been almost suffocated by a thousand dreary sermons, by a fanatic idolatry, by intense sectarian controversy, and by what he demonstrates to be an absurd superstructure of pseudoscientific theology. In some places even now there is a powerful antipathy to biblical literature, born of fatigue and disgust at absurd sectarian commentary; Arnold's criticism can still refresh and renew the texts.

41. See especially Ludwig Wittgenstein, *Lectures and Conversations on Aesthetics, Psychology, and Religious Belief* (Oxford: Basil Blackwell, 1966).

42. Philip Sidney, *Apologie for Poetrie* (1595).

43. *Note-Books*, p. 509. Datable items near it in the *Note-Books* are from things published in 1877 and 1878.

The theory of fictions, which I now propose to review because I think it helps us to grasp the significance of Arnold's thought, developed out of the German *Bildung*-complex that Arnold appropriated. Nietzsche more than any other came to terms with the new relativity of the century, and he proposed that any theory of "truth" is constrictive. His purpose was to free consciousness from any such absolute and, in the words of Hayden White, to "return consciousness to the enjoyment of its Metaphorical powers, its capacity to 'frolic in images,' to entertain the world as pure phenomena, and to liberate, thereby, man's poetic consciousness to an activity more pure, for being more self-conscious, than the naive Metaphor of primitive man."[44] The theory of fictions proper was formulated in German by Hans Vaihinger in *Die Philosophie des Als-Ob* (1911).[45] English readers have a particular advantage here, however: the work was translated by C. K. Ogden, *The Philosophy of As If* (1932), in consultation with Vaihinger himself after Ogden had introduced him to the early theory of fictions of Jeremy Bentham (c. 1815).[46] Ogden quotes Bentham: "To language, then—to language alone—it is that fictitious entities owe their existence; their impossible, yet indispensable existence."[47] This complements Vaihinger's theory, at the same time as it reverses it—making language the means to the other fictions.

Vaihinger was much interested in the theory of evolution and emphasized the biological function of mind, its survival power.[48] F. A. Lange had said, "Man needs to supplement reality by an ideal world of his own creation"; Vaihinger expanded this view and applied it to science, metaphysics, theology, social ideals, and morality. It is both necessary and useful to act on the basis of fictions known to be false,

44. Hayden White, *Metahistory: The Historical Imagination in Nineteenth-Century Europe* (Baltimore: Johns Hopkins University Press, 1973), p. 334.

45. Hans Vaihinger, *Die Philosophie des Als-Ob* (Berlin, 1911); trans. C. K. Ogden, in consultation with Vaihinger, *The Philosophy of As If* (New York, 1924), p. 19n.

46. Jeremy Bentham, *Bentham's Theory of Fictions*, passages selected and edited by C. K. Ogden, with a valuable introduction of 152 pp. (1932; reprint ed., London: Routledge and Kegan Paul, 1951; Patterson, N.J.: Littlefield, Adams, 1959).

47. Ibid., xxxii.

48. For this summary I adapt the article on Vaihinger by Rollo Handy in the *Macmillan Encyclopedia of Philosophy* (New York: Macmillan, 1967), vol. 8, pp. 221–24.

fictions that contradict observed reality or that are self-contradictory
(as in the case of light and its waves or particles). The fiction is an
auxiliary construct, a circuitous approach, a scaffolding afterward
to be demolished.[49] To take "God" and "immortality" for examples:
it may be a great convenience to act as if the cosmos were orderly and
created by an all-powerful and all-good God, and as if man were immortal. In physics, the atom has been a useful fiction; in biology
"vital force"; in mathematics $\sqrt{-1}$; in sociology the notion of a
social contract. Intellectually, practically, and morally we need false
but expedient fictions to cope with the world. "Thought is an adapt-
able, pliant, and adjustable organic function."

Mind, however, Vaihinger holds, sets itself problems that cannot
be solved: questions about the origin of the world, the formation of
matter, the origin of motion, the meaning of the world, and the purpose of life. It is experience and intuition that give us the harmonious
unity that reason cannot supply; there seem to be, that is, nonrational
solutions to questions that have no rational answer. Senseless questions may be explained by looking backward into their psychological
origin. Vaihinger deplores "practical atheism," understood as the
failure to act so as to make the world better. Religion becomes a mode
of behavior rather than the acceptance of certain theoretical views. He
hold that the striving toward the Kingdom of God is what matters,
not the achieving of it.

I think it will be obvious that Arnold anticipated much of this Vaihingerian philosophy. Here is Arnold's relativism, the sea of more-or-
less and of constant change, that German historicism cast him into.
Here is *Bildung*, by which process we never arrive at a final absolutism
but develop by stages, ever provisionally positing the best hypotheses
of our time and culture, cultivating our "negative capability" and our
language, metaphors, myths—or fictions. "For *the days of Israel are
innumerable* . . . . culture must not fail to keep its flexibility, and to
give to its judgments [a] passing and provisional character" (V: 255).
His idea of *adequacy* as a criterion for literature (the Greeks are,
above all, *adequate*; I: 32–38) nicely represents value as provisional
and nonabsolute. Here is Arnold's "esprit ondoyant et divers" (V:

49. Theorists used to distinguish hypotheses from fictions in that it is expected
that hypotheses are to be *proved*. As I understand it, however, most scientists now
posit even their best hypotheses as provisional.

174); as John Holloway indicates Arnold "mediates not a view of the world but a habit of mind."[50] Church and religion are to be valued and maintained. Religion is a matter of conduct, shaped (made non-random, noncapricious) by the direction of the movement toward perfection ("Be ye perfect!"), which is the metaphor of the Kingdom of God. "The object of religion is conduct; and if a man helps himself in his conduct by taking an object of hope and presentiment *as if* [my emphasis] it were an object of certainty, he may even be said to gain thereby an advantage" (VI: 232). To demythologize as Arnold does is to look back into the psychological need that the myth has answered to. *The not-ourselves which makes for righteousness* is the result of such research, representing the experience that imperiously demanded expression, an invention, a noble fiction, a personification —God.

The poet Wallace Stevens was deeply impressed by Vaihinger's theory, and it is to Stevens, I think, that we owe the extension of the concept of fictions to aesthetics. Nietzsche and Vaihinger shape Stevens's own aesthetic, which is often the subject of his poetry as well as his prose. For him, man's fiction-making power is "the necessary angel" by which he survives; man creates "ideas of order"—in art, in science, in everything; God is the "Supreme Fiction." Stevens also perpetuates by no means incidentally a strong Arnoldian line. His ideal is cosmopolitan; he cultivates the Arnoldian disinterestedness and the Arnoldian kind of "negative capability."[51] And he takes what I think of as an Arnoldian interest in metaphor, and allies it with Vaihingerian fiction-theory.[52]

Frank Kermode, in turn, who is familiar with Stevens and his

50. John Holloway, *The Victorian Sage* (London: Macmillan, 1953), p. 207.

51. The Henry E. Huntington Library in San Marino, Ca., has Stevens's marked copy of Arnold's *Essays in Criticism, First Series* (London: Macmillan, 1895). He marks criticism as "the free play of mind" and "disinterestness," and the whole sentence, "The paramount virtue of religion is, that it has lighted up morality; that it has supplied the emotion and inspiration needful for carrying the sage along the narrow way perfectly, for carrying the ordinary man along it at all" ("Marcus Aurelius," Stevens's copy, p. 346; III: 134). Stevens was apparently reading the book in 1898–1900.

52. Terence Hawkes in his handbook *Metaphor*, number 25 in the Critical Idiom Series (London: Methuen, 1972), recognizes Stevens's appreciation of metaphor as the unit of fiction. See pp. 1, 6, 16, 57, 90, 91.

sources in Nietzsche and Vaihinger, builds on Stevens's theory "the nicer knowledge of belief, that what it believes in is not true."[53] Just as it is Stevens who extends fiction theory to aesthetics, so it is Kermode who extends fiction theory to include literary fictions, such as "plots"—from Creation through to Apocalypse, from the abdication of King Lear to the death of Cordelia, all novels and their reactive antinovels, our poems, our very modes of perception itself. In most minimal terms, we *hear* "tick-tick-tick-tick" and *make* it as we hear it into the plot of "tick-*tock*, tick-*tock*"; maximal terms would be Genesis through to Revelation, or alternatively, the physicists' Big Bang through to—the big Whimper, or Black Hole, or whatever it is that is being currently hypothesized by the world's prophetic soul, dreaming on things to come. Kermode's *The Sense of an Ending, or Studies in the Theory of Fiction*, has been welcome to many as a fresh and satisfactory theory of art, and he himself in his own readings of literary texts demonstrates its fruitfulness.[54] And of course it is the more valuable because it is not mere aesthetic theory but a theory of the human condition, even more broad than Susanne Langer's.

It is in this largest perspective of fictions that the significance of metaphor becomes apparent, even the sense of metaphor that Arnold discovers in his biblical criticism. He apprehends that metaphor is the heart of the matter in religion. It has been recognized that in this Arnold anticipates Rudolf Bultmann, Karl Jaspers, Paul Tillich, and others.[55] As Bultmann says, "Myth is the expression of man's conviction that the origin and purpose of the world in which he lives are to be sought not within it but beyond it. . . . Myth is also an expression of man's awareness that he is not lord of his own being."[56] David Tracy

53. Frank Kermode, *The Sense of an Ending, or Studies in the Theory of Fiction* (New York: Oxford University Press, 1966), p. 34.

54. See my "Frank Kermode and the Invented World," *Novel* 1 (Winter 1968): 171–77.

55. Nathan A. Scott claims Arnold's "immense relevance to modern theology" with some very informed arguments, but then misses the significance Arnold lays on literary criticism and metaphor. "Arnold's Version of Transcendence—the *Via Poetica*," *Journal of Religion* 59 (July 1979): 261–64.

56. Rudolf Bultmann, quoted in San Juan, "Matthew Arnold and the Poetics of Belief," pp. 109–10. He quotes from *Kerygma and Myth*, trans. R. H. Fuller (London: Society for the Propagation of Christian Knowledge, 1941). Jerold Savory gives an interesting account of discovering in Arnold the ideas he first encountered in a seminary context in Bultmann, Paul Tillich, Reinhold Niebuhr, and even Diet-

tells us, "That all major religions are grounded in certain root metaphors has become a commonplace in modern religious studies."[57]
These metaphors present the "enigma and promise of the human
situation" and prescribe certain courses of action. Heretofore, he says,
too little attention has been paid to the relationship between the poetic
and religious function of the human spirit, with certain notable exceptions, such as George Santayana and Jacques Maritain (surely we
can add Arnold). Metaphors should not be considered reductively,
as mere decorative substitutes for ideas or literal "meanings"; in fact,
analysis of metaphor has shifted from substitute theory to "a theory
of tension or interaction." Paul Ricoeur, he continues, "representing
the emerging consensus in New Testament scholarship," describes
parable as "the conjunction of a narrative form and a metaphorical
progress." (I think Arnold understood this thoroughly.) The parable,
Tracy continues in the modern idiom, is a model, a heuristic fiction; its
fictiveness is declared sometimes in the "radical disclaimers"—"The
Kingdom of God is like." Finally, Tracy says, the study of metaphor
"is hardly the luxury item" many theologians have thought it. "It
moves to the very center of contemporary theological studies."[58] Paul
Ricoeur himself builds, as he says, on the conception of language of
Humboldt and Ernst Cassirer (and we understand also Herder and
the whole expressionist school), the conception that it is language
that gives form to experience. He sees metaphor as essential to religious discourse; it is as a "model" is to science—it is a "heuristic
fiction." Metaphor, moreover, teaches us to see "as if."[59]

The main line of scholarly biblical criticism today appears to be
Arnoldian.

For recent general theory of metaphor we can turn to Wayne Booth,
as he continues the line of *The Rhetoric of Fiction*[60] into "Metaphor

---

rich Bonhoeffer and Martin Buber ("The Gospel According to Arnold: *Literature
and Dogma* and *God and the Bible*," *The Arnoldian* 5 [Winter 1978]: 15–21).

57. David Tracy, "Metaphor and Religion: The Test Case of Christian Texts,"
Critical Inquiry 5 (Autumn 1978): 91–106, especially p. 91.

58. Ibid., p. 106.

59. Paul Ricoeur, "Biblical Hermeneutics" (1. The Narrative Form; 2. The
Metaphorical Process; 3. The Specificity of Religious Language), *Semeia* 4
(1975): 27–148, especially pp. 79, 81, 85.

60. Wayne Booth, *The Rhetoric of Fiction* (Chicago: University of Chicago
Press, 1961).

as Rhetoric."[61] For him, the recent explosion of interest in metaphor, in the social and natural sciences as in the humanities, reveals the difficulty of making definitions, and he feels pretty sure that all the things we call metaphor cannot go under one definition. But, as he says, we can posit that with all metaphors more is communicated than the words literally say; what the *more* is, is the difficulty. Aristotle and others have called it energy. Booth tentatively draws up some criteria for effective metaphors: 1) They are *active*; they lend energy to the less energetic or to the abstract (compare Arnold's *motor*, or morality *lit up*). 2) They are concise (but of course: Arnold's *God*, for instance, for the not-ourselves, etc.). 3) They are appropriate ("Clouds and darkness are round about him, righteousness and judgment are the habitation of his seat"). 4) They are accommodated to the audience (and so, as Arnold says, we must study the Jews and Israel). 5) They build the proper ethos for the speaker's character (consider, as Arnold explains, Jesus' use of Isaiah's metaphor of the suffering servant; VII: 319 et passim).

Booth continues: "The metaphors we care for most are always embedded in metaphoric structures that finally both depend on and constitute selves and societies." Booth moves, he says, toward "an immense thesis: the quality of any culture will in part be measured both by the quality of the metaphors it induces or allows and the quality of the judges of metaphor that it educates and rewards."[62] Literary critics, Booth continues, discriminate among metaphors, "those that diminish us from those that enlarge us." In our world of advertising we have a host of metaphors at work that tends to diminish us, keeping our vision centered on possessions. But the great poets seem to say: "My vision of what *stands for* human happiness is itself the activity of sharing pictures of what human life is or can be." "Metaphor in this view," Booth continues, and I italicize, *"is not a means to other ends but one of the main ends of life; sharing metaphors becomes one of the experiences we live for."*[63]

Now he writes:

It is no doubt that this inherent aspiration of all literature to metaphoric truth accounts for our tendency in modern times, as the old religious meta-

61. Booth, "Metaphor as Rhetoric," pp. 49–72.
62. Ibid., p. 64.
63. Ibid., p. 69.

phors have weakened their hold on us, to turn literature to overt religious uses. When critics like Matthew Arnold found themselves treating poetry as the religion of the future, they were in fact simply expressing a kind of rivalry that was implicit in all secular metaphoric enterprises. . . . My story, though it may present no visible Gods and no expressions of piety, inevitably rivals yours that begins, "In the beginning was the Word." [64]

Here, I should like for Arnold's sake, if not for critics *like* Arnold, to insist that though he may appear to suggest a rivalry, as, most clearly, where he challenges St. Francis and Luther to "beat" Sophocles, he in fact, as the critic and man of culture recommending the best that has been thought and known in the world, envisages a coexistence of "rival" metaphor systems: we need Sophocles *and* St. Francis, Homer *and* the Bible. He sees the "rival" metaphor systems as mutually enriching: to know only one is to know none and to be in danger of literalism. He by no means would agree that "the old religious metaphors have weakened their hold on us"; he sees, rather (to borrow Hayden White's words on Nietzsche), the liberation of "man's poetic consciousness to an activity more pure, for being more self-conscious, than the naive Metaphor of primitive man." [65] The great biblical metaphors mean *more*, not less, than they do to the literal mind—the metaphors of creation, of the epic release from Egypt and journey to the Promised Land, of the stupendous perspective of the Whirlwind in Job, the poignancy of the Psalmist's "I am a stranger here on earth; O, hide not thy commandments from me"; the insights of the parables of Jesus, or the parable that his life itself constitutes. How can these things be diminished, except in a context of enervating dogma? We do not stop singing the great music, or turn our backs on the Old Masters, or pull down the great churches. Even in Moscow, in a metaphor-impoverished culture, the church buildings remain, to sweeten and grace the drab city.

Arnold consistently strives in his criticism to be as "scientific" as he can possible be, and there isn't much "science" to apply. The best he can do is refer to his own experience and to the accumulated experience of literature and its critics, of which his own knowledge was vast. He fastened on likely interpretations, and good hunches, like

64. Ibid., pp. 70–71.

65. Hayden White, *Metahistory* (Baltimore: Johns Hopkins University Press, 1973), p. 334.

Coleridge's "The Bible *finds me* at greater depth of my being." There may be now some hard scientific evidence to endorse such a hunch. Scientists have tested the brain waves of persons reading,

first, dry technical text and then fiction full of imagery. The brain signals indicated activity on the left side of the brain during both tasks, as would be expected, but more activity on the right side when the reading matter was fiction than when it was dry and technical.[66]

It may quite possibly be, then, that dogma, the "dry technical text," can never engage us wholly, while "fiction full of imagery" engages not only the verbal mathematical left-brain part of us but also the spatial, musical, face-recognizing, possibly "altruistic" right-brain part of us.[67] It is proposed moreover that while in childhood the connection (*corpus callosum*) between the two brains matures,

the childhood development of anatomical connections between brain subsystems may in fact be related to the parallel development of integration between mental subsystems, such as parts of the personality, leading to unity of the self.[68]

It would seem, then, that dogma leaves us incomplete, calling into play as Carlyle says the "*mere* argumentative region" of us. But literature— metaphor, and its extension into myth, fable, legend, allegory, epic, lyric, all fictions great and small—not only engages that other side of us but exploits the *corpus callosum* and put us all together.

While "images" or metaphors may be earning a place in psychology, the philosophers who often have given metaphor a bad name now seem to grant at least some grudging acknowledgment. At most, it may seem essential. Iris Murdoch, returning to Plato, insists that he himself was a "poet." "Of course he used metaphor, but philosophy needs metaphor and metaphor is basic; how basic is the most basic philosophical question."[69]

66. Harold M. Schmeck, Jr., " 'Two Brains' of Man: Complex Teamwork," *New York Times*, January 8, 1980, p. C3.

67. Ibid.

68. Ibid.

69. Iris Murdoch, *The Fire and the Sun: Why Plato Banished the Artists* (Oxford: Clarendon Press, 1977), p. 88.

XI

Practical Criticism:
God and the Bible
and Isaiah

A RNOLD'S theory of religion-literature is complete and whole in *Literature and Dogma*. It gives him his point of leverage, and the ensuing writings are more expansive and assured. *God and the Bible*, though announced merely as "a review of the objections to *Literature and Dogma*," has value and power of its own, and Arnold himself felt it included some of his best writing (VII: 439).[1]

The first three chapters, "The God of Miracles," "The God of Metaphysics," and "The God of Experience," are Arnold's definitive dismissal of the personal God. In "The God of Miracles," Arnold modifies his thesis on the literal-figurative dichotomy—as indeed it becomes increasingly clear we all must—the "literal" turns out so regularly to be a lesser degree or different kind of "figurative." And so Arnold must grant that when the Bishop of Gloucester asserts "the blessed truth that the God of the universe is a person," he is indeed using figurative language just as Arnold has claimed Israel does with his "high and holy one that inhabiteth eternity." The Bishop writes bad poetry, however, and the insidious trouble with it is that it is intended as science. Arnold reexplains the psychology of anthropomorphosis: "We make persons of the sun, wind, love, envy, war, fortune; in some languages every noun is male or female. But this we know is figure and personification. Being ourselves alive and thinking and having sex, we naturally invest things with these our abilities" (VII:

1. See Jerold Savory, "Matthew Arnold and 'the Author of *Supernatural Religion*': The Background to *God and the Bible*," *Studies in English Literature* 16 (Autumn 1976): 677–91.

162).[2] "In general, as God is said to have made man in his own image,
... man has returned the compliment. . . . We construct a magnified
and non-natural man" (VII: 162). We cannot accept the miracle, or
"fairy-tale" ground of support either for this image of God or for the
Bible. In a noteworthy piece of demythologizing exegesis, Arnold suggests that "a clue . . . of fact, there probably was to every miracle. . . .
The story of the feeding of the thousands may well have had its rise in
the suspension, the comparative extinction, of hunger and thirst during hours of rapt interest and intense mental excitement" (VII: 171).

When we turn to "The God of Metaphysics":

> At the mention of that name *metaphysics*, lo! essence, existence, substance,
> finite and infinite, cause and succession, something and nothing, begin to
> weave their eternal dance before us; with the confused murmur of their com-
> binations filling all the region governed by *her*, who far more indisputably
> than her late-born rival, political economy, has earned the title of the Dismal
> Science.
>
>   (VII: 173)

To deal with all this, Arnold turns from the "great" men, Hegel and
other sage professors, to—with much ironic play—himself, a "mere"
professor of *words*. It is not German philosophy but German *philology*, he says, that will reveal our errors, the science of Curtius,
Gesenius—and here he also cites the Rothschild tutor and friend Marcus Kalisch.[3] He demonstrates, as Wittgenstein would, that the God-
statements are non-sense, exclaiming: "To such a degree do words
make man, who invents them, their sport!" (VII: 188). He insists on
man's "plastic and personifying power," the anthropomorphic or
what we can now call the fiction-making process: we men "transfer
by a figure the phenomena of our bodily life to all law and operation"
(VII: 193). He dismisses the famous "proofs" of God—Anselm's,
Descartes's, and the "argument from design": "We know nothing
about the matter, it is altogether beyond us." If we abandon with

2. If there are any readers of Arnold who have objected to the phallocracy of
Jehovah it should be observed that Arnold's god-definitions—the not-ourselves, the
stream-of-tendency—are very satisfactorily asexual.

3. VII: 186 and 455n. He is also called variously Moritz M. Kalisch, Marcus
Moritz Kalisch, Moritz Kalisch. He published his *Historical and Critical Commentary on the Old Testament* in London in 1858.

regret the belief in the existence of God drawn from miracles because it comforted many, the belief "drawn from metaphysics one dismisses, on the other hand, with sheer satisfaction" (VII: 198–99).

But in "The God of Experience"—it is here that he felt was some of his best writing—he elaborates his claim that there can be a valid scientific way to talk about God. He discriminates among Higher Criticisms. Much of German biblical criticism employs overmuch of "rigour and vigour," assuming that "people do not vary; people do not contradict themselves; people do not have undercurrents of meaning; people do not divine" (VII: 203). And these critics reduce religion to an absurdity and declare us enfranchised from it all, and dismiss God, the Bible, and religion in general. But Arnold traces some of the processes of developing religion as part of man's distinctive humanness, taking cultural differences and historical change into account and working comparatively. "From Pindar, Aeschylus and Sophocles, may be quoted sentences as religious as those we find in Job or Isaiah" (VII: 209). Early Hellenic righteousness, however, did not last, but the Hebrews made it their central concern, and their poetry, because it is such superlative poetry, maintains the righteousness. The Psalms everywhere indicate both the intensity of the religious experience and the nature of the religion. Here again Arnold borrows the eloquence of these extraordinarily passionate poems to make his argument in a way that in turn illuminates the texts. These Psalms and prophetic writings, he might have said in the Herderian fashion, are at once the most characteristic expression and the most precious possession of the nation:

So powerfully did the inmost chords of its being vibrate to them, so entirely were they the very truth it was born to and sought to find utterance for, that it adopted them, made them its standards, the documents of that most profound and authentic expression of the nation's consciousness, its religion. Instead of remaining literature and philosophy, isolated voices of sublime poets and reforming free-thinkers, these glorifications of righteousness became Jewish religion, matters to be read in the synagogue every Sabbath-day.

(VII: 214)

This is literature *becoming* religion. The implication is that this literature can still become religion for us now—or, rather, it is *both*, undifferentiatedly—a continuum. He calls Xenophanes up out of obscurity to witness the process of development: "The gods did not from the first show to men all things; but in time, by searching, men came to a discovery of the better" (VII: 217). So are born ideas of moral order.

During man's chaotic and rudimentary time, these ideas must have been at work; and as they were no conscious creation of man's will, but solicited him and ripened in him whether he would or no, we may truly and fitly call them the Spirit of God brooding over chaos, moving silently upon the human deep. . . . We give an explanation which is natural. But we say that this natural explanation is yet grander than the preternatural one.

(VII: 217, 218, 220)

This is demythologization, this is literary criticism, making the brooding Spirit-of-God figure here new with meaning. For a Herderian-developmentalist, Darwin has no terrors; he answers, rather, to the Herderian's prophetic soul and adds a dimension to Arnold's exegesis of the Spirit of God "moving silently upon the human deep." Here is Carlyle's Natural Supernaturalism and his religious "Wonder" coming to flower in a new Bible criticism. "Liturgy," Arnold proposes, has its origin "in the stirrings we call aesthetic" (VII: 218), and he returns to a figure frequent in the Psalms and Prophets that in virtue we feel more alive (following the law of our being), in lack of virtue we are less stable, less real, less existent:

As the whirlwind passeth, so is the wicked no more, but the righteous is an everlasting foundation. As righteousness tendeth to life, so he that pursueth evil pursueth it to his own death.

(VII: 231, Proverbs 10: 25, 11: 19)

The passages are beautifully chosen to bear out his central New Testament exegesis of the Kingdom of God on earth.

The rest of *God and the Bible* is more technical: a chapter on "the Bible canon" and two long chapters on the Gospel of John, one "from without"—or, on external evidence—and one "from within"—on internal evidence. These three chapters constitute an education in the subjects and can still be recommended as authoritative. Study of the history of the canon must always work against bibliolatry, simply because it reminds us of the thoroughly human agents who made the selection. Here and there are points where new evidence has shifted since Arnold's time the history of the canon or some understanding of

John, but by and large Arnold was in possession of the current learning, which has not increased or changed much, and the presentation is thoroughly readable as well as sound critically. "Disinterestedness" is not quite so possible a thing as Arnold implies, and yet his own account here is one of the very few instances where biblical criticism is not obviously and oppressively sectarian, or "interested." Super quotes the authority F. Crawford Burkitt writing in 1901:

For my own part I have found Matthew Arnold's remarks . . . to be much the most illuminating investigation of the origins and character of the Gospel according to St. John which has yet appeared. Most literary people do not know how well-equipped he was for the work. He had the habit and experience of literary criticism, and an excellent knowledge not only of the works of modern theologians, but—what is of much more importance—of the ancient sources also. Few professed theologians know how to quote as well as Matthew Arnold from Eusebius or Philosophumena.[4]

Most literary people still do not know this. Nor do the theologians know, so far as I can tell. There are perhaps not many scholars with the phenomenally broad learning that enabled Burkitt to give this judgment.[5] Arnold in a way defies criticism by bridging the two fields of expertise, but literary scholars should be informed that the main principle of Arnold's theory of John, that it was written by a later writer using memoirs of the apostle John and the apostle's collection of *logia*, seem to be the main principles of Rudolf Bultmann's respected commentary.[6] From the survey of Johannine scholarship in the recent *Interpreter's Bible*, it appears that Arnold's line has become the main line.[7]

4. Super, *Prose* VII: 440–41; F. Crawford Burkitt, *Two Lectures on the Gospels* (London, 1901), pp. 54–56, 67.

5. For Burkitt's credentials, see *Dictionary of National Biography* (supplement of 1949), and the *Oxford Dictionary of the Christian Church*, ed. F. L. Cross (London: Oxford University Press, 1957).

6. Rudolf Bultmann, *Das Evangelium des Johannes* (Göttingen, Ger.: Vanderhoeck und Ruprecht, 1941). See *Interpreter's Bible*, ed. Nolan B. Harmon, et al., 12 vols. (New York: Abingdon Press, 1952), 8: 460 and note.

7. *Interpreter's Bible*, 8: 437–63. Frank Kermode, like Arnold, holds that the gospel writers failed to understand Jesus even while reporting his sayings. *The Genesis of Secrecy* (Cambridge, Mass: Harvard University Press, 1979), p. 17 et passim. Kermode does not mention Arnold's biblical criticism.

The two books of the Bible that combine the greatest sustained art with the greatest devotional feelings are—most literary people would agree—the book of Job and the prophetic book of Isaiah. As early as 1848, in an interesting letter to Clough, Arnold tells of recognizing Carlyle by his manner: "The thoughts extracted and arbitrarily stated, are every newspaper's: it is the style and feeling by which the beloved man appears. Apply this, Infidel, to the Oriental Poem [the *Bhagavad-Gita*, which Clough seemed to resist]. How short could Mill write Job?" (*Clough* 75). This gnomic question seems to say that a Utilitarian summary of the events of Job would be as nothing. Style and art are part of the meaning. He advises Clough to write "plainer. . . . Read the Bible: Isaiah, Job, &c" (*Clough* 103). In *God and the Bible* he was to explain further the Hebrew "gnomic" way as opposed to the way the Greeks "had come to dovetail their thoughts into each other, to join their sentences by articulations, just as we do now with ours; indeed, it is from the Greeks that the world has learned to do it" (VII: 308, 327). Above all, Arnold was to show as few biblical commentators have his thorough understanding of Hebrew parataxis, both its logic and its artistic effect.[8] In 1862, Arnold was apparently contemplating doing a translation of Job himself, and Renan's French version of Job figures frequently in the reading lists.[9]

The Job project was never realized; it was Isaiah that he did do a version of. In the "attempt conservative and the attempt religious" he goes so far as to make some of the most glorious poetry in English available to the widest audience in England—schoolchildren. We get a glimpse of his motivation in some advice to pupil-teachers: "Open their minds," he would say; "take them into the world of Shakespeare, and try to make them feel that there is no book so full of poetry and beauty as the Bible."[10] England was at last moving toward a comprehensive state education; in view of the crippling disputes as to what kind of religion would be taught in government schools, it seemed a likely solution to circumscribe religion and possibly excise the Bible. In his inspector's report of 1869 he had strongly urged an element of

8. See, for example, VII: 57.

9. See Park Honan, *Matthew Arnold: A Life* (New York: McGraw-Hill, 1981), p. 320.

10. Dean Boyle, quoted by Fred G. Walcott in his *The Origins of Culture and Anarchy: Matthew Arnold and Popular Education in England* (Toronto: University of Toronto Press, 1970), p. 139.

Bible study in the secular school curriculum, as "the only chance for saving the one elevating and inspiring element in the scanty instruction of our primary schools from being sacrificed to a politico-religious difficulty" (IV: 376–77). Again, he writes with urgency, "The Bible is for the child in an elementary school almost his only contact with poetry and philosophy. What a course of eloquence and poetry (to call it by that name alone) is the Bible in a school which has and can have but little eloquence and poetry!" (VII: 504). "The friends of physics," he goes on to explain,

> do not content themselves with extolling physics; they put forth schoolbooks. . . . Any one who believes in the civilising power of letters and often talks of this belief, to think that he has for more than twenty years got his living by inspecting schools for the people, has gone in and out among them, has seen that the power of letters never reaches them at all and that the whole study of letters is thereby discredited and its power called in question, . . . may well desire to do something to pay his debt to popular education . . . , to serve it . . . where he has always said its need was sorest.
>
> (VII: 505)

The literature of the Bible is the one foreign literature for which the ordinary people have had some preparation. The Old Testament is the most suitable for this *literary* study, since it exhibits Hebrew literature in its perfection, while the New Testament purports only "to be a plain record of events, or else epistles . . . [not] aspiring to the literary qualities of poetry, rhythm and eloquence" (VII: 506).

Arnold's choice of the Deutero-Isaiah is perfect. It is accessible, and its choice represents the poet Arnold's informed critical values. "After all," he says, "Isaiah is immensely superior to Milton's *Comus* in all the more essential qualities of a literary production, even as literature."[11] The little book *A Bible Reading for Schools*, comprising the Deutero-Isaiah, or Isaiah 40–66, came out, then, in 1872 and achieved a modest success. This was reissued in 1875 for the general reader, with an introduction and some additions; Arnold was then instigated to add Isaiah 1–39, "Isaiah of Jerusalem," and he published the whole work in 1883 with an introduction. Super gives us both introductions, and—in an appendix—the whole text of Arnold's version and his notes.[12]

11. From a letter to William Steward, quoted VII: 413.
12. VII: 51–72; X: 100–130; Appendix 259–447.

Isaiah is a great artistic achievement, but it is also a notorious problem for scholars, the text being frequently defective or obscure, and
the whole impossible to ascribe to one author. The first thirty chapters
are ascribed to the historical "Isaiah of Jerusalem," *floruit* 740–701
B.C., though even some of this section appears to be later accretion,
and chapters 40 to 66 belong to the period 537–520 B.C., easily dated
by the clear references to Cyrus. These are sometimes thought of as
a collection of prophecies, sometimes considered the work of a single
or multiple author known conventionally as the "Deutero-Isaiah."
The problems of text and author have drawn many scholars: as Arnold writes, Aben-Ezra (Ibn Ezra, 1092–1167), the Dutch Vitringa
(1649–1722), and Robert Lowth (his text and commentary appeared
in 1778) are the most important until the German scholars took the
problems in hand. Arnold's work takes place against the background
of the work on the English Revised Version, 1881–85, which was in
progress from 1870. T. K. Cheyne, one of the company appointed to
the Old Testament Revision, brought out his own version and arrangement of Isaiah with apparatus in 1870 and another more scholarly
edition in 1880. Both he and Arnold were thoroughly conversant with
the German scholarship; Cheyne of course was the better Hebraist,
while Arnold was an amateur, with possibly more literary sense.

Arnold's introduction to Isaiah 40–66 for the general reader declares his editorial principles and his thoroughly guarded and modest
aim: to choose among the options offered by scholarship for the obscure parts; he would be most gratified "to find that a reader had gone
from the beginning of the chapters to the end without noticing anything different from what he was accustomed to, except that he was
not perplexed and thrown out as formerly" (VII: 416). He subscribes
to the principle of minimal change, just as the Revision was charged
to, but he feels his version is not obliged to as many corrections as the
Revision: if the sense runs smoothly that will be sufficient. Other
things being equal, Arnold will respect the version of Isaiah as quoted
in the New Testament, where available. He reminds us that Isaiah of
course is quoted in the New Testament more than any other Old
Testament book: Gesenius gives thirty-four passages, of which
twenty-one are from these last chapters. (Arnold's sustained work
on Isaiah was actually a useful accompaniment to his New Testament
studies in *God and the Bible*.) He explains his connection of certain
passages from Isaiah of Jerusalem to this Deutero-Isaiah text—and he

follows Cheyne in this (VII: 416), as indeed standard modern commentaries do.[13] At times he uses his knowledge of parallel structure to
determine the preferred reading. He acclaims Lowth's criticism but
deplores his version at points: certainly "Speak ye comfortably to
Jerusalem" is hardly improved by Lowth's "Speak ye animating words
to Jerusalem"! (VII: 62). Cheyne's version aims at the greatest accuracy combined with conservatism, but he is insensitive to the King
James Version style and frequently loses some good rhythm or effect
unnecessarily. It is a delicate matter, Arnold insists. In his explana-
tory and interpretive notes he expects the historical and linguistic
scholarship to be acceptable to Anglican, Roman Catholic, or Jew.
For he confines himself to the "local and temporary side of those
prophecies"; the other side, with its "secondary, eternal scope," must
be more important ultimately, but he insists that this second sense will
only be grasped when we understand the historical and literary
aspects. Goethe was, he tells us, "so constant a reader of the Bible
that his free-thinking friends reproached him for wasting his time
over it," and he quotes Goethe, translating the passage he had copied
in his *Note-Books*, to the effect that the better one knows the local and
circumstantial in the Bible the more beautiful it becomes, and the
more insights it affords into our lives and wants (VII: 68, *Note-Books*
168). He pays tribute to the scholarship of Gesenius and Ewald but
says nevertheless that in their interpretations they often fail, blighted
by dogma, or bent by interest to support a theory in which there has
been a professional investment, as it were. We must not press our
conjectures too far: "The best critic is he who does not insist on
being more precise than his text." The interesting "servant" concept
in the Deutero-Isaiah, for instance, for which there have been so many
theories, had better remain as unspecified and unexplained by the
literary critic as it is in the text.

   Finally in this introduction Arnold returns to the central mission of
his career, that answer to the "need for joy" stated in "Obermann
Once More." These Isaiah chapters are marked by "boundless ex-
hilaration."

Much good poetry is profoundly melancholy; now the life of the generality
of people is such that they require joy. And if ever that "good time coming,"

13. See *Interpreter's Bible*, vol. 5, pp. 151–64; 297; 381–419.

for which we all of us long, was presented with energy and magnificence, it is
in these chapters; it is impossible to read them without catching its glow.

(VII: 71)

Many of us, he says, have a sort of "centre-point" in the distant past
to which we relate our ideas.

Our education is such that we are strongly led to take this centre-point in the
history of Greece or Rome; but it may be doubted whether one who took the
conquest of Babylon and the restoration of the Jewish exiles would not have
a better. Whoever began with laying hold on this series of chapters as a whole,
would have a starting point and lights of unsurpassed value for getting a conception of the course of man's history and development. . . . What an extending of their horizons, what a lifting them out of the present, what a sug-
gestion of hope and courage!

(VII: 71–72)

Some grasp of "the history of the human spirit" apparently can take
us out of the vertigo of our own contemporary "multitudinousness."
So he concludes with a golden sentence from Jerome's translation of
the Psalms: "Cogitavi dies antiquos, et annos aeternos in mente
habui." [14]

Arnold's edition of *Isaiah of Jerusalem* with an introduction came
out in 1883; "I have never done a piece of work that pleases me more,"
he told his publisher (X: 484). This is so, undoubtedly, simply because he is making more accessible one of the greatest texts he knows.
"I rate the value of the operation of poetry and literature upon men's
minds extremely high," he says in this introduction—and by now we
know he does indeed value them as religion. "And from no poetry
and literature, not even from our own Shakespeare and Milton, great
as they are and our own as they are, have I, for my own part, received
so much delight as from Homer and Isaiah." He continues here his
strategy of not only asserting the "literary" value of the Bible but also
of *classifying* Bible authors with poets, consistently asserting that
continuum of which I have spoken. And the Bible most conveniently
supplies the needed literature other than one's own. It *has* been a

14. Psalms 77:5 (Vulgate 76:6). "I have thought on ancient days, and the
eternal years have I kept in mind." The King James Version has "I have considered the days of old, the years of ancient times."

cultural enlargement for Christian nations. And it is the more accessible for the great fact that it is more translatable:

The effect of Hebrew poetry can be preserved and transferred in a foreign language, as the effect of other great poetry cannot. The effect of Homer, the effect of Dante, is and must be in great measure lost in translation, because their poetry is a poetry of metre, or of rhyme, or both; and the effect of these is not really transferable. . . . Isaiah's, on the other hand, is a poetry, *as is well-known, of parallelism.* [My emphasis]

(X: 102)

The truth is that the principle was and is little known, and it is grossly neglected not only by exegetes but also by literary critics.[15] Arnold's negligent "as is well-known" is part of his ironic game, so little appreciated here that his great insight has virtually been ignored. It is an insight, I think, that only a critic well trained in literary discipline could declare with its due emphasis. This poetry, then,

depends not on metre and rhyme, but on a balance of thought, conveyed by a corresponding balance of sentence; and the effect of this can be transferred to another language.

(X: 102)

We can take possession of this great poetry, then, more completely than we can Homer's or Dante's in translation. It is perhaps a little surprising that Arnold does not have his version of Isaiah printed as verse. He had the example of Renan's edition of Job, apparently one of his most read books from 1866 on.[16] Renan not only prints the couplets as couplets but in his introduction discourses brilliantly on parallelism, the "rime des pensées," the "rhyme of thoughts"; and he uses parallelism for exegesis, defending an emendation with "sens conseillé par le parallélisme," a "meaning counselled by the parallelism."[17]

15. At last Stanley Gewirtz demonstrates some of these patterns of parallelism by the biblical poets, and declares: "To be indifferent towards their art is to risk indifference for the meaning." *Patterns in the Early Poetry of Israel,* Studies in Ancient Oriental Civilization, no. 32 (Chicago: University of Chicago Press, 1963), p. 97. And see my "Old Testament Poetry: The Translatable Structure," *Publications of Modern Language Association* 92 (October 1977): 987–1004.

16. See *Note-Books* 579, 581, 597, 600, 603, 605.

17. Ernest Renan, *Le Livre de Job, traduit de l'hebreu, avec une étude sur l'âge*

Arnold shows himself here a little more willing to change the King James Version: we *must* alter to correct—but what skill it takes!—to alter so as not to lose the quality of the translation made in the "great flowering-time" of our literature, to which are attached such "deep and powerful sentiments" (X: 103). The word *Jehovah* instead of *The Lord*, for instance, is inadmissible, for it has a "mythological sound." The old translators, interpreting prophecy to be predictive, used more future tense than is correct in translating the Hebrew tense-less verb, and yet where they mingle, as frequently, preterites, pre-sents, and futures "the general sense is adequately given [as though the confusion of tenses *results* in a Hebraic timelessness], and nothing is gained by endangering the rhythm of these fine verses through turn-ing all the tenses into presents" (X: 105).

And then what must we know to enjoy these texts? Arnold pro-ceeds to give what is still a readable, useful, and correct summary in a few pages of the historical setting. "Of the final scope of Isaiah's ideas, so far as we can apprehend it, and of the character and grandeur of his prophetic deliverances, I do not here speak" (X: 108). In the magazine version of this sentence, Arnold had said that on this mat-ter of Isaiah's ideas, "I may speak at more length hereafter" (X: 558), an intention not fulfilled. He might have been instigated by a letter from Newman of 1872. Newman has just read Arnold's preface to the Deutero-Isaiah and tells him he thinks the idea of such a book is excellent and that he accepts Arnold's dating of the chapters. But he writes—and this puts the case *against* the Bible-as-Literature—"I should dread to view it as literature. . . . A devout mind, which loves the objects which are its ultimate scope, and which instinctively sees

---

et le caractère du poème, 7th ed. (Paris: Calmann-Lévy, 1922), p. vi note. Renan writes:

> Since the rhythm of Hebraic poetry consists uniquely of the symmetrical
> division of parts of the sentence, it has always seemed to me that the true
> manner of translating these poetic works is to conserve this parallelism, which
> our processes of versification, founded on rhyme, quantity, and rigorous
> syllable-count, entirely disfigure. I have therefore made all efforts to keep in
> my translation something of the sonorous cadence that gives so much
> charm to the Hebrew. It is certain that, since the metrics of these old poems
> consisted solely in a sort of rhyme of thoughts, all careful translations should
> present this rhyme as the original does.

our Lord moving among the successive prophetical announcements, may and will (if cultivated) go on to admire its wonderful poetry, and will bear safely, in a critical and scholarlike way, to investigate its literal or first meanings."[18] The Newman-Arnold exchanges follow a pattern: Arnold insists to Newman on what they have in common; Newman in return insists on their differences.[19] Arnold: "We both love Christianity"; Newman (with full cognizance of his own wit): "I am praying for you!" Newman's stance here on the interpretation of Isaiah shows the difference, which is—simply—that Newman is a supernaturalist, and the *first* importance of Isaiah for him is its Christian doctrine. Newman recommended to Arnold that he produce a popular edition of 1 Samuel, "which is a perfect poem, epic or tragedy."[20] There is no doubt that 1 Samuel is superb narrative and would make a splendid little book (someone *should* do it), but Newman's remark shows either an ignorance of what technically constitutes an Old Testament "poem" or an insouciance as to the whole question.

Arnold's arrangement of chapters aims to answer to the historical circumstances. To claim, as evangelicals do, that Isaiah of Jerusalem (fl. 740–701 B.C.) foresaw and described the events in the Deutero-Isaiah which clearly belong to the period 537–520 B.C. is "simply bewildering." Cheyne, he says, has turned over-conservative on this matter of chapter rearrangement of Isaiah; Ewald is one of those who, having proved that a thing *might* have been so and so, then "jumps straight to the conclusion . . . that so and so it *must* have been; Lowth was rash, and took liberties" (X: 123–24). The principle is "respect for existing facts, and . . . dread of the fantastic" (X: 125). In sum, he conserves, he gives the necessary historical information, he rearranges enough to make sense in accord with history. One is reminded of Arnold's fable from Burnouf, and the mission accomplished: "Go then, O Pourna. Having been delivered, deliver; having been consoled, console; being arrived thyself at the farther bank, enable others to arrive there also" (I: 19). That was à propos of translating Homer; here again we find him involved with that important element of transmission—translation itself.

18. Quoted in Matthew Arnold, *Unpublished Letters*, ed. Arnold Whitridge (New Haven: Yale University Press, 1923), p. 63.

19. Ibid., for instance, pp. 55, 59.

20. Ibid., p. 64.

Arnold's text, on the whole, has about as few changes from the King James Version as the Revision has,[21] and most of his changes are the same or move in the same direction as the Revision's. He prints the prose in paragraphs and leaves the poetry in conventional "verse" form; that is, each numbered verse is a new paragraph. The King James Version's italics, by which the translators meticulously indicated the interpolations making the terse Hebrew into idiomatic English, Arnold prints in ordinary type. And he adds punctuation—the appropriate quotation marks and rather a lot of exclamation marks. The limits of his knowledge of Hebrew are perhaps given away when he leaves a plain mistake in the King James Version: *seraphims* for the plural of *seraph* (6: 2, 6), *seraphim* of course being the correct plural.

Although he disdains Lowth in his introduction, he does follow him frequently.[22] In 5: 25 where the King James Version has "their carcasses were torn in the midst of the streets," Lowth has "their carcasses became as dung," and Arnold follows suit, but the Revised Version merely writes that they "were as refuse." In 6: 10 where the King James Version has "Make the heart of this people fat," Lowth substitutes *gross* for *fat;* Arnold does as Lowth, and the Revised Version returns to *fat.* For the famous *burden* of chapters 15 ff., Lowth had put *oracle,* which perhaps is easier to understand. Arnold chooses

---

21. In 1870 the Convocation of Canterbury appointed a committee that included some nonconformists and some Americans to revise the King James Version (KJV, or, in England, AV for Authorized Version). The principles were "to introduce as few alterations as possible into the text of the AV, consistently with faithfulness," and "to limit as far as possible, the expression of such alterations to the language of the Authorized and earlier English versions." Of scholars who otherwise figure in this study of Arnold, the Old Testament Committee included Connop Thirlwall, who died in 1875 before it was completed, and T. K. Cheyne. The New Testament was published in 1881, the Old Testament in 1885. The American Standard Version (ASV, 1901) incorporates into this Revised Version (RV) certain renderings preferred by American scholars who had cooperated. A revision of the ASV, called the RSV, came out 1946–52 and has become widely accepted both in America and Britain, by Roman Catholics (in the U.S.A. in 1965) as well as Protestants. See the short account in the *Oxford Dictionary of the Christian Church* (London: Oxford University Press, 1974), under "Bible, English Versions," sect. 4. See also Allen Wikgren, "The English Bible," sects. 14–17, in *Interpreter's Bible* 1: 95–101; and Luther A. Weigle, "English Versions Since 1611," *The Cambridge History of the Bible*, 3 vols. (Cambridge: Cambridge University Press, 1963), 3: 361–82.

22. Robert Lowth, *Isaiah, A New Translation,* with commentary (Albany: Charles R. and George Webster, 1794).

to keep *burden;* the Revised Version chooses *oracle,* but Arnold explains in his note that *burden* means "oracular sentence of doom" (X: 385). There are many such slight variations among the versions. Most important, perhaps, are the simple corrections of mistakes in the King James Version: in 1: 25 "I will take away all thy tin" is corrected to "all thy alloy" by Lowth, Arnold, and the Revised Version, with clear advantages. Similarly, the King James Version 1: 31, "The strong shall be as tow, and the maker of it as a spark," Lowth corrects to "The strong shall be as tow, and his work as a spark of fire"; Arnold follows, omitting "of fire." So too, the Revised Version. Where 1: 27 in the King James Version is obscure: "Zion shall be redeemed through judgment, and her converts with righteousness," Lowth changes the last part to "her captives in righteousness" —still obscure; but Arnold simply puts "her converts *through* righteousness," which makes sense (*and* makes a parallelism). The Revised Version spells it out more specifically: "those in her who report, by righteousness." In the marvelous passage on the extravagance of women's dress:

Because the daughters of Zion are haughty and walk with stretched forth necks and wanton eyes, walking and mincing as they go, and making a tinkling with their feet: Therefore the Lord will smite with a scab the crown of the head of the daughters of Zion. . . . In that day the Lord will take away the bravery of their tinkling ornaments about their feet, and their cauls, and their round tires like the moon, the chains, and the bracelets, and the mufflers, the bonnets, and the ornaments of legs, and the headbands, and the tablets, and the earrings, the rings, and the nose jewels, the changeable suits of apparel, and the mantles, and the wimples, and the crisping pins, the glasses, and the fine linen, and the hoods, and the veils.

(3: 17–23)

we are pleased to recognize some of the paraphernalia of England in 1611; and students love to learn that *crisping pins* are curlers. Lowth appeared to have visions of Oriental harems: *crisping pins* become *little purses, hoods* become *turbans,* and *glasses* become *transparent garments.* With Arnold, *cauls* become *headbands, earrings* become *chains, headbands* become *girdles, tablets and earrings* become *scent-bottles and amulets,* the *crisping pins* become *pockets!* (the Revised Version has *handbags*), and the *glasses* (helpfully) become *looking-glasses* (but the Revised Version has *garments of gauze,* which appears to corroborate Lowth's reading). It is pleasant to see Arnold coping with these details. One wonders if he saw "round tires like the moon" as Victorian hoop-skirts.

But generally Arnold makes just those corrections that clear up King James Version obscurities, as the Revised Version does. He uses *coast* for *isle*, as the Revised Version does when it makes sense (e.g., 20: 6) but keeps *isles* when the places are really distant, as in the case of Tarshish (60: 9). In the famous "Butter and honey shall he eat," Arnold substitutes *milk-curd* for *butter*, loosing a rhythm but probably gaining historical accuracy. (*I* think it must have been yogurt.) The Revised Version, however, sacrifices the inversion and the rhythm: "He shall eat curds and honey." In 52: 14 Arnold is suddenly quainter than the King James Version: he writes *astonied* for the King James Version's *astonished*. Is it a slip, or was he using one of the versions older than the King James? He corrects 40: 3, "The voice that crieth in the wilderness, Prepare ye the way of the Lord," to "A voice of one that crieth! In the wilderness prepare ye the way of the Lord"; but a few verses later he follows Handel's version, "O thou that bringest good tidings to Zion," rather than the King James Version, "Oh Zion that bringest good tidings," which reading the Revised Version confirms. Some passages, it seems, were hallowed for Arnold by Handel's music, as they might be for us also. Arnold's translation of the Hebrew names improves meaning; as he explains in his introduction, we must understand the name of the son of Isaiah, Shear-jashub, "The-remnant-shall-return," for it governs the whole book (X: 107, 110), and where the King James Version has: "Thou shalt be called Hephzibah, and thy land Beulah: for the Lord delighteth in thee, and thy land shall be married" (62: 4), Arnold has: "Thou shalt be called My delight is in thee, and thy land Married; for the Lord delighteth in thee, and thy land shall be married" (as also in Revised Version).

In his notes, Arnold gives only such historical and literary information as makes the text intelligible; he fastidiously, of course, eschews dogma. He quotes a traveler's report to explain the frail loneliness of "a lodge in a garden of cucumbers" (1: 8);[23] he gives a brief and clear explanation of the nature of the Septuagint, the Vulgate, and the Chaldaic version and sums up scholarship conveniently. He quotes once from the Vulgate, where Jerome's version is irresistibly superb:

23. I too have seen in the Near East these lonely little platforms for the guard of the ripening crop.

"Thou hast heard; see all this" (*Quae audisti, vide omnia!*). But he burdens the student-reader with no learned apparatus, German or other.

On the delicate matter of chapter 53 ("A virgin shall conceive"), he writes in his note: "The application of this well-known chapter to Jesus Christ will be in every one's mind. But it must be our concern here to find out its primary historical import, and its connexion with the discourse where it stands" (X: 418). Nothing could be more firm, and yet nothing more discreet. He notes that the Vulgate "translates so as to heighten the identification with Christ" and that "the old Latin version which the Vulgate superseded is more faithful to the original than the Vulgate itself" (X: 420). On 26: 20, "The earth shall bring forth the dead," he notes, "It may easily be conceived how this magnificent verse, taken literally, became a signal text for the doctrine of the resurrection of the dead which from this time onward began to prevail among the Jews" (X: 446). The ploy here is rather clever: the term "magnificent verse," rather than "central doctrine" or whatever, certainly suggests a figurative reading and discreetly sustains his values of literature over dogma. And then in his text at 59: 20, for the King James Version's "the Redeemer" Arnold puts "a redeemer," with obvious implications.

We see Arnold coping at times with propriety: in 46: 3 the King James Version has "borne by me from the belly," and Arnold (and the Revised Version) puts "borne by me from the birth," which may represent a bowdlerizing of *belly*. But he retains the King James Version's "the sounding of thy bowels" (63: 15) and makes it worse with his note: "The metaphor is from strings tightly stretched, and giving, therefore, a louder and deeper sound." The schoolchildren would be fools to believe *this*, and would be sure to giggle. The Revised Version gives up, and puts "the yearning of thy heart." In 30: 22, however, Arnold had a harder problem. The subject is idols, and the King James Version writes, "Thou shalt cast them away as a menstruous cloth!" which witnesses the strong nerves of King James's committee as well as their appreciation of metaphor. Lowth wrote "polluted garment"; Arnold writes "defiled cloth." The modern versions also lose their nerve: the Jerusalem has "something polluted," while the New English Bible goes as far as "a foul discharge." Arnold's solution is fair enough.

He must have remembered the shy Iberians of the "Scholar-Gipsy" when he wrote his note on Tarshish (60: 9) : "The Greek Tortessus, a Phoenician settlement at the mouth of the Guadalquivir. . . . It was the port whence the rich mineral produce of Spain was shipped by the Phoenicians" (X: 429). The many glorious parts he barely touches: in 44: 23 where the King James Version has "lower parts of the earth," Arnold changes only "lower parts" to "foundations," with good effect:

Sing, O ye heavens, for the Lord hath done it: shout, ye foundations of the earth: break forth into singing, ye mountains, O forest, and every tree therein!

He once takes a little liberty: in the sublime "Comfort ye" passage, he concludes "that she receiveth of the Lord's hand double for all her rue"—*rue* instead of the *sin* in all the other versions. *Rue* seems to me a poet's word, and tender, a little rebellion against the harsh Hebraism. And he appears to take a liberty in the passage about the earthquake (24: 20); he writes: "The earth doth reel to and fro like a drunkard, and doth sway like a hammock." All the other English versions seem to have, instead of *hammock*, a *cottage*, or *hut*, or *shack*. *Hammock* is good, if unauthorized. In 60: 2 I think Arnold deals with tenses better than the King James or Revised Version: Arnold writes, "Behold darkness doth cover the earth, and gross darkness the nations! but the Lord shall arise upon thee, and his glory shall be seen upon thee." Both the King James and the Revised Version have "shall cover" instead of "doth cover"; Arnold's is the more immediate and dramatic.

His rearrangement of the sections of the text seems to me unexceptionable given the tremendous textual problems of Isaiah, and since this is something the Revised Version or other regular translations can hardly do, it makes the Arnold version a highly satisfactory one for reading. The last sections of Isaiah as ordered in the Bible seem to be left-over fragments, or discrete poems or prophecies, that hardly fit in well anywhere, and the last chapter ends fortuitously on a horrific note: carcasses and abhorrence. For a book chiefly characterized by a glorious vision of hope fulfilled, this is an unsatisfactory ending. Arnold, with perfect tact, and without changing the King James text, puts chapter 27 at the end:

Ye shall be gathered one by one, O ye children of Israel! And it shall come to pass in that day, that the great trumpet shall be blown, and they shall come which were forlorn in the land of Assyria, and the outcasts in the land of Egypt, and shall worship the Lord in the holy mount at Jerusalem.

XII

The National Institution

ARNOLD'S *Last Essays on Church and Religion* (1876) elaborates his doctrine in its ecclesiastical context: that of the Church of England and its great men. "Bishop Butler and the *Zeit-Geist*" (VIII: 11–62) confirms Arnold's mature sense of Butler's authority. When young he had inveighed against Butler's faculty psychology (51); he is now more tender toward fictions proper to their time; he places Butler in historical context—the Deist controversies—and acclaims him after all for applying the scientific method, for his effort to do in moral philosophy what Newton had done in physics. His faculty psychology was useful in its time, "corresponding with facts of which we are all conscious, [which] if practically acted upon would be found to work satisfactorily" (VIII: 31); it was what we can call in Glanvill's term "a convenient supposal" or in our own term a *heuristic fiction*. He pays tribute to the stupendous metaphor of Butler's *Analogy of Religion*, the world as metaphor for spirit, but because the work is bound to the *Zeitgeist* and blighted by dogma, it has, "even in Butler's own judgment . . . [a] puny total outcome" (VIII: 56). He turns away from it to be "refreshed" in the immediacy of biblical poetry, whose metaphors survive the vagaries of the *Zeitgeist*: "The Eternal is the strength of my life!" "The foundation of God standeth sure!" (VIII: 57).

In the lecture at Sion College on "The Church of England" (VIII: 63–86) he confronts the clergy directly, to explain how, as Super puts it, "a critic so apparently destructive of Christian dogma could be so warm a supporter of the Church establishment." According to reports, he was successful in the defense of his position and "carried" his clerical audience; he told his sister that those "who had come to curse, remained to bless" (VIII: 394–95, *Letters* II: 147). He maintains in his own terms the ecclesiastical principles that were his father's: the Church of England is not a private sect but a national institution, "a great national society for the promotion of what is commonly called *goodness*, and for promoting it through the most effectual means possible, the only means which are really and truly effectual for the object: through the means of the Christian religion and of the Bible" (VIII: 65). He counters the arguments for disestablishment: the Church is not, as alleged, a bulwark of rank and property. Let us judge the Church by its representative great men, Isaac Barrow, for instance—and he quotes a magnificent sermon passage against distinctions of wealth and rank. It is the business of the clergy, Arnold says, to preach renovation here and now—"God's will, as in heaven, so on earth," interpreting the primitive gospel of Christ to mean the Kingdom of God on *this earth*. And so Arnold endorses his father's activism, and his own, and the motivations of the Christian Socialists. The secularist predictions that religion will rapidly wither away in the light of science are proving, he says, untrue. We have, instead, a wave of religious reaction. And he argues, with Butler, that if Christianity does not stand ready to fill the spiritual needs of humankind, all sorts of evil superstition will rush in to fill the vacuum. Butler insisted on respect for rationality, and Arnold argues that the people of England have a tradition of good sense and integrity—unlike, he makes clear, Roman Catholic populations—and in accord with their integrity have an Establishment that is reasonable. Besides Butler and Barrow he calls in two of the Cambridge Platonists to witness:

Sir Matthew Hale, the most moderate of men and the most disposed to comprehension, said: "Those of the separation were good men, but they had narrow souls, who would break the peace of the church about such inconsiderable matters as the points in difference were." Henry More, that beautiful spirit [here again is the German idea of the *schöne Seele*] is exactly to the same effect. "A little religion may make a man schismatical, but a great deal will surely make a man decline division where things are tolerable, which is the case of our English Church."

                                                                    (VIII: 83)

Arnold predicts that the Church will prevail, by maintaining the original ideal of the Gospel as he understands it, by fidelity to rea-

son, and by stressing *goodness* rather than dogma. Whether Arnold
was right in his predictions is, I suppose, still moot. The Establishment has endured, but there seem to be many "redundant" churches.
There are, however, certainly some moves in the Arnoldian direction: new saints, for instance, are now to be added to the roster in the
forthcoming prayer book without supernatural paraphernalia, without "miracles" and even without conforming: William Wilberforce,
the Roman Catholic martyr Sir Thomas More, and the Methodist
Wesleys.

The issue in "A Last Word on the Burials Bill" (VIII: 87–110) is
a lesser issue, and more dated. In country places the churchyard was
the sole legal place of burial, and the Church of England was insisting
on the Prayer Book burial service—to the consternation of the Nonconformists. Arnold argues for conformity in burials, typically asserting the importance of *style*: let it be done *worthily*, without
ignobleness or *vulgarity* (VIII: 90). He counts one hundred and
thirty-eight sects of Nonconformists, including "Ranters, Recreative
Religionists, and Peculiar People," and suggests some minimal
changes in the Anglican burial service to make it acceptable and
truly *common* to all these, for "a fixed and noble form, consecrated
by use and sentiment" is of the highest value to society—educative.
A lost cause, no doubt, perhaps well lost. The most interesting thing
in this essay is Arnold's sense of the function of ritual: baptism is
figure of spiritual cleansing and the new life; the Anglican burial
service eschews personal emphasis on the dead individual, thereby
in its ritual instigating us all to celebrate our own deaths.

By far the most important of *Last Essays* is "A Psychological Parallel" (VIII: 111–47), for it is a comprehensive reprise of his religious
writings, from the perspective of his continuing meditations on the
Gospels (as the *Note-Books* indicate) and of a renewed study of the
"latitude men" of the seventeenth century. These "latitude men," including the Cambridge Platonists, precursors of Thomas Arnold and
the Broad Church, are the subject of a book Arnold was reading in
1876, John Tulloch's "delightful," "excellent," and "serious" book,
*Rational Theology and Christian Philosophy in England in the Seven-
teenth Century.*[1]

1. VIII: 121–22. This two-volume work was published in Edinburgh and London in 1872, with a second edition in 1874. Basil Willey models part of his important *Seventeenth Century Background* (London: Chatto and Windus, 1949) on

"A Psychological Parallel" starts out with a consideration of the belief in witchcraft in the seventeenth century, and a particular case, the trial of Rose Cullender and Amy Duny as witches, "because it shows us so clearly how to live in a certain atmosphere of belief will govern men's conclusions from what they see and hear" (VIII: 116). "The atmosphere of belief" is, of course, what Glanvill had called "climate of opinion," what Herder understood as the arbitrary uniqueness of a culture, and what Arnold generally thinks of as the "breath

---

it. Tulloch's later work, *Movements of Religious Thought in Britain in the Nineteenth Century* (London: Longmans, Green, 1885; reprint ed., Leicester: Leicester University Press; New York: Humanities Press, 1971), gives Willey the basic outline for his own *Nineteenth Century Studies* (London: Chatto and Windus, 1949).

Tulloch slights Matthew Arnold in *Movements*, a slight that Willey so magisterially makes up for in his *Nineteenth Century Studies*. Tulloch gives considerable space to Thomas Arnold, and more to Carlyle, whose teaching was "negative," he says, on certain points: the denial of miracle, the denial of the "Divine Personality," and his disposition to exalt might at the expense of meekness; but he "was great as a Moral Teacher in so far as he preserved certain elements of his early creed" (p. 206). He speaks of Carlyle's way of referring to God impersonally, as "The Divine" or "The Immensities," and then in a disapproving note observes:

This odd phase of religious thought is known to every student of its history not only in Stoicism but in Gnosticism. . . . We fear it must be said that to Carlyle in some respect is due the modern habit, conspicuously exemplified in *Natural Religion* and Mr. Matthew Arnold's writings, of using the name of God without any note of its Christian meaning,—a habit in every respect pernicious, as both leading to moral confusion and ignoring the living growth of moral and religious ideas. (p. 207).

Later in the book he classifies Arnold with Herbert Spencer, John Tyndall, and Thomas Huxley, as contrasted with the "Theistic" thinkers like James Martineau (p. 329). Tulloch simply does not accept Arnold's claim for a third position, of a "Christian" who rejects on the one hand reductive science and on the other a literalist Christianity, although in conscience if he acclaims much of Carlyle he should acclaim much of Arnold. I think, moreover, Tulloch may have been influenced more than he admits by *Literature and Dogma*: he grants dogma to be "divisive" in rather Arnoldian terms (p. 335). For a good account of Tulloch, see Mrs. Oliphant's *Memoir of Principal Tulloch* (Edinburgh: Blackwood, 1888).

Another noteworthy contemporary rejection of Arnold is Richard Holt Hutton's. Although very appreciative of Arnold as a poet, Hutton dismisses Arnold's retailored Christianity: Arnold's "curious earnestness and ability in attempting the impossible will soon, I believe, be a mere curiosity of literature" (*Essays on Some of the Modern Guides of English Thought in Matters of Faith* [London: Macmillan, 1887], p. 130).

of the *Zeit-Geist.*" The sophisticated and sensible people of the time who believed in witches: Sir Matthew Hale, Henry More (and he might have mentioned Glanvill), and even Sir Thomas Browne, cannot be called imbecile or credulous. "The belief in witchcraft was in the very atmosphere which Hale breathed, as the belief in miracles was in the very atmosphere which St. Paul breathed" (VIII: 121).

At this time, the Cambridge Platonists—Ralph Cudworth, John Hales, Benjamin Whichcote, Henry More, John Smith—were formulating "their extraordinarily simple, profound, and just conception of religion" as a *temper*, a *behavior.* Their conception, for a long time obscured, though occasionally appreciated, by Bishop Wilson for instance, is now "a boon for the religious wants of our own time" (VIII: 123). He wishes Tulloch would publish an anthology of their writings (and he himself projected one [VIII: 123, 409n.]). For the time being, he introduces us to John Smith's *Select Discourses.* "Their grand merit is that they insist on the profound *natural truth* of Christianity, and thus base it upon a ground which will not crumble under our feet" (VIII: 123). This John Smith was required for a certain occasion to preach a sermon against witchcraft. Smith is much concerned with the devil and his works, and the evil arts, rites, and ceremonies connected therewith, but explains: "When we say the devil is continually busy with us, I mean not only some apostate spirit as one particular being, but that spirit of apostasy which is lodged in all men's natures." Arnold comments, "Here, in this *spirit of apostasy which is lodged in all men's natures,* Smith had what was at bottom experimental and real." Arnold recognizes in Smith a man who rightly understood the anthropomorphosizing process; Smith says:

He that allows himself in any sin, or useth an unnatural dalliance with any vice, does nothing else in reality than entertain an *incubus demon.* . . . As men's love to God is ordinarily nothing else but the mere tendency of their natures to something that hath the name of God put upon it, without any clear or distinct apprehension of him, so their hatred of the devil is commonly nothing else but an inward displacency of nature against something entitled by the devil's name.

(VIII: 126)

Moreover

Where we find wisdom, justice, loveliness, goodness, love, and glory in their highest elevations and most unbounded dimensions, that is He; and where we find any true participation of these, there is a true communication of God; and a defection from these is the essence of sin and the foundation of hell.

(VIII: 127)

It is clear that what Arnold loves in Smith is his devout and intelligent participation in the demythologizing process. The fact that he believed in witchcraft "proves nothing against his being a man of veracity, judgment, and mental power." Accepting this erroneous belief, he at the same time sees into the meaning of it, what it represents, as in a figure, of the human condition.

And this is precisely the case of Paul, with respect to resurrection. Paul as a man of his time shared the current belief in literal raising from the dead, and "as is well known [or as is claimed by Matthew Arnold in *St. Paul and Protestantism*], by a prodigy of religious insight seized another aspect for the resurrection than the aspect of physical miracle. He presented resurrection as a spiritual rising which could be appropriated and enacted in our own living experience" (VIII: 128). Jesus' own figurative understanding of resurrection was "overlaid and effaced" by the popular belief in miraculous bodily resurrection, which Paul shares, for it was part of the climate of opinion. And Paul is not therefore "an imbecile and credulous enthusiast." For "even while affirming such preternatural incidents, he may with profound insight seize the true and natural aspect of them, the aspect which will survive and profit when the miraculous aspect has faded" (VIII: 129). Arnold's analogy, his "parallel" between Smith and St. Paul, supports his previously published religious argument precisely where—in my view—it is weakest; one understands why he was delighted to seize on the case of double-mindedness in this seventeenth-century divine to bolster his own possibly doubtful argument for the double-mindedness of Paul.

He goes on to consider the adjustment of literalism and metaphorical understanding in the Book of Common Prayer, including the Thirty-nine Articles, and reiterates his theory of a language "thrown out" at forces that engage affection and awe, and defy referential statement. As Butler prayed, let us be delivered "from *offendiculum* of scrupulousness" (VIII: 132). And when we are agreed on the function of the Church in its largest sense, as the "national society for the promotion of goodness," we can understand liturgy as figure, or "poetry." "It is a great error to think that whatever is thus perceived to be poetry ceases to be available in religion. The noblest races are those which know how to make the most serious use of poetry" (VIII: 132). We cannot, he goes on, dispense with a liturgy hallowed by centuries. The two Creeds, for instance, the Apostles' in its "concrete imagery," the Nicene Creed, in its "imaginative play of abstract ideas," elaborate nothing other than the truth of "Salvation through Jesus Christ."

As such, they are poetry for us; and poetry consecrated, moreover, by having been on the tongue of all our forefathers for two thousand years, and on our own tongue ever since we were born. As such, then, we can *feel* them, even when we no longer take them literally; while, as approximations to a profound truth, we can *use* them. [Arnold's emphasis]
(VIII: 136)

One remembers his idea, borrowed from Polybius early in his career as a critic, the idea of *pragmatic* poetry (I: 7). Perhaps we ourselves might feel, with the erosion of traditional liturgy in our own time, a sharp sense of loss. "The practical lesson to be drawn from all this," Arnold says, "is that we should avoid violent revolution in the words and externals of religion" (VIII: 142).

The essay ends with a return to the sayings of Jesus, culled by Arnold from the Gospels and made into an arrangement of his own, in a translation of his own. His edition of Isaiah can reflect only the scholarship of other men, and he could only choose among alternatives made available by Hebraists. But here in translating the New Testament he is on his own ground, being trained up since Rugby days in New Testament Greek. The *Note-Books* for 1875–76 show a high proportion of transcriptions of the New Testament Koine, and his own translations and ordering represent his meditations on the figurative language as reported of Jesus, with an effort to get behind the simplicity of the reporters that he described in *God and the Bible*. It makes an interesting and challenging collection.

I am the good shepherd; the good shepherd lays down his life for the sheep. And other sheep I have, which are not of this fold; them also must I bring, and they shall be one flock, one shepherd. Fear not, little flock, for it is your Father's good pleasure to give you the kingdom.

> My kingdom is not of this world; the kingdom of God cometh not with
> observation; behold, the kingdom of God is *within* you! [Arnold's emphasis]
> Whereunto shall I liken the kingdom of God? It is like a grain of mustard seed
> . . . ; It is like leaven. . . .
>   (VIII: 144; John 10: 11, 10: 16; Luke 12: 32; John 18: 36)

The juxtaposition of these passages is strategic: first the indisputably
figurative shepherd passage, last the mustard seed and leaven, figures
frankly acknowledged in the simile-presentation, the *likening*. In
between comes the Kingdom of God; so placed, it cannot be a literal
jaspers-and-emerald afterlife. The literal interpretation would be as
absurd as the *real* shepherd, the *real* mustard seed, the *real* leaven.
He concludes the essay with St. Augustine's figure of man as a
wanderer "through the waste places fertile in sorrow, seeking rest
and finding none," and a passage from Hebrews, "In all things I
sought rest. . . . And so I was established in Sion; likewise in the beloved city he gave me rest, and in Jerusalem was my power" (VIII:
147). Arnold's argument depends on the degree to which the biblical
figures and Augustine's actually do function, on the pragmaticality
of the poetry—and it would be hard to dismiss that.

The ingratiating essay "Falkland" (1877) (VIII: 188–207) is best
considered along with "A Psychological Parallel," for it also has its
impetus in Tulloch's *Rational Theology*, though of course Tulloch's
and Arnold's main source is *The History of the Rebellion* (1702–4)
by Edward Hyde, Earl of Clarendon. The account of Falkland's ideal
society at Great Tew, the *convivium philosophicum*, must touch all
who have ever loved an academic cloister. The society included some
of the "latitude men" and Cambridge Platonists; the historian Hugh
Trevor-Roper in a recent study explains what held them together:

All their writings and discussions show that they were the students and disciples of Erasmus and Hooker, and that their philosophy for their own time
was . . . a constructive scepticism which led, in religion, to ecumenicism: to
a religion which, having shed sectarian differences, justified itself by natural
reason and historical continuity.[2]

This helps to explain Arnold's sympathy with the group, and endorses his understanding of the time as being something like his own,

2. Hugh Trevor-Roper, "Clarendon," *Times Literary Supplement*, January 10,
1975, pp. 31–33.

a time of growing skepticism; hence it is that Arnold felt their "rational theology" was a "boon" for the nineteenth century. Falkland, the leader, he sees as a martyr to "sweetness and light," a very Arnoldian tragic hero, as John Farrell has pointed out, a victim of historical change like Empedocles.[3] History demanded allegiance either to the Stuarts or the Puritans, and neither cause was sound. "Falkland had lucidity enough to see it. He gave himself to the cause which seemed to him least unsound, and to which 'honesty,' he thought, bound him; but he felt that the truth was not there, any more than with the Puritans,—neither the truth nor the future." His "lucidity of mind and largeness of temper . . . are his great title to our veneration. They are what make him ours; what link him to the nineteenth century. He and his friends . . . kept open their communications with the future" (VIII: 204). The Puritan triumph at the time led to the "moral anarchy of the Restoration . . . and the long discredit of serious things, to the dryness of the eighteenth century," and the religious middle class "entered the prison of Puritanism, and had the key turned on their spirit there for two hundred years" (VIII: 201).[4] But the martyrdom of Falkland was not in vain—and Arnold ends with one of his prose poems: "The day will come when this nation shall be renewed by it. But, O lime-trees of Tew, and quiet Oxfordshire field-banks where the first violets are even now raising their heads!—how often, ere that day arrive for Englishmen, shall your renewal be seen!" (VIII: 207).

The *very* last essay Arnold wrote on Church and Religion is the preface to *Last Essays on Church and Religion*, written just before the book was published in March of 1877. It is an envoi to his religious writings but at the same time a strong statement of the continuity between religion and literature. "In returning to devote to literature, more strictly so-called, what remains to me of life and strength and leisure, I am returning, after all, to a field where work of the most important kind has to be done, though indirectly, for religion" (VIII: 148). He takes up two continental assessments of *Literature and Dogma*, explaining how on the Continent the intellectuals have dismissed religion and are astonished that any liberal at all should want to preserve it. In a way Arnold holds this out as a

3. John Farrell, "Matthew Arnold's Tragic Vision," *Publications of Modern Language Association* 85 (January 1970): 107–17.

4. Arnold is quoting himself here; see III: 121, VI: 390.

sort of threat: the Continent *has* rejected Christianity because of its
defective grounding in miracle; take *my* way, or we will follow suit
and lose both the Bible and Christianity. He refines and rephrases his
idea of the two selves, or forces, contending for the mastery in us:

one, a movement of first impulse and more involuntary . . . ; the other, a
movement of reflection and more voluntary, leading us to submit inclination
to some rule, and called generally a movement of man's higher or enduring
self, of reason, spirit, will.

(VIII: 154)

Christianity best sustains us in this better self, as we move toward the
Kingdom of God. He notes that modern science ascribes all our passions to two instincts: the reproductive instinct and the instinct of
self-preservation. Christianity answers perfectly with the corresponding virtues of chastity and charity. Something like the necessity for
charity is broadly accepted now, he says, in modern philosophers'
and sociologists' idea of human *solidarity*, and "finely touched souls,"
he declares, see a similar kind of *natural truth*, and necessity, in
chastity. He quotes Goethe's "prayer" for *pureness* (*die Idee des
Reinen*) perhaps as much as to say, *even* Goethe recognizes the
principle (VIII: 157–58). He describes the melancholy doctrine of
Schopenhauer, newly in fashion; it is un-human and somehow absurd; Arnold still insists instead on that need for joy so poignantly
expressed in his poetry and insists that righteousness answers to this
need. "Human life is a blessing and a benefit, and constantly im-
provable, because in self-renunciation is a fount of joy, 'springing
up into everlasting life.' Not only, 'it is more *right* to give than to
receive,' more rational, more necessary; but, 'It is more *blessed* to
give than to receive' " (VIII: 160). He concludes with a passage from
Jowett, introducing Plato's *Protagoras*: "The moral and intellectual
are always dividing, yet they must be reunited, and in the highest
conception of them are inseparable" (VIII: 162). This short essay
is perhaps Arnold's most homiletic, and it succinctly states the
Arnoldian creed. The faith that man's most developed intellectual
achievements—as in literature—have ultimately a necessary connection with virtue may serve as the justification of literary study, and
it embodies in the broadest terms Arnold's sense of the unity of
religion and poetry.

XIII

Last Essay on
Arnold and God

MILTON'S power of style . . . has for its great character *elevation;* and Milton's elevation clearly comes, in the main, from a moral quality in him—his pureness. 'By pureness, by kindness!' says St. Paul. These two, pureness and kindness, are, in very truth, the two signal Christian virtues, the two mighty wings of Christianity, with which it winnowed and renewed, and still winnows and renews, the world." This is, so far as I know, Arnold's own figure, and it is the work of a poet. It borrows a little of the grotesqueness of the Old Testament cherubim and seraphim, and at the same time it calls to mind the "metaphysical" figures of those English poets who wrote in the age of "Rational Theology." It can stand as a sort of "emblem" in the seventeenth-century manner over the rest of Arnold's career as literary critic, coming as it does in his essay on Edmond Scherer, "A French Critic on Milton," which sets the perspective of this later phase of his criticism.[1]

It is hard for the English to detach themselves from the old Puritan issue in Milton studies, and so we do well to look to a foreign critic, says Arnold, for disinterestedness; and in Scherer the French critic we have, moreover, a great "firmness and sureness of judgment" (VIII: 175). He recognizes Scherer's historical method as reaching out toward a responsible criticism, but now he finds that the histori-

---

1. VIII: 165–87. The "wings of Christianity" passage is on p. 184. Super writes in his introductory note, "As an essay on critical method, it stands in much the same relation to Arnold's later critical essays as 'The Function of Criticism' to the earlier" (p. 419).

cal method, "the old story of the man and the milieu,"[2] one of the basic ideas of "The Function of Criticism at the Present Time" (III: 261), is not altogether sufficient. "It is a perilous doctrine" that this historical method will yield of itself the right judgment or evaluation (VIII: 175). The curious case of *Paradise Lost* sets a problem for critics because the poem depends on a theological thesis that is absurd, and hence, as Scherer says, it is in a sense "false," "grotesque," "tiresome." But Scherer recognizes *Paradise Lost*, nevertheless, as "immortal," for the great passages that are part of the "poetical patrimony of the human race" (VIII: 181–82), for the incomparable lines, the incomparable imagery, and finally above all the sustained level of *style*. But this is not quite all, for Arnold. The style itself comes from a moral quality. Kindness, or charity, is not one of Milton's signal virtues, but pureness, or chastity, *is*, as Arnold's splendid citation from "Smectymnuus" reminds us. This essay on Milton presents the Arnoldian principle that has been formed by his writings on dogma, on God, and on the Bible, the principle that literary criticism must ultimately take account of morals, which is the domain of religion. Just as all Arnold's early literary criticism contributed to the shaping of his religious thought, so does now the religious thought go to shape and direct the literary criticism.

I should like in conclusion to review a few of the later essays in which the "religious" element is conspicuous, ranging from the comparativist interest of "A Persian Passion Play" to the great influence of his youth in "George Sand," the social-educational concern of "Literature and Science," the social-ecclesiastical concern of "A Comment on Christmas," his old love of the mystics in "A Friend of God," to new interests in "Amiel" and "Tolstoi."

"A Persian Passion Play" (1871) is a rather daring piece of education. The Oberammergau Passion Play had been revived in 1871 and was much talked of, and for Arnold to take up the celebration of the martyrdom of Hassan and Hussein and call it a "Passion Play" is very comparative indeed. Arnold alleges that the increasing tolerance of Protestants for Roman Catholics is part of "the spread of larger conceptions of religion, of man, and of history, than were current formerly" (VII: 13), and this essay will appeal to that larger interest in religion. He recounts the history of the split of Islam into

2. Of course Arnold is referring to Hippolyte Taine.

the Shiah and the Suni sects, and with quotations from Gibbon recounts the martyrdom at Kerbela of Hassan and Hussein, the grandsons of Mahomet, which is celebrated by the Shiite Moslems. The self-flagellation that accompanies the season of the dramas, Arnold relates back to ancient practices "on this old Asiatic soil, where beliefs and usages are heaped layer upon layer and ruin upon ruin" (VII: 20), back to the priests of Baal cutting themselves with knives. His description of the dramas, thanks in part to Gobineau, is vivid, pathetic, and compelling. But where Gobineau ascribes the appeal of the plays to patriotism, Arnold ascribes it to the way they answer, as Christianity does, to "the urgent wants of human nature" (VII: 35). He tells how when Jaffer, Mahomet's cousin, took refuge among the Christian Abyssians and described his religion there, the Abyssian king found that in all essentials it was like Christianity—not a straw's difference. Arnold sees more than a straw: he declares the Bible is superior to the Koran, and Christianity superior to Islam, but nevertheless, he says, these martyrdom plays do acclaim the very same "mildness and self-sacrifice" that was being celebrated at Oberammergau (VII: 39). In fact, Islam itself in acclaiming these virtues does in a way witness the excellence of Jesus who embodies them supremely. This last rather spoils the disinterestedness of the essay, as much as to say that if *even* this inferior religion has a place for mildness and self-sacrifice, how much better must be the religion to which they are central! And Arnold writes as though Christianity were later, more *developed* than Islam, when of course Islam arose late as a kind of reformation of the Judaeo-Christian line. But if the essay is a little weak as comparative religion, it is very strong in vividness and sympathy. The fact that events of our own time have made it particularly interesting and informative witnesses the Arnoldian ideal of cultural breadth and transmission.[3]

The "George Sand" essay (1877) looks back on what had been a passionate interest of his youth, and in explaining her power explains his own development. Her "principal elements" are: "the cry of agony and revolt, the trust in nature and beauty, the aspiration towards a purged and renewed human society" (VIII: 220). With

3. Recent history has made them of great interest now; as we all know they are still performed in Shiite Iran. An excellent collection of learned essays on them has recently been published: Peter J. Chalkowski, ed., *Ja'ziyeh: Ritual and Drama in Jran* (New York: New York University Press and Soroush Press, 1979).

Arnold, the "cry of agony and revolt" had given way to the philosophical Aurelian melancholy of his poems, but otherwise his characterization of George Sand is a characterization of himself. Like
him, she had early freed herself by rejecting the orthodox, literal,
anthropomorphic God, "made in our image, silly and malicious, vain
and puerile, irritable or tender, after our fashion" (VIII: 228). She
wrote:

It is an addition to our stock of light, this detachment from the idolatrous conception of religion. It is no loss of the religious sense, as the persisters in
idolatry maintain. It is quite the contrary, it is a restitution of allegiance to the
true Divinity. It is a step made in the direction of this Divinity, it is an ab-
juration of the dogmas which did him dishonour.

(VIII: 228–29, 438n.)

George Sand's vague phrase "Divine sense," Arnold says, stands for
"all the best thoughts and best actions of life, suffering endured, duty
achieved, whatever purifies our existence, whatever vivifies our love"
(VIII: 229). Because Madame Sand is a Frenchwoman, that is to
say odd, un-English, and peculiar—says the smiling Arnold—"her
religion is therefore, as we might expect, with peculiar fervency social"
(VIII: 229). As he goes on to play with this peculiar French and
foreign idea, we know of course that it has become in Matthew
Arnold an English idea, and it runs through all his work.

George Sand is quoted in the essay "Equality" (1878): "The human ideal, as well as the social ideal, is to achieve equality" (VIII:
279). If the earlier "Democracy" (1861) (II: 3–29) had not made
Arnold's political views abundantly clear, "Equality" must, altogether unequivocally and consistently with his whole career. "When
we talk of man's advance towards his full humanity, we think of an
advance, not along one line only, but several" (VIII: 286); Bildung-
Culture is the way of the advance, and it is an advance for all. Humanity—Herder's Humanität—is marked by its recognition of every
human being as an aggregation of infinite possibilities, and it is for
Arnold as for Herder the inevitable and best corollary of the Christian doctrine of the uniqueness and value of the individual.

"Literature and Science" (1882) is much anthologized and much
loved for its enduring defense of humane letters, even the study of
Greek—even now! The education consisting of natural science, which
Thomas Huxley was advocating, "leaves one important thing out of

... account: the constitution of human nature" (X: 61). And human nature has an imperious need to satisfy "the sense for conduct, the sense for beauty"; what speaks to this need is something bigger than mere religion. He starts with Plato on education, "those studies which result in [man's] soul getting soberness, righteousness and wisdom," not a bad idea of education, he says, whether you are going into the House of Lords or the pork trade in Chicago (X: 55). And he continues to draw on Greek literature for examples of the broadest and most humane culture, still the best to help us relate the new discoveries of science to the rest of our lives—"So strong . . . is the demand of religion and poetry to have their share in a man, to associate themselves with his knowing, and to relieve and rejoice it" (X: 66). The standard idea of Arnold, made all too current by T. S. Eliot, is that he proposed to substitute culture for religion—and that idea was anathema to T. S. Eliot. Arnold's idea rightly understood would still be anathema to T. S. Eliot, but it is by no means a simple idea of exchange. In this essay, medieval education and the Church that controlled it, both held up to scorn by Huxley, are presented by Arnold as a sort of temporary substitute for culture, the broad humane culture as the Greeks understood it. It was a legitimate substitute because while it neglected both humane letters and science it answered to that imperious "sense for conduct, the sense for beauty" (X: 66). And now "the importance of humane letters in a man's training becomes not less, but greater, in proportion to the success of modern science in extirpating what it calls 'mediaeval thinking.' " (X: 67). Arnold sees science as part of culture, and literary criticism as partaking of science, and right here he brings science to literature in the experimental mode, with an exhibit in the line of the paired statements of *Literature and Dogma*. Again, the heart of the matter appears to be metaphor. Compare, he says, the maxim "Patience is a virtue" with Homer: "For an enduring heart have the destinies appointed to the children of men" (X: 67–68). The maxim is all very well, but does nothing for us. But when we suffer, or are disoriented, or are emotionally bereft by some prodigious advance of modern thought, we might be advantaged by calling Homer's line to mind. Arnold tactfully leaves it unexplicated, but in the interests of a scientific criticism we might imagine its function. In the figure "the children of men" we sense the long continuity of human experience and feel a sustaining solidarity; in the "destinies" we recognize the three dark sisters as an acknowledged personification of the force-not-our-selves, and we do not have to stop to ask whether we "believe" in them or not as we might with some Christian text; personified, they can be imagined as "appointing" us certain tremendous emotional powers of endurance, *because*, we can all too easily infer, there may be so very much to endure. We know we are not evading with some sentimentality the sadness of our human lot, and we can feel there-fore the satisfaction of courage, and a kind of decorum in things. And so Arnold can conclude that the " 'hairy quadruped furnished with a tail and pointed ears, probably arboreal in his habits,' this good fellow carried hidden in his nature, apparently, something destined to develop into a necessity for humane letters. Nay, more; we seem finally to be even led to the further conclusion that our hairy ancestor carried in his nature, also, a necessity for Greek" (X: 72).

"A Comment on Christmas" (1885) (X: 218–38) reviews the theory of miracle as symbol or figure; this time Arnold recounts the legend of the miraculous birth of Plato (ever implying that Chris-tianity is not unique), taking it as a symbol of Plato's purity. But Plato did not found a religion and so the legend died. Jesus founded a religion (and Paul established it), and so the legend of virgin birth remained functional, and functions still as a symbol of the idea of purity—this is what we celebrate at Christmas. Lent, with the legend of the miracle of the temptation, celebrates the idea of self-conquest and self-control; Whitsuntide, with the miracle of the tongues of fire, celebrates the idea of inspiration. The two greatest ideas of Chris-tianity are pureness and charity: France is now rather weak on purity (in her worship of the great goddess "Lubricity"), England is weak in charity. Even the Church of England has been associated too much with station and property and forgets that "Blessed are the poor in spirit," which is interpreted to mean blessed are those who are indif-ferent to riches. This point leads Arnold directly into the interpreta-tion of the Christian virtue of charity as an obligation to extend economic equality: "It shall be required *of this generation*." R. H. Super connects this essay with Arnold's "Lay Sermon" (1884) (X: 249–55) celebrating the "saints" of the Anglican Church who gave themselves to social work in London's East End.[4] Both confirm once

4. One of these saints was celebrated in his sonnet of 1867, "East London," *Poems* 486.

more Arnold's faithfulness to his father's ideal of the Broad activist Church, working toward the Kingdom of God on earth.

The essay "A Friend of God" (XI: 180–89) was written as a service for a friend but represents a real interest of Arnold's—the mystic Tauler, who was associated with the fourteenth-century Swiss mystical sect, the *Gottesfreunde*, "Friends of God"; their name they took from the biblical epithet for Abraham, "the friend of God."[5] Arnold had known Tauler early in a French version as the *Note-Books* show;[6] in the later *Note-Books* and in this essay he quotes the English translation by his friend Morell:

Sin killeth nature, but nature is abhorrent of death; therefore sin is against nature, therefore sinners can never have a joy.

(XI: 181, *Note-Books* 536)

and acclaims the "natural truth" of such statements. He deplores the recent "crude and turbid" recrudescence of mythology in the spectacle of the Salvation Army, but insists nevertheless that even the common people are rejecting the mythological and irrational in religion, and this change creates a situation favorable to the true "Friends of God"—the Latitude Men, Butler, Wilson—Wilson whose glory Arnold says is his living and abiding sense that "sin is against nature"—and he was "the most exemplary of Anglican Churchmen" (X: 185). The change is favorable likewise to the mystics, "whom their heart prompted to rest religion on natural truth rather than on mythology" (XI: 186). Jesus' words, "How hardly shall they that have riches enter into the kingdom of heaven," are interpreted by narrow literalists to mean, "If you trust in riches . . . you cannot enter after death into the paradise above the sky." But "our mystic" understood the words rightly (demythologizing): "How hardly shall they that have riches follow me and my life, live naturally, be happy" (XI: 187).

Arnold continued through his life to practice the doctrine of *Bildung*; he continued, we know by his reading lists, to read regularly in "the best," and he continued to develop himself and turn to new ideas, new writers. The *Note-Books* reveal in some touching excerpts

5. See 2 Chronicles 20: 7, John 15: 14, James 2: 23.
6. *Note-Books* 13. There was an English version of 1857, done by Susanna Winkworth, a disciple of Bunsen.

his determination not to yield up *Bildung* to old age; he quotes
Sainte-Beuve on the Swiss moralist Charles-Victor de Bonstetten:

Cette vigilance du dedans, cette éducation continuelle . . . fait qu'on ne se
fige pas à un certain âge, qu'on ne se rouille pas, et que de toute la force de
son esprit on repousse le *poids* des ans.

(Note-Books 460)

This inward vigilance, this continual education keeps him from congealing at
a certain age, from rusting, so that with all the force of his spirit he spurns the
weight of years. [Arnold's emphasis]

He also transcribes Bonstetten's own words:

Ce n'est pas parce qu'on est jeune que l'on apprend quelque chose, mais parce
que dans la jeunesse on vous tient au travail et qu'on vous fait suivre avec
méthode une pensée. Dites-vous que votre inapplication et l'irrégularité ou
la nullité sont la véritable cause de la stagnation de vos idées, que vous attri-
buez faussement à l'âge.

(Note-Books 485)

It is not because one is young that one learns, but because in youth one is held
to work and made to follow out a thought with method. Tell yourself that your
inapplication, irregularity, and vacancy are the true cause of the stagnation of
your ideas, which you falsely attribute to age.

"Bonstetten died at 86," Arnold adds to the entry. And then there is
a motto from Goethe frequent in the *Note-Books* from 1877 on:

Das Hervorbringen selbst ein Vergnügen und sein eigner Lohn ist.

(Note-Books 286 et passim)

Creation is a gratification in itself and is its own reward.

Hervorbringen (creation) is surely to be understood as Carlyle understood it and translated it: Produce! Produce!

The essay "Amiel" makes reference to this discipline. He had rejected Henri-Frédéric Amiel for some time as less than "tonic" (XI:
265) and at first explains that he will still reject his poetry as a sort
of inferior "Obermann" and will reject the speculative philosophy of
the *Journals* as a bedazzled and futile Buddhism that led Amiel in
fact to incapacity, to his acknowledged "increasing isolation, inward
disappointment, enduring regrets, a melancholy neither to be consoled
nor confessed, a mournful old age, a death in the desert" (XI: 272–

73). Amiel refused to seek out the ideas that combat the paralysis of indeterminacy: "The ideas to live with . . . are ideas staunchly counteracting and reducing the power of the infinite and indeterminate" (XI: 272). But Arnold finds nevertheless that Amiel's *Journals* are admirable when he turns specific and critical, when he does perhaps manage that discipline of creative thought. No doubt he won Arnold by his appreciation of the office of critic. Arnold quotes:

Like Plato's sage, it is only at fifty that the critic is risen to the true height of his literary priesthood, or, to put it less pompously, of his social function.

(XI: 274)

He appreciates Amiel's comparativist insight, quoting him:

Learning and even thought are not everything. A little *esprit*, point, vivacity, imagination, grace, would do no harm. . . . The Germans heap the faggots for the pile, the French bring the fire.

(XI: 278)

And he is much interested in Amiel's sense of the social necessity for religion and his rejection of orthodox Christianity.

The whole Semitic dramaturgy has come to seem to me a work of the imagination. . . . The apologetics of Pascal, Leibnitz, Secrétan appear to me no more convincing than those of the Middle Age, for they assume that which is in question—a revealed doctrine, a definite and unchangeable Christianity. Pious fiction is still fiction. Truth has superior rights.

(XI: 280–81)

With such critical insights, it is doubly to be lamented that Amiel failed in discipline. Arnold writes:

Toils and limits composition indeed has; yet all composition is a kind of creation, creation gives . . . pleasure, and, when successful and sustained, more than pleasure, joy. . . . Sainte-Beuve's motto, as Amiel himself notices, was that of the Emperor Severus: *Laboremus*. "Work," Sainte-Beuve confesses to a friend, "is my sore burden, but it is also my great resource."

(XI: 276)

I think in this passage we find an element of Arnold's autobiography.

It is a pretty irony of history that Arnold records in a letter to his mother of 1861: he thanks her for forwarding mail including "a note returning a letter (of no importance) of a Russian count who had been sent with a letter to me" (Letters I: 155). Count Leo Tolstoi was in England in 1861, particularly interested in visiting the schools, and had been recommended to the attention of Inspector Matthew Arnold. The letter "of no importance" seems important now, and one yearns to know if there was any personal exchange between Arnold and Tolstoi. There was exchange later, by way of books. Tolstoi greatly admired "The Function of Criticism at the Present Time,"[7] and then: "Tolstoi," records a memoirist,

speaks with great praise of the religious books of Matthew Arnold. According to his words, there is an established opinion that the first place in the works of Matthew Arnold is occupied by poetry, the second by critical works, the third by religious works. It would be more correct, however, to arrange everything in reverse order. The religious works of Arnold are the best and most significant part of his works.[8]

Ernest J. Simmons records that in 1884 Tolstoi was urging his friends to read Literature and Dogma, "a remarkable production" that, he said, contained many of his own thoughts. Arnold "will bring you great satisfaction because he particularly insists on destroying the notion of God as something outside us, a 'magnified man' as he calls him."[9] And he had had his friend Chertkov present Arnold in England with a French translation of What I Believe. He was much taken with Arnold's "sweet reasonableness" as a term for the Christian principle he wanted to exercise in his own (much tried) family.[10] And in 1890–91 we find him rereading Literature and Dogma, a "favorite" work.[11]

    7. John Bayley comments on this, Tolstoy and the Novel (1966; New York: Viking Press, 1968), pp. 11–12.

    8. L. N. Tolstoy v vospominanijax sovremennikov, eds. S. N. Golubov, V. V. Grigorenko, N. K. Gudzij, S. A. Makašin, Ju. G. Oksman, vol. 1 (Moscow, 1960), pp. 437–38. I owe this citation to Mary Frances Wogec. There is a partial translation of this book by Margaret Wettlin, Reminiscences of Lev Tolstoi by His Contemporaries (Moscow: Foreign Languages Publishing House, c. 1960).

    9. Ernest J. Simmons, Leo Tolstoi (London: John Lehmann, 1949), pp. 437–38. In just this period we find him planning to read Epictetus, Marcus Aurelius, Lao-Tse, Buddha, Pascal, the Gospels (p. 439). The list might suggest some Arnoldian influence, although all these authors have been read without it.

    10. Ibid., p. 423.

    11. Ibid., p. 502.

Arnold, in his turn, was in some degree aware of Tolstoi since 1861; in 1887 he was reading *Anna Karénine, Ma Religion* (What I Believe), *Que Faire?* and *Ma Confession*, all in French.[12]

Partisans of the novel as genre may take umbrage at Arnold's critical neglect of it—except for the case of George Sand. But he read novels: the *Note-Book* reading lists and *Letters* reveal a wide-ranging and pretty steady novel habit: Fielding, Sterne, Goldsmith, Austen, Scott (a positive flurry of rereading in 1873), Bulwer, Charlotte Brontë, Dickens, Thackeray, George Eliot, Trollope, Kingsley, Disraeli, Collins, Hawthorne, Stowe, Cooper, Howells, Bret Harte, George Sand (early, late, and widely), Hugo, Stendhal, Daudet, Balzac, Flaubert, Zola, Turgenev, and, before the end, Stevenson, Hardy, and James. The partisans of the novel may forgive him all critical neglect at last for the sake of his important and perspicacious essay "Count Leo Tolstoi" (1887), which really marks the beginning of Tolstoi's reputation in England. He explains in a letter: "I had a special reason for writing about Tolstoi, because of his religious ideas; in general I do not write about the literary performances of living contemporaries or contemporaries only recently dead" (*Letters* I: 438).

He begins by greeting the genre with Sainte-Beuve's observation: the age of George Sand and the "lyric, ideal" novel is over; now in Flaubert's *Madame Bovary* we have the novel of "severe and pitiless truth" (XI: 282). The great English novelists are gone, Arnold says (Thackeray died in 1863, Dickens in 1870, George Eliot 1880, Trollope 1882), the French novel has lost ground, and it is now the Russian novel that becomes preeminent. The Russian nature "seems marked by an extreme sensitiveness, a consciousness most quick and acute for what the man's self is experiencing, and also for what others in contact with him are thinking and feeling" (XI: 282). He turns to Tolstoi, but not to *War and Peace*, for "in the novel one prefers, I think, to have the novelist dealing with the life he knows from having lived it" (XI: 284). *Vanity Fair* is to be preferred to *The Virginians*, *Anna Karénine* to *War and Peace*. *Anna Karénine* has too many characters, too many incidents, for artistic unity, but it is not to be taken as a "work of art" but rather as a "piece of life" (XI: 285).

12. See Super, *Prose* XI: 467. I follow Arnold's French spelling of the names. *Anna Karenina* was published serially in Russia 1875–77; a French translation appeared in 1885, and an English one in New York the next year.

He *sees* and *lives with* Anna, Karénine, Stiva, Dolly, and the rest. He recounts how Levine at last marries Kitty and they are profoundly happy—"Well, and who could help being happy with Kitty? So I find myself adding impatiently" (XI: 288).

And the truth is, Arnold loves Anna. And this love makes something of a problem for him. We English are a nation "qui sait se gêner" (XI: 289), who know how to control ourselves. "Perhaps in the Slav nature this valuable faculty is somewhat wanting"; even in English high society there may be some laxity.

But in general an English mind will be startled by Anna's suffering herself to be so overwhelmed and irretrievably carried away by her passion, by her almost at once regarding it, apparently, as something which it was hopeless to fight against. . . . It is the triumph of Anna's charm that it remains paramount for us nevertheless; that throughout her course, with its failures, errors, and miseries, still the impression of her large, fresh, rich, generous, delightful nature, never leaves us—keeps our sympathy, keeps even, I had almost said, our respect.

(XI: 289–90)

This does not create much of a critical problem for us now; it is interesting that, for Arnold, it did, and he must work it out. The solution is that Tolstoi never caters to the French goddess "Lubricity,"[13] as Flaubert does, whose Emma Bovary follows a course similar to Anna's. Such catering, Arnold says, as Burns said of promiscuity, *petrifies feeling.* And *Madame Bovary* is a work of *petrified feeling.* "The treasures of compassion, tenderness, insight . . . are wanting to Flaubert. He is cruel" (XI: 293).

In recounting Levine's conversion, as Arnold says, Tolstoi had recounted his own; Levine avows at the end of the novel: he will probably continue to be imperfect,

but my inner life has won its liberty; it will no longer be at the mercy of events, and every minute of my existence will have a meaning sure and profound which it will be in my power to impress on every single one of my actions, that of *being good.*

(XI: 295)

13. Super in a delightful note observes that, nevertheless, "in his description of Anna's costume at the ball Arnold omits the word 'low-necked.' "

Since finishing the novel, Tolstoi has gone on to write more autobiography, recounting his religious experience in more detail.

The idea of *life* is his master idea. . . . Moral life is the gift of God, is God, and
this true life, this union with God to which we aspire, we reach through Jesus.
. . . This doctrine is proved true for us by the life in God, to be acquired
through Jesus, being what our nature feels after and moves to, by the warning
of misery if we are severed from it, the sanction of happiness if we find it. . . .
Sound and saving doctrine, in my opinion, this is.

(XI: 297)

But it might have been gathered, says Arnold, from the novel. Tolstoi, though, has gone on to work out for himself what he calls "the
positive doctrine of Jesus," a scheme of five new "commandments"
to replace the decalogue, which five, if all were observed, would
create a new world. We cannot fail to be moved by Tolstoi's uncompromising dedication to his new ideal in every slightest element of
his own life: "Whatever else we have or have not in Count Tolstoi,
we have at least a great soul and a great writer" (XI: 302). But Arnold has one single objection: "Christianity cannot be packed into
any set of commandments. . . . Christianity is a *source*; no one supply of water and refreshment that comes from it can be called the
sum of Christianity" (XI: 302).[14] Tolstoi falls into dogma, in fact.
"Jesus paid tribute to the government and dined with the publicans.
. . . Perhaps Levine's *provisional solution* [my emphasis], in a society like ours, was nearer to 'the rule of God, of the truth,' than the
more trenchant solution which Count Tolstoi has adopted for himself since" (XI: 303). Dogma, for Arnold, always runs the risk of its
self-righteousness and absoluteness. The world as we know it does
not allow the absolute. And Jesus, for Arnold, teaches this lesson
against absolutes. In the continual flux of human development, we
must make do with the *provisional*, the "convenient supposal" of
Glanvill, the fiction of metaphor and myth, as we try to "be good."

Arnold's recognition of Levine's *provisional* proclaims the connection of this Tolstoi essay with *Literature and Dogma*. The novelist
can have, like Jesus, a secret and a method, but let him not go in for
dogma. Conduct is by far the greater part of religion, and the best
conduct is the imitation of Jesus. The novelist, then, can participate

14. Part of this is restatement of *Literature and Dogma*, VI: 299.

in the imitation by extending charity to the humblest or the greatest sinner. Arnold sees Tolstoi's novels as a better "imitation" than anything that can be done in doctrinal writings. Above all, by extending his love to his characters he makes us know and love them. Insofar as Arnold is impressed in his English way with Anna's sin, and even so loves her, just so far does he recognize the art of this novelist. He does not mention the Gospel episode of the woman taken in adultery, but he might have. Tolstoi presents us with Anna, and turns to us saying, "He that is without sin among you, let him first cast a stone." *There*, now, is a phenomenological theory of the novel waiting to get out of this essay of Arnold's—the reader is implicated, possibly "surprised by sin."[15]

Tolstoi, we are told, "considered Arnold's article . . . to contain well-formulated and justified criticism."[16] Nevertheless, he notoriously exercises a kind of Christian *interestedness*, and frequently it is as though he cannot help being the great writer in spite of it. Oddly, I think one may see the effect of *Literature and Dogma* in his novel *Resurrection* (1899). He began it in the period when he was rereading *Literature and Dogma* (1890–91), and it can be viewed as a kind of Arnoldian paradigm. Nekludoff is compact of two Arnoldian "selves"; *resurrection* is understood in Arnold's way as the metaphor for a new life on earth, and joy is the result of righteousness. But despite all its merit and interest, we must grant as Arnold would (he did not live to read it) that because of the conspicuous doctrine it fails of greatness. *War and Peace* and *Anna Karénine* stay with the provisional and are great *fictions* in more than one sense.

Finally, I think the question of Arnold and God is no other than the question of Arnold and fictions. For him, the time was out of joint, and to set it right was to readjust the religious side of life to the actual and scientific side. The Germans had posited *development* as the way of things, and it became apparent that to accept *development* is to forgo absolute "truth" and to make do with the *provisional*— convenient supposals, fictions. Theological dogma, in claiming to be "true," puts itself forward as science, misapprehending science itself.

15. John Bayley's *The Characters of Love* is perhaps the best statement of the theory (New York: Macmillan, 1960).

16. *L. N. Tolstoy*, p. 438. Translated by Mary Frances Wogec.

For the propositions of science, as Glanvill knew and as was becoming more apparent in Arnold's time, are by their nature provisional: new discoveries are perpetually invalidating them, and we must be willing to abandon them and come up with new propositions more "adequate" to the state of knowledge at the time. Since Arnold's time, limitation results and uncertainty principles—relativity, in fact—have obliged scientists more and more to underwrite the principle of provisionality. A hypothesis must not be a creed but a policy, which we adopt temporarily as the best basis for the next stage of investigations. The "best" hypothesis, or fiction, is the one that best fits the present sense of the way things are and best meets our needs for action. Arnold's words for value in literature, *pragmatic* and *adequate*, perfectly catch this relativity of value in our fictions.

For Arnold, the greatest challenge of his career was the rationalization of religion; accordingly it is in his religious books that he best realizes his central principle of provisionality, and so they best reveal the principle of all his work. All dogma is vulnerable because presented as absolute. But what is blessedly *invulnerable* is literature (or poetry, or art), because it acknowledges its fictionality. It cannot date; rather, it makes past and distant civilizations accessible to us and so extends human community: in Carlyle's words, "It is thus that the Wise Man stands ever encompassed, and spiritually embraced, by a cloud of witnesses and brothers." *Bildung* is the mode that best suits this relative, becoming, provisional world, for *Bildung* acknowledges the flux, recognizes human capacity as distinctively infinite, and wills perpetual cultivation of all distinctively human capacities. Arnold's idea of Culture, then, embracing *Bildung*, subsumes all humane activities: science, politics, art, literature, and religion, all understood in a basically Herderian expressionist way as a series of human constructs. All Arnold's works turn on the great pole not of Bacon's "truth" but of the provisional. *Poetry*, and the word is used more and more in the course of his career to equal *the metaphorical mode*, is the mode of the provisional or of fictions; it is the human way of survival. "I am a stranger here on earth: O hide not thy commandments from me." Poetry *will* prevail. "Currency and supremacy are insured to it, not indeed by the world's deliberate and conscious choice, but by something far deeper,—by the instinct of self-preservation in humanity" (IX: 188).

Index

Designer: Randall Goodall
Compositor: Heritage Printers
Text: Linotype Weiss
Display: Weiss Initials Series I,
              Weiss, and Weiss Italic
Printer: Heritage Printers
Binder: The Delmar Company